SpringerBriefs in Law

More information about this series at http://www.springer.com/series/10164

Valsamis Mitsilegas

The Criminalisation of Migration in Europe

Challenges for Human Rights and the Rule of Law

Springer

Valsamis Mitsilegas
Department of Law
Queen Mary University of London
London
UK

ISSN 2192-855X ISSN 2192-8568 (electronic)
ISBN 978-3-319-12657-9 ISBN 978-3-319-12658-6 (eBook)
DOI 10.1007/978-3-319-12658-6

Library of Congress Control Number: 2014953305

Springer Cham Heidelberg New York Dordrecht London

Printed on acid-free paper

Springer is part of Springer Science+Business Media (www.springer.com)

Acknowledgments

This book develops further ideas and arguments expressed in a number of recent publications. Chapter 3 is an updated and extended version of V. Mitsilegas, 'The Changing Landscape of the Criminalisation of Migration in Europe. The Protective Function of European Union Law' published in M. Guia, M. Van der Woude and J. Van der Leun (eds.), *Social Control and Justice. Crimmigration in an Age of Fear*, Eleven International Publishing, 2012, pp. 87–114. Parts of Chap. 4 develop further ideas and arguments presented in V. Mitsilegas, 'Solidarity and Trust in the Common European Asylum System' published in *Comparative Migration Studies*, vol. 2, 2014, pp. 231–253 and V. Mitsilegas, 'Immigration Detention, Risk and Human Rights in the Law of the European Union. Lessons from the Returns Directive' to be published in M. Guia, V. Mitsilegas and R. Koulish (eds.), *Immigration Detention, Risk and Human Rights*, Springer, forthcoming.

This book is dedicated to my EU Justice and Home Affairs LLM students and to the group of brilliant Queen Mary Ph.D. candidates currently researching their theses on migration and criminal law under my supervision. You are inspirational.

Contents

Chapter 1
Conceptualising the Criminalisation of Migration

Recent years have witnessed a growth in scholarly interest in the phenomenon of the criminalisation of migration. Academic interest in the field has followed the proliferation of state enforcement practices in immigration control on both sides of the Atlantic, with a number of leading scholars offering different conceptualisations of and approaches to the criminalisation of migration and its legal implications. In the United States, Stephen Legomsky has highlighted the use of criminal law to punish immigration violations, combined in parallel with the attachment of immigration law consequences to criminal convictions.[1] This twofold link, underpinned by what Legomsky has called importing criminal law enforcement strategies in the field of immigration control, has also been highlighted by Juliet Stumpf under her analysis of the now widely used term of 'crimmigration', which also encompasses an analysis of the impact of the criminalisation of migration on inclusion and exclusion.[2] In the United Kingdom, a recent study by Ana Aliverti has focused on the criminal prosecution and punishment of migrants in domestic law,[3] while Lucia Zedner has highlighted the potential consequences of the criminalisation of migration for fundamental principles of criminal law.[4] From a European perspective, Elspeth Guild, writing for the Council of Europe Commissioner for Human Rights, has adopted a more general approach including within the criminalisation of migration the adverse consequences for migrants in terms of residence and social rights, including employment rights,[5] while I have explored the criminalisation of migration at EU level in a narrower sense by focusing on the relationship between the use of substantive criminal law and European Union law in this context.[6] Issues related to the criminalisation of immigration have also been addressed by a number

[1] Legomsky (2007).
[2] Stumpf (2006).
[3] Aliverti (2013).
[4] Zedner (2013).
[5] Issue paper prepared by Guild (2009).
[6] Mitsilegas (2012a).

V. Mitsilegas, *The Criminalisation of Migration in Europe*,
SpringerBriefs in Law, DOI 10.1007/978-3-319-12658-6_1

of scholars in the United States and Europe within wider analyses of the link between migration and illegality,[7] as well as of the process of the securitisation of migration and its legal implications.[8] Research on the criminalisation of migration has not been confined only to academic lawyers, with important insights being provided by scholars in international relations, political sociology[9] and, more recently, criminology.[10]

Informed by these contributions and the diversity of approaches contained therein, the analysis in this book will be based on a conceptualisation of the criminalisation of migration based primarily on the use of the law in this process and the legal consequences of such criminalisation. Criminalisation will thus be understood in a narrow sense as including the use of substantive criminal law to regulate migration (in particular via the creation of immigration-related criminal offences and the imposition of criminal sanctions for these offences), but will also encompass more generally the use of criminal law tools including surveillance[11] and detention[12] to deal with migrants. The definition of the criminalisation of migration will also include the recent shift observed in both crime and immigration control towards prevention, leading to what has been characterised as a model of preventive justice.[13] **The criminalisation of migration for the purposes of this book will be understood as the threefold process whereby migration management takes place via the adoption of substantive criminal law, via recourse to traditional criminal law enforcement mechanisms including surveillance and detention, as well as via the development of mechanisms of prevention and pre-emption.**

The book will analyse the main elements of such criminalisation in the law of the European Union, by focusing on the position of migrants who do not have a link otherwise with EU law (by being, for instance, family members of EU nationals). The book will address the consequences of the criminalisation of migration for human rights and the rule of law. The analysis of the rule of law will include implications for legal certainty, arbitrariness, gaps in the law and legality (which, in the case of European Union law, also includes competence). Affected human rights are in particular the rights to liberty, to seek asylum, to private life and data protection and to non-discrimination. The structure of the book aims to reflect the migrant trajectory and align instances of criminalisation with the different stages of

---

[7] Dauvergne (2008).

[8] See inter alia Chacón (2007), Mitsilegas (2007), and for a comparative analysis, Mitsilegas (2012b).

[9] On the international relations/political sociology nexus see the work of Bigo (1996) on the securitisation of migration.

[10] See a number of contributions in Aas and Bosworth, *call out.*

[11] See Mitsilegas, *call out. (references in note 8).*

[12] See Joao Guia (2015).

[13] See Ashworth and Zedner (2014).

migrant experience. The book will thus be structured on the basis of three stages of the migrant experience: before entry (and before migrants reach the border); during stay (looking at how substantive criminal law is used to regulate migration in the territory); and after entry and towards removal (examining efforts to exclude and remove migrants from the territory and jurisdiction of EU Member States). The book will thus aim to provide a holistic typology of the criminalisation of migration in the law of the European Union.

References

Aliverti, A. (2013). *Crimes of mobility: Criminal law and the regulation of Migration*. Abingdon: Routledge.

Ashworth, A., & Zedner, L. (2014). *Preventive justice*. Oxford University Press: Oxford.

Bigo, D. (1996). *Polices en Réseaux L'Expérience Européenne*. Paris: Presses Sciences Po.

Chacón, J. M. (2007). Unsecured borders: Immigration restrictions, crime control and national security. *Connecticut Law Review, 39*, 1827–1891.

Dauvergne, C. (2008). *Making people illegal. What globalisation means for migration and law*. Cambridge: Cambridge University Press.

Guild, E. (2009). *Criminalisation of migration in Europe: Human rights implications*. Strasbourg: Council of Europe Commissioner for Human Rights.

Joao Guia, M., Mitsilegas, V., & Koulish, R. (Eds.). (2015). *Immigration detention, risk and human rights*. New York: Springer (forthcoming).

Legomsky, S. H. (2007). The new path of immigration law: Asymmetric incorporation of criminal justice norms. *Washington and Lee Law Review, 64*, 469–528.

Mitsilegas, V. (2007). Border security in the European Union: Towards centralised controls and maximum surveillance. In E. Guild, H. Toner, & A. Baldaccini (Eds.), *Whose freedom, security and justice? EU immigration and Asylum Law and policy* (pp. 359–394). Oxford: Hart Publishing.

Mitsilegas, V. (2012a). The changing landscape of the criminalisation of migration in Europe. The protective function of European Union Law. In M. Guia, M. Van der Woude, & J. Van der Leun (Eds.), *Social control and justice: Crimmigration in an age of fear* (pp. 87–114). The Hague: Eleven International Publishing.

Mitsilegas, V. (2012b). Immigration control in an era of globalisation: Deflecting foreigners, weakening citizens, strengthening the state. *Indiana Journal of Global Legal Studies, 19*(1), 3–60.

Stumpf, J. (2006). The crimmigration crisis: Immigrants crime, and sovereign power. *American University Law Review, 56*, 367–419.

Zedner, L. (2013). Is the criminal law only for citizens? A problem at the borders. In K. Franko Aas, & M. Bosworth (Eds.), *The borders of punishment: Migration, citizenship, and social exclusion* (pp. 40–57). Oxford: Oxford University Press.

Chapter 2
Before Entry: Criminalisation as Prevention

2.1 Introduction

A key element in the immigration enforcement strategy adopted by the European Union in recent years has been the focus on preventing migrants from reaching the territory of the European Union in the first place, with the aim of shielding the European Union and Member States from assuming legal obligations towards migrants. This emphasis on prevention has been reflected in a two-fold change from traditional immigration control on the physical border.[1] The first change is temporal, with border controls taking place *before* an individual has reached the actual physical border. The second change is spatial, with border controls taking place increasingly extraterritorially, outside the territory of the European Union, most commonly on the high seas or in the territory of third states.[2] This chapter will analyse how migrants are being criminalised before reaching the borders of Europe (i.e. the external borders of the European Union) by presenting a typology of preventive criminalisation through categorising four main levels of criminalisation as prevention and highlighting the human rights and rule of law challenges such preventive approach entails. The chapter will thus focus on: the link between criminalisation and prevention in extraterritorial immigration control; the emergence of a prevention paradigm via the use of delegation by European Union law, to both the private sector (the privatisation of immigration control) and to specialised agencies (and in particular the European Borders Agency, FRONTEX); and the link between prevention, criminalisation and securitisation, by focusing on preventive immigration control via the growing recourse to technology, databases and invasive surveillance using a wide range of personal data (including sensitive data such as biometrics) and allowing access to immigration data to law

---

1 See Mitsilegas (2015a).
2 See Ryan and Mitsilegas (2010).

V. Mitsilegas, *The Criminalisation of Migration in Europe*,
SpringerBriefs in Law, DOI 10.1007/978-3-319-12658-6_2

enforcement authorities. The analysis of this multi-level paradigm of criminalisation as prevention will be accompanied by a critical analysis of legislative and judicial responses to the rule of law and human rights challenges it entails.

2.2 The Rise of Extraterritorial Immigration Control

The rise of extraterritorial immigration control has presented a number of challenges to the rule of law and human rights. Extraterritorial immigration control practices have been linked with attempts by the European Union and its Member States to evade legal responsibility for migrants wishing to reach the external border of the European Union, by conducting border control operations on the high seas or in the territory of third states. This practice runs the risk of creating gaps in the rule of law and the applicability of European human rights standards in operations conducted extraterritorially. The rule of law and human rights challenges of extraterritorial immigration control, linked with the broader question of the extraterritorial application of European human rights law and in particular the European Convention on Human Rights (ECHR) have been addressed by the European Court of Human Rights. On a number of occasions, the Strasbourg Court has attempted to clarify the extent of state responsibility for complying with the European Convention on Human Rights when acting extraterritorially. In its ruling in *Al-Skeini,* the court confirmed that in certain circumstances, the use of force by a State's agents operating outside its territory may bring the individual thereby brought under the control of the State's authorities into the State's jurisdiction under Article 1 of the Convention.[3] Reiterating its earlier case law, the Court added that "[w]hat is decisive in such cases is the exercise of physical power and control over the person in question."[4] A case cited in *Al-Skeini* which is of particular relevance to the issue of extraterritorial immigration control is *Medvedyev*.[5] The Court ruled there that the ECHR applied extraterritorially in enforcement actions by France in a case of suspected drug trafficking on the high seas. As this was a case of France having exercised "full and effective control" over the boat in question and its crew, "at least de facto, from the time of its interception, in a continuous and uninterrupted manner until they were tried in France, the applicants were effectively within France's jurisdiction for the purposes of Article 1 of the Convention".[6] The case is of relevance for extraterritorial immigration control not only because it involved the use of force and actual interception at sea, but also because this happened in a relative legal vacuum with few developed international law rules in the field. The court recognized this vacuum by stating that "it is regrettable ... that the international effort to combat drug

---

[3] *Al-Skeini v. United Kingdom,* App. No. 55721/07, Eur. Ct. H.R. 1 (2011).

[4] Paragraphs 58–59.

[5] *Medvedyev v. France*, App. No. 3394/03 Eur. Ct. H.R. (2010).

[6] Paragraph 67.

trafficking on the high seas is not better coordinated bearing in mind the increasingly global dimension of the problem"[7] and found "that the deprivation of liberty" in this case "was not 'lawful' … for lack of a legal basis of the requisite quality to satisfy the general principle of legal certainty".[8] The court rejected the French Government's claim that interception on the high seas is a special case, stating that

> The special nature of the maritime environment relied upon by the Government in the instant case cannot justify an area outside the law where ships' crews are covered by no legal system capable of affording them enjoyment of the rights and guarantees protected by the Convention which the States have undertaken to secure to everyone within their jurisdiction, any more than it can provide offenders with a "safe haven".[9]

The European Court of Human Rights has thus attempted to address the rule of law and fundamental rights issues arising from the existence of gaps in legal protection in extraterritorial state acts by expanding state jurisdiction under the Convention. The case-law of the Court is particularly relevant in cases of extraterritorial immigration control, as the Court's approach, in effect, exports the border to places and instances where the state exercises enforcement action.[10] This has been characterised as a functional approach to border control focusing not on a general test of personal or geographical control, but rather on the specific power or authority assumed by the state acting extraterritorially in a given capacity.[11]

The Court of Human Rights had the opportunity to address the human rights challenges of extraterritorial immigration control directly in its ruling in the case of *Hirsi*.[12] The case involved eleven Somali nationals and thirteen Eritrean nationals who were part of a group of about two hundred individuals who left Libya aboard three vessels with the aim of reaching the Italian coast. On 6 May 2009, when the vessels were 35 nautical miles south of Lampedusa, that is, within the Maltese Search and Rescue Region of responsibility, they were intercepted by three ships from the Italian Revenue Police (Guarda di Finanza) and the Coastguard. The occupants of the intercepted vessels were transferred onto Italian military ships and returned to Tripoli and handed over to the Libyan authorities.[13] The Strasbourg Court had no difficulty in asserting jurisdiction. It stated that Italy cannot circumvent its jurisdiction under the Convention by describing the events at issue as rescue operations on the high seas[14] and noted that, while in *Medvedyev* the events took place on board of a vessel flying the flag of a third state, here the events took place entirely on board ships of the Italian armed forces, the crews of which were

[7] Paragraph 101.

[8] Paragraph 102.

[9] Paragraph 81.

[10] See Mitsilegas (2012).

[11] See Gammeltoft-Hansen (2011).

[12] *Hirsi Jamaa and Others v Italy*, Application no. 27765/09. For an analysis, see Mitsilegas, callout (The Law of the Border), whereupon the part on Hirsi is based.

[13] Paragraphs 9–12.

[14] Paragraph 79.

composed exclusively of Italian military personnel. In the Court's opinion, in the period between boarding the ships of the Italian armed forces and being handed over to the Libyan authorities, the applicants were under the continuous and exclusive de jure and de facto control of the Italian authorities. Speculation as to the nature and purpose of the intervention of the Italian ships on the high seas would not lead the Court to any other conclusion.[15]

Having established jurisdiction, the Court found that Italy was in breach of both Article 3 ECHR (prohibition of inhuman and degrading treatment) and of Article 4 of Protocol number 4 (prohibition of collective expulsion of aliens). As regards Article 3, the Court rejected Italy's claim that Libya was a safe third country. It noted that the mere ratification of international treaties by a third country is not by itself a guarantee of compliance with human rights[16] and added that Italy cannot evade its own responsibility by relying on its obligations arising out of bilateral agreements with Libya.[17] The Court added that the Italian authorities knew or should have known that, as irregular migrants, they would be exposed in Libya to treatment in breach of the Convention and that they would not be given any kind of protection in that country and that it was for the national authorities, faced with a situation where human rights were being systematically violated as described above, to find out about the treatment to which the applicants would be exposed after their return.[18] In the present case substantial grounds have been shown for believing that there was a real risk that the applicants would be subjected to treatment in Libya contrary to Article 3 of the Convention.[19] The Court also found a violation of Article 3 on account of the fact that the applicants were exposed to the risk of arbitrary repatriation to Eritrea and Somalia. According to the Court, when the applicants were transferred to Libya, the Italian authorities knew or should have known that there were insufficient guarantees protecting the parties concerned from being arbitrarily returned to their countries of origin.[20] More importantly, Italy is not exempt from complying with its obligations under Article 3 of the Convention because the applicants failed to ask for asylum or to describe the risks faced as a result of the lack of an asylum system in Libya. The Court reiterates that the Italian authorities should have ascertained how the Libyan authorities fulfilled their international obligations in relation to the protection of refugees.[21]

As regards Article 4 of Protocol number 4 on the prohibition of collective expulsion of aliens, the Court developed its case-law by stating the following:

> It is therefore clear that, while the notion of 'jurisdiction' is principally territorial and is presumed to be exercised on the national territory of States, the notion of expulsion is also

[15] Paragraphs 79–80.

[16] Paragraph 128.

[17] Paragraph 129.

[18] Paragraphs 130–131.

[19] Paragraph 136.

[20] Paragraph 156.

[21] Paragraph 157.

> principally territorial, in the sense that expulsions are most often conducted from national territory. Where, however, as in the instant case, the Court has found that a Contracting State has, exceptionally, exercised its jurisdiction outside its national territory, it does not see any obstacle to accepting that the exercise of extraterritorial jurisdiction by that State took the form of collective expulsion. To conclude otherwise, and to afford that last notion a strictly territorial scope, would result in a discrepancy between the scope of the application of the Convention as such and that of Article 4 of Protocol No. 4, which would go against the principle that the Convention should be interpreted as a whole. Furthermore, as regards the exercise by a State of its jurisdiction on the high seas, the Court has already stated that the special nature of the maritime environment cannot justify an area outside the law where individuals are covered by no legal system capable of affording them enjoyment of the rights and guarantees protected by the Convention which the States have undertaken to secure to everyone within their jurisdiction (*Medvedyev* para 81).[22]

In the light of the above, the Court found that the removal of aliens carried out in the context of interceptions on the high seas by the authorities of a State in the exercise of their sovereign authority, *the effect of which is to prevent migrants from reaching the borders of the State or even to push them back to another State*, constitutes an exercise of jurisdiction within the meaning of Article 1 of the Convention which engages the responsibility of the State in question under Article 4 of Protocol No. 4.[23] The Court found that the transfer of applicants to Libya was carried out without any form of examination of each applicant's individual situation and that there was therefore a violation of Article 4.[24]

Hirsi is of great importance in affirming the extraterritorial application of human rights law and emphasising that states cannot evade their human rights responsibilities towards migrants by exercising extraterritorial immigration control including by cooperating with third states. Following its reasoning in its earlier case-law in *M.S.S.* (concerning the transfer of asylum seekers within the EU under the Dublin Regulation),[25] as reflected in the subsequent ruling of the Court of Justice of the European Union in *N.S.*,[26] the Court affirmed the positive obligations of states to ascertain whether the fundamental rights of affected migrants are protected in the state to which the migrant is to be transferred to. Moreover, in an extremely important finding, the Court extended the protection of migrants under the ECHR in cases of collective expulsion. As den Heijer has noted, the Court's reasoning allows for an interpretation that any interception activity that factually prevents migrants from effectuating an entry may be construed as expulsion.[27] In *Hirsi*, the Court applied the Convention in cases where state action has resulted to the deflection of migrants, i.e. to acts the effect of which is to prevent migrants from reaching the borders of the State or even to push them back to another State. State jurisdiction applies here even if the migrant has not

---

22 Paragraph 178.

23 Paragraph 180, emphasis added.

24 Paragraphs 185–186.

25 *M.S.S.* v. *Belgium and Greece*, judgment of 21 January 2011, Application No 30696/09.

26 Joined Cases C-411/10 and C-493/10, *N. S. and M. E.*, judgment of 21 December 2011. For further details, see Chap. 4.

27 See den Heijer (2013).

reached the physical, territorial border of the state. States can no longer hide behind deflection techniques under a logic of prevention. In *Hirsi,* the Court reiterated the importance of the rule of law and the rejection of 'areas outside the law'. In doing so, it focused heavily on the impact of immigration control by the state on the affected individuals in what has been eloquently characterised the 'individualisation of jurisdiction'.[28] By placing the individual at the heart of the system of protection of the Convention, the European Court of Human Rights had to address the borders of the law related to extraterritorial immigration control operations.

While *Hirsi* is extremely important and has already been influential in the development of EU legislation in the field,[29] it involves a situation where there has been clear state intervention on migrants. What is less evident the extent to which the Court's reasoning would apply in cases where there is no actual state enforcement action taking place, but where there are attempts to deflect movement via the use of surveillance extraterritorially (for instance via the use of EUROSUR) or in cases where the attribution of responsibility is difficult because multiple authorities are involved. This is in particular in cases of FRONTEX operations, including operations on the high seas and cooperation with third states.[30] An expansive interpretation of jurisdiction will address these issues and remedy the legal uncertainty stemming from gaps in legal responsibility arising from delegation in border control in this context. As Guy Goodwin-Gill has noted, interception operations are initiated and coordinated by the EU agency, FRONTEX, and collaboratively or individually by EU Member States. Directly *or indirectly*, they affect the rights of individuals, some or many of whom may be in need of international protection. Within the terms of the ILC articles on state responsibility, particularly Articles 4 and 6, interceptions continue to be carried out in the exercise of governmental authority by the state, or in the equivalent exercise of its executive competence by the EU's agency.[31] Nothing in the evidence of practice to date, Goodwin-Gill continues, reveals any break in the chain of liability. Neither the on-board presence of a third-state official, nor the use of joint patrols in which actual interception is undertaken by a third state, disengage the primary actor from responsibility for setting the scene that allows the result, if nothing more. In each case, the EU agency or Member States exercise a sufficient degree of effective control; it may not be solely liable for what follows, but it is liable nonetheless.[32] This view is strengthened the finding of the Court in *Hirsi* as regards collective expulsion, where the Court established jurisdiction under the ECHR in cases of attempts to prevent migrants reaching the EU external border. It is also strengthened, as will be seen below, by the recently adopted EU legislation on surveillance and search and rescue at sea with regard to FRONTEX operations.

---

28 See Nussberger (2012).

29 See part on FRONTEX below.

30 See Baldaccini (2010).

31 See Goodwin-Gill (2011).

32 Ibid.

2.3 Delegation of Immigration Control to Specialised Agencies: The Case of FRONTEX

The geopolitical and legal changes in Europe resulting in the abolition of internal border controls within the European Union on the one hand, and the extension of EU territory via the successive enlargements of the EU (in particular the eastward enlargements) on the other, have led to the establishment of a European agency responsible for border controls (FRONTEX).[33] The establishment of FRONTEX has been to a great extent a product of the lack of trust of 'old' EU Member States towards the new EU members from Central and Easter Europe with regard to their capacity to guard effectively the new external border of the European Union.[34] The establishment of FRONTEX has aimed to strengthen the powers of EU Member States, and the European Union as a whole, to manage its external border. As such, FRONTEX has been perceived as largely a security agency, aiming at managing migrants as perceived risks.[35] Rather than diluting state sovereignty in the field of immigration control, the establishment of FRONTEX has strengthened, rather than weakened, the border control powers of Member Stares by establishing an additional layer of control.[36] Establishing a border management agency at European Union level has however posed a number of significant challenges for the reconfiguration of immigration control in Europe. First of all, the discussion of delegation of powers from the state to agencies must be viewed in the specific light of EU law, where the additional layer of the contested relationship between the competence of the Union (and its agencies) and the Member States exists. This aspect is particularly relevant in the field of immigration control, traditionally linked to state sovereignty. In this context, a key questions as regards the delegation of immigration control powers at EU level is who has the power, and thus the legal responsibility, for immigration control: is it the Member States of the EU, or the EU agency (FRONTEX)? As will be demonstrated below, the lines between national and Union competence in the field are on many occasions blurred, resulting in gaps in the legal protection of those affected by immigration control at EU level. These gaps in upholding the rule of law and fundamental rights are particularly acute when FRONTEX conducts joint operations extraterritorially.

---

[33] See Council Regulation 2007/2004 establishing a European Agency for the 'management of operational cooperation at the external borders of the Member States of the European Union, [2004] OJ L 349/1, 25 November 2004.

[34] For a background, see Mitsilegas (2007a).

[35] On the securitisation aspect, see also Neal (2009).

[36] Mitsilegas (*Immigration Control in an Era of Globalisation*).

2.3.1 The 2004 FRONTEX Regulation

The difficult task of establishing a European agency for immigration control while respecting state sovereignty in the field is reflected in the careful articulation of the Agency's powers. The opening Article to the initial FRONTEX Regulation states that the aim of the Agency is to improve the integrated management of the external borders of the Member States of the EU.[37] While the responsibility for the control and surveillance of external borders lies with Member States, the provision continues, the Agency will facilitate and render more effective the application of EC measures by co-ordinating Member States' actions in the implementation of these measures, thereby contributing to 'an efficient, high and uniform level of control on persons and surveillance of the external borders of the Member States.'[38] To achieve this, the main tasks of the Agency are: to co-ordinate operational co-operation between Member States, including the evaluation, approval and co-ordination of proposals for joint operations and pilot projects and the launching, in agreement with Member States concerned, of initiatives for such operations and projects[39]; to assist Member States with training of border guards[40]; to carry out risk analysis by developing a common risk analysis model[41]; to follow up research development on border control[42]; to assist Member States in circumstances requiring increased technical and operational assistance at external borders[43]; and to provide Member States with the necessary support in organising joint return operations.[44]

The key to the question of the extent to which FRONTEX has replaced national border controls is to determine the extent of the Agency's coordination powers.[45] Two main questions arise in this context. The first is whether Agency staff will have enforcement powers in the territory of Member States (and consequently which rules will apply to them); secondly, whether the Agency has coercive powers over Member States when organising joint operations. As to the first question, Article 10 of the FRONTEX Regulation states that the 'exercise of executive powers by the

37 Article 1(1).

38 Article 1(2).

39 Articles 2(1)(a) and 3(1).

40 Articles 2(1)(b) and 5. In this context, developments such as the Community Borders Code are particularly relevant. Regulation (EC) No. 562/2006 of the European Parliament and of the Council of 15 March 2006 establishing a Community Code on the rules governing the movement of persons across borders (Schengen Borders Code), [2006] OJ L105/1, 13 April 2006.

41 Articles 2(1)(c) and 4.

42 Articles 2(1)(d) and 6.

43 Articles 2(1)(e) and 8–8(2)(b) which calls for the deployment of the Agency's experts to support national authorities.

44 Articles 2(1)(f) and 9.

45 The Preamble further confirms that the development of policy and legislation on external border control and surveillance remains a responsibility of the EU institutions, in particular the Council. Recital 20.

Agency's staff and the Member States' experts acting on the territory of another Member State shall be subject to the national law of that Member State.'[46] What constitutes 'executive power' in this context is not defined in the Regulation. The latter however avoids explicitly excluding operational powers of Agency staff from its scope, a view that is reinforced by the similar treatment of Agency staff with experts from Member States. There is less ambiguity with regard to the second question, i.e. whether the Agency can compel Member States to participate in joint operations without their agreement. Article 3(1) second indent states that the Agency may itself, and *in agreement with the Member State(s) concerned*, launch initiatives for joint operations and pilot projects.[47] Thus, Member States cannot be made to participate in joint projects without their agreement. Article 20(3) of the Regulation provides an additional safeguard by stating that proposals for decisions on specific activities to be carried out at, or in the immediate vicinity of, the external border of any particular Member State requires a vote in favour of their adoption by the Member of the Management Board representing that Member State.

2.3.2 *The 2007 RABITS Regulation*

The powers of FRONTEX were further developed via the amendment of its legal basis to allow for the deployment of so-called Rapid Border Intervention Teams Regulation (RABITS).[48] There is a greater pooling of state sovereignty and a greater clarity and detail as to the tasks of these teams, which are deployed for the purposes of providing rapid operational assistance for a limited period to a requesting EU Member State facing a situation of urgent and exceptional pressure.[49] The tasks and powers of these teams, the first of which was deployed at the request of Greece in the autumn of 2010 on the Greek-Turkish land border,[50] are described in Article 6 of the RABITs Regulation, which states that Members of the teams shall have the capacity to perform all tasks and exercise all powers for border checks or border surveillance in accordance with the Schengen Borders Code and that are necessary for the realisation of the objectives of that Regulation[51] and that

---

[46] It is noteworthy and indicative of the sensitivity of the issue that in his evidence before the House of Lords EU Committee on the role of the Agency on returns of irregular immigrants, the Director, Mr Laitinen, stated that they 'do not have executive powers.' See House of Lords EU Select Committee, *Illegal Migrants: Proposals for a Common EU Returns Policy*, 32nd Report, Session 2005–2006, HL Paper 166 (Q581).

[47] Emphasis added.

[48] Regulation 863/2007 establishing a mechanism for the creation of Rapid Border Intervention Teams and amending Council Regulation 2007/2004 as regards that mechanism and regulating the tasks and powers of guest officers.

[49] Article 1(1) of the RABITs Regulation.

[50] For details, see the *FRONTEX General Report 2011*, at pp. 29–30.

[51] Article 6(1).

they may only perform tasks and exercise powers under instructions from and, as a general rule in the presence of border guards of the host Member State.[52] The RABITs Regulation further contributes towards the militarisation of the EU external border, as they are allowed to carry weapons[53] and to use force, including weapons.[54] According to the provision on applicable law, while performing the tasks and exercising the powers, the members of the teams shall comply with Community law and the national law of the host Member State.[55]

The RABITs Regulation has added detail on the legal framework of some aspects of FRONTEX operations, and represents a clear shift from purely national to EU border control involving executive measures and coercive powers. However, a number of concerns with regard to gaps in the accountability and legal responsibility of the Agency remained. Delegation of immigration control to an EU agency increases enforcement powers by providing an additional layer of immigration control and its actions may have significant consequences for the individuals affected, with FRONTEX already being actively coordinating Member State action in the field.[56] However, the extent of the powers and accountability of the agency are unclear. FRONTEX has been established as a management agency, and its annual reports are dominated by management-speak and management-style targets—something that may lead to a depoliticisation of border controls at EU level and fundamental decisions on EU borders strategy being taken on the basis of the FRONTEX operational plan and the decisions of its management board rather than on the basis of a more open debate.[57] Decisions on FRONTEX operations have been shrouded in secrecy,[58] with transparency as to its operational plans lacking. Moreover, while its parent Regulation has emphasised coordination as a key FRONTEX task, it is not clear whether such coordination of national responses leads to FRONTEX responsibility. FRONTEX is officially a 'management' agency

---

52 Article 6(2).

53 According to Article 6(5) of the RABITs Regulation 'while performing their tasks and exercising their powers, members of the teams may carry service weapons, ammunition and equipment as authorised according to the home Member State's national law. However, the host Member State may prohibit the carrying of certain service weapons, ammunition and equipment, provided that its own legislation applies the same prohibition to its own border guards'.

54 According to Article 6(6), 'While performing their tasks and exercising their powers, members of the teams shall be authorised to use force, including service weapons, ammunition and equipment, with the consent of the home Member State and the host Member Sate, in the presence of border guards of the host Member State and in accordance with the national law of the host Member State.' However, the following paragraph allows the use of weapons, ammunition and equipment 'in legitimate self-defence and in legitimate defence of members of the teams or of other persons, in accordance with the national law of the host Member State' (Article 6(7)).

55 Article 9.

56 For details of FRONTEX planning and coordinating of joint border control operations see their annual Reports at www.frontex.europa.eu.

57 On FRONTEX and depoliticisation, see Mitsilegas, *Border Security in the European Union, call-out.*

58 See Moreno-Lax (2011).

but cannot fit in easily with the various typologies of Union agencies,[59] which have been established primarily in a market regulation context.[60] The emphasis on management in the FRONTEX Regulation cannot mask the fact that FRONTEX is essentially an operational agency, involved in actions with a significant impact on the relationship between the individual and the State.[61]

Notwithstanding the growth in FRONTEX activities in recent years, it has been increasingly difficult to pin down its responsibilities when it comes to its action. FRONTEX may be operational in practice, yet it may also claim that it has no legal responsibility for border controls, as it has merely a 'co-ordinating' role. This may lead to a situation where FRONTEX denies any responsibility claiming that the exercise of border controls are for Member States,[62] while Member States frame controls at their external borders as controls by FRONTEX—with Member States increasingly viewing FRONTEX as an answer to their expectations with regard to their border control responsibilities.[63] The potential to the creation of gaps in the legal responsibility of actors in FRONTEX operations is magnified if one looks at the legal framework underpinning the relations between FRONTEX one the one hand and other bodies and agencies (in particular law enforcement agencies) and third countries on the other. The FRONTEX Regulation provides for cooperation between the Agency and international organisations (including Europol) and third countries on the basis of 'working arrangements.'[64] FRONTEX has already entered in a number of such 'working arrangements' with security/law enforcement agencies both within[65] and outside the EU,[66] as well as with a number of third states.[67] The ambiguity regarding the legal force of working arrangements and the lack of transparency with regard to their negotiation and content may lead to the emergence of FRONTEX as an actor in a securitised, global system of immigration control

---

59 For attempts at categorisation of EU agencies, see inter alia Chiti (2000), Kreher (1997), see also the overview by Vos (2000).

60 See in particular Majone (1997).

61 V. Mitsilegas, 'Extraterritorial Immigration Control in the 21st Century: the Individual and the State Transformed', in Ryan and Mitsilegas, *call-out*, pp. 39–66. As Curtin notes, it can be argued that in the case of FRONTEX the Council did not delegate its own existing executive powers but rather the tasks in question had been exercised by Member States—Curtin (2009).

62 See in this context the striking FRONTEX news release according to which FRONTEX 'would like to state categorically that the agency has not been involved in diversion activities to Libya', the latter being based on a bilateral agreement between Italy and Libya—http://www.frontex/europa.eu/newsroom/news_releases/art70.htm.

63 See for instance the July 2009 statement of the then Press Secretary of the Greek Government: 'We have to strengthen FRONTEX activities': in http://www.kathimerini.gr/4Dcgi/_w_articles_kathremote_1_16/07/2009_289089.

64 Articles 13 and 14 of the FRONTEX Regulation respectively.

65 See the Strategic Co-operation Agreement between FRONTEX and Europol, at https://www.europol.europa.eu/sites/default/files/flags/frontex.pdf.

66 See *Frontex signs Working Arrangement with Interpol*, News Release of 29 May 2009, at http://www.frontex.europa.eu/newsroom/news_releases/art63.html.

67 See *Frontex. External Relations* at http://www.frontex.europa.eu/external_relations/.

without being accompanied by clearly defined standards of legal responsibility either for itself or for its interlocutors.

2.3.3 The 2011 FRONTEX Regulation

In the light of these challenges, the FRONTEX legal framework was revised for a third time in 2011 to address inter alia sustained criticism with regard to the lack of emphasis on the protection of human rights of migrants as well as concerns regarding accountability and the rule of law in FRONTEX operations.[68] Regulation (EU) No 1168/2011[69] has amended the FRONTEX Regulation to include detailed rules governing FRONTEX operations but also a series of specific provisions on human rights and accountability. The Regulation states expressly that FRONTEX will fulfil its tasks in full compliance with the relevant Union law, including the Charter; the relevant international law, including the Geneva Convention; obligations related to access to international protection, in particular the principle of *non-refoulement* and fundamental rights.[70] The Regulation further states that no person shall be disembarked in, or otherwise handed over to the authorities of, a country in contravention of the principle of *non-refoulement*, or rom which there is a risk of expulsion or return to another country in contravention of that principle and that the special needs of children, victims of trafficking, persons in need of medical assistance, persons in need of international protection and other vulnerable persons shall be addressed in accordance with Union and international law.[71] Fundamental rights will also be respected via procedural and governance developments. The Regulation calls upon the Agency to draw up and further develop and implement its Fundamental Rights Strategy and to put in place an effective mechanism to monitor the respect for fundamental rights in all the activities of the Agency.[72] The Regulation further calls for the establishment of a Consultative Forum by the Agency to assist the Executive Director and the Management Board in fundamental rights matters[73] and for the designation by the Management Board of a Fundamental Rights Officer.[74] The protection of fundamental rights is further addressed in the context of

[68] For an overview of these challenges, see Council of Europe Parliamentary Assembly, *Frontex: Human Rights Responsibilities*, Report, Committee on Migration, Refugees and Displaced Persons, 8.4.2013 (*Rapporteur:* Mikael Cederbratt). See also the ensuing Resolution 1932(2013).

[69] Regulation (EU) No 1168/2011of the European Parliament and of the Council of 25 October 2011 amending Council Regulation (EC) No 2007/2004 establishing a European Agency for the Management of Operational Cooperation at the External Borders of the Member States of the European Union, OJ L304/1, 22.11.2011.

[70] Amended Article 1(2) of Regulation 2007/2004: second indent.

[71] New Article 2(1a).

[72] Article 26a(1).

[73] Article 26a(2).

[74] Article 26a(3).

broader rule of law and accountability innovations. The Regulation calls for the drawing up by FRONTEX of a Code of Conduct applicable to all operations coordinated by the Agency. The Code of Conduct will lay down procedures intended to guarantee the principles of the rule of law and respect for fundamental rights with particular focus on unaccompanied minors and vulnerable persons, as well as on persons seeking international protection, applicable to all persons participating in the activities of the Agency. FRONTEX will develop the Code of Conduct in cooperation with the aforementioned Consultative Forum.[75] In a further move towards greater transparency and accountability, the Regulation provides for the drawing up by the Executive Director of an operational plan for FRONTEX joint operations and pilot projects.[76] The operational plan will include inter alia, in cases of operations at sea, specific information on the application of the relevant information and legislation in the geographical area where the rapid intervention takes place, including references to international and Union law regarding interception, rescue at sea and disembarkation.[77]

The 2011 Regulation goes some way towards addressing criticisms regarding the lack of emphasis on the protection of the rights of migrants in FRONTEX operations, as well as concerns with regard to transparency and the accountability of the agency. The Regulation represents an attempt to incorporate and mainstream fundamental rights in the work of FRONTEX, and the requirement to draw up an operational plan enhances accountability by setting out in detail the role of FRONTEX in specific operations. However, these developments do not address fully questions of the legal responsibility of FRONTEX in joint operations, especially when these operations have an impact on the fundamental rights of migrants. In particular, the FRONTEX legal framework in its various iterations continues not to grant a specific and express avenue of complaint or remedy for affected migrants within the FRONTEX structure. This gap has been addressed in detailed inquiries by the European Ombudsman. In an inquiry conducted in 2012, the Ombudsman found that FRONTEX had no mechanism in place by which it could deal with individual incidents of breaches of fundamental rights alleged to have occurred in the course of its work. The Ombudsman saw the lack of an internal complaints mechanism as a significant gap in FRONTEX's arrangements and recommended to FRONTEX that it should take any possible action to enable the FRONTEX Fundamental Rights Officer to consider dealing with complaints on infringements of fundamental rights in all FRONTEX activities submitted by persons individually affected by the infringements and also in the public interest.[78] FRONTEX decided not to accept this recommendation. A key element in the position being adopted by

---

[75] New Article 2a.

[76] New Article 3a(1).

[77] Amended Article 8e(1).

[78] European Ombudsman, *Draft Recommendation of the European Ombudsman in his inquiry into complaint OI/5/2012/BEH-MHZ against the European Agency for the Management of Operational Cooperation at the External Borders (Frontex)*, 9.4.2013, point M.

FRONTEX is that individual incidents, which become the subject of complaint, are ultimately the responsibility of the particular Member State on whose territory the incident occurred. In a follow-up Report, the Ombudsman did not accept that FRONTEX does not carry responsibility for the actions of staff operating under its banner and that it is not tenable that FRONTEX has no responsibility and that, thus, it should not deal with complaints arising from actions in which it is involved.[79] According to the European Ombudsman, FRONTEX would be the logical first resort for submitting complaints.[80] The Ombudsman recommended that FRONTEX should establish a mechanism for dealing with complaints about infringements of fundamental rights in all FRONTEX-labelled joint operations. The mechanism should receive complaints from persons who claim to be individually affected, or who complain in the public interest. This role could be entrusted to the FRONTEX Fundamental Rights Officer, who should be resourced accordingly. The recommendations of the European Ombudsman are based on the acceptance that FRONTEX has legal responsibility for its operations and cannot hide behind the responsibility of Member States. The recommendations will strengthen the human rights scrutiny of FRONTEX operations in providing a remedy for affected migrants *within* the structure of FRONTEX. This remedy will be in addition to the avenue provided by the Treaty of Lisbon which grants the Court of Justice jurisdiction to review the legality of acts of bodies, offices and agencies of the Union intended to produce legal effects vis-à-vis third parties.[81] This provision is certainly applicable to FRONTEX operations but the additional lodging of complaints within FRONTEX will facilitate the speedy investigation of human rights issues and enable a thorough assessment of FRONTEX operations on the ground and closer to the time of the FRONTEX operations affecting migrants.

2.3.4 FRONTEX and Rules on Sea Border Operations and Search and Rescue at Sea

The existence of legal responsibility of FRONTEX when conducting joint operations with Member States is further confirmed by EU law governing sea border operations and search and rescue at sea. The European Union first adopted rules in the field in 2010, not via a further amendment of the FRONTEX Regulation, but on the basis of the comitology procedure established by Article 12(5) of the Schengen Borders Code. The relevant Council Decision[82] introduced in Annexes rules for sea

---

[79] Special Report of the European Ombudsman in own-initiative inquiry OI/5/2012/BEH-MHZ concerning Frontex, 7.11.2013.

[80] Point 43.

[81] Article 263(1) TFEU.

[82] Council Decision of 26 April 2010 supplementing the Schengen Borders Code as regards the surveillance of the sea external borders in the context of operational cooperation coordinated by

border operations coordinated by FRONTEX and mere guidelines for search and rescue situations for disembarkation in the context of sea border operations coordinated by the Agency. The adoption of the Decision raised important rule of law issues. Important rules relating to FRONTEX operations at sea with potentially significant consequences for the human rights of affected migrants were adopted not via the ordinary EU legislative procedure (which would ensure the application of the full scrutiny powers of the European Parliament) but via the more opaque comitology procedure: rules on FRONTEX operations have thus been treated as non-essential, merely technical rules. The European Parliament challenged the legality of the adoption of the Decision before the Court of Justice.[83] The Court emphasised the principle that the adoption of rules essential to the subject-matter is reserved to the legislature of the European Union adding that the essential rules governing the matter in question must be laid down in the basic legislation and may not be delegated.[84] In relation to the specific case before it, the Court found that although the Schengen Borders Code, which is the basic legislation in the matter, states in Article 12(4) that the aim of such surveillance is to apprehend individuals crossing the border illegally, it does not contain any rules concerning the measures which border guards are authorised to apply against persons or ships when they are apprehended.[85] The adoption of such rules constitutes a major development in the Schengen Borders Code system.[86] The impact of these rules on fundamental rights was a crucial factor in the Court's finding that these are essential and constitute a major development of the Schengen Borders Code. According to the Court, provisions on conferring powers of public authority on border guards—such as the powers conferred in the contested decision, which include stopping persons apprehended, seizing vessels and conducting persons apprehended to a specific location—mean that the fundamental rights of the persons concerned may be interfered with to such an extent that the involvement of the European Union legislature is required.[87] The Court confirmed that parts I and II of the Annex of the contested Decision contain essential elements of external maritime border surveillance and found that, notwithstanding the Decision's reference to 'guidelines' on search and rescue, this reference cannot affect their classification as essential rules: the Court noted in this context that this part of the Annex forms part of the FRONTEX operational plan and that since the conditions provided for by that plan must be complied with, it necessary follows that the rules in paras 1.1 and 2.1 of Part II to the Annex of the contested decision are intended to produce binding legal

(Footnote 82 continued)
the European Agency for the Management of Operational Cooperation at the External Borders of the Member States of the European Union (2010/252/EU), OJ L111/20, 4.5.2010.

83 Case C-355/10, European Parliament v Council, judgment of 5 September 2012.

84 Paragraph 64.

85 Paragraph 73.

86 Paragraph 76.

87 Paragraph 77.

effects.[88] The Court's ruling is significant from a rule of law perspective not only by stopping Member States and the Commission hiding behind the comitology procedure in shielding key rules on FRONTEX operations from scrutiny but also by treating these rules as essential on the basis of their impact on fundamental rights and by treating rules on FRONTEX operations—regardless of how they are labelled—as legally binding.

The Court's ruling triggered a fresh round of negotiations for new EU legislation on the surveillance of the EU external border, taking place this time under the ordinary legislative procedure with the full involvement of the European Parliament. The ensuing Regulation[89] contains detailed legally binding rules on the surveillance of the EU external sea borders in the context of FRONTEX operations. It includes special rules on detection,[90] interception in the territorial sea,[91] interception on the high seas,[92] interception in the contiguous zone,[93] search and rescue situations[94] and disembarkation.[95] The Regulation contains three major developments aimed at addressing gaps in the protection of fundamental rights and the rule of law: it includes a series of detailed provisions aimed at ensuring respect with fundamental rights and refugee law, in particular when third countries are involved in sea operations; it places emphasis on the assessment of the human rights situation in third countries; and it introduces a series of provisions aiming at enhancing the accountability of FRONTEX, most notably as regards the drawing up of operational plans and the reporting of FRONTEX. The Regulation contains a number of strong Preambular provisions related to compliance with human rights when third countries are involved. When cooperation with third countries takes place on the territory or the territorial sea of those countries, the Member States and the Agency should comply with norms and standards *at least equivalent to those set by Union law*.[96] Moreover, in a provision reflecting the judgment of the European Court of Human Rights in *Hirsi*, it is stated explicitly that the possible existence of an arrangement between a Member State and a third country does not absolve Member States from their obligations under Union and international law, in particular as regards compliance with the principle of *non-refoulement*, whenever they are aware or ought to be aware that systemic deficiencies in the asylum procedure and in the reception conditions of asylum seekers in that third country amount to substantial

---

88 Paragraphs 78–82.

89 Regulation (EU) No 656/2014 of the European Parliament and of the Council of 15 May 2014 establishing rules for the surveillance of the external sea borders in the context of operational cooperation coordinated by the European Agency for the Management of Operational Cooperation at the External Borders of the Member States of the European Union, OJ L189/93, 27.6.2014.

90 Article 5.

91 Article 6.

92 Article 7.

93 Article 8.

94 Article 9.

95 Article 10.

96 Preamble, recital 5. Emphasis added.

grounds for believing that an asylum seeker would face a serious risk of being subjected to inhuman and degrading treatment or where they are aware of ought to be aware that that third country engages in practices in contravention of the principle of *non-refoulement.*[97] Protection of fundamental rights and the principle of *non-refoulement* is also upheld expressly in the body of the Regulation which states that no person shall, in contravention of the principle of *non-refoulement*, be disembarked in, forced to enter, conducted to or otherwise handed over to the authorities of a country where, inter alia, there is a serious risk that he or she would be subject to the death penalty, torture, persecution or other inhuman or degrading treatment or punishment, or where his or her life or freedom would be threatened on account of his or her race, religion, nationality, sexual orientation, membership of a particular social group or political opinion, or from which there is a serious risk of an expulsion, removal or extradition to another country in contravention of the principle of *non-refoulement.*[98] This is a welcome and broad provision which is applicable to a wide range of FRONTEX operations. As Peers has noted, the European Parliament successfully insisted on adding the words 'forced to enter' and 'conducted to' in this Article, which clearly covers push-backs.[99]

These express commitments to protect fundamental rights and the principle of *non-refoulement* are backed up by detailed and concrete provisions aiming on the one hand to ensure a detailed assessment of the level of human rights protection in a third country, and on the other hand to provide a series of procedural safeguards to the affected migrants during sea operations. When considering the possibility of disembarkation in a third country, in the context of planning a sea operation, the host Member State, in coordination with participating Member States and the Agency, must take into account the general situation in that third country. In a passage reminiscent of the practice of the European Court of Human Rights in *M.S. S.* and of the Court of Justice in *N.S.*[100] the Regulation further states that the assessment of the general situation in a third country will be based on information derived from a broad range of sources, which may include other Member States, Union bodies, offices and agencies, and relevant international organisations. Intercepted or rescued persons shall not be disembarked, forced to enter, conducted to or otherwise handed over to the authorities of a third country when the host Member State or the participating Member States are aware or ought to be aware that that third country engages in practices as described in Article 4(1).[101] In terms of procedural safeguards, the Regulation stipulates that during a sea operation, before the intercepted or rescued persons are disembarked in, forced to enter, conducted to or otherwise handed over to the authorities of a third country and taking into account the assessment of the general situation in that third country in

---

[97] Preamble, recital 13.

[98] Article 4(1). See also Preamble, recital 12.

[99] See Peers (2014).

[100] For an overview, see Chap. 4.

[101] Article 4(2).

accordance with para 2, the participating units must use all means to identify the intercepted or rescued persons, assess their personal circumstances, inform them of their destination in a way that those persons understand or may reasonably be presumed to understand and give them an opportunity to express any reasons for believing that disembarkation in the proposed place would be in violation of the principle of *non-refoulement*. For those purposes, further details must be provided for in the operational plan including, *when necessary*, the availability of shore-based medical staff, interpreters, legal advisers and other relevant experts of the host and participating Member States.[102] According to the Preamble, the operational plan should include procedures ensuring that persons with international protection needs, victims of trafficking in human beings, unaccompanied minors and other vulnerable persons are identified and provided with appropriate assistance, including access to international protection.[103] It has been pointed out by a Report prepared for the Parliamentary Assembly of the Council of Europe that this assessment can take place during operations at sea and that it can be questioned if this is a meaningful assessment if safeguards such as legal aid or an effective remedy against a negative decision are not in place.[104] It has also been pointed out that the Regulation ultimately allows FRONTEX and Member States to let migrants disembark in third countries.[105] While such gaps in protection may still exist, the Regulation constitutes a decisive step forward compared with previous EU law in the field. The Regulation enhances accountability and transparency in FRONTEX operations at sea by enhanced requirements for operational plans.[106] The Regulation further includes specific fundamental rights commitments[107] backed up by robust requirements of assessment of the situation in third countries during FRONTEX operations as well as by provisions granting expressly some procedural rights to migrants affected by operations at sea. Article 4(3) will assume particular importance in future FRONTEX operations as it must in turn be interpreted in accordance with the Charter of Fundamental Rights. Most importantly, the

---

[102] Article 4(3). Emphasis added.

[103] Preamble, recital 17.

[104] Council of Europe Parliamentary Assembly, *The 'Left-to-Die' Boat: Actions and Reactions*, Report, Committee on Migration, Refugees and Displaced Persons, *Rapporteur*: Tineke Strik, para 64.

[105] Ibid.

[106] See also the reporting requirements in Article 13 of the Regulation according to which the yearly FRONTEX Report will include a description of the procedures put in place by the Agency to apply this Regulation in practice, including detailed information on compliance with fundamental rights and the impact on those rights, and any incidents which may have taken place (Article 13(2)).

[107] The emphasis on protecting fundamental rights is further reiterated in Article 4(7) of the Regulation which states expressly that Article 4 will apply to all measures taken by Member States or FRONTEX in accordance with the Regulation.

Regulation confirms the legal responsibility of FRONTEX in operations at sea and affirms the applicability of EU human rights standards in instances of operational cooperation between FRONTEX and Member States with third countries in the context of migrant push-backs.

2.4 Delegation and the Privatisation of Immigration Control

Another key strand of delegation of immigration control in European Union law involves the adoption of a series of legislative measures imposing liability to carriers who fail to comply with immigration control-related obligations. Issues surrounding delegation from the state to the private sector in the context of carriers' liability have been analysed extensively in the literature.[108] This part will examine the detail of such privatisation and attempt to demonstrate that, rather than asking the private sector *to replace* state functions in the field, privatisation in the field of immigration control means that the state delegates *additional* tasks (such as the examination and assessment of identity documents) to the private sector. This process of privatisation is reminiscent of what has been deemed in the field of crime control as the 'responsibilisation' strategy, whereby the state co-opts the private sector in order to achieve crime control and security governance objectives.[109] In this manner, the involvement of the private sector serves to add an extra layer of immigration control, in addition to the exercise of expanding state powers in the field.[110] This chapter will examine the preventative aspect of the privatisation of immigration control, by examining legislation placing duties on carriers aiming to identify and transmit information on passengers *before* they reach the border. Preventive privatisation in this context entails criminalisation, in pushing carriers, when in doubt, not to allow the travel of passengers deemed as a risk to immigration control (and, as will be seen below, security). This paradigm of preventive privatisation is complemented by the privatisation of immigration control *ex post*, once migrants have reached the territory of the European Union. The key example of this paradigm are measures on employers' sanctions, which will be analysed later in this volume.[111]

---

[108] See inter alia: Lahav (1998), Guiraudon (2001), and in the UK context, Nicholson (1997).

[109] The term was introduced by Garland (1996).

[110] Mitsilegas, *call-out* (*Immigration Control in an Era of Globalisation*).

[111] Directive 2009/52/EC providing for minimum standards on sanctions and measures against employers of illegally staying third-country nationals, OJ L168, 30 June 2009, p. 24. See Chap. 3.

2.4.1 *Carriers' Liability*

The original flagship measure of the privatisation of immigration control in European Union law is the Carriers liability Directive.[112] The Directive takes forward the provisions of Article 26 of the Schengen Implementing Convention and imposes two main duties on carriers: to take all the necessary measures to ensure that an alien carried out by air or sea is in possession of the travel documents required for entry into the territories[113]; and to assume responsibility for third country nationals who have been refused entry into the territory, including their return or assuming the cost of their return.[114] If carriers transport third country nationals who do not possess the necessary travel documents, they face a series of financial sanctions.[115] In this manner, carriers are asked to provide an extra layer of immigration control in identifying passengers and checking travel documents. EU law also privatises immigration control at the level of enforcement, by requiring carriers to take charge or bear the cost of the return of third country nationals whom they have transported into EU territory.[116] In addition to the carriers' liability Directive, EU Member States adopted in 2003 on a Directive requiring the transmission by carriers of passenger data, but this Directive covered the transmission of data for journeys to the EU, and required the transmission of much more limited categories of personal data (API data, namely data which can be found primarily on the passport).[117] Notwithstanding the fact that the API Directive was adopted under Title IV and its stated aim was to combat illegal immigration, there have been attempts by the UK Government during negotiations to frame it also as a national security and counter-terrorism matter and thus align it with its domestic approach on border security and e-borders.[118]

---

[112] Council Directive 2001/51/EC supplementing the provisions of Article 26 of the Convention implementing the Schengen Agreement of 14 June 1985, OJ L187, 10 July 2001, p. 45.

[113] Article 26(1)(b) of the Schengen Implementing Convention.

[114] Articles 2 and 3 of the Directive and Article 26(1)(a) of the Schengen Implementing Convention.

[115] Articles 4 and 5 of the Directive and 26(2) of the Schengen Implementing Convention.

[116] For an overview of the challenges facing carriers in the implementation of the Directive, see Scholten (2014).

[117] Council Directive 2004/82/EC of 29 April 2004 on the obligation of carriers to communicate passenger data [2004] OJ L 261/24, 6 August 2004. For an analysis of the Directive see Mitsilegas (2005).

[118] Caroline Flint, then a Home Office Minister, argued that the proposal 'is all about border control, whether it is illegal immigration or criminals coming in, or people who are a threat to national security' See her evidence in see House of Lords, EU Committee, *Fighting illegal immigration: should carriers carry the burden?*, 5th Report, session 2003–2004, HL Paper 29, at para 9.

2.4.2 The Collection and Transfer of Passenger Name Record (PNR) Data

The link between privatisation, prevention and securitisation has been provided expressly in EU law by introducing obligations to air carriers to transfer Passenger Name Records (PNR) to state authorities not of EU Member States, but of third states starting primarily with the United States.[119] The imposition of duties to air carriers to collect and transfer to state authorities of PNR data has been a key component of US Homeland Security strategy post-9/11, in the light of the way in which the 9/11 attacks occurred.[120] Carriers flying to the US from Europe were thus placed under duties imposed by unilateral US legislation to transfer PNR data to the US authorities and concerns were raised that compliance with US requirements would render carriers in breach of EU law and domestic Member States' law on data protection.[121] In order to address this conflict of interest, EU institutions proceeded to conclude an agreement between the European Community and the United States authorities legitimising the transfer of PNR data to the US. On the basis of a Decision by the Commission confirming the adequacy of US data protection standards,[122] a transatlantic agreement on the transfer of PNR data to the US Bureau of Customs and Border Protection was signed in 2004. The Agreement was subsequently litigated before the Court of Justice of the European Union, with the European Parliament bringing an action for annulment of the Decision authorising the conclusion of the Agreement on grounds of legality, proportionality and infringement of the fundamental rights of privacy and data protection. In what can be characterised as a 'pyrrhic victory' for the European Parliament, the Court annulled the measure on legality (competence) grounds, but without examining the substance of the Parliament's fundamental rights non-compliance allegations.[123] The annulment of the Agreement resulted in the conclusion of an interim third pillar Agreement, and eventually in 2007 of a third pillar EU–US PNR Agreement.[124]

---

[119] See the Agreement between the European Union and Australia on the processing and transfer of European Union sourced PNR data by air carriers to the Australian Customs Service (OJ L186, 14.7.2012, p. 4). The European Union and Canada have signed a new PNR Agreement on 25 June 2014 (*Signature of the EU–Canada agreement on Passenger Name Records (PNR)*, Council doc. 10940/14, Brussels, 25 June 2014, PRESSE 339), The Agreement is expected to replace its pre-Lisbon predecessor (OJ L82, 21.3.2006).

[120] Mitsilegas *call-out (Immigration Control in an Era of Globalisation)*.

[121] Mitsilegas *call-out (Controle des Etrangers)*.

[122] Commission Decision of 14 May 2004 on the adequate protection of personal data contained in the Passenger Name Record of air passengers transferred to the United States' Bureau of Customs and Border Protection, [2004] OJ L 235/11, 6 July 2004. The Undertakings of the US Homeland Security Department are annexed in pp. 15–21. The list of PNR data is annexed in p. 22.

[123] Joint cases C-317-04 and C-318/04 *European Parliament v Council*, judgment of 30 May 2006.

[124] For details, see Mitsilegas (2007b).

The entry into force of the Lisbon Treaty meant that the European Parliament, which had a limited role with regard to the conclusion of international agreements under the old third pillar, was called to consent to the 2007 EU–US PNR Agreement. The Parliament expressed concerns about the compatibility of the Agreement with EU privacy and data protection law and called upon the Commission to put forward a single set of principles to serve as a basis for negotiations with third countries.[125]

The new EU–US PNR Agreement was eventually approved by the European Parliament in early 2012 and took effect on June 1, 2012.[126] The legal bases for the Decisions to sign and conclude the Agreement are Articles 82(1)(d) and 87(2)(a) in conjunction with Article 218(6)(a) TFEU.[127] The Agreement will remain in force for a period of 7 years after its entry into force and, unless one of the Parties notifies of its intention not to renew further, will be renewable for subsequent 7 year periods.[128] Its structure is a significant improvement from a rule of law perspective, as the main provisions and safeguards are set out largely in the text of the EU–US Agreement itself, rather than in a Letter by the US to the EU, as was the case with the 2007 Agreement. The purpose of the Agreement is defined in rather broad terms: 'to ensure security and to protect the life and safety of the public.'[129] This broad wording may challenge calls for the inclusion of strict purpose limitation safeguards under the Agreement. It applies to a wide range of carriers: to carriers operating passenger flights between the European Union and the United States[130] as well as to carriers incorporated or storing data in the European Union and operating passenger flights to or from the United States.[131] The Agreement establishes an obligation for carriers to provide PNR data contained in their reservation systems to the US Department of Homeland Security (DHS) as required by DHS standards and consistent with the Agreement.[132] Data transmission will occur initially 96 h before departure and additionally either in real time or for a fixed number of routine and scheduled transfers as specified by DHS.[133] The Agreement defines PNR data by

[125] European Parliament Resolution of 5 May 2010 on the launch of negotiations for Passenger Name Record (PNR) agreements with the United States, Australia and Canada P7_TA(2010)0144.

[126] On entry into force, see Article 27(1) of the Agreement.

[127] Council Decision of 13 December 2011 on the signing, on behalf of the European Union, of the Agreement between the United States of America and the European Union on the use and transfer of Passenger Name Records to the United States Department of Homeland Security, OJ L215/1, 13.8.2012; Council Decision of 26 April 2012 on the conclusion of the Agreement between the United States of America and the European Union on the use and transfer of Passenger Name Records to the United States Department of Homeland Security, OJ L215/4, 13.8.2012.

[128] Article 26(1) and (2).

[129] Article 1(1).

[130] Article 2(2).

[131] Article 2(3).

[132] Article 3.

[133] Article 15(3). But see exceptions in Article 15(5).

reference to the Guidelines of the International Civil Aviation Organisation (ICAO).[134] As with the previous transatlantic PNR Agreements, the actual categories of PNR data to be transferred to the US Homeland Security Department are listed in an Annex to the Agreement. The Annex contains 19 categories of PNR data, which include broad categorisations such as frequent flier information, payment information, travel itinerary, travel status, seat number, general remarks and historical changes. DHS will retain PNR in an active database for up to 5 years.[135] After this active period, PNR shall be transferred to a dormant database for a period of up to 10 years.[136] Following the dormant period, data retained must be rendered fully anonymised.[137] However, data related to a specific case or investigation may be retained in an active PNR database until the case or investigation is archived and even so, this paragraph is without prejudice to data retention requirements for individual investigation or prosecution files.[138] Moreover, the Agreement does allow the onward transfer to PNR data to third countries.[139]

The Agreement thus maintains the paradigm of the privatisation of crime control set out in earlier Agreements and imposes extensive obligations on carriers to transmit a wide range of everyday personal data to the US Homeland Security Department. It constitutes a key example of the trend towards generalised, pre-emptive surveillance, whereby masses of every day personal data is collected by the private sector and transferred to state authorities in order to enable them to predict future behaviour and manage risk.[140] The transfer of PNR data affects every passenger, migrants and citizens alike.[141] The surveillance system the Agreement establishes poses grave challenges to fundamental rights, in particular the rights to privacy and data protection. These challenges are compounded by calls for the European Union to internalise the US approach on pre-emptive surveillance by mirroring the US system in creating a system whereby airlines flying into the EU are required to collect and transfer PNR data to European authorities before travel. The EU–US PNR Agreement itself envisages the potential establishment of such an EU PNR system states that if and when an EU PNR system is adopted, the Parties will consult to determine whether this Agreement would need to be adjusted accordingly to ensure full reciprocity. Such consultations will in particular examine whether any future EU PNR system would apply less stringent data protection

---

[134] Article 2(1).

[135] Article 8(1).

[136] Article 8(3). According to Article 8(6), the Parties agree that, within the framework of the evaluation as provided for in Article 23(1), the necessity of a 10-year dormant period of retention will be considered.

[137] Article 8(4).

[138] Article 8(5).

[139] Article 17(1)—The US may transfer PNR to competent government authorities of third countries only under terms consistent with this Agreement and only upon ascertaining that the recipient's intended use is consistent with those terms. See also Article 17(2).

[140] See Mitsilegas (2015b).

[141] See Mitsilegas (2009).

safeguards than those provided for in this Agreement and whether, therefore, this Agreement should be amended.[142] The European Commission tabled a proposal for a Framework Decision on an EU PNR system as early as 2007.[143] The Commission explained that the proposal was a result of the "policy learning" from inter alia the existing EU PNR Agreements with the United States and Canada.[144] Agreement on the proposal was not reached before the entry into force of the Lisbon Treaty, a fact which led the Commission to table new legislation post-Lisbon, this time in the form of a Directive.[145] The Commission justified the establishment of a European system of PNR transfer as necessary for law enforcement purposes due to its potential for risk assessment of passengers and proposed a system which is very similar to the US PNR system, at least as regards the categories of transferred data[146] and the emphasis on risk assessment.[147] In parallel to such calls for the establishment of an EU PNR system and negotiations by the EU to conclude PNR agreements with other third countries including Australia and Canada, the Commission has also been calling for the development of a global regime for the collection and transfer of PNR data. In its Communication on a Global Approach to Transfers of PNR Data to Third Countries,[148] the Commission called upon the European Union to consider initiating discussions with international partners that use PNR data and those that are considering using such data in order to explore whether there is common ground between them for dealing with PNR transfers on a multilateral level. In this manner, a system of generalized pre-emptive surveillance of mobility based on the involvement of the private sector which has been imposed unilaterally by the United States as an emergency post-9/11 response potentially becomes normalised via EU action on a global scale, notwithstanding the persistent concerns with regard to the compatibility of such a system with European human rights law.[149]

---

[142] Article 20(2). See also the wording of the US Letter to the EU within the framework of the 2007 Agreement according to which DHS expected not to be asked to undertake data protection measures in its PNR system that are more stringent than those applied by the US for its PNR system—point IX, para 1—see also Preamble of the Agreement, recital 5.

[143] *Commission Proposal for a Council Framework Decision on the Use of Passenger Name Record (PNR) for Law Enforcement Purposes*, COM (2007) 654 final (Nov. 6 2007).

[144] *Id.* at 2.

[145] *Commission Proposal for a Directive of the European Parliament and of the Council on the Use of Passenger Name Record Data for the Prevention, Detection, Investigation, and Prosecution of Terrorist Offences and Serious Crimes*, COM (2011) 32 final (Feb. 2, 2011).

[146] Requested data includes all forms of payment information, including billing address, travel status of passenger (including confirmations), check-in status, no show or go show information, seat number and other seat information, number and other names of travelers on PNR, and "general remarks".

[147] V. Mitsilegas, *call-out* (*Immigration Control in an Era of Globalisation*).

[148] COM (2010) 492 final, 21.9.2010.

[149] Mitsilegas, *call-out* (*The Transformation of Privacy*).

2.5 Immigration Control as Security Governance

The imposition to carriers of obligations to transfer PNR data to the authorities of third states is only one example of the securitisation of migration at EU level. The development of EU law and policy in recent years has been marked by growing linkages between immigration control and security governance. In this two-fold process of securitisation of migration, immigration control is used to achieve security objectives, while security and crime governance methods are being used to conduct border and immigration controls. Conceived in both sides of the Atlantic as 'border security', this process of securitisation of migration has a strong preventive aspect.[150] In addition to the collection and transfer of a wide range of personal data emanating from every day legitimate activity to state authorities responsible for security and crime prevention and control that PNR transfer systems entail, the securitisation of migration in Europe has also taken the form of the establishment of large scale EU immigration databases and mobility surveillance systems, as well as efforts to interlink and make interoperable these databases. The establishment of databases is linked with the focus on the collection by the state of a wide range of personal data from migrants, including sensitive data such as biometrics. Securitisation is also strongly premised upon negating the specificity of the purpose of the collection by state authorities of personal data of migrants (which is immigration control) and arguing that this purpose is not only immigration control but also security governance. This attack on purpose limitation has led to EU law now allowing access to a wide range of immigration data collected in EU databases to authorities responsible for crime control and security. A multi-layered system of securitisation and criminalisation of migration has thus been established.

2.5.1 Migration and Security in EU Law and Policy

The link between immigration control and security was clearly articulated in the 5 year Programme for EU Justice and Home Affairs law and policy agreed by the European Council in 2004 (the Hague Programme). According to the latter,

> the management of migration flows, including the fight against illegal immigration should be strengthened by establishing *a continuum of security measures* that effectively links visa application procedures and entry and exit procedures at external border crossings. Such measures are also of importance for the prevention and control of crime, in particular terrorism. In order to achieve this, a coherent approach and harmonised solutions in the EU on biometric identifiers and data are necessary.[151]

---

[150] On the emergence of the concept of Border Security see Mitsilegas, *call-out* (*Border Security in the European Union*); Mitsilegas (2011).

[151] Paragraph 1.7.2. Emphasis added.

In this manner, the wording of the Hague Programme represents the creation of what scholars have already identified in the 1990s as the so-called '(in)security continuum' which consists of linking, in law and policy discourse, the disparate and very different aims of controlling immigration on the one hand and fighting 'security threats' such as crime and terrorism on the other.[152] Intervention *before* entry, prevention and the collection and exchange of personal data (including biometrics) are all key in this context. The renewal of such (in)security continuum emerged at EU level following attacks in a European capital, Madrid. In the Declaration on combating terrorism of 25 March 2004 following these attacks, the European Council linked the monitoring of the movement of people with counter-terrorism by stressing that 'improved border controls and document security play an important role in combating terrorism'. There were two elements in this approach: the inclusion of biometrics in EU visas and passports, which should be prioritised and relevant measures be adopted by the end of 2004; and the enhancement of the interoperability between EU databases and the creation of 'synergies' between existing and future information systems (such as the Schengen Information System II, the Visa Information System and Eurodac) in order to exploit their added value within their respective legal and technical frameworks in the prevention and fight against terrorism.[153]

The emphasis on the use of technology in the securitisation of migration in the European Union was clearly reflected in a Commission Communication on the 'interoperability' of databases.[154] The purpose of the Communication was to highlight how, beyond their present purposes, databases 'can more effectively support the policies linked to the free movement of persons and serve the objective of combating terrorism and serious crime'.[155] On the basis of this approach, the Commission argued strongly in favour of access of authorities responsible for internal security to immigration databases including the Visa Information System.[156] The Communication provided a definition of 'interoperability', which is the 'ability of IT systems and of the business processes they support to exchange data and to enable the sharing of information and knowledge'.[157] According to the Commission, interoperability is a technical rather than a legal/political concept.[158]

---

[152] See Bigo (1996).

[153] See V. Mitsilegas, *call-out* (*Contrôle des étrangers*).

[154] *Communication on Improved Effectiveness, Enhanced Interoperability and Synergies among European Databases in the Area of Justice and Home Affairs,* COM (2005) 597 final, Brussels, 24 November 2005.

[155] Ibid., p. 2.

[156] Ibid., p. 8. The Commission also took the opportunity to float proposals for longer-term developments, including the creation of a European Criminal Automated Fingerprints Identification System, the creation of an entry-exit system and introduction of a border crossing facilitation scheme for frequent border crossers, and European registers for travel documents and identity cards (pp. 8–9).

[157] Ibid., p. 3.

[158] Ibid.

This attempt to treat interoperability, which is a term now increasingly used by EU institutions,[159] as a merely technical concept, while at the same time using the concept to enable maximum access to databases containing a wide range of personal data (which become even more sensitive with the sustained emphasis on biometrics) is a striking attempt to depoliticise the issue and shield developments from the enhanced scrutiny that the adoption of legislation in the field would provide.[160]

2.5.2 The Visa Information System

A key example of the preventive securitisation of migration in Europe via the establishment of an EU database containing a wide range of personal data (including biometrics) which is also accessible by law enforcement authorities is the development of the Visa Information System (VIS). The VIS is a management tool of the EU instrument of extraterritorial immigration control *par excellence,* the visa.[161] The Justice and Home Affairs Council adopted detailed conclusions on the development of VIS in February 2004, stating clearly that one of the purposes of the system would be to 'contribute towards improving the administration of the common visa policy and towards internal security and combating terrorism.'[162] It also called for access to VIS to be granted to border guards and 'other national authorities to be authorised by each Member State such as police departments, immigration departments and services responsible for internal security.'[163] In June 2004, the Council adopted a Decision forming the legal basis for the establishment of VIS[164] and negotiations began to define its purpose and functions and formulate rules on access and exchange of data. The Commission subsequently tabled a draft Regulation aiming to take VIS further by defining its aims and rules on data access and exchange.[165] The Justice and Home Affairs Council of 24 February 2005 called for access to VIS to be given to national authorities responsible for 'internal

---

[159] See for instance the Justice and Home Affairs Council Conclusions of 5–6 June 2008 'on the management of the external borders of the member states of the European Union', where it is stated that pilot projects developing future EU border management measures should allow for 'maximum interoperability' (para 16).

[160] See Mitsilegas, *call-out* (*Extraterritorial Immigration Control in the 21st Century*).

[161] See Guild (2003).

[162] Doc 5831/04 (Presse 37). The Council called for the inclusion in VIS of biometric data on visa applicants.

[163] Ibid.

[164] Council Decision of 8 June 2004 establishing the Visa Information System (VIS), [2004] OJ L 213/5, 15 June 2004.

[165] Proposal for a Regulation of the European Parliament and of the Council concerning the VIS and the exchange of data between Member States on short-stay visas, COM (2004) 835 final, 28 December 2004.

security', when exercising their powers in investigating, preventing and detecting criminal offences, including terrorist acts or threats and invited the Commission to present a separate, third pillar proposal to this end.[166] The Commission tabled such a proposal in November 2005.[167] The two texts were linked and thus negotiated in parallel (co-decision was required formally for the first pillar Regulation, while for the third pillar Decision the European Parliament had a consultation role).[168] Agreement on both proposals was confirmed at the Justice and Home Affairs Council of 12–13 June 2007[169] and they were published in the Official Journal in August 2008.[170]

Reflecting the logic of the Conclusions of the 2005 Justice and Home Affairs Council, the VIS Regulation expressly states that one of the purposes of the Visa Information System is to contribute to the prevention of threats to internal security of the Member States.[171] The Regulation also contains a bridging clause to the third pillar Decision allowing access to VIS by Europol within the limits of its mandate and when necessary for the performance of its tasks, and by the relevant national authorities 'if there are reasonable grounds to consider that consultation of VIS data will substantially contribute' to the prevention, detection or investigation of terrorist offences and of other serious criminal offences.[172] The terms of access of internal security authorities and Europol to the VIS are set out in detail in the third pillar Decision.[173] The VIS will also include biometric data.[174] Some detail with regard to the introduction of biometrics to EU visas can be found in a Regulation amending the Common Consular Instructions.[175] The link between the collection and use of biometrics on the one hand and the identification of the visa holder on the other is made clear already in the Preamble to the Regulation.[176] The Regulation calls upon Member States to collect biometric identifiers comprising the facial image and 10 fingerprints from the applicant.[177] The development of the Visa Information System constitutes a paradigm in EU law of the routine inclusion of biometrics in EU

---

166 Doc. 6228.05 (Presse 28), pp. 15–16.

167 COM (2005) 600 final, 24 November 2005.

168 For further details see V. Mitsilegas, '*Human Rights, Terrorism and the Quest for Border Security*', *call-out.*

169 Council doc. 10267/07 (Presse 125).

170 Regulation (EC) No 767/2008, OJ L218, 13 August 2008, p. 60; Decision 2008/633/JHA, OJ L218, 13 August 2008, p. 129.

171 The Regulation also enables the recording of biometric data into VIS—see Article 5(1).

172 Article 3(1).

173 In particular Articles 5–7.

174 Regulation, Preamble recital 10, Articles 5 and 9.

175 Regulation (EC) No 390/2009, L131, 28 May 2009, p. 1.

176 'The integration of biometric identifiers in the VIS is an important step towards the use of new elements, which establish a more reliable link between the visa holder and the passport in order to avoid the use of false identities'—recital 2.

177 Amended Part III point 1.2(a). See also the exceptions in Part III point 1.2(b).

immigration databases[178] as well as of legitimising the tenuous link between extraterritorial immigration control via the imposition of visa requirements and security and crime control imperatives. The inclusion of biometrics in EU databases lies also at the core of EURODAC, the EU database containing information on individuals lodging an asylum application in EU Member States. Following intense inter-institutional debate, the new post-Lisbon EURODAC Regulation now allows access to the system by law enforcement authorities.[179] EU law has also introduced —under an immigration legal basis—an obligation for Member States to introduce biometrics in EU passports.[180] The use of biometrics is also key to current proposals for the establishment of an EU entry-exit system, with access to this system by law enforcement authorities being a possibility.[181] The securitisation of migration has thus been normalised.

2.5.3 The Entry-Exit System and Registered Traveller Programme

Another example of the new generalised surveillance based on monitoring movement, applying to both EU and third country nationals, is the collection of sensitive personal data has been the new move by the European Commission to propose the creation of an entry-exit system at the external borders of the European Union, coupled with facilitation of border crossings for *bona fide* travellers and the creation of an electronic travel authorisation system.[182] The entry/exit system would be a new database, applying to third country nationals admitted for a short stay; bona

[178] On the use of biometrics in EU immigration databases, see Baldaccini (2008), see also Brouwer (2007).

[179] Regulation (EU) No 603/2013 of the European Parliament and of the Council of 26 June 2013 on the establishment of 'Eurodac' for the comparison of fingerprints for the effective application of Regulation (EU) No 604/2013 establishing the criteria and mechanisms for determining the Member State responsible for examining an application for international protection lodged in one of the Member States by a third-country nationals or a stateless person and on requests for the comparison with Eurodac data by Member States' law enforcement authorities and Europol for law enforcement purposes, and amending Regulation (EU) No 1077/2011 establishing a European Agency for the operational management of large-scale IT systems in the area of freedom, security and justice, OJ L180/1, OJ 29.6.2013. For a critical analysis, see Vavoula (2015).

[180] Council Regulation (EC) No 2252/2004 of 13 December 2004 on standards for security features and biometrics in passports and travel docs issued by Member States, [2004] OJ L 385/1, 29 December 2004. For a critical analysis, including on the legality of the Regulation, see Mitsilegas, *call-out* (*The Borders Paradox*).

[181] See *Draft Regulation of the European Parliament and of the Council establishing an Entry/ Exit System (EES) to register entry and exit data of third country nationals crossing the external borders of the Member States of the European Union—Access for law enforcement purposes*, Council doc. 10720/14, Brussels, 12 June 2014.

[182] Commission Communication on *Preparing the Next Steps in Border Management in the European Union*, COM (2008) 69 final, Brussels, 13 February 2008.

fide travellers would be 'low risk' third country nationals, but also EU citizens—both would cross external borders via 'automated gates'. The Electronic Travel Authorisation System (ETA) would apply to third country nationals not subject to a visa requirement who would be required to make an electronic application in advance of travelling. These proposals are similar to the US model of border security, and are reminiscent of the recommendation by the 9/11 Commission to 'balance' the collection of biometrics by US citizens with measures aimed at speeding 'known travellers'.[183] Both interoperability and the use of biometrics is central to these proposals, in particular to the proposals for the establishment of a system of border crossings via automated gates. The Commission noted that:

> In the run-up to *full introduction of biometric passports*, the current legal framework allows for schemes based on voluntary enrolment to be deployed by Member States, under the condition that the criteria for enrolment correspond to those for minimum checks at the borders *and that the schemes are open for all persons enjoying the Community right to free movement*. Such schemes should be *interoperable* within the EU, based on common technical standards, which should be defined to support the *widespread and coherent use of automated border control systems*.[184]

The added value of a new database on an entry-exit system for third country nationals is however not evident, especially in the light of the recent setting up of the Visa Information System. Moreover, and along with the evident proportionality concerns, there have been serious legality concerns with regard to the extension of legislation on the management of the EU external border to EU citizens.[185] However, the momentum for the establishment of an entry-exit system along these lines is currently high. The European Council invited the Commission to present proposals for an entry/exit and registered traveller system by the beginning of 2010,[186] and agreed in the European Pact on Immigration and Asylum (endorsed by the European Council in October 2008) to deploy 'modern technological means to ensure that systems are interoperable' and stated that from 2012 the focus should be 'on establishing electronic recording of entry and exit, together with a fast-track procedure for European citizens and other travellers'.[187] The political prioritisation of the establishment of an entry-exit system has been reaffirmed in the 5 year plan succeeding the Hague Programme, the Stockholm Programme, which emphasised once more the link between security, mobility and technology.[188]

---

[183] For an overview of US initiatives, see Mitsilegas, *call-out* (*Immigration Control in an Era of Globalisation*).

[184] Ibid., p. 7. Emphasis added.

[185] For further details on this point, see V. Mitsilegas, *call-out* (*The Borders Paradox*).

[186] Presidency Conclusions of the Brussels European Council of 19/20 June 2008, Council doc. 11018/08, Brussels, 20 June 2008, para 10.

[187] Council doc. 13440/08, Brussels, 24 September 2008, point III(e).

[188] European Council, *The Stockholm Programme—An Open and Secure Europe Serving and Protecting Citizens,* OJ C 115, 4 May 2010, p. 1.

The opening sentence of the Stockholm Programme chapter entitled 'access to Europe in a globalised world' states that '[t]he Union must continue to facilitate legal access to the territory of its Member States while in parallel taking measures to counteract illegal immigration *and cross-border crime* and maintaining a high level of security.'[189] Noting that the possibilities of 'new and interoperable technologies hold great potential for rendering border management more efficient as well as more secure but should not lead to discrimination or unequal treatment of passengers' the European Council invited the Commission to present proposals for an entry/exit system alongside a fast track registered traveller programme with a view to such a system becoming operational as soon as possible; to prepare a study on the possibility and usefulness of developing a European system of travel authorisation and, where appropriate, to make the necessary proposals; and to continue to examine the issue of automated border controls and other issues connected to rendering border management more efficient.[190] The Commission Action Plan on the implementation of the Stockholm Programme envisaged the tabling of legislative proposals setting up an Entry Exit System and a Registered Traveller Programme in 2011.[191] The Commission has now published two draft Regulations on the establishment of an Entry-Exit System[192] and on the establishment of a Registered Traveller Programme[193] respectively. They both apply to third-country nationals only.

By establishing an entry-exit system—which is remarkably similar to developments in US law analysed above—the EU introduces a system of surveillance of movement based on automaticity, interoperability, and the collection and consultation of sensitive personal data such as biometrics. As I have noted elsewhere, merging the logic of risk prevention with the logic of border security, this model has far-reaching consequences for the protection of fundamental rights and the relationship between the individual and the State.[194] Movement is monitored on the basis of profiling—and the establishment of individual, subjective assessments on each traveller. Migrants are criminalised as they can be deemed as 'suspects' under these assessments, and their freedom of movement curtailed accordingly. The introduction of the concept of 'bona fide' traveller is extremely worrying in this context. As the European Data Protection Supervisor has noted in his preliminary comments on the initial Commission proposals:

---

189 Chapter 5, para 5.1, emphasis added.

190 Ibid.

191 Commission Communication, *Delivering an Area of Freedom, Security and Justice for Europe's Citizens. Action Plan Implementing the Stockholm Programme,* COM (2010) 171 final, p. 44.

192 Proposal for a Regulation of the European Parliament and of the Council establishing an Entry/Exit System (EES) to register entry and exit data of third country nationals crossing the external borders of the Member States of the European Union, COM (2013) 95 final, Brussels, 28.2.2013.

193 Proposal for a Regulation of the European Parliament and of the Council establishing a Registered Traveller Programme, COM (2013) 97 final, Brussels, 28.2.2013.

194 Mitsilegas, *call-out* (*The Borders Paradox*).

> The underlying assumption in the communications (especially in the entry/exit proposal) is worrying: all travellers are put under surveillance and are considered a priori as potential law breakers. For instance in the Registered Travellers system, only the travellers taking specific steps, through ad hoc registration and provision of detailed personal information, will be considered 'bona fide' travellers. The vast amount of travellers, who do not travel frequently enough to undergo such a registration, are thus, by implication, de facto in the 'mala fide' category of those suspected of intentions of overstay.[195]

Concerns with regard to the discriminatory impact of the Registered Traveller Programme, as well as with regard to the necessity and proportionality of the new Commission proposals, have also been expressed by the European Data Protection Supervisor in his Opinion on the two draft Regulations tabled by the Commission in 2013.[196]

2.5.4 EUROSUR

The nexus between the preventive turn in border control via shifts in time and space, the move towards delegation and the use of technology and risk management in the securitisation of migration are all clearly reflected in the recently adopted European Union Regulation establishing the European Border Surveillance System (EUROSUR).[197] EUROSUR is a common framework for the exchange of information and for the cooperation between Member States and FRONTEX in order to improve situational awareness and to increase reaction capability at the external borders of the Member States of the Union for the purpose of detecting, preventing and combating illegal immigration and cross-border crime and contributing to ensuring the protection and saving the lives of migrants.[198] A key component of the system is the development of situational pictures at national and EU level[199] and, importantly, a common pre-frontier intelligence picture which will be maintained by FRONTEX in order to provide the national coordination centres with effective, accurate and timely information and analysis on the pre-frontier area.[200] The latter is defined as the geographical area beyond the external borders.[201] Key to the operation of EUROSUR is the common application of surveillance tools which will be coordinated by FRONTEX.[202] FRONTEX will provide a national coordination

---

195 Opinion of 3 March 2008, pp. 5–6.

196 Opinion of 18 July 2013.

197 Regulation No 1052/2013, OJ L295/11, 6.11.2013.

198 Article 1.

199 Articles 8–10.

200 Article 11(1).

201 Article 3g.

202 Article 12(1).

centre, at its request, with information on the external borders of the requesting Member State and on the pre-frontier area which may be derived from inter alia: selective monitoring of designated third-country ports and coasts which have been identified through risk analysis and information as being embarkation or transit points for vessels or other craft used for illegal immigration or cross-border crime; tracking of vessels or other craft over high seas which are suspected of, or have been identified as, being used for illegal immigration or cross-border crime; monitoring of designated areas in the maritime domain in order to detect, identify and track vessels and other craft being used for, or suspected of being used for, illegal immigration or cross-border crime; and selective monitoring of designated pre-frontier areas at the external borders which have been identified through risk analysis and information as being potential departure or transit areas for illegal immigration or cross-border crime.[203] The system also provides for exchange of information with neighbouring third countries.[204] EUROSUR is thus designed to be a system of supranational extra-territorial surveillance, involving information gathering outside the border and in third states, based on technology, with the aim of in essence providing intelligence which will help prevent or deflect migration flows to the EU external border.[205] The terms of its establishment are yet another example of the prioritisation of security considerations in EU immigration control policy.[206]

2.5.5 Pre-emptive Surveillance, Privacy and the Rule of Law

The securitisation of immigration control with an emphasis on the prevention of migrant flows has significant consequences for migrants. EU law has created a multi-layered system of pre-emptive surveillance whereby a vast array of personal data (including every day data emanating from legitimate activities such as applying for a visa or booking a flight ticket and sensitive data such as biometrics) is collected on a routine basis and ending into databases which are accessible by law enforcement and security authorities.[207] State authorities have thus access to a wealth of personal data enabling practices such as profiling and data mining. The impact of state intervention on the individual is intensified when one considers the

---

[203] Article 12(2).

[204] Article 20.

[205] For a critical analysis of the use of technology in the development of EUROSUR, see Jeandesboz (2011).

[206] See also the concerns expressed in the United Nations General Assembly, Report of the Special Rapporteur on the human rights of migrants, Francois Crépeau: *Regional Study: Management of the External Borders of the European Union and its impact on the human rights of migrants,* 24 April 2013, para 44.

[207] On the concept of pre-emptive surveillance for counter-terrorism purposes see de Goede (2012).

potential of combining personal data from different databases collected for different purposes in order to create a profile of risk or dangerousness. In addition to the substantive privacy challenges these developments pose, risk assessment in these terms poses acute rule of law challenges in reconfiguring the place of the individual in a democratic society.[208] Key in this context is what has been deemed as the adiaphorisation in surveillance: according to Lyon,

> Data from the body (such as biometrics, DNA) or triggered by the body … are sucked into databases to be processed, analysed, concatenated with other data, then spat out again as a 'data double.' The information that proxies for the person is made up of 'personal data' only in the sense that it originated with a person's body and may affect their life chances and choices. The piecemeal data double tends to be trusted more than the persontrans-formation of privacy in an era of.[209]

The use of personal data in these terms leads to a process whereby individuals embarking on perfectly legitimate everyday activities are constantly being assessed and viewed as potentially dangerous without having many possibilities of knowing or contesting such assessment. At any time, anybody can be a 'trusted' or a 'suspect' passenger. As Amoore has noted, 'read in this way the border becomes a condition of being that is always in the act of becoming, it is never entirely crossed, but appears instead as a constant demand for proof of status and legitimacy.'[210] In this manner, EU law creates a permanent system of risk assessment and categorisation of individuals, leading to the normalisation of practices of inclusion and exclusion.[211] These practices are manifestly deficient from a rule of law perspective as they undermine legal certainty and the legitimate expectations individuals have from the state. As Solove has noted, predictive determinations about one's future behaviour are much more difficult to contest than investigative determinations about one's past behaviour.[212] To the extent that these practices are applicable also to citizens of the Union, they challenge fundamentally the bond between the citizen and the state and the relationship of trust inherent in citizenship.[213]

In addition to rule of law challenges, the securitisation of migration via the normalisation of pre-emptive surveillance poses acute challenges to the rights of privacy and data protection. Everyday personal data is collected and transferred to state authorities and EU databases *en masse* and the principle of purpose limitation as regards the use of personal data for immigration control purposes is largely inapplicable under the logic that 'it is all about security.' The danger of profiling in such a system of constant data collection and risk assessment is present. A significant step forward towards addressing these challenges has been made by the

[208] See Mitsilegas (2014).

[209] See Bauman and Lyon (2013).

[210] See Amoore (2006).

[211] See Franco Aas (2011).

[212] See Solove (2008).

[213] On the applicability of border surveillance to EU citizens, see V. Mitsilegas, *The Borders Paradox, call-out.*

European Court of Human Rights in the case of *Marper*,[214] where the retention of DNA data by the British police of individuals not associated with any crime was deemed contrary to Article 8 of the ECHR (private and family life). In *Marper* the European Court of Human Rights examined the compatibility with the ECHR of the systemic and indefinite retention of DNA profiles and cellular samples of persons who have been acquitted or in respect of whom criminal proceedings have been discontinued in the UK. The Court found that such blanket and indiscriminate retention of data is disproportionate and thus non-compliant with Article 8 of the Convention. The ruling is important in rejecting the retention of DNA data *per se*: according to the Court, the mere retention and storing of personal data by public authorities, however obtained, are to be regarded as having a direct impact on the private-life interest of an individual concerned, irrespective of whether subsequent use is made of the data.[215] It is also important in highlighting the broader impact of retention on the affected individuals and in particular the risk of stigmatisation, stemming from the fact that persons in the position of the applicants, who have not been convicted of any offence and are entitled to the presumption of innocence, are treated in the same way as convicted persons.[216]

A further significant step forward in setting limits to surveillance has been made by the Court of Justice of the European Union in a case concerning the compatibility with human rights of the EU Directive on data retention, which introduced the obligation of blanket retention of a series of telecommunications data to mobile phone providers.[217] Following up to a number of significant rulings by national constitutional courts in Europe finding that the implementation of the Directive was unconstitutional in their respective legal orders,[218] in its landmark ruling in the case of *Digital Rights Ireland*,[219] the Court of Justice annulled the data retention Directive on the grounds that the EU legislature has exceeded the limits imposed by compliance with the principle of proportionality in the light of Articles 7, 8 and 52 (1) of the Charter. The Court developed its ruling in six main steps.[220] The first step has been to focus on proportionality and to emphasise the importance of the principle by reference to CJEU case-law,[221] but also by reference to the Strasbourg

---

[214] Case of *S. And Marper v. The UK*, Application nos. 30562/04 and 30566/04.

[215] Paragraph 121.

[216] Paragraph 122.

[217] Directive 2006/24/EC of the European Parliament and of the Council of 15 March 2006 on the retention of data generated or processed in connection with the provision of publicly available electronic communications services of public communications networks and amending Directive 2002/58/EC, OJ L 105, 13 April 2006, p. 54.

[218] For an overview see Mitsilegas, *call-out* (*The Value of Privacy in an Era of Security*).

[219] Joined Cases C-293/12 and C-594/12, *Digital Rights Ireland and Seitlinger*, judgment of 8.4.2014.

[220] See Mitsilegas, *call-out* (*The Transformation of Privacy*).

[221] According to the settled case-law of the Court, the principle of proportionality requires that acts of the EU institutions be appropriate for attaining the legitimate objectives pursued by the legislation at issue and do not exceed the limits of what is appropriate and necessary in order to

jurisprudence in *Marper*.[222] The second step has been to view data protection as a means of protecting privacy: according to the Court, it should be noted that the protection of personal data resulting from the explicit obligation laid down in Article 8(1) of the Charter is especially important for the right to respect for private life enshrined in Article 7 of the Charter.[223] The third and key step has been to focus on the generalised and unlimited collection of personal data under the Directive. According to the Court, the directive requires the retention of all traffic data concerning fixed telephony, mobile telephony, Internet access, Internet e-mail and Internet telephony. It therefore applies to all means of electronic communication, the use of which is very widespread and of growing importance in people's everyday lives. Furthermore, in accordance with Article 3 of Directive 2006/24, the directive covers all subscribers and registered users. It therefore entails an interference with the fundamental rights of practically the entire European population.[224] In this respect, it must be noted, first, that Directive 2006/24 covers, in a generalised manner, all persons and all means of electronic communication as well as all traffic data without any differentiation, limitation or exception being made in the light of the objective of fighting against serious crime.[225] The Court further noted that Directive 2006/24 affects, in a comprehensive manner, all persons using electronic communications services, but without the persons whose data are retained being, even indirectly, in a situation which is liable to give rise to criminal prosecutions. It therefore applies even to persons for whom there is no evidence capable of suggesting that their conduct might have a link, even an indirect or remote one, with serious crime.[226] Neither does the Directive require any relationship between the data whose retention is provided for and a threat to public security and, in particular, it is not restricted to a retention in relation (i) to data pertaining to a particular time period and/or a particular geographical zone and/or to a circle of particular persons likely to be involved, in one way or another, in a serious crime, or (ii) to persons who could, for other reasons, contribute, by the retention of their data, to the prevention, detection or prosecution of serious

---

(Footnote 221 continued)
achieve those objectives (see, to that effect, Case C-343/09 *Afton Chemical* EU:C:2010:419, para 45; *Volker und Markus Schecke and Eifert* EU:C:2010:662, para 74; Cases C-581/10 and C-629/10 *Nelson and Others* EU:C:2012:657, para 71; Case C-283/11 *Sky Österreich* EU:C:2013:28, para 50; and Case C-101/12 *Schaible* EU:C:2013:661, para 29)—para 46.

[222] With regard to judicial review of compliance with those conditions, where interferences with fundamental rights are at issue, the extent of the EU legislature's discretion may prove to be limited, depending on a number of factors, including, in particular, the area concerned, the nature of the right at issue guaranteed by the Charter, the nature and seriousness of the interference and the object pursued by the interference (see, by analogy, as regards Article 8 of the ECHR, Eur. Court H.R., *S. and Marper v. the United Kingdom* [GC], nos. 30562/04 and 30566/04, § 102, ECHR 2008-V)—para 47.

[223] Paragraph 53.

[224] Paragraph 56.

[225] Paragraph 57.

[226] Paragraph 58.

offences.[227] The fourth step for the Court has been to focus on the absence of meaningful limits on access to personal data in the Directive[228] and on the fact that no prior authorisation by a judicial or independent administrative authority is required.[229] The fifth step has been to highlight the shortcomings in the Directive's provisions on the length of data retention.[230] The sixth step for the Court, which is of great importance in the light of moves towards data transfer to third countries and the globalisation of surveillance, has been to highlight the absence of safeguards on data security and protection especially in the light of the lack of geographical limits to data retention: the Court has pointed out that the Directive does not require the data in question to be retained within the European Union, with the result that it cannot be held that the control, explicitly required by Article 8(3) of the Charter, by an independent authority of compliance with the requirements of protection and security, as referred to in the two previous paragraphs, is fully ensured. Such a control, carried out on the basis of EU law, is an essential component of the protection of individuals with regard to the processing of personal data.[231]

The implications of the rulings in *Marper* and *Digital Rights Ireland* for the reconfiguration of the relationship between pre-emptive surveillance and privacy cannot be underestimated. These rulings place considerable limits to the surveillance powers of the state. Courts have emphasised that the very retention of personal data as such can challenge the right to privacy; that the retention of data by the state on individuals who have not been convicted of a criminal offence leads to stigmatisation and discrimination; and that generalised surveillance by the general retention of everyday personal data changes fundamentally the relationship between

---

[227] Paragraph 59.

[228] Paragraph 61: Article 4 of the directive, which governs the access of those authorities to the data retained, does not expressly provide that that access and the subsequent use of the data in question must be strictly restricted to the purpose of preventing and detecting precisely defined serious offences or of conducting criminal prosecutions relating thereto; it merely provides that each Member State is to define the procedures to be followed and the conditions to be fulfilled in order to gain access to the retained data in accordance with necessity and proportionality requirements.

[229] Paragraph 62: access by the competent national authorities to the data retained is not made dependent on a prior review carried out by a court or by an independent administrative body whose decision seeks to limit access to the data and their use to what is strictly necessary for the purpose of attaining the objective pursued and which intervenes following a reasoned request of those authorities submitted within the framework of procedures of prevention, detection or criminal prosecutions. Nor does it lay down a specific obligation on Member States designed to establish such limits.

[230] Article 6 of Directive 2006/24 requires that those data be retained for a period of at least 6 months, without any distinction being made between the categories of data set out in Article 5 of that directive on the basis of their possible usefulness for the purposes of the objective pursued or according to the persons concerned. Furthermore, that period is set at between a minimum of 6 months and a maximum of 24 months, but it is not stated that the determination of the period of retention must be based on objective criteria in order to ensure that it is limited to what is strictly necessary (paras 63–64).

[231] Paragraph 68.

the individual and the state by placing affected individuals under a constant state of suspicion. All these findings are applicable to the collection of personal data for border control purposes, and become even more relevant in cases where border controls are used for security purposes. Privacy challenges along the lines articulated by the judiciary in Europe are particularly acute in systems involving the mass collection and exchange of personal data (such as the PNR and entry-exit systems), as well as in the development of massive immigration databases such as the Visa Information System and in the collection and use of sensitive personal data such as biometrics. The limits to state power to collect and use personal data for border control purposes have been highlighted by the Court of Justice in its recent ruling in *Schwarz*.[232] The Court found that the EU Regulation on the inclusion of biometric data in the passports of EU citizens met both legality and human rights standards as set out in Articles 7 and 8 of the Charter. However, the Court put forward two important findings in relation to the collection of biometrics: that persons applying for passports cannot be deemed to have consented to the processing of their fingerprints[233]; and that since the Regulation does not provide for the storage of fingerprints except within the passport itself, and does not provide for any other form or method of storing those fingerprints, it cannot in and of itself be interpreted as providing a legal basis for the centralised storage of data collected thereunder or for the use of such data for purposes other than that of preventing illegal entry into the European Union.[234] The Court's ruling in favour of the compatibility of the Regulation with fundamental rights was based largely on this finding. As with the cases analysed above, the ruling of the Court of Justice in *Schwarz* raises serious questions regarding the compatibility of the blanket and multi-purpose collection and storage of personal data, including biometrics, in centralised large-scale EU and national databases (such as the Visa Information System or databases containing PNR data) with the right to privacy.[235]

2.6 Conclusion

The preventive turn in immigration control in European Union law has led to a significant increase in the powers of the state and the parallel targeting of migrants. The emphasis on extraterritorial immigration control revealed Member States' efforts (with the help of FRONTEX) to shield their jurisdictions from the legal obligations towards migrants and demonstrated the serious rule of law gaps extraterritorial immigration control entails. EU law has further strengthened the hand of the state by delegating immigration control-related responsibilities to the

232 *Michael Schwarz v Stadt Bochum*, Case C-291/12, judgment of 17 October 2013.

233 Paragraph 32.

234 Paragraphs 60–61.

235 Mitsilegas, call-out (The Law of the Border).

private sector and to the European Border Agency (FRONTEX). The increase in the reach of the state in this context has been accompanied by a decrease in its accountability, with serious rule of law questions arising with regard to the allocation of legal responsibility for immigration control to the delegated level. These gaps in the rule of law have been accompanied by a strong criminalisation/securitisation agenda, whereby EU law (via the establishment of databases, surveillance systems, the normalisation of biometrics as a form of immigration control, the imposition of obligations to transfer personal data to the state by the private sector and the blurring of the boundaries between the purposes of immigration control and security governance) has led to the proliferation of measures targeting migrants, again with the aim to prevent them reaching the jurisdiction of EU Member States. As it has been demonstrated throughout the chapter, the proliferation of these measures of control before the border has profound implications for human rights, most strongly for the rights to seek asylum, privacy, data protection and non-discrimination. On both the rule of law and human rights grounds, this 'criminalisation as prevention' paradigm has been challenged by the European judiciary. The European Court of Human Rights in *Hirsi* has upheld the rule of law and underpinned extraterritorial immigration control by legal guarantees. *Hirsi* is of further significance in that it has led and influenced law reform at European Union level. The Strasbourg Court also addressed privacy and data protection concerns in *Marper,* which, while not an immigration ruling, has set clear limits on the legality of the collection and retention by the state of sensitive personal data of individuals not been convicted of a criminal offence. *Marper* is clearly applicable to EU immigration law, as is *Digital Rights Ireland*, where the Luxembourg Court struck down the blanket retention of mobile phone data set out in the data retention Directive. The Luxembourg Court has established further limits on state surveillance in the *Schwarz* ruling which is directly related to immigration control. All these rulings challenge the legitimacy, legality and scope of the current far-reaching EU legal instruments establishing large-scale databases and systems of surveillance at European Union level. The follow-up to *Hirsi* and to *Digital Rights Ireland*, where the Court of Justice did not hesitate to invalidate the data retention Directive, demonstrates that judicial intervention is bound to lead to a rethinking of the 'criminalisation as prevention' paradigm and the reform of legislation in order to address the acute challenges to human rights and the rule of law this paradigm entails. Such rethinking is urgent. The legality of the maintenance at EU level of large-scale databases including sensitive personal data without further specifications and of systems and arrangements entailing the blanket transfer of personal data and the development of new initiatives such as a European PNR system—the adoption of which the European Council has again prioritised in the recent post-Stockholm Guidelines on the Area of Freedom, Security and Justice-[236] is highly questionable after *Marper* and *Digital Rights Ireland.*

---

[236] European Council Conclusions, 26/27 June 2014, point 10 (Council document EUCO 79/14, Brussels, 27.6.2014).

References

Amoore, L. (2006). Biometric borders: Governing mobilities in the war on terror. *Political Geography, 25*, 336–351, 348.
Baldaccini, A. (2008). Counter-terrorism and the EU strategy for border security: Framing suspects with biometric documents and databases. *European Journal of Migration and Law, 10*, 31–49.
Baldaccini, A. (2010). Extraterritorial border controls in the EU: The role of frontex in operations at sea. In V. Mitsilegas & B. Ryan (Eds.), *Extraterritorial immigration control: Legal challenges* (pp. 229–256). Dordrecht: Nijhoff.
Bauman, Z., & Lyon, D. (2013). *Liquid surveillance* (p. 8). Cambridge: Polity.
Bigo, D. (1996). *Polices en Réseaux. L'Éxperience Européenne.* Paris: Presses de Sciences Po.
Brouwer, E. (2007). The use of biometrics in EU databases and identity documents. In J. Lodge (Ed.), *Are you who you say you are? The EU and biometric borders* (pp. 45–66). Nijmegen: Wolf Legal Publishers.
Chiti, E. (2000). The emergence of a community administration: The case of European agencies. *Common Market Law Review, 37*, 309–343.
Curtin, D. (2009). *Executive power of the European Union. Law, practices, and the living constitution* (p. 164). Oxford and New York: Oxford University Press.
de Goede, M. (2012). *Speculative security.* Minnesota: University of Minnesota Press.
den Heijer, M. (1013). Reflections on *Refoulement* and collective expulsion in the *Hirsi* case. *International Journal of Refugee Law, 25*, 265–290, 283.
Franco Aas, K. (2011). Crimmigrant' bodies and bona fide travelers: Surveillance. Citizenship and global governance'. *Theoretical Criminology, 15*, 331–346.
Gammeltoft-Hansen, T. (2011). *Access to asylum. International Refugee Law and the globalisation of migration control* (p. 124). Cambridge: Cambridge University Press.
Garland, D. (1996). The limits of the sovereign state: Strategies of Crime Control in contemporary society. *The British Journal of Criminology, 36*, 445–471.
Goodwin-Gill, G. (2011). The right to seek asylum: Interception at sea and the principle of non-refoulement. *International Journal of Refugee Law, 23*, 443–457, 453.
Guild, E. (2003). The border abroad—visas and border controls. In K. Groenendijk, E. Guild & P. Minderhoud (Eds.), *In search of Europe's borders* (pp. 87–104). Dordrecht: Nijhoff.
Guiraudon, V. (2001). De-nationalizing control: Analyzing state responses to constraints on migration control. In V. Guiraudon & C. Joppke (Eds.), *Controlling a new migration world* (pp. 29–64). London: Routledge.
Jeandesboz, J. (2011) Beyond the tartar steppe: EUROSUR and the ethics of European border control practices. In J. P. Burgess & S. Gurtwith (Eds.), *A threat against Europe? Security, migration and integration* (pp. 111–132). Brussels: VUB Press.
Kreher, A. (1997). Agencies in the European community—a step towards administrative integration in Europe. *Journal of European Public Policy, 4*, 225–245.
Lahav, G. (1998). Immigration and the state: The devolution and privatisation of immigration control in the EU. *Journal of Ethnic and Migration Studies, 24*, 675–694.
Majone, G. (1997). The new European agencies: regulation by information. *Journal of European Public Policy, 4*, 262–273.
Mitsilegas, V. (2005). Contrôle des étrangers, des passagers, des citoyens: Surveillance et anti-terrorisme. *Cultures et Conflits 58*, 155–182.
Mitsilegas, V. (2007a). Border security in the European Union. Towards centralised controls and maximum surveillance. In E. Guild, H. Toner, & A. Baldaccini (Eds.), *Whose freedom, security and justice? EU immigration and asylum law and policy* (pp. 359–394). Portland: Hart Publishing.
Mitsilegas, V. (2007b). The external dimension of EU action in criminal matters. *European Foreign Affairs Review, 12*, 457–497.

Mitsilegas, V. (2009). The borders paradox. The surveillance of movement in a union without internal frontiers. In H. Lindahl (Ed.), *A right to inclusion and exclusion? Normative faultlines of the EU's area of freedom, security and Justice* (pp. 33–64). Oxford and Portland, Oregon: Hart.

Mitsilegas, V. (2011). Human rights, terrorism and the quest for "border security". In M. Pedrazzi, et al. (Eds.), *Individual guarantees in the European Judicial Area in criminal matters* (pp. 85–112). Brussels: Bruylant.

Mitsilegas, V. (2012). Immigration control in an era of globalisation: Deflecting foreigners, weakening citizens, strengthening the state. *Indiana Journal of Global Legal Studies, 19*(1), 3–60.

Mitsilegas, V. (2014). The value of privacy in an era of security. Embedding constitutional limits on pre-emptive surveillance. *International Political Sociology, 8*, 104–108.

Mitsilegas, V. (2015a). The Law of the Border and the Borders of Law. Rethinking Border control from the perspective of the individual. In: L. Webber (Ed.), *Rethinking Border control for a globalising world*, Routledge (forthcoming).

Mitsilegas, V. (2015b). The transformation of privacy in an era of pre-emptive surveillance. *Tilburg Law Review* (forthcoming).

Moreno-Lax, V. (2011). Seeking asylum in the mediterranean: Against a Fragmentary reading of EU member states' obligations accruing at sea'. *International Journal of Refugee Law, 23*, 174–220, 184.

Neal, A. (2009). Securitization and risk at the EU border: The origins of FRONTEX'. *Journal of Common Market Studies, 47*, 333–356.

Nicholson, F. (1997) Implementation of the immigration (Carriers' Liability) Act 1987: Privatising immigration functions at the expense of international obligations? *International and Comparative Law Quarterly, 46*, 586–634.

Nussberger, A. (2012). The concept of 'Jurisdiction' in the jurisprudence of the European Court of Human Rights. *Current Legal Problems, 65*, 241–268, 265.

Peers, S. (2014). *New EU rules on maritime surveillance: Will they stop the deaths and push-backs in the mediterranean?* EU Law Analysis. Retrieved June 27, 2014 from http://eulawanalysis.blogspot.co.uk/2014/06/new-eu-rules-on-maritime-surveillance.html.

Ryan, B. & Mitsilegas, V. (Eds.). (2010) *Extraterritorial immigration control: Legal challenges.* Dordrecht: Nijhoff.

Scholten, S. (2014) *Privatisation of immigration control? A socio-legal study on the role of private transport companies in the Netherlands and the United Kingdom.* Ph.D., dissertation defended on 21.3.2014. Nijmegen: University of Nijmegen.

Solove, D. J. (2008). Data mining and the security-liberty debate. *University of Chicago Law Review, 343–362*, 359.

Vavoula, N. (2015). The reacts Eurodac Regulation: Are asylum-seekers treated as suspected criminals? In C. Bauloz, M. Ineli Ciger, S. Singer & V. Stoyanova (Eds.), *Seeking asylum in the European Union*, Dordrecht: Nijhoff (forthcoming).

Vos, E. (2000). Reforming the European commission: What role to play for EU agencies? *Common Market Law Review, 37*, 1113–1134.

Chapter 3
In the Territory: The Use of Substantive Criminal Law to Regulate the Presence of Migrants

3.1 Introduction

The past decade witnessed a growing emphasis on the use of substantive criminal law as a means of enforcing immigration control in Europe. This chapter will map the evolution and content of such criminalisation at the European Union and national level, by exploring the intersection between migration law and criminal law at the level of the European Union and by examining the challenges that criminalisation poses for the relationship between European Union law and national immigration law. For these purposes, the chapter will employ a narrow definition of criminalisation, which is defined as the use of substantive criminal law to treat conduct related to migration flows as a criminal offence and to impose sanctions for the breach of criminal law. The analysis will take place at two levels: at the level of criminalisation of migration in the law of the European Union; and at the level of the criminalisation of migration by European Union Member States. The first part of the chapter will thus examine the various ways in which European Union law has employed criminal law in order to deal with immigration enforcement. The second part will examine the ways in which Member States of the European Union have criminalised migration and will highlight the limits that European Union law has posed on state sovereignty and the power of the state to criminalise. The chapter will thus test the protective function of European Union law, in setting limits to state power and safeguards for the migrants who fall within the reach of criminal law.

V. Mitsilegas, *The Criminalisation of Migration in Europe*,
SpringerBriefs in Law, DOI 10.1007/978-3-319-12658-6_3

3.2 The Criminalisation of Migration in the Law of the European Union

The European Union legislator has adopted a number of measures dealing with the criminalisation of migration. However, and unlike recent trends in certain EU Member States, European Union law has not criminalised the conduct of migrants as such. Rather, the law has focused primarily at targeting individuals who facilitate in one way or another irregular migration. Such criminalisation has been founded on a broader process of securitization of migration, with phenomena of human trafficking and human smuggling viewed as global security threats linked to the threat of transnational organized crime. A second wave of criminalisation measures has been linked with the broader trend towards the privatisation of immigration control, whereby the private sector (including in this case employers) are co-opted by the State to assist in immigration control and to prevent irregular movement or stay. While such criminalisation does not necessarily lead to the imposition of criminal sanctions on migrants themselves, it has potentially a significant impact on their rights and their visibility vis-à-vis the State.

3.2.1 Criminalisation as Securitisation: The Criminalisation of Human Trafficking

The criminalisation of human trafficking and human smuggling in European Union law follows closely the approach adopted by the 2,000 United Nations Convention on Transnational Organised Crime (the Palermo Convention), with the European Union playing a key part in its negotiation.[1] The Convention includes two Protocols, one on human trafficking and one on human smuggling. The first major global effort to legislate on immigration control was thus made possible on the basis of security considerations.[2] According to Gallagher, "[w]hile human rights concerns may have provided some impetus (or cover) for collective action, it was clearly the sovereignty/security issues surrounding trafficking and migrant smuggling, as well as the perceived link with organized criminal groups operating across national borders, that provided the true driving force behind such efforts."[3] Rather than focusing on the rights of migrants, the Trafficking and Smuggling Protocols were justified primarily on the basis of the need to protect states from transnational criminality. This securitisation approach has been criticized heavily for effectively criminalizing migration and extending the reach of the state, with James Hathaway arguing that "the focus of the transnational effort against human trafficking on the

[1] See Mitsilegas (2011).

[2] See Mitsilegas (2012).

[3] Anne T. Gallagher, The International Law of Human Trafficking 71 (2010).

prevention of cross-border movements created a legal slippery slope in which it proved possible to set a transnational duty to criminalize not only 'human trafficking' … but also the much broader phenomenon of human smuggling,"[4] and that the U.N. intervention is really a pretext for the globalization of border control.[5]

The first major legal instrument criminalising human trafficking at EU level has been the 2002 Framework Decision on combating trafficking in human beings.[6] The Framework Decision put forward a comprehensive criminalisation framework[7]: it established criminal offences for the trafficking in human beings which mirrored to a great extent the definitions of trafficking included in the Palermo Convention[8] and called upon Member States to punish these offences with substantial sanctions.[9] The Framework Decision prioritised criminalisation and enforcement over the rights of the victims of trafficking, containing only limited and general provisions on the protection of victims.[10]

A similar approach to victims' rights was also reflected in the subsequent Directive on Residence Permits to Victims of Trafficking,[11] which was adopted with the specific purpose "to define the conditions for granting residence permits of limited duration, linked to the length of the relevant national proceedings, to third-country

---

[4] James C. Hathaway, *The Human Rights Quagmire of "Human Trafficking,"* 49 Va. J. Int'l L. 1, 5 (2008). *But see* Anne T. Gallagher, *Human Rights and Human Trafficking: Quagmire or Firm Ground? A Response to James Hathaway* 49 Va. J. Int'l L. 789 (2009).

[5] Hathaway, supra note 4, at 25–35.

[6] COUNCIL FRAMEWORK DECISION of 19 July 2002 on combating trafficking in human beings (2002/629/JHA) L203/1, 1.8.2002.

[7] For an analysis of the 2002 Framework Decision see Obokata (2003).

[8] Article 1(1) of the Framework Decision calls upon Member States to take the necessary measures to ensure that the following acts are punishable: the recruitment, transportation, transfer, harbouring, subsequent reception of a person, including exchange or transfer of control over that person, where: (a) use is made of coercion, force or threat, including abduction, or (b) use is made of deceit or fraud, or (c) there is an abuse of authority or of a position of vulnerability, which is such that the person has no real and acceptable alternative but to submit to the abuse involved, or (d) payments or benefits are given or received to achieve the consent of a person having control over another person *for the purpose of exploitation of that person's labour or services, including at least forced or compulsory labour or services, slavery or practices similar to slavery or servitude, or for the purpose of the exploitation of the prostitution of others or other forms of sexual exploitation, including in pornography.*

[9] See in particular Article 3(2) which called for high levels of sanctions (imprisonment with a maximum penalty of no less than 8 years) if any of the following aggravating circumstances have occurred: (a) the offence has deliberately or by gross negligence endangered the life of the victim; (b) the offence has been committed against a victim who was particularly vulnerable (a victim shall be considered to have been particularly vulnerable at least when the victim was under the age of sexual majority under national law and the offence has been committed for the purpose of the exploitation of the prostitution of others or other forms of sexual exploitation, including pornography) (c) the offence has been committed by use of serious violence or has caused particularly serious harm to the victim; (d) the offence has been committed within the framework of a criminal organisation.

[10] See Article 7.

[11] Council Directive 2004/81, 2004 O.J. (L 261) 19 (EC).

nationals who cooperate in the fight against trafficking in human beings or against action to facilitate illegal immigration".[12] The Directive places a duty on Member States to consider issuing a residence permit for victims of trafficking if the following conditions are met: the opportunity presented for the victim to prolong his or her stay on its territory for the investigations or the judicial proceedings; the demonstration by the victim of a clear intention to cooperate; and the victim having severed all relations with those suspected of human trafficking.[13] The residence permit provided is entirely conditional upon the progress of the criminal proceedings—it will not be renewed if the above conditions cease to be satisfied or if a decision adopted by the competent authorities has terminated the relevant proceedings.[14] Security of residence may thus be provided to victims only if they facilitate the prosecution of suspected traffickers.

The relationship between the enforcement and protective aspects of EU trafficking legislation has been somewhat rebalanced after the entry into force of the Lisbon Treaty by the recent adoption of the 2011 Directive on Trafficking in Human Beings.[15] The Directive, which is the outcome of a co-decision process between the Council of Ministers and the European Parliament replaces the 2002 Framework Decision in relation to Member States who participate in it.[16] The Directive extends and intensifies criminalisation, in particular by expanding the concept of exploitation in the definition of the trafficking offences,[17] by raising the penalty levels for trafficking in human beings[18] and by expanding the concept of vulnerability as an

[12] See Article 1.

[13] See Article 8.

[14] See Article 13(1).

[15] Council Directive 2011/36, 2011 O.J. (L 101) 1 (EU). DIRECTIVE 2011/36/EU OF THE EUROPEAN PARLIAMENT AND OF THE COUNCIL of 5 April 2011 on preventing and combating trafficking in human beings and protecting its victims, and replacing Council Framework Decision 2002/629/JHA (OJ L101/1, 15.4.11).

[16] Article 21.

[17] Article 2(3) of the Directive calls for the punishment of the recruitment, transportation, transfer, harbouring or reception of persons, including the exchange or transfer of control over those persons, by means of the threat or use of force or other forms of coercion, of abduction, of fraud, of deception, of the abuse of power or of a position of vulnerability or of the giving or receiving of payments or benefits to achieve the consent of a person having control over another person, for the purpose of exploitation. Exploitation includes, as a minimum, the exploitation of the prostitution of others or other forms of sexual exploitation, forced labour or services, including begging, slavery or practices similar to slavery, servitude, or the exploitation of criminal activities, or the removal of organs (Article 2(5)).

[18] The Directive now provides for a penalty threshold for all trafficking offences defined therein (a maximum penalty of at least 5 years of imprisonment). The sentence level rises to a maximum penalty of at least 10 years of imprisonment where one of the following aggravating circumstances occur: the offence was committed against a victim who was particularly vulnerable, which, in the context of this Directive, shall include at least child victims; the offence was committed within the framework of a criminal organization; the offence deliberately or by gross negligence endangered the life of the victim; or was committed by use of serious violence or has caused particularly serious harm to the victim. Member States must also treat the commission of trafficking by public officials in the performance of their duties is regarded as an aggravating circumstance (Article 4).

aggravating circumstance enhancing the penalty threshold for trafficking.[19] However, at the same time it includes a wide range of provisions on the rights of victims of trafficking. The Directive includes provisions on the protection of victims of trafficking in human beings in criminal investigation and proceedings[20]; on assistance, support and protection measures for child victims of trafficking in human beings[21]; on assistance and support to child victims[22]; on protection of child victims of trafficking in human beings in criminal investigations and proceedings[23]; on assistance, support and protection for unaccompanied child victims of trafficking in human beings[24]; on compensation to victims and access to national compensation schemes[25]; and on the non-prosecution or imposition of penalties on victims for their involvement in criminal activities they have been compelled to commit as a direct consequence of being subjected to trafficking.[26] The new trafficking Directive thus combines a strong criminalisation focus with an emphasis on the need to protect victims of trafficking. The Directive provisions must also be viewed in the light of the judgment of the European Court of Human Rights in *Rantsev*, where the Court held that trafficking was prohibited by Article 4 of the ECHR (on the prohibition of slavery and forced labour) and stressed that compliance with Article 4 requires Member States to comply with a series of positive obligations to protect victims of trafficking.[27] However, and notwithstanding these developments, it should be noted that a number of the victims' provisions in the new trafficking Directive continue to be framed in whole or in part under a logic of prosecutorial efficiency.[28] Moreover, the fact remains that victim protection continues, after the adoption of the 2011 Directive, to be disassociated from security of residence as the 2004 Directive on residence permits for victims of trafficking remains in force.

---

[19] A position of vulnerability is defined generally as a situation in which the person concerned has no real or acceptable alternative but to submit to the abuse involved (Article 2(4)).

[20] Article 12.

[21] Article 13.

[22] Article 14.

[23] Article 15.

[24] Article 16.

[25] Article 17.

[26] Article 8.

[27] *Rantsev v Cyprus and Russia,* judgment of 7 January 2010, Application no. 25965/04. For a critical analysis, see Stoyanova (2012).

[28] Referring to the justification for Article 8 of the Directive, the Preamble states that, "[t]he aim of such protection is to safeguard the human rights of victims, to avoid further victimisation *and to encourage them to act as witnesses in criminal proceedings against the perpetrators.*" (emphasis added) *Id.* at 3.

3.2.2 *Criminalisation as Securitisation: The Criminalisation of the Facilitation of Unauthorised Entry, Transit and Residence*

An extensive criminalisation approach has been adopted in the context of the aim of combating human smuggling (or, in more neutral EU terminology, the facilitation of unauthorized entry, transit and residence), with a key question in this context being whether the criminalisation of smuggling would lead to the criminalisation of smuggled migrants themselves. This issue has been partly addressed by the Palermo Convention Protocol on the Smuggling of Migrants. While the Protocol expressly states that migrants will not become liable to criminal prosecution for the fact of having been the object of smuggling,[29] the provision on the criminalisation of smuggling expressly states that it does not prevent states from taking measures against a person whose conduct constitutes an offense under their domestic law.[30] The Smuggling Protocol thus does not prevent states from treating illegal entry, stay, or residence as such as criminal offenses under their domestic law.[31] Moreover, the Smuggling Protocol does not exclude the criminalisation of individuals or organizations providing assistance to individuals for the purposes of them accessing or remaining in the territory of states in order to lodge an application for asylum.

An expansive approach to the criminalisation of human smuggling is reflected in EU law. The relevant legal framework is set out by a Directive defining what is called in EU law the "facilitation of unauthorized entry, transit and residence"[32] accompanied—in the light of the first pillar competence limits regarding criminalisation at the time[33]—by a third pillar Framework Decision confirming that conduct which is defined as facilitation in the Directive will be treated as a criminal offence.[34] The EU Directive goes further than the Smuggling Protocol in that it dispenses with the condition of obtaining a financial or other material benefit for the smuggling offence to be established.[35] The Directive calls upon member states to adopt criminal sanctions for "any person who intentionally assists a person who is not a national of a Member State to enter, or transit across, the territory of a Member State in breach of the laws of the State concerned on the entry or transit of aliens … ". The Framework Decision contains a general obligation for Member

---

[29] *Id.* at 7.

[30] Protocol Against the Smuggling of Migrants by Land, Sea and Air, Supplementing the Convention Against Transnational Organized Crime Article 6(4), Nov. 15, 2000, *available at* http://www.unhcr.org/refworld/docid/479dee062.html [hereinafter Smuggling Protocol].

[31] *Id.*

[32] Council Directive 2002/90, 2002 O.J. (L 328) 19 (EC).

[33] See Mitsilegas (2009).

[34] COUNCIL FRAMEWORK DECISION of 28 November 2002 on the strengthening of the penal framework to prevent the facilitation of unauthorised entry, transit and residence (2002/946/JHA), L 328/1, 5.12.2002.

[35] *See* Article 1(1)(a), *id.*

States to criminalise such conduct[36] and imposes specific high levels of sanctions only when certain aggravating circumstances occur.[37] In spite of the lack of specificity as regards the level of criminal sanctions to be imposed by Member States,[38] it is clear that the scope of criminalization at EU level is very broad as it can cover any form of assistance to enter or transit the territory of an EU Member State in breach of what is essentially administrative law (such as cases where the migrant is traveling without travel documents).

Such broad criminalisation may have a negative impact on the position of third-country nationals seeking access to the European Union in order to apply for international protection. The scope of the criminal offences prescribed in EU law may lead to the prosecution of any individual or member of an organisation who provides advice or assistance to migrants. The Directive does attempt to address this issue by providing Member States the option not to impose sanctions for human smuggling by applying their national law and practice for cases where the aim of the behavior is to provide humanitarian assistance to the person concerned.[39] However, this provision is discretionary and its value in redressing the balance set out by the broad definition and criminalisation of human smuggling under EU law is questionable. By using the threat of criminal sanctions, the EU measures on human smuggling essentially aim at deterring individuals and organisations from coming into contact and assisting any third-country national wishing to enter the territory of EU Member States. As has been noted in an issue paper published by the Council of Europe Commissioner for Human Rights, "the message which is sent is that contact with foreigners can be risky as it may result in criminal charges."[40]

---

[36] According to the Framework Decision, Each Member State shall take the measures necessary to ensure that the infringements defined in Articles 1 and 2 of the Directive are punishable by effective, proportionate and dissuasive criminal penalties which may entail extradition (Article 1 (3)). Article 1(6) of the Framework Decision further states that If imperative to preserve the coherence of the national penalty system, the actions defined in para 3 shall be punishable by custodial sentences with a maximum sentence of not less than 6 years, provided that it is among the most severe maximum sentences available for crimes of comparable gravity.

[37] According to Article 1(3), Member States must ensure that,when committed for financial gain, the infringements defined in Article 1(1)(a) and, to the extent relevant, Article 2(a) of Directive 2002/90/EC are punishable by custodial sentences with a maximum sentence of not less than 8 years where they are committed in any of the following circumstances: the offence was committed as an activity of a criminal organization; and the offence was committed while endangering the lives of the persons who are the subject of the offence.

[38] According to the European Commission, this has led to a wide range of penalties imposed by Member States in the transposition of the Framework Decision—*Report from the Commission based on Article 9 of the Council Framework Decision of 28 November 2002 on the strengthening of the penal framework to prevent the facilitation of unauthorised entry, transit and residence*, COM (2006) 770 final, Brussels, 6.12.2006.

[39] See Article 1(2), Council Directive 2002/90, supra note 28.

[40] Elspeth Guild, *Criminalisation of Migration in Europe: Human Rights Implications*, Council of Eur., Comm'r Hum. Rts. 39 (2009).

3.2.3 Criminalisation as Privatisation: The Introduction of Employers' Sanctions

A more recent expansion of the criminalisation of migration at EU level concerns the imposition of criminal sanctions on employers of irregular migrants. This move is part of a general trend towards the privatisation of immigration control, whereby the private sector is co-opted by the state in order to conduct what are essentially state functions of immigration control.[41] Thus far the privatisation of immigration control has focused primarily on the prevention of entry into the territory by requiring the private sector (in particular carriers) to conduct immigration controls *before* entry into the territory—with privatisation acting thus as a form of extra-territorial immigration control.[42] The imposition of criminal sanctions on employers of irregular migrants extends the privatisation of immigration control *after* entry in the territory, thus multiplying the criminal law enforcement avenues for those deemed to facilitate irregular residence. However, and along with the broader question of whether the private sector can legitimately be asked to assume immigration control duties, the extent to which *criminal* law is the most effective and proportionate means of privatising immigration control is contested.

The debate on the extent to which criminalisation is the optimal way forward towards privatising immigration control by imposing obligations on employers is reflected in the content of the recently adopted EU Directive on employers' sanctions.[43] The Directive prohibits the employment of 'illegally staying' third-country nationals.[44] An 'illegally staying' third-country national are defined as 'a third-country national present on the territory of a Member State, who does not fulfil, or no longer fulfils, the conditions for stay or residence in that Member State.'[45] The scope of the Directive is thus broad, apparently including the employment of both third-country nationals who have entered the territory of a Member State irregularly, and the employment of overstayers. In addition to this prohibition, the Directive imposes a series of extensive immigration-related duties upon employers, including identification, record-keeping and reporting duties on employers.[46] Sanctions for the infringement of the prohibition to employ 'illegally staying' third-country nationals are mainly financial,[47] but the Directive provides also for alternative sanctions such as exclusion from public procurement.[48] Failure to comply

---

[41] See Mitsilegas in *Indiana Journal of Global Legal Studies, call-out.*

[42] Mitsilegas (2010).

[43] Council Directive 2009/52, 2009 O.J. (L 168) 24 (EC).

[44] See Article 3(1). However, Member States are granted the discretion not to apply this provision to illegally staying third-country nationals whose removal has been postponed and who are allowed to work in accordance with national law (Article 3(3)).

[45] Article 2(b).

[46] See Article 4(1).

[47] See Articles 5–6.

[48] See Article 7.

with the identification and reporting duties imposed by Article 4(1) of the Directive also triggers liability for the infringement of the prohibition of illegal employment set out in Article 3: the Directive obliges Member States to ensure that employers who have fulfilled these obligations are not held liable for an infringement of the prohibition of illegal employment unless the employers knew that the document presented as a valid residence permit or another authorization for stay was a forgery.[49] The Directive thus attempts to strike a balance between the aim of rendering employers responsible for checking and recording residence permits of third-country nationals on the one hand, and the aim of addressing the employers' concerns that they are in no position to proactively identify forged documents on the other. However, it is clear that by equating liability for illegal employment with liability for failure to comply with identification obligations, the Directive aims at establishing a far-reaching layer of privatised control of third-county nationals residing in the territory of EU Member States.

While the employers' sanctions Directive imposes a wide range of duties to the private sector, the use of criminal law for the breach of these duties is limited to specific circumstances. Criminal law sanctions apply only for the intentional infringement of the prohibition of illegal employment under Article 3 (and not for the breach of the identification, recording and reporting obligations set out in Article 4 of the Directive); in accordance with the limits to the then first pillar (Community) criminal law competence set by the Court of Justice in its ship-source pollution ruling,[50] the level of criminal sanctions is not specified (infringements are punishable in general by effective, proportionate and dissuasive criminal penalties)[51]; and criminal sanctions apply only if the following aggravating circumstances occur as regards the infringement of Article 3: the infringement continues or is persistently repeated; is in respect of the simultaneous employment of a significant number of illegally staying third-country nationals; is accompanied by particularly exploitative working conditions; is committed by an employer who, while not having been charged with or convicted of a human trafficking offence, uses work or services exacted from an illegally staying third-county national with the knowledge that he or she is a victim of trafficking in human beings; or relates to the illegal employment of a minor.[52] The Directive thus uses criminal law to address not only traditional aggravating circumstances (such as persistent offending) but also as a means of acknowledging the need to protect vulnerable migrants who are subject to various forms of exploitation.

---

[49] Article 4(3).

[50] *Commission v. Council, Case C-440/05* ECR [2007] I-9097. For an analysis, see Mitsilegas (2009).

[51] Article 10(1). This approach may lead to considerable differences in national implementing law. For an initial overview of implementation trends, see Commission Staff Working Paper accompanying the Commission's Annual Report on Immigration and Asylum (2010), SEC (2011) 620 final, Brussels, 24.5.2011, pp. 27–28.

[52] Article 9(1).

The proclaimed focus of the Directive on tackling exploitation[53] is also reflected in the insertion of further provisions aimed at targeting the private sector when employing irregular migrants under exploitative conditions. At the heart of these provisions is an effort to make irregular migrants come forward and report instances of exploitation. In this light, the Directive places Member States under the duty to ensure that there are effective mechanisms through which third-country nationals in illegal employment may lodge complaints against their employers, directly or through third parties designated by Member States such as trade unions or other associations or a competent authority of the Member State.[54] Member States must ensure in this context that third parties which have a legitimate interest in ensuring compliance with the Directive, may engage either on behalf of or in support of an illegally employed third-country national, with his or her approval, in any administrative or civil proceedings provided for with the objective of implementing the Directive.[55] However, the legal position of third parties who assist irregular migrants in this context is uncertain, as, was analysed earlier in the chapter, they may be held criminally liable for facilitating unauthorised residence. Acknowledging this risk of criminalisation, the employers' sanctions Directive includes a safeguard clause according to which providing assistance to third-country nationals to lodge complaints will not be considered as facilitation of unauthorized residence under Directive 2002/90/EC.[56]

The Directive does not stop there, but includes a call to irregular migrants *themselves* to cooperate with state authorities with the view of tackling employer exploitation. Adopting a strategy similar to the content of the Directive on residence permits on victims of trafficking (analysed earlier in the chapter), the employer sanctions Directive states that, in respect of criminal offences covered by Article 9 (1)(c) (the infringement is accompanied by particularly exploitative working conditions) or (e) (the infringement relates to the illegal employment of a minor), Member States will define in national law the conditions under which they may grant, *on a case-by-case basis, permits of limited duration, linked to the length of the relevant national proceedings*, to third-country nationals involved, under arrangements comparable to those applicable to third-country nationals who fall within the scope of Directive 2004/81/EC (residence permits for victims of trafficking).[57] As with the Directive on residence permits for victims of trafficking, the employer sanctions Directive provides with extremely limited safeguards on security of residence: residence permits will be granted on a case-by-case basis (thus subject to state discretion), will be of limited duration, and are again framed purely within a logic of prosecutorial efficiency (they are linked to the relevant national proceedings). The Directive thus asks migrants in an irregular situation to

53 See also recital 13 of the Preamble.

54 Article 13(1).

55 Article 13(2).

56 Article 13(3).

57 Article 13(4). Emphasis added.

come forward and present themselves to the state without offering any legal certainty as to the rights which will be conferred to them if they cooperate and without excluding the prospect of their subsequent return. It remains to be seen whether this provision when implemented by Member States will have any real impact, especially in view of the fact that the vulnerability of exploited workers is not necessarily reflected in detail in EU law compared to the vulnerability of victims of trafficking.

The above analysis demonstrates a double contradiction at the heart of the employer sanctions Directive: the Directive's main objective is to apply what Garland has called the 'responsibilisation strategy'[58] to the private sector, by requiring employers to (pro)actively cooperate with the state in tackling irregular employment. Employers are thus viewed as allies to the state, but at the same time they are viewed as targets: irregular migrants, trade unions and other organizations are urged to come forward and denounce exploitation in the workplace. This contradiction is also replicated with regard to migrants themselves: irregular migrants are seen as allies to the state (in being helpful in denouncing exploitation) but they are also obviously the main targets of the Directive, whose aim is to make it more and more difficult for these migrants to find work. This double contradiction poses real obstacles to the Directive achieving its stated aims. It is compounded by the fact that the criminalisation of migration in other EU law instruments provides few safeguards for migrants and citizens alike. The extensive criminalisation of the facilitation of unauthorised entry and residence has the potential of minimising contact by NGOs, other organisations and individuals with migrants under the threat of criminal prosecution. On the other hand, migrants are offered with extremely limited rights as a reward for them cooperating with the state to tackle irregular migration. As will be seen in the next part, however, the disassociation of this law and policy area from pure state discretion and the very existence of secondary EU law in these fields may be a step forward towards providing safeguards from migrants, when interpreted in the light of European Union constitutional law and its general principles.

3.3 European Union Law as a Limit to the Criminalisation of Migration by EU Member States

While European Union law has not explicitly treated breaches of immigration requirements by migrants themselves as criminal offences as such, such trends have been increasingly prevalent in the national legislation of a number of EU Member States. Key examples in this context have been the treatment of irregular entry and residence per se as a criminal offence; and the criminalisation of the failure to comply with return instructions. This punitive turn at the national level has posed

[58] Garland (1996).

considerable challenges for European Union law. The shared competence between Member States and the European Union in the field of migration law raises complex issues with regard to the degree of sovereignty or discretion left to Member States when they legislate on irregular migration and when they promote legislative choices resulting in the criminalisation of migration. A key question in this regard is whether European Union law poses limits to the power of Member States to adopt national legislation in the field. This part of the chapter will examine the limits that European Union law places on domestic criminal law in general. The analysis will then focus on two recent judgments of the Court of Justice of the European Union focusing specifically on the compatibility of national legislation criminalizing migration with European Union law. The limits posed to the national legislator by EU law will be dissected, and the protective function of European Union law as regards the position of the migrant will be highlighted.

3.3.1 The Limits of EU Law on National Criminal Law

The debate on the existence and extent of a role for the European Union in the field of criminal law has been long-standing.[59] It appeared long before Member States decided to confer express powers to the European Union (but not to the then European Community) to legislate in criminal matters (in the Maastricht Treaty) and certainly before the entry into force of the Lisbon Treaty which abolished the third pillar and streamlined to a great extent Union powers in the field. Already in the days of the Treaty of Rome, it became clear that it was impossible to draw a neat distinction between legislation related to the four freedoms and the single market on the one hand, and criminal law on the other. While the European Community at the time did not possess express competence to adopt criminal offences and sanctions at EC level, the European Court of Justice confirmed in a number of occasions that Community law places limits on the application of *national* criminal law. The Member States of the European Union are not entirely free to adopt national criminal law but are bound by their EU law obligations when doing so. The Court of Justice has placed limits on domestic criminal law measures if the latter would have as its effect to limit disproportionately rights established by Community law, in particular rights related to free movement. As early as 1981, the Court stated in *Casati* that

> In principle, criminal legislation and the rules of criminal procedure are matters for which the Member States are still responsible. However, it is clear from a consistent line of cases decided by the Court, that Community law also sets *certain limits* in that area as regards the control measures which it permits the Member States to maintain in connection with the free movement of goods and persons. The administrative measures or penalties must not go beyond what is strictly necessary, the control procedures must not be concerned in such a

[59] For an overview, see Mitsilegas (2009).

> way as to restrict the freedom required by the Treaty and they must not be accompanied by a penalty which is so disproportionate to the gravity of the infringement that it becomes an obstacle to the exercise of that freedom.[60]

The Court justified this approach on the grounds of the necessity to prevent the erosion of Community law freedoms by national measures.[61] The Court's approach is based on the principle of proportionality.[62] In subsequent cases, and in order to ensure the effective exercise of Community rights, the Court has not hesitated to check the compatibility with Community law of domestic criminal laws penalising conduct as diverse as driving without a licence in the host Member State (resulting from failure to exchange within the time limits prescribed by the law of the host State the home state driving licence with the host state licence),[63] and pursuing the organised activity of collecting bets without a licence or a police authorisation.[64] In addition to prescribing limits to the imposition of criminal sanctions by Member States, the Court has also found that Community law had an influence in the conduct of domestic criminal proceedings—more specifically, national autonomy in prescribing the language of criminal proceedings may be limited in order to ensure non-discrimination against persons to whom Community law grants equal treatment rights, as well as free movement.[65] It is clear from these cases that the fundamental Union law objective of free movement places considerable limits to national sovereignty in legislating in criminal matters, with European Union law acting as a safeguard against overcriminalisation at national level.[66]

This general overview of the limits European Union law places on the power of Member States to criminalise suggests that similar limits apply to the power of Member States to treat breaches of immigration rules as criminal offences. The existence of such limits has now been confirmed by the Court of Justice in two judgments concerning the compatibility of national law criminalising migrants with European Union law. What is significant in these judgments (which will be analysed in detail below), is that the Court examined the compatibility of domestic criminal law not with European Union law on free movement, but with European Union immigration law, and in particular legislation dealing with the enforcement of immigration law (the Returns Directive).

---

[60] Case 203/80, [1981] ECR 2595, para 27. Emphasis added.

[61] Paragraph 28.

[62] Tridimas (2006).

[63] Case C-193/94 *Skanavi and Chryssanthakopoulos* [1996] ECR I-929.

[64] Joint Cases C-338/04, C-359/04 and C-360/04, *Placanica, Palazzese and Sorricchio*, ECR [2007] I-1891. The Court referred therein to the case of *Calfa*, Case 48/96 [1999] ECR I-11, where it was held that the penalty of expulsion of a Community national found guilty of drug possession for personal use was precluded by Articles 48, 52 and 59 of the EC Treaty and Article 3 of Directive 64/221/EC. Being a tourist, Calfa was deemed by the Court to be a recipient of services following the earlier *Cowan* ruling (Case 186/87 *Cowan v Trésor Public* [1989] ECR 195).

[65] Case C-274/96 *Bickel and Franz*, ECR [1998] I-7637.

[66] See also Mitsilegas (2014).

3.3.2 *The Limits of EU Migration Law on National Criminal Law—the El Dridi Ruling*

In the case of *El Dridi*[67] the Court of Justice examined a preliminary reference request made in proceedings brought against Mr El Dridi, who was sentenced to 1 year's imprisonment for the offence of having stayed illegally on Italian territory without valid grounds, contrary to a removal order made against him by the Questore di Udine. He appealed against that decision before the Corte d'appello di Trento (Appeal Court, Trento). That court was in doubt as to whether a criminal penalty may be imposed during administrative procedures concerning the return of a foreign national to his country of origin due to non-compliance with the stages of those procedures, since such a penalty seems contrary to the principle of sincere cooperation, to the need for attainment of the objectives of Directive 2008/115 (the returns Directive) and for ensuring the effectiveness thereof, and also to the principle that the penalty must be proportionate, appropriate and reasonable. The Court of Appeal noted in particular that the criminal sanction provided for in Italian law came into play *subsequently* to the finding of an infringement of an intermediate stage of the gradual procedure for implementing the return decision, provided for by the returns Directive and that the level of penalty imposed by national law (a term of imprisonment of 1–4 years) seems, to be *extremely severe*. In those circumstances, the Corte d'appello di Trento decided to stay the proceedings and to refer the following question to the Court of Justice for a preliminary ruling:

> In the light of the principle of sincere cooperation, the purpose of which is to ensure the attainment of the objectives of the directive, and the principle that the penalty must be proportionate, appropriate and reasonable, do Articles 15 and 16 of Directive 2008/115 … preclude:
>
> - the possibility that criminal penalties may be imposed in respect of a breach of an intermediate stage in the administrative return procedure, before that procedure is completed, by having recourse to the most severe administrative measure of constraint which remains available?
> - the possibility of a sentence of up to 4 years' imprisonment being imposed in respect of a simple failure to cooperate in the deportation procedure on the part of the person concerned, in particular where the first removal order issued by the administrative authorities has not been complied with?[68]

3.3.2.1 The Ruling of the Court of Justice

The Luxembourg Court summed up the referring court's question as asking whether Directive 2008/115, in particular Articles 15 and 16 thereof, must be interpreted as precluding a Member State's legislation, such as that at issue in the main

[67] Case C-61/11 PPU, *Hassen El Dridi, alias Karim Soufi*, Judgment of 28 April 2011.

[68] Paragraphs 22–25 of the judgment.

proceedings, which provides for a sentence of imprisonment to be imposed on an illegally staying third-country national on the sole ground that he remains, without valid grounds, on the territory of that State, contrary to an order to leave that territory within a given period. The CJEU noted in this context the emphasis placed by the national court on the principle of sincere cooperation and on the objective of ensuring the effectiveness of EU law.[69] In the light of this question, the CJEU followed a step-by-step approach in order to assess the compatibility of Italian law with EU migration law (the returns Directive).

3.3.2.2 Step 1: Interpreting the Returns Directive Restrictively in the Light of Fundamental Rights

The first step in the Court's reasoning in *El Dridi* was to provide an interpretation of the returns Directive, which will inform the implementation of the Directive by Member States. The Court confirms a restrictive interpretation of the coercive provisions of the Directive, stressing from the outset that the Directive pursues the establishment of an effective removal and repatriation policy, based on common standards, for persons to be returned in a humane manner and with full respect for their fundamental rights and also their dignity.[70] Member States can depart from the common standards and procedures established by the Directive only as provided for therein.[71] In any case, although Article 4(3) of the Directive allows Member States to adopt or maintain provisions that are more favourable than Directive 2008/115 to illegally staying third-country nationals provided that such provisions are compatible with it, that directive *does not allow those States to apply stricter standards* in the area that it governs.[72] The Court further observes that the returns Directive sets out specifically the procedure to be applied by each Member State for returning illegally staying third-country nationals and fixes the order in which the various, successive stages of that procedure should take place.[73] It is only in particular circumstances, such as where there is a risk of absconding, that Member States may, first, require the addressee of a return decision to report regularly to the authorities, deposit an adequate financial guarantee, submit documents or stay at a certain place or, second, grant a period shorter than 7 days for voluntary departure or even refrain from granting such a period.[74] In the latter situation, but also where the obligation to return has not been complied with within the period for voluntary departure, Article 8(1) and (4) of Directive 2008/115 provides that, in order to ensure effective return procedures, those provisions require the Member State which has issued a

---

[69] Paragraphs 29–30.

[70] Paragraph 31.

[71] Paragraph 32.

[72] Paragraph 33. Emphasis added.

[73] Paragraph 34. For a detailed overview of these stages see paragraphs.

[74] Paragraph 37.

return decision against an illegally staying third-country national to carry out the removal by taking all necessary measures including, where appropriate, coercive measures, *in a proportionate manner and with due respect for, inter alia, fundamental rights.*[75] Following from recital 16 in the Preamble to the directive and from the wording of Article 15(1) that the Member States must carry out the removal *using the least coercive measures possible*. It is only where, *in the light of an assessment of each specific situation*, the enforcement of the return decision in the form of removal risks being compromised by the conduct of the person concerned that the Member States may deprive that person of his liberty and detain him.[76] Articles 15 and 16 of the Directive places strict limits on detention.[77]

In the light of the above discussion, the Court of Justice confirmed that the return procedure established by the Directive corresponds to a *gradation* of the measures to be taken in order to enforce the return decision, a gradation which goes from the measure which allows the person concerned the most liberty, namely granting a period for his voluntary departure, to measures which restrict that liberty the most, namely detention in a specialised facility. The Court adds that the principle of proportionality must be observed throughout those stages.[78] Even the use of the latter measure, which is the most serious constraining measure allowed under the directive under a forced removal procedure, is strictly regulated, inter alia *in order to ensure observance of the fundamental rights of the third-country nationals concerned.*[79] It is in the light of those considerations that it must be assessed whether the common rules introduced by the returns Directive preclude national legislation such as that at issue in the main proceedings.[80] The assessment of the compatibility of national law with EU migration law (the returns Directive) must thus take into account the need to ensure proportionality and the respect of the fundamental rights of third-country nationals.

3.3.2.3 Step II: Confirming the Direct Effect of the Relevant Provisions of the Returns Directive

Having established the need to assess the compatibility of Italian criminal law in the light of the returns Directive (and taking into account the need to observe proportionality and fundamental rights), the Court was faced with an additional challenge: while Italy had introduced domestic criminal law affecting directly third-country nationals who had not complied with return orders, it had not transposed

---

[75] Paragraph 38.

[76] Paragraph 39. Emphasis added.

[77] Paragraph 40.

[78] Paragraph 41. Emphasis added.

[79] Paragraph 42. Emphasis added. See also the references to relevant human rights instruments and case-law in para 43.

[80] Paragraph 44.

the returns Directive into Italian law.[81] The question thus arises whether the relevant provisions of the returns Directive (Articles 15 and 16) were applicable in Italy in the first place. The Court did not hesitate to grant to these provisions direct effect, meaning that even in the absence of national implementation, Mr El Dridi (whose situation falls within the scope of the Directive) can rely upon Articles 15 and 16 of the returns Directive against the State.[82] The Court thus sends a clear message that Member States cannot act unilaterally while at the same time disregarding their obligations under EU law. The Court noted in particular that the removal procedure provided for by the Italian legislation at issue in the main proceedings is significantly different from that established by the Directive.[83]

3.3.2.4 Step III: Assessing National Criminalisation Legislation in the Light of the Returns Directive: Asserting the Principles of Effectiveness and Loyal Cooperation

Having set out the interpretative parameters of the returns Directive and confirming that the Directive provisions relevant to the case have direct effect, the Court went on to assess the compatibility of national law with the Directive. The Court began by granting a certain degree of freedom to Member States to adopt national criminal law aimed inter alia at dissuading those nationals from remaining illegally on those States' territory: however, this freedom arises only if it is clear that the coercive measures Member States may adopt in implementing the returns Directive have not led to the expected result being attained, namely, the removal of the third-country national against whom they were issued.[84] The Court went on to limit Member States freedom further. By evoking settled case-law mentioned earlier in the chapter (see inter alia the cases of *Casati* and *Cowan*), the Court reiterated its finding that although in principle criminal legislation and the rules of criminal procedure are matters for which the Member States are responsible, this branch of the law may nevertheless be affected by European Union law.[85] While neither the legal basis of the Directive (or its Lisbon successor) nor the Directive itself precludes the Member States from having competence in criminal matters in the area of irregular immigration and irregular stays, they must adjust their legislation in that area in order to ensure compliance with European Union law.[86]

The Court based the limits on the power of Member States to adopt criminal law upon the principles of effectiveness and loyal cooperation. It reiterated that Member States may not apply rules, even criminal law rules, which are liable to jeopardise

[81] Paragraph 45.

[82] Paragraphs 46–48.

[83] Paragraph 50.

[84] Paragraph 52.

[85] Paragraph 53.

[86] Paragraph 54.

the achievement of the objectives pursued by a Directive and, therefore, deprive it of its effectiveness.[87] It also confirmed the applicability of the principle of loyal cooperation as expressed in the second and third subparagraphs respectively of Article 4(3) TEU, according to which Member States inter alia 'shall take any appropriate measure, general or particular, to ensure fulfilment of the obligations arising out of the Treaties or resulting from the acts of the institutions of the Union' and 'shall … refrain from any measure which could jeopardise the attainment of the Union's objectives', including those pursued by Directives.[88]

Applying these principles to the specific case before it, the Court found that Member States may not, in order to remedy the failure of coercive measures adopted to carry out removals under Article 8(4) of the returns Directive (measures which are subject to the principle of proportionality) provide for a custodial sentence *on the sole ground* that a third-country national continues to stay illegally on the territory of a Member State after an order to leave the national territory was notified to him and the period granted in that order has expired; rather, they must pursue their efforts to enforce the return decision, which continues to produce its effects.[89] Such a custodial sentence risks jeopardising the attainment of the objective pursued by that directive, namely, the establishment of an effective policy of removal and repatriation of illegally staying third-country nationals as it is liable to frustrate the application of the measures referred to in Article 8(1) of Directive 2008/115 and delay the enforcement of the return decision.[90] The returns Directive, and in particular Articles 15 and 16 thereof, must thus be interpreted as precluding a Member State's legislation, such as that at issue in the main proceedings, which provides for a sentence of imprisonment to be imposed on an illegally staying third-country national on the sole ground that he remains, without valid grounds, on the territory of that State, contrary to an order to leave that territory within a given period.[91]

This finding does not preclude the possibility for Member States to adopt 'provisions' (note that there is no express reference to criminal law provisions) regulating the situation in which coercive measures have not resulted in the removal of a third-country national staying illegally on their territory. However the adoption of these measures must occur with respect for the principles and objective of the returns Directive (which thus continues to provide the benchmark for the adoption of national criminal law).[92] In the light of the above, the national court is called upon to apply and give full effect to the provisions of EU law, to refuse to apply any provision of the Italian law in question which is contrary to the result of the returns

---

[87] Paragraph 55.

[88] Paragraph 56.

[89] Paragraphs 57–58. Emphasis added.

[90] Paragraph 59.

[91] Paragraph 62.

[92] Paragraph 60.

Directive taking due account of the principle of the retroactive application of the more lenient penalty.[93]

3.3.2.5 European Union Law as a Limit to the Criminalisation of Migration: The Impact of El Dridi

El Dridi is a landmark judgment on two levels: on the level of constitutional law, it reiterates—based on settled case-law in the field—that EU law places limits to the power of EU Member States to criminalise, limits which stem from the obligation of Member States to comply with the EU law principles of effectiveness and loyal cooperation; on the level of migration law, it confirms that EU law, and EU migration law specifically, places limits upon Member States' power to criminalise migration. *El Dridi* in this context marks a departure from earlier case-law: while traditionally, in rulings like *Casati,* the Court of Justice has placed limits on national criminal law in order to achieve free movement objectives, in *El Dridi* these limits are justified in order to achieve the effectiveness of an *enforcement* measure, namely the EU returns Directive whose potential negative impact on the position of migrants has been criticised.[94] Following *El Dridi,* the returns Directive plays a two-fold protective role for the affected migrants: being interpreted in the light of proportionality and fundamental rights, it places limits to Member States' criminalisation powers; and, more generally, it has the potential of bringing the full effect of European Union law on a wide range of Member States' choices to criminalise migration, with domestic criminal law being subject to an assessment in the light of EU law when all aspects of the return of third-country nationals come into play. While the Court is careful to leave a degree of discretion to Member States by stating that the latter retain the power to adopt provisions in cases where coercive measures provided for by EU law have not resulted in the return of the third-country nationals, it adds that these measures must occur with respect for the principles and objective of the returns Directive.

3.3.3 The Limits of EU Migration Law on National Criminal Law—the Case of Achughbabian

The extent to which European Union law places limits on the power of EU Member States to criminalise migration was tested again post-*El Dridi* in the case of *Achughbabian.*[95] The judgment was in response to a reference for a preliminary ruling

[93] Paragraph 61.

[94] For a critical analysis, see Baldaccini (2009).

[95] Case C-329/11, *Alexandre Achughbabian v Préfet du Val-de-Marne*, judgment of 6 December 2011.

from the Cour d'Appel de Paris and concerned the compatibility of French law criminalising migration with EU law. The case differs from *El Dridi* in that it concerns the criminalisation and imposition of criminal sanctions by French law for irregular entry or residence per se. The applicant was placed in police custody for being suspected of having committed the offence described above. An order obliging the applicant to leave France was already imposed in 2009, and a deportation order was issued in 2011. The applicant argued that the provision criminalising irregular entry and residence was incompatible with EU law in the light of *El Dridi.* The *Cour d'Appel* decided to stay the proceedings and refer the following question to the Court for a preliminary ruling:

> Taking into account its scope, does Directive [2008/115] preclude national legislation, such as Article L. 621-1 of [Ceseda], which provides for the imposition of a sentence of imprisonment on a third-country national *on the sole ground of his illegal entry or residence* in national territory?[96]

3.3.3.1 Step I: Determining the Applicability of the Returns Directive to National Law Criminalising Irregular Stay

Achughbabian differs from *El Dridi* in that the question referred to Luxembourg concerns the compatibility with EU law of national law concerning the criminalisation of migration *prima facie unrelated to a returns procedure.* The French legislation in question criminalised irregular entry or residence as such. It is thus not surprising that the Court of Justice commenced addressing the question by the *Cour d'Appel* by examining the extent to which the returns Directive applies in this context. The Court confirms that Member States retain a degree of sovereignty in adopting criminal sanctions for the breach of immigration law: the returns Directive is not designed to harmonise in their entirety the national rules on the stay of foreign nationals (note the use by the Court of the term 'stay' and not 'residence' here) and thus does not preclude the law of a Member State from classifying an illegal stay as an offence and laying down penal sanctions to deter and prevent such an infringement of the national rules on residence.[97] Neither does the Directive (which concerns only the adoption of return decisions and the implementation of those decisions) preclude a third-country national being placed in detention with a view to determining whether or not his stay is lawful.[98]

However, the above findings do not mean that national action to criminalise or detain third-country nationals necessarily falls outside the scope of the returns Directive. Firstly, the Court states that national authorities are required, in order to prevent the objective of the returns Directive from being undermined, to act with diligence and take a position without delay on the legality or otherwise of the stay

---

96 Paragraph 25. Emphasis added.

97 Paragraph 28.

98 Paragraphs 29–30.

of the person concerned. The finding that the stay is illegal will lead in principle, according to the returns Directive, to a return decision.[99] Detention is thus inextricably linked with the outcome of the return of the third-country national concerned. Secondly, and notwithstanding state power to criminalise or detain along the lines set out above, it needs to be examined whether the returns Directive precludes the criminalisation of irregular entry or residence under French law *in so far as it is capable of leading to an imprisonment in the course of the return procedure* governed by the said Directive.[100] In that respect, the Court reiterated its ruling in *El Dridi* that Member States cannot apply criminal legislation capable of imperilling the realisation of the aims pursued by the said directive, thus depriving it of its effectiveness.[101] The Court thus envisages the possibility that national law criminalising irregular entry or residence is assessed in the light of the returns Directive.

3.3.3.2 Step II: Applying the Returns Directive to National Law Criminalising Irregular Stay—the Return of Effectiveness and Loyal Cooperation

Having concluded that national law criminalising irregular entry or stay may be assessed in the light of the returns Directive, the Court found that in the present case the situation of the applicant in the main proceedings fell indeed within that referred to in Article 8(1) of that directive.[102] It is clear to the Court that the imposition and implementation of a sentence of imprisonment during the course of the return procedure provided for by the returns Directive does not contribute to the realisation of the removal which that procedure pursues, namely the physical transportation of the person concerned outside the Member State concerned and that such a sentence does not therefore constitute a 'measure' or a 'coercive measure' within the meaning of Article 8 of the Directive.[103] The Court went on to highlight the differences between national criminalisation and the system put forward by the returns Directive: it is undisputed that the national legislation at issue in the main proceedings, in that it provides for a term of imprisonment for any third-country national aged over 18 years who stays in France illegally after the expiry of a period of 3 months from his entry into French territory, is capable of leading to an imprisonment whereas, following the common standards and procedures set out in Articles 6, 8, 15 and 16 of the returns Directive, such a third-country national must, as a matter of priority, be made the subject-matter of a return procedure and may, as

[99] Paragraph 31.

[100] Paragraph 32. Emphasis added.

[101] Paragraph 33.

[102] Paragraphs 34–36.

[103] Paragraph 37.

regards deprivation of liberty, be subject at most to placing in detention.[104] National legislation such as that at issue in the main proceedings is, consequently, likely to thwart the application of the common standards and procedures established by the returns Directive and delay the return, thereby, like the legislation at issue in *El Dridi*, undermining the effectiveness of the said directive.[105]

Linking the criminalisation of irregular stay with the return of the third-country national enabled the Court to apply *El Dridi* in this case which prima facie involved the criminalisation of irregular stay per se. A key factor in the Court's reasoning was the self-standing nature of criminalisation. The Court noted that in the particular case there was nothing in the evidence before the Court to suggest that Mr Achughbabian has committed any offence other than that consisting in staying illegally on French territory. The situation of the applicant in the main proceedings could not therefore be removed from the scope of the returns Directive, as Article 2 (2)(b) of the latter clearly cannot, without depriving that directive of its purpose and binding effect, be interpreted as making it lawful for Member States not to apply the common standards and procedures set out by the said directive to third-country nationals who have committed only the offence of illegal staying.[106] The finding of the applicability of the returns Directive led to the Court to apply its *El Dridi* reasoning and stress that the principles of effectiveness and loyal cooperation must be respected in order to ensure the objectives of the returns Directive, in particular that return must take place as soon as possible.[107] That would clearly not be the case if, after establishing that a third-country national is staying illegally, the Member State were to preface the implementation of the return decision, or even the adoption of that decision, with a criminal prosecution followed, in appropriate cases, by a term of imprisonment. Such a step would delay the removal and does not appear amongst the justifications for a postponement of removal referred to in Article 9 of the returns Directive.[108]

3.3.3.3 Step III: Affirming the Power of Member States to Criminalise in Cases Where the Returns Directive has been Applied Unsuccessfully

In *Achughbabian*, the Court of Justice affirmed the fact that national legislative choices to criminalise migration are constrained by Member States' obligations to respect European Union law. Mindful of the impact of this ruling on state sovereignty and in order to address Member States' concerns that EU law limitations

[104] Paragraph 38.
[105] Paragraph 39.
[106] Paragraph 41.
[107] Paragraphs 43–45.
[108] Paragraph 45.

would put an end to the possibility of Member States deterring illegal stays,[109] the Court went on to confirm its finding in *El Dridi* that Member States retain the power to criminalise when the procedure provided for in the returns Directive was applied but did not lead to the return of third-country nationals. According to the Court, while Member States bound by the returns Directive cannot provide for a term of imprisonment for illegally-staying third-country nationals in situations in which the latter must, by virtue of the common standards and procedures established by that directive, be removed and may, with a view to preparation and implementation of that removal at the very most be subject to detention, that does not exclude the possibility of Member States adopting or maintaining provisions, which may be of a criminal nature, governing, in compliance with the principles of the said directive and its objective, the situation in which coercive measures have not enabled the removal of an illegally staying third-country national to take place.[110] The returns Directive does not preclude penal sanctions being imposed, following national rules of criminal procedure, on third-country nationals to whom the return procedure established by that directive has been applied and who are illegally staying in the territory of a Member State without there being any justified ground for non-return.[111] However, the Court added a further limit to such criminalisation stating that the imposition of the sanctions mentioned in the previous paragraph is subject to full compliance with fundamental rights, particularly those guaranteed by the European Convention for the Protection of Human Rights.[112]

3.3.3.4 The Impact of Achughbabian—Affirming the Protective Function of European Union Law

Achughbabian is an important follow-up to *El Dridi* in two respects: in reiterating the Court's finding that Member States are not entirely free to adopt domestic criminal law, but when doing so they are under the obligation to respect European Union law, and the returns Directive in particular; and in extending the scope of *El Dridi* to bring within the ambit of EU law national legislation which at first sight does not appear to be directly related to the returns Directive. It is true that the Court was mindful to leave Member States a degree of freedom to legislate in criminal matters in this context—the Court has followed this strategy in the past in the ship-source pollution ruling,[113] when it affirmed an inroad to state sovereignty in criminal matters (by confirming the earlier ruling in the environmental crime case[114] that the Community had competence to adopt criminal offences and

[109] Paragraph 47.

[110] Paragraph 46. See also the reference to El Dridi, paras 52 and 60.

[111] Paragraph 48.

[112] Paragraph 49.

[113] See part 3.3.3.2 above.

[114] Commission v Council, Case C-176/03 ECR [2005] I-7879.

sanctions) but at the same time left Member States the choice to adopt specific sanctions levels unanimously under the third pillar.[115] However, Member States' freedom to criminalise is placed under strict EU law limits. national criminal law must still be in compliance with the objectives and provision of the returns Directive, as well as with fundamental rights. Moreover, and crucially, the reasoning of the Court leads to the conclusion that it is very unlikely that criminalisation at national level (in particular the criminalisation of irregular entry or stay) can be viewed independently from the returns Directive. As is clear from *Achughbabian*, the criminalisation of irregular entry or stay cannot be an aim in itself but is ultimately linked to the objective of the return of the third-country national affected—thus bringing into play the application of EU law. In this manner, the Court managed to use EU law (and remarkably an enforcement measure such as the returns Directive) in order to protect third-country nationals from extensive criminalisation in Member States.

3.3.4 The Limits of EU Migration Law on National Criminal Law—the Case of Sagor

The case of *Sagor*[116] concerned a reference for a preliminary ruling from the Tribunale di Rovigo in Italy on the compatibility of Returns Directive with national law which penalises illegal stay by third-country nationals by means of a fine which may be replaced by an order for expulsion or home detention. Unlike *Achughbabian*, where the Court was asked to rule on the compatibility of the Directive with national law criminalising irregular stay by the imposition of custodial sentences, *Sagor* addressed the question of the compatibility of the Returns Directive with alternative forms of criminalisation, i.e. the imposition of fines which may be replaced by an expulsion order or home detention. The Court reiterated its finding in *Achughbabian* that in principle the Returns Directive does not preclude the criminalisation of illegal stay by Member States[117] but qualified this statement by reiterating its finding in both *Achughbabian* and *El Dridi* that Member States may not apply criminal law rules which are liable to undermine the application of the common standards and procedures established by the Returns Directive and thus to deprive it of its effectiveness.[118] The Court proceeded by distinguishing criminalisation leading to imprisonment from criminalisation under the facts of the present case leading to a fine or to an expulsion order. According to the Court, legislation which provides for a criminal prosecution which can lead to a fine for which an expulsion order may be substituted *has markedly different effects* from those of

115 Mitsilegas, EU Criminal Law, Chap. 2.

116 Case C-430/11.

117 Paragraph 31.

118 Paragraph 32.

legislation providing for a criminal prosecution which may lead to a term of imprisonment during the course of the return procedure.[119] The key factor here is the impact of such criminalisation on the functioning of the Returns Directive: according to the Court the possibility that *a criminal prosecution as prescribed by the Italian legislation under review may lead to a fine is not liable to impede the return procedure* established by the Returns Directive—the imposition of a fine does not in any way prevent a return decision from being made and implemented in full compliance with the conditions set out in Articles 6–8 of the Directive, nor does it undermine the common standards relating to deprivation of liberty set out in Articles 15 and 16 of the directive.[120] Moreover, the option given to the criminal court of replacing the fine with an expulsion order accompanied by an entry ban of at least 5 years, is also not, in itself, prohibited by the Directive, which does not preclude the decision imposing the obligation to return from being taken—in certain circumstances as determined by the Member State concerned—in the form of a criminal judgment.[121] The Court noted in this context that Article 7(4) of the Directive allows the Member States to refrain from granting a period for voluntary departure, *in particular where there is a risk that the person concerned may abscond* in order to avoid the return procedure.[122] The discourse of risk enabled the Court here to adopt a harsh interpretation of the Returns Directive as regards the process of return, privileging automatic enforced removal over voluntary return.

However, the Court did apply its findings on the link between imprisonment and the effectiveness of the Returns Directive on the imposition by national law of a fine for which a home detention order may be substituted. The Court reiterated its finding in *Achughbabian* that it follows both from the duty of loyalty of the Member States and from the requirements of effectiveness referred to in the Directive that the obligation imposed on the Member States by Article 8 of that directive to carry out the removal must be fulfilled as soon as possible.[123] According to the Court, the imposition and enforcement of a home detention order during the course of the return procedure provided for by the Directive clearly do not contribute to the achievement of the removal which that procedure pursues, namely the physical transportation of the relevant individual out of the Member State concerned. Such an order does not therefore constitute a 'measure' or a 'coercive measure' within the meaning of Article 8 of the Returns Directive.[124] The Court added that the home detention order is liable to delay, and thus to impede, the measures, such as deportation and forced return by air, which can be used to achieve removal. Such a risk of undermining the return procedure is present in

---

119 Paragraph 34. Emphasis added.

120 Paragraph 36.

121 Paragraphs 37–39.

122 Paragraph 41, emphasis added. But the Court added that such assessment must be done on an individual basis.

123 Paragraph 43.

124 Paragraph 44.

particular where the applicable legislation does not provide that the enforcement of a home detention order imposed on an illegally staying third-country national must come to an end as soon as it is possible to effect that person's removal.[125] The Returns Directive thus precludes national legislation which allows illegal stays by third country nationals to be penalised by means of a home detention order without guaranteeing that the enforcement of that order must come to an end as soon as the physical transportation of the individual concerned out of that Member State is possible. The Directive aim of speedy return thus prevails upon national criminalisation which may take the form of home detention.

3.3.5 *The Compatibility of National Criminal Sanctions with the Returns Directive in the Context of the Imposition of Re-entry Bans—Filev and Osmani*

In its recent ruling in *Filev* and *Osmani,*[126] the Court examined the compatibility with the returns Directive of German legislation imposing criminal sanctions for irregular entry following the imposition of an entry ban of unlimited duration predating the Directive. In the case of *Osmani*, an additional element has been that initial removal has been a consequence of a criminal conviction for drug trafficking.[127] The referring court made clear that Mr Filev did not appear to pose a serious threat to public policy, public security or national security within the meaning of Article 11(2) of the returns Directive.[128] The Court was called to answer two questions concerning the compatibility of national criminal law with the Directive. The first question involves the compatibility of the imposition of national criminal sanctions for breach of an entry ban. Following its classic effectiveness reasoning in *El Dridi* and *Achughbabian*, the Court reiterated that Member States may not apply criminal legislation capable of imperilling the achievement of the objectives pursued by the Directive, thus depriving it of its effectiveness.[129] The application of this reasoning in the present case led to the conclusion that a Member State may not impose criminal sanctions for breach of an entry ban falling within the scope of the returns Directive if the continuation of the effects of that ban does not comply with Article 11(2) of the Directive.[130] Moreover, Article 11(2) of the Directive precludes a continuation of the effects of entry bans of unlimited length made before the date on which the Directive became applicable, beyond the maximum length of entry ban laid down in that provision, except where those entry bans were made against

[125] Paragraph 45.
[126] Case C-297/12, judgment of 19 September 2013.
[127] Paragraphs 15–18.
[128] Paragraph 21.
[129] Paragraph 36.
[130] Paragraph 37.

third-country nationals constituting a serious threat to public order, public security or national security. As mentioned by the referring court, Mr Filev did not appear to constitute such threat.

The Court was also called upon to answer a second question, on a different aspect of the relationship between the returns Directive and national criminal law. The referring Court asked whether an expulsion order which predates by 5 years or more (i.e. the maximum period of the entry ban) the period between the date on which the Directive should have been implemented and the date on which it was actually implemented may subsequently be used as a basis for criminal proceedings, where that order was based on a criminal sanction within the meaning of Article 2 (2)(b) of the Directive.[131] Article 2(2)(b) allows Member States to decide not to apply the Directive to third-country nationals who are the subject of, inter alia, return as a criminal law sanction or as a consequence of a criminal law sanction in accordance with the provisions of national law.[132] This question is of relevance as regards Mr Osmani, whose conviction for drug trafficking framed him as a high risk third country national. The Court accepted that the Directive will not apply to third-country nationals referred to in Article 2(2)(b) in cases where Member States use the discretion conferred to them by this provision at the latest upon expiry of the period for implementing the returns Directive.[133] By contrast, if Member States have not made use of such discretion after the expiry of the implementation deadline, in particular because of the fact that they have not yet implemented the Directive in national law, they may no longer restrict the scope of the persons covered by the Directive.[134] According to the Court, allowing Member States to use their discretion after the implementation deadline against a third country national such as Mr Osmani in the present case *who could already directly rely* on the relevant provisions of the returns Directive would be to worsen that person's situation.[135] Member States can thus not exclude third-country nationals, whatever the risk they pose, from the scope of the returns Directive and the protection it may offer if they do not loyally enforce EU law. European constitutional law, as reflected in the duty of loyal cooperation as far as Member States are concerned, and the principle of direct effect as far as the affected individual is concerned, has come here to the rescue of a presumably in the eyes of the German authorities high risk third country national.

---

131 Paragraph 46.

132 See para 40.

133 Paragraph 52.

134 Paragraph 53.

135 Paragraph 55. Emphasis added.

3.4 Conclusion: The Protective Function of European Union Law

The intervention of the European Union legislator in terms of using criminal law to control immigration has focused both on preventing the irregular entry of third-country national into the European Union (via the criminalisation of trafficking in human beings and facilitation of unauthorised entry) and on identifying and sanctioning irregular stay and residence after entry (via the criminalisation of the facilitation of unauthorised transit and residence and the imposition of criminal sanctions on employers if a series of aggravating circumstances with regard to the employment of migrants in an irregular situation occur). The criminalisation of trafficking and facilitation of unauthorised entry, transit and residence reflects a confluence of policy objectives between the European Union and the global community, with criminalisation at EU level reflecting the securitisation of migration at global level and the establishment in policy and law of a link between migration and organised crime. This securitisation approach has resulted in the prioritisation of criminal law enforcement needs with little emphasis placed on the impact of these measures on migrants themselves. While it should be noted that the European Union legislator has not chosen to criminalise irregular entry, transit or residence per se, the broad scope of criminalisation (in particular as regards the facilitation offences) and the logic of law enforcement and prosecutorial efficiency as regards the granting of rights to migrants have resulted in a legal framework leading to limited safeguards and legal certainty for vulnerable migrants and significant adverse consequences for access to the EU by those who wish to claim international protection. This securitisation approach has been toned down somewhat in the second wave of criminalisation measures. The Directive on employers' sanctions outs forward a more limited and carefully circumscribed criminalisation approach, and addresses to some extent the precarious situation of irregular migrants. The situation of the migrant is also addressed by the revised Directive on trafficking in human beings, which contains a plethora of provisions on the rights of victims of trafficking. While neither Directive provides with a high level of legal certainty for migrants (in particular as regards security of residence), their provisions (in particular those granting rights to third-country nationals) have the potential to offer significant protection to migrants when interpreted by national courts or by the Court of Justice. The protective function of these measures will be enhanced when interpreted in the light of EU constitutional law which privileges the protection of fundamental rights and the respect of the principle of proportionality.

The protective function of European Union law is already evident as regards the second aspect of the criminalisation of migration in Europe, namely the criminalisation of migration not at the EU level, but by individual Member States. Unlike the European Union legislator, a number of Member States including France and Italy have chosen to criminalise conduct deemed contrary to national immigration law—thus criminalising migrants directly. In the light of the political sensitivity of the issue and the potential the impact of state sovereignty the determination of whether Member States were free to adopt such legislation was crucial, in particular given the shared competence on migration between the Union and Member States. The Court of Justice was called upon to rule on the relationship between national criminal law and European Union law in this context. Its findings confirmed the limits that European Union law places upon national criminal law. In a departure from earlier case-law, the Court assessed national law in the light of European Union law dealing not with free movement, but with the enforcement of migration law (the returns Directive). In this manner, the Court found a way to apply the protective provisions of European Union law to third-country nationals. The protective function of EU law is expressed in this context in two ways: by reminding Member States that even EU law on immigration enforcement such as the returns Directive must be interpreted in accordance with fundamental principles of EU law including the protection of fundamental rights and the principle of proportionality; and, crucially, by linking national criminalisation of migration, and in particular the criminalisation of breaches of national immigration law such as irregular stay, with the implementation of the returns Directive. Member States cannot shield their criminal law by claiming that the criminalisation of irregular entry or stay is self-standing or an end in itself. Such criminalisation is inevitably linked with the ultimate objective of return, which signifies the applicability of European Union law. The Court's approach signifies a direct challenge to the employment of symbolic criminal law by Member States and makes it increasingly hard for Member States to evade the control of EU institutions and law when they make criminalisation choices in the field. Imprisonment for its own sake or as an end in itself is incompatible with EU law as it is not designed to lead to the eventual return of irregular migrants in accordance with proportionality and fundamental rights, even when these migrants are deemed to be high-risk. In all these ways, the Court has highlighted repeatedly the capacity of European Union law to act as a limit to the criminalisation of migration at the national level.

References

Baldaccini, A. (2009). The return and removal of irregular migrants under EU law: An analysis of the returns directive. *European Journal of Migration and Law, 11*, 1–17.

Garland, D. (1996). The limits of the Sovereign State: Strategies of crime control in contemporary society. *British Journal of Criminology, 36*, 445–471.

Mitsilegas, V. (2009). *EU criminal law*. Chapter 2. Oxford: Hart.

Mitsilegas, V. (2010). Extraterritorial immigration control in the 21st century: The individual and the state transformed. In V. Mitsilegas & B. Ryan (Eds.), *Extraterritorial immigration control: Legal challenges* (pp. 39–66). Leiden: Martinus Nijhoff/Brill.

Mitsilegas, V. (2011). The EU and the rest of the world: Criminal law and policy interconnections. In M. Evans & P. Koutrakos (Eds.), *Beyond the established orders. Policy Iiterconnections between the EU and the rest of the world* (pp. 149–178). Oxford: Hart.

Mitsilegas, V. (2012). Immigration control in an era of globalisation: Deflecting foreigners, weakening citizens, strengthening the state. *Indiana Journal of Global Legal Studies, 19*, 3–60.

Mitsilegas, V. (2014). From overcriminalisation to decriminalisation. The many faces of effectiveness in European criminal law. *New Journal of European Criminal Law*, (3) (forthcoming).

Obokata, T. (2003). EU council framework decision on combating trafficking in human beings: A critical appraisal. *Common Market Law Review, 40*, 917–936.

Stoyanova, V. (2012). Dancing on the borders of article 4: Human trafficking and the European court of human rights in the *Rantsev* case. *Netherlands Quarterly of Human Rights, 30*, 163–194.

Tridimas, T. (2006). *The general principles of EU law* (2nd ed.) (p. 234). Oxford: Oxford University Press.

Chapter 4
After Entry: Criminalisation as Risk Management, Detention and Removal

4.1 Introduction

In addition to the use of substantive criminal law to enable the prosecution of immigration-related offences, a key strand of the criminalisation of migration is the emphasis on the exclusion of migrants from the legal safeguards applicable in the jurisdiction once they have entered the territory and the strong priority for the EU and its Member States of the removal of irregular migrants from their territory. Exclusion and removal have far-reaching negative human rights and rule of law implications for migrants, especially in cases where the latter are considered to be high-risk. This chapter will analyse the implications of the criminalisation of migration in the context of exclusion and deportation by focusing on two main aspects of criminalisation. The first part will focus specifically on the exclusion and removal of asylum-seekers, either via their exclusion from refugee status or via mechanisms whereby EU Member States have attempted to shield their jurisdiction from the responsibility of examining asylum applications via the transfer of asylum seekers either to other European Union Member States (under the system established by the Dublin Regulation) or, in accordance with the provisions of the asylum procedures Directive, to countries outside the European Union considered to be 'safe'. Attempts by the European Union and Member States to prevent asylum seekers from reaching the EU external border analysed in Chap. 2 are here thus coupled with attempts to evade legal responsibilities with regard to the examination of asylum claims in cases where asylum seekers have made it into the European Union. The second part will examine criminalisation in the context of removal, by focusing in particular on the evolution and provisions of the EU Returns Directive. Following the analysis of the impact of the Court's case-law on using the Returns Directive to limit national criminalisation powers in Chap. 3, this chapter will focus on the impact of the case-law of the Court of Justice in interpreting and shaping the

V. Mitsilegas, *The Criminalisation of Migration in Europe*,
SpringerBriefs in Law, DOI 10.1007/978-3-319-12658-6_4

provisions of the Directive in the light of human rights law. The chapter will focus in particular on the interpretation by the Court of Justice of the provisions of the Returns Directive on the detention of migrants and examine the extent to which the Court has placed limits to the criminalisation of migration such detention powers entail.

4.2 The Exclusion of Asylum-Seekers

The development of the Common European Asylum System has been marked by efforts to disassociate the legal systems of EU Member States from obligations to examine in detail asylum claims in instances where such claims are deemed to be undeserving. There are three main examples of this trend: the inclusion in European asylum law of provisions allowing for exclusion from refugee status of individuals deemed as posing a security risk to EU Member States under the refugee qualification Directive; the refusal to examine an asylum application combined with the automatic transfer of an asylum seeker to another EU Member State under the system established by the Dublin Regulation; and the treatment of asylum applications in an accelerated procedure in cases involving inter alia asylum seekers who are deemed to be high risk or uncooperative and the non-examination of asylum applications if applicants can be transferred to third countries outside the European Union which are considered to be safe under the system put forward by the asylum procedures Directive. These elements of European asylum law have survived the move from the post-Amsterdam minimum standards in asylum law to the post-Lisbon measures entailing a higher level of harmonisation and leading to a Common European Asylum System. What all these instances have in common is the criminalisation of the asylum seeker on the basis of the perception of the latter and the asylum claims submitted as a security risk, abusive, or posing an unreasonable burden to the asylum system of EU Member States. What all these three instances have in common is the exclusion of the asylum seeker from the asylum determination system of EU Member States, with the Dublin Regulation and the safe third country provisions of the asylum procedures Directive ultimately aiming to remove asylum seekers and their claims to the responsibility of other countries, inside or outside the European Union. While preventive immigration control as analysed in Chap. 2 aims at shielding the territory and jurisdiction of Member States from the very arrival of asylum seekers *before* entry, the measures analysed in this chapter complete this picture of deflection by aiming to exclude asylum seekers from the jurisdiction of Member States and expel them from their territory *after* these asylum seekers have managed to gain entry into the European Union.

4.2.1 Exclusion from Refugee Status

Like the minimum standards Directive it has replaced,[1] the post-Lisbon refugee qualification Directive has maintained the possibility for Member States to exclude third-country nationals from refugee status.[2] Exclusion is linked primarily with the perception of the asylum seeker as a risk to society and to the political system of Member States. While provisions on exclusion from refugee status do exist in international refugee law,[3] efforts to exclude third country nationals from being refugees have intensified post-9/11, within the emergence of a general climate of securitisation of migration and stigmatisation of foreigners.[4] This securitisation of asylum seekers has also been reflected in the adoption of counter-terrorism Resolutions by the United Nations Security Council.[5] According to the refugee qualification Directive, a third-country national is excluded from being a refugee inter alia where there are serious reasons for considering that he or she has committed a serious non-political crime outside the country of refuge prior to his or her admission as a refugee[6] and if he or she has been guilty of acts contrary to the purposes and principles of the United Nations.[7] The Directive further provides for the exclusion of third-country nationals from subsidiary protection, adding that exclusion can happen if the third country national constitutes a danger to the community or to the security of the Member State in which he or she is present[8] or if, without further specification in the text, he or she has committed a serious crime.[9] The consideration of third country nationals as a security risk may also lead to the revocation of refugee status. Member States may inter alia revoke, end or refuse to renew refugee status when here are reasonable grounds for regarding him or her as a danger to the security of the Member State in which he or she is present[10] and when the third country national having been convicted by a final judgment of a particularly serious crime, constitutes a danger to the community of that Member State.[11] As Guild and Garlick have noted, exclusion and revocation on

---

[1] Council Directive 2004/83/EC of 29.4.2004 on minimum standards for the qualification and status of third country nationals or stateless persons as refugees, OJ L304, 30.9.2004, p. 12.

[2] Directive 2011/95/EU of the European Parliament and of the Council of 13 December 2011 on standards for the qualification of third-country nationals or stateless persons as beneficiaries of international protection, for a uniform status for refugees or for persons eligible for subsidiary protection, and for the content of the protection granted, OJ L337/9, 20.12.2011.

[3] For an overview see Guild and Garlick (2011).

[4] For an overview, see Goodwin-Gill (2008).

[5] See Mathew (2008).

[6] Article 12(2)(b).

[7] Article 12(2)(c).

[8] Article 17(1)(d).

[9] Article 17(1)(b).

[10] Article 14(4)(a).

[11] Article 14(4)(b).

grounds of the third country national constituting a security threat relate not to the past acts of an asylum seeker, but to prospective and hypothetical future acts.[12] The text of the Directive appears to leave open the exclusion of asylum seekers from refugee status on the basis of subjective assessments by the State of them constituting a security risk. This subjectivity and potential exclusion on the basis of labelling third-country nationals as security risks poses significant challenges to human rights and the rule of law, in particular when such assessments are made in a blanket and automatic way without being based on concrete evidence or on the assessment of individual cases.

The rule of law challenges arising from the provisions on exclusion from refugee status have been addressed by the Court of Justice in its ruling in *B and D.*[13] The Court was asked to interpret the exclusion criteria set out in the first refugee qualification Directive in cases where third country nationals were considered to fall under the exclusion grounds falling currently under Article 12(2)(c) of the new refugee qualification Directive on the basis of their membership of an organisation which has been prescribed as a terrorist group under a separate listing EU Common Position. The Court found that the fact that a person has been a member of an organisation which, because of its involvement in terrorist acts, is on the list forming the Annex to Common Position 2001/931 which implemented Security Council Resolution 1373 (2001), and that that person has actively supported the armed struggle waged by that organisation does not automatically constitute a serious reason for considering that person has committed a serious non-political crime or acts contrary to the purposes or principles of the United Nations. It added that the finding in such a context that there are serious reasons for considering that a person has committed such a crime or has been guilty of such acts is conditional on *an assessment on a case-by-case basis of the specific facts*, with a view to determining whether the acts committed by the organisation concerned meet the conditions laid down in those provisions and whether *individual responsibility for carrying out those acts can be attributed to the person concerned*, regard being had to the standard of proof required under Article 12(2) of the directive.[14] The Court's ruling thus introduces important rule of law safeguards. While the Court has accepted that the competent authorities of the Member States can also apply Article 12(2)(c) of Directive 2004/83 to a person who, in the course of his membership of an organisation which is on the list forming the Annex to Common Position 2001/931, has been involved in terrorist acts with an international dimension[15] it went on to stress that the mere fact that the person concerned was a member of such an organisation cannot automatically mean that person must be excluded from refugee

[12] Guild and Garlick, *call-out*, p. 74.

[13] Joined Cases C-57/09 and C-101/09, *B and D*, judgment of 9 November 2010. For a recent commentary, see Drywood (2014).

[14] Paragraph 99. Emphasis added.

[15] Paragraph 84.

status.[16] Participation in the activities of a terrorist group cannot come necessarily and automatically within the grounds of exclusion laid down in 12(2)(b) and (c) of the Directive.[17] These provisions presuppose a full investigation into all the circumstances of each individual case.[18] Exclusion from (and revocation of) refugee status must thus be based on a full investigation and an assessment on a case-by-case basis of the specific facts which will lead to the attribution of individual responsibility for specific acts to the third country nationals involved. Member States are thus not allowed to exclude third country nationals from refugee status merely by labelling them as 'terrorists.' The EU legislator has attempted to reintroduce this element of subjectivity in the Preamble to the new refugee qualification Directive, which states that the notion of national security and public order also covers cases in which a third-country national belongs to an association which supports international terrorism or supports such an association.[19] However, this provision must be applied in compliance with the Court's ruling in *B and D* which requires an individual assessment on a case-by-case basis based on specific facts and an individual attribution of responsibility for specific acts.

4.2.2 Intra-EU Transfers of Asylum-Seekers: The Dublin Regulation

EU harmonisation measures on asylum have been accompanied by a cooperative system of intra-EU allocation of responsibility for the examination of asylum claims. Such a system had already been established in public international law shortly after the fall of the Berlin Wall by the 1990 Dublin Convention,[20] which was replaced post-Amsterdam by the Dublin Regulation.[21] Placed in the broader context of the construction of an Area of Freedom, Security and Justice, the Dublin Regulation has been designed to serve not only asylum policy, but also broader border and immigration control objectives. According to the Preamble to the Regulation, 'the progressive creation of an area without internal frontiers in which free movement of persons is guaranteed in accordance with the [then] Treaty establishing the European Community and the establishment of [the then] Community policies regarding the conditions of entry and stay of third country nationals, including common efforts towards the management of external borders,

[16] Paragraph 88.

[17] Paragraph 92.

[18] Paragraph 93.

[19] Preamble, recital 37.

[20] For a background see Blake (2001).

[21] Regulation 343/2003 establishing the criteria and mechanisms for determining the Member State responsible for examining an asylum application lodged in one of the Member States by a third-country national, OJ L50/1, 25.2.2003.

makes it necessary *to strike a balance between responsibility criteria in a spirit of solidarity*'.[22]

The significance of border control considerations is evident in the formulation of the criteria established by the Regulation to allocate responsibility for the examination of asylum applications by Member States. The Regulation puts forward a hierarchy of criteria to determine responsibility.[23] While on top of this hierarchical list one finds criteria such as the applicant being an unaccompanied minor,[24] family reunification considerations[25] or a legal relationship with an EU Member State (such as the possession of a valid residence document or a visa),[26] following these criteria one finds the criterion of irregular entry into the Union: if it is established that an asylum seeker has irregularly crossed the border into a Member State having come from a third country, this Member State will be responsible for examining the application for asylum.[27] Irregular entry thus triggers state responsibility to examine an asylum claim. The very occurrence of the criteria set out in the Dublin Regulation sets out a system of automatic inter-state cooperation which has been characterised as a system of negative mutual recognition.[28] Recognition can be viewed as negative here in that the occurrence of one of the Dublin criteria creates a duty for one Member State to take charge of an asylum seeker and thus recognise the refusal of another Member State (which transfers the asylum seeker in question) to examine the asylum claim. The Dublin Regulation thus introduces a high degree of automaticity in inter-state cooperation. Member States are obliged to take charge of asylum seekers if the Dublin criteria are established to apply, with the only exceptions to this rule (on the basis of the so-called sovereignty clause in Article 3 (2) and the humanitarian clause in Article 15 of the Regulation) being dependent on the action of the Member State which has requested the transfer. As in the case of the application of the principle of mutual recognition in criminal matters,[29] automaticity in interstate cooperation is accompanied with the requirement of speed, which is in this case justified on the need to guarantee effective access to the asylum procedure and the rapid processing of asylum applications.[30]

Notwithstanding the claim of the Dublin Regulation that one of its objectives is to facilitate the processing of asylum applications, it is clear that the Regulation has been drafted primarily with the interests of the state, and not of the asylum seeker, in mind. The Regulation establishes a mechanism of automatic interstate cooperation aiming to link allocation of responsibility for asylum applications with border

---

22 Preamble, recital 8. Emphasis added.

23 Chapter III of the Regulation, Articles 5–14.

24 Article 6.

25 Articles 7 and 8.

26 Article 9.

27 Article 10.

28 Guild (2004).

29 Mitsilegas (2006).

30 Article 17(1) and Preamble, recital 4.

controls and in reality to shift responsibility for the examination of asylum claims to Member States situated at the EU external border. The specificity of the position of individual affected asylum seekers is addressed by the Regulation only marginally, with the Regulation containing limited provisions on remedies: a non-suspensive remedy to the asylum seeker with regard to the decision not to examine his or her application[31] and the decision concerning his or her taking back by the Member State responsible to examine the application.[32] The asylum determination system envisaged by the Dublin Regulation has been a system aiming at speed. This objective has recently been confirmed by the Court of Justice which in the case of *Abdullahi*[33] stated that one of the principal objectives of the Dublin Regulation is the establishment of a clear and workable method for determining rapidly the Member State responsible for the processing of an asylum application so as to guarantee effective access to the procedures for determining refugee status and not to compromise the objective of the rapid processing of asylum claims.[34] Privileging the interests of the state in relation to the position of the asylum seeker is linked to the perception that the abolition of internal borders in the Area of Freedom, Security and Justice will lead to the abuse of domestic systems by third-country nationals. The terminology of abuse can be found in cases before the Court of Justice of the European Union, with Advocate General Trstenjak recently stating that the purpose of the hierarchy of criteria in the Dublin Regulation is first to determine responsibility on the basis of objective criteria and to take into account of the objective of preserving the family *and secondly to prevent abuse in the form of multiple simultaneous or consecutive applications for asylum.*[35] In the political discourse, this logic of abuse has been encapsulated in the terminology of 'asylum shopping'. Giving evidence before the House of Lords European Union Committee on the draft Dublin Regulation, the then Home Office Minister Angela Eagle stated that the underlying objectives of the Regulation were 'to avoid asylum shopping by individuals making multiple claims in different Member States and to address the problem known as 'refugees in orbit'…it is in everybody's interests to work together to deal with some of the issues of illegal migration and to get some coherence into the asylum seeking issue across the European Union'.[36] Under this logic of abuse, the Regulation aims largely to automatically remove the unwanted, third-country nationals who are perceived as threats to the societies of the host Member States. The legitimate objective of applying for asylum is thus securitised in the law of the European Union.

[31] Article 19(2).

[32] Article 20(1)(e).

[33] Case C-394/12, *Abdullahi*, judgment of 10 December 2013.

[34] Paragraph 59.

[35] Opinion of Advocate General Trstenjak Case C-245/11, *K*, Opinion of 27 June 2012, para 26, emphasis added.

[36] House of Lords Select Committee on the European Union (2001–2002) *Asylum Applications—Who Decides?*, 19th Report, session 2001–2002, para 27.

As mentioned above, the system of interstate cooperation established by the Dublin Regulation is based on a system of negative mutual recognition. Mutual recognition creates extraterritoriality[37] and presupposes mutual trust[38]: in a borderless Area of Freedom, Security and Justice, mutual recognition is designed so that the decision of an authority in one Member State can be enforced beyond its territorial legal borders and across this area speedily and with a minimum of formality. As in EU criminal law, in the field of EU asylum law automaticity in the transfer of asylum seekers from one Member State to another is thus justified on the basis of a high level of mutual trust. This high level of mutual trust between the authorities which take part in the system is premised upon the presumption that fundamental rights are respected fully by all EU Member States across the European Union. In asylum law, as evidenced in the Preamble of the Dublin Regulation, such mutual trust is based additionally upon the presumption that all EU Member States respect the principle of *non-refoulement* and can thus be considered as safe countries for third-country nationals.[39] In its extreme, this logic of mutual recognition premised upon mutual trust absolves Member States from the requirement to examine the individual situation of asylum applicants and disregards the fact that fundamental rights and international and European refugee law may not be fully respected at all time in all cases in EU Member States, especially in the light of the increased pressure certain EU Member States are facing because of the emphasis on irregular entry as a criterion for allocating responsibility under the Dublin Regulation. Interstate cooperation resulting to the transfer of asylum seekers from EU Member State to EU Member State thus occurs almost automatically, without many human rights questions being asked by the authorities examining requests for Dublin transfers.

This system of interstate cooperation based on automaticity and trust in the field of European asylum law was challenged in Luxembourg in the joint cases of *N.S.* and *M.E.*[40] The Court of Justice was asked to rule on two references for preliminary rulings by the English Court of Appeal and the Irish High Court respectively. The referring courts asked for guidance on the extent to which the authority asked to transfer an asylum seeker to another Member State is under a duty to examine the compatibility of such transfer with fundamental rights and, in the affirmative, whether a finding of incompatibility triggers the 'sovereignty clause' in Article 3(2) of the Dublin Regulation. In a seminal ruling, the Court found that an application of the Dublin Regulation on the basis of the conclusive presumption that the asylum seeker's fundamental rights will be observed in the Member State primarily responsible for his application is incompatible with the duty of the Member States to interpret and apply the Regulation in a manner consistent with fundamental

---

37 Nicolaidis (2007).

38 Mitsilegas, *call-out* (*The Constitutional Implications of Mutual Recognition*).

39 Preamble, recital 2.

40 Joined Cases C-411/10 and C-493/10, *N.S. and M.E.*, judgment of 21 December 2011, hereinafter *N.S.*

rights.[41] Were the Regulation to require a conclusive presumption of compliance with fundamental rights, it could itself be regarded as undermining the safeguards which are intended to ensure compliance with fundamental rights by the European Union and its Member States.[42] Most importantly, such presumption is rebuttable.[43] If it is ascertained that a Dublin transfer will lead to the breach of fundamental rights as set out in the judgment, Member States must continue to apply the criteria of Article 13 of the Dublin Regulation.[44] The Member State in which the asylum seeker is present must, however, ensure that it does not worsen a situation where the fundamental rights of that applicant have been infringed by using a procedure for determining the Member State responsible which takes an unreasonable length of time. If necessary, that Member State must itself examine the application in accordance with the procedure laid down in the sovereignty clause set out in Article 3(2) of the Regulation.[45] *N.S.* followed the ruling of the European Court of Human Rights in the case of *M.S.S.*[46] In *M.S.S.,* the Strasbourg Court found Dublin transfers from Belgium to Greece incompatible with the Convention and importantly found both the sending and the receiving states in breach of the Convention in this context.[47] *M.S.S.,* which as seen in Chap. 2 has also proven to be influential on subsequent Strasbourg case-law on onward transfers to third countries[48] has contributed to the Court of Justice in opposing the automaticity in the operation of the Dublin Regulation by not accepting the non-rebuttable assumption of compatibility of EU Member States action with fundamental rights.

The Court's rejection of the conclusive presumption that Member States will respect the fundamental rights of asylum seekers has admittedly been accompanied by the establishment by the Court of Justice of a high threshold of incompatibility with fundamental rights: a transfer under the Dublin Regulation would be incompatible with fundamental rights if there are substantial grounds for believing that there are systemic flaws in the asylum procedure and reception conditions for asylum applicants in the Member State responsible, resulting in inhuman or degrading treatment, within the meaning of Article 4 of the Charter (on the prohibition of torture and inhuman or degrading treatment or punishment), of asylum seekers transferred to the territory of that Member State.[49] Member States, including the national courts, may not transfer an asylum seeker to the Member State responsible within the meaning of the Regulation where they cannot be

41 Paragraph 99.

42 Paragraph 100.

43 Paragraph 104.

44 Paragraphs 95–97.

45 Paragraph 98.

46 *M.S.S.* v. *Belgium and Greece*, judgment of 21 January 2011, Application No 30696/09.

47 Moreno-Lax (2012).

48 *Hirsi Jamaa*, Application no. 27765/09, concerning the transfer of asylum seekers from Italy to Libya.

49 Paragraph 85.

unaware that systemic deficiencies in the asylum procedure and in the reception conditions of asylum seekers in that Member State amount to substantial grounds for believing that the asylum seeker would face a real risk of being subjected to inhuman or degrading treatment within the meaning of Article 4 of the Charter.[50] This high threshold is justified on the basis of the assumption that all Member States respect fundamental rights and by the acceptance of the existence, in principle, of mutual trust between Member States in the context of the operation of the Dublin Regulation. According to the Court, it is precisely because of that principle of mutual confidence that the European Union legislature adopted the Dublin Regulation in order to rationalise the treatment of asylum claims and to avoid blockages in the system as a result of the obligation on State authorities to examine multiple claims by the same applicant, and in order to increase legal certainty with regard to the determination of the State responsible for examining the asylum claim and thus to avoid forum shopping, it being the principal objective of all these measures to speed up the handling of claims in the interests both of asylum seekers and the participating Member States.[51] It cannot be concluded that any infringement of a fundamental right will affect compliance with the Dublin Regulation,[52] as at issue here is the *raison d'etre* of the European Union and the creation of an area of freedom, security and justice and, in particular, the Common European Asylum System, based on mutual confidence and a presumption of compliance by other Member States with EU law and in particular fundamental rights.[53] The Court found that it would not be compatible with the aims of the Dublin Regulation were the slightest infringement of other measures in the Common European Asylum System to be sufficient to prevent the transfer of an asylum seeker to the Member State primarily responsible under the Dublin Regulation[54] and reiterated the objectives of the Dublin Regulation to establish a clear and effective method for dealing with asylum applications by allocating responsibility speedily and based on objective criteria.[55]

N.S. constitutes a significant constitutional moment in European Union law and introduces a fundamental change in the development of interstate cooperation in European asylum law. The rejection by the Court of the conclusive presumption of fundamental rights compliance by EU Member States signifies the end of automaticity in interstate cooperation. The end of automaticity operates on two levels. Firstly, national authorities (in particular courts) which are asked to execute a request for a transfer under the Dublin Regulation are now under a duty to examine, on a case-by-case basis, the individual circumstances in each case and the human rights implications of a transfer in each particular case. Automatic transfer of

[50] Paragraph 94.

[51] Paragraph 78.

[52] Paragraph 81.

[53] Paragraph 83.

[54] Paragraph 84.

[55] Paragraphs 84 and 85.

individuals is no longer allowed under EU law. Secondly, national authorities are obliged to refuse to execute such requests when the transfer of the affected individuals will result in the breach of their fundamental rights within the terms of *N.S.* The ruling in *N.S.* has thus introduced a fundamental rights mandatory ground for refusal to transfer an asylum seeker in the system established by the Dublin Regulation.[56] While the Court of Justice in N.S. placed limits to the automaticity in the operation of the Dublin Regulation, it was careful not to condemn the Dublin system as a whole. The requirement for Member States to apply the Regulation in compliance with fundamental rights did not lead to a questioning of the principle behind the system of allocation of responsibility for asylum applications between Member States. There are three main limitations to the Court's reasoning: Firstly, the Court used the discourse of the presumption of the existence of mutual trust between Member States, although as seen above this discourse has been used thus far primarily in the context of cooperation in criminal matters and not in the field of asylum law, where the Dublin Regulation has co-existed with a number of EU instruments granting rights to asylum seekers.[57] Secondly, a careful reading of N.S. also demonstrates a nuanced approach to the sovereignty clause in Article 3(2) of the Regulation: the Court stressed that, prior to Member States assuming responsibility under 3(2), they should examine whether the other hierarchical criteria set out in the Regulation apply. Thirdly, it should be reminded again that the threshold set out by the Court for disapplying the system is high: mere non-implementation of EU asylum law is not sufficient to trigger non-return, systemic deficiencies in the national asylum systems must occur leading to a real risk of breach of fundamental rights.[58]

In addition to its contribution to questioning automaticity in the Dublin system, the Court's ruling in *N.S.* is important in highlighting that the adoption of legislative measures conferring rights to asylum seekers may not be on its own adequate to ensure the effective protection of fundamental rights in the asylum process. *N.S.* has demonstrated that the existence of EU minimum harmonisation on rights may not prevent systemic deficiencies in the protection of fundamental rights in Member States. Monitoring and extensive evaluation of Member States' implementation of European asylum law and their compliance with fundamental rights is essential in this context. In addition to the standard constitutional avenues of monitoring compliance with EU law at the disposal of the European Commission as guardian of the treaties, the Lisbon Treaty includes an additional legal basis in Article 70 TFEU for the adoption of measures laying down the arrangements whereby Member States, in collaboration with the European Commission, conduct objective and impartial evaluation of the Union policies in the field of the Area of Freedom, Security and Justice, in particular in order to facilitate full application of the principle of mutual recognition. The Justice and Home Affairs Council has called

56 Mitsilegas (2012).

57 Labayle (2011).

58 Mitsilegas, *call-out* (*The Limits of Mutual Trust*).

recently for the establishment of evaluation mechanisms in the field of EU asylum law.[59] On the basis of the findings of European courts in *M.S.S.* and *N.S.*, the work of organisations such as the UNHCR and civil society actors must be central in the processes of monitoring the situation of international protection on the ground in EU Member States. However, the question of the value of the findings of civil society organisations and the UNHCR as evidence before national and European authorities remains open. While both the Luxembourg and the Strasbourg Courts have referred to the work of UNHCR in their rulings, the Court of Justice found in a recent ruling[60] that the Member State in which the asylum seeker is present is not obliged, during the process of determining the Member State responsible, to request the UNHCR to present its views where it is apparent from the documents of that Office that the Member State indicated as responsible by the criteria in Chap. III of the Dublin Regulation is in breach of the rules of European Union law on asylum. However, work done by civil society and UNHCR, the transparency their presence creates and the information produced and its use by national and European authorities, including courts, is key in shifting the focus of solidarity towards the asylum seeker and in contributing towards the establishment of evidence-based trust in the Common European Asylum System.

Following the Court's ruling in *N.S.*, the revision of the Dublin Regulation post-Lisbon has been eagerly awaited. The adoption of the new instrument (the so-called 'Dublin III' Regulation)[61] may come as a disappointment to those expecting a radical overhaul of the Dublin system. The Regulation maintains intact the system of allocation of responsibility for the examination of asylum applications by EU Member States under the same list of hierarchically enumerated criteria set out in its pre-Lisbon predecessor.[62] However, the Dublin III Regulation has introduced an important systemic innovation to take into account the Court's ruling in *N.S.*: according to Article 3(2) of the Regulation, second and third indent,

> Where it is impossible to transfer an applicant to the Member State primarily designated as responsible because there are substantial grounds for believing that there are systemic flaws in the asylum procedure and in the reception conditions for applicants in the Member State, resulting in a risk of inhuman or degrading treatment within the meaning of Article 4 of the Charter of Fundamental Rights of the European Union, the determining Member State shall continue to examine the criteria set out in Chap. III in order to establish whether another Member State can be designed as responsible.
> Where the transfer cannot be made pursuant to this paragraph to any Member State designated on the basis of the criteria set out in Chap. III or to the first Member State with

[59] 3151st Justice and Home Affairs Council meeting, Brussels, 8 March 2012.

[60] Case C-528/11, *Halaf v Darzhavna agentsia za bezhantiste pri Ministerskia savet,* judgment of 30 May 2013.

[61] Regulation (EU) No 604/2013 of the European Parliament and of the Council of 26 June 2013 establishing the criteria and mechanisms for determining the Member State responsible for examining the application for international protection lodged in one of the Member States by a third-country national or a stateless person (recast), OJ L180/31, 29.6.2013.

[62] See Chap. III of the Regulation, Articles 7–15.

which the application was lodged, the determining Member State shall become the Member State responsible.

The European legislator has thus attempted to translate the Court's ruling in *N.S.* to establish an exception to the Dublin system. The high threshold adopted by the Court in the specific case has been adopted in Dublin III, with the transfer of an asylum applicant being impossible when there are substantial grounds to believe that there are systemic flaws in the asylum system of the receiving Member State which will result in a risk of specifically inhuman and degrading treatment (and not necessarily as regards the risk of the breach of other fundamental rights). Even when such risk has been established, responsibility does not automatically fall with the determining Member State, which only becomes responsible if no other Dublin criterion enabling the transfer of the applicant to another Member State applies. While it could be argued that the new Dublin Regulation could require expressly a higher level of protection of human rights when designing the Dublin system, the legislative recognition of the *N.S.* principles is important in recognising the end of the automaticity in Dublin transfers and placing national authorities effectively under the obligation to examine the substance of the applicants' relevant human rights claims prior to authorising a transfer. Article 3(2) places thus an end to the automatic presumption of human rights compliance by EU Member States and reconfigures the relationship of mutual trust between national executives.

A greater emphasis on the rights of the asylum seeker is also evident in other, specific, provisions of the new Regulation. The provisions on remedies have been strengthened, in particular as regards their suspensive effect.[63] The rights of minors and family members are highlighted, with the Regulation containing strong provisions on evidence in determining the Dublin criteria[64] and in emphasising the possibility of Member States to make use of the discretionary provision which enables them to assume the examination of an asylum claim (the former 'sovereignty clause in Article 3(2) which has morphed into a 'discretionary clause' in Article 17), in particular when this concerns family reunification.[65] The emphasis on the protection of the rights of family reunification and of minors has also been evident in the case-law of the Court of Justice in relation to the pre-Lisbon Dublin Regulation. In a case involving unaccompanied minors, the Court has held that since unaccompanied minors form a category of particularly vulnerable persons, it is important not to prolong more than it is strictly necessary the procedure for determining the Member State responsible which means that, as a rule, unaccompanied minors should not be transferred to another Member State.[66] The Court has also extended the scope of the Dublin criterion of examination of a family asylum application on humanitarian grounds, giving a broad meaning to the humanitarian

---

[63] Article 27(3).

[64] Article 7(3).

[65] Article 17(2).

[66] Case C-648/11, *MA, BT and DA v Secretary of State for the Home Department*, judgment of 6 June 2013, para 55.

provisions of the Regulation.[67] The interpretation of humanitarian, human rights and family reunification clauses in an extensively protective manner by the Court signifies another inroad to the automaticity in interstate cooperation which the Dublin system aims to promote and reiterates the required emphasis on the examination of the substance of individual claims.

4.2.3 Removal of Asylum-Seekers Outside the EU: From the Management of Risk to the Safe Third Country Concepts

As seen above, the main aim of the Dublin Regulation is to establish a system which shields the asylum systems of EU Member States from examining asylum applications by a great number of third country nationals by ensuring their transfer to another State within the European Union which will assume responsibility for the examination of asylum applications. In addition to this system of intra-EU transfers of asylum-seekers, European asylum law has established an additional layer of rules aiming to absolve Member States from their responsibilities to examine fully asylum applications either by providing that these applications are dealt with by accelerated procedures or by providing that applications will not be examined at all if applicants can be further transferred to so-called safe third countries. This additional system of negating the responsibility of Member States to examine fully asylum applications was firmly established post-Amsterdam by the Directive on minimum standards on asylum procedures[68] and has been maintained in principle—albeit with a number of procedural improvements—post-Lisbon by the new asylum procedures Directive.[69] The Directive allows Member States to put forward accelerated examination procedures and/or procedures conducted at the border or in transit zones.[70] These procedures apply inter alia when the applicant is from a safe country of origin.[71] Moreover, as is the case with the Dublin Regulation, the choice to depart from the ordinary process of examining asylum application here is applicable to a great extent to address applications which are deemed by Member States to be abusive or *mala fide*. Accelerated or border procedures may thus apply

[67] Case C-245/11, *K v Bundesasylamt*, judgment of 6 November 2012.

[68] Council Directive 2005/85/EC of 1 December 2005 on minimum standards on procedures in Member States for granting and withdrawing refugee status, OJ L326/13, 13.12.2005.

[69] Directive 2013/32/EU of the European Parliament and of the Council of 26 June 2013 on common procedures for granting and withdrawing international protection (recast), OJ L180/60, 29.6.2013.

[70] Article 31(8).

[71] Article 31(8)(b). The Directive expands on the concept of safe country of origin in Article 36.

when asylum seeker is deemed to be uncooperative[72] or to be acting in bad faith[73] or in a misleading manner.[74] They may also apply in cases where the applicant may, for serious reasons, be considered a danger to the national security or public order of the Member State, or the applicant has been forcibly expelled for serious reasons of public security or public order under national law.[75] The reference to the applicant being a danger to national security is reminiscent of the grounds for exclusion under the refugee qualifications Directive. The Court's ruling in *B and D*, requiring an assessment on a case-by-case, factual basis, is also applicable in the present context. The requirement for an assessment of whether an application for asylum would fall under an accelerated procedure where a safe country of origin is allegedly involved is also confirmed by the Preamble to the Directive, according to which it is important that, where the applicant shows that there are valid reasons to consider the country not to be safe *in his or her particular circumstances*, the designation of the country as safe can no longer be considered relevant for him or her.[76] Ruling on the legality of accelerated procedures established in the 2005 asylum procedures Directive, the Court of Justice emphasised the requirement that the reasons which led a national authority to examine the merits of the application under such a procedure can be subject to judicial review.[77]

The asylum procedures Directive further provides for cases where Member States are not required to examine asylum applications. This is the case where applications are deemed to be inadmissible,[78] including cases where 'a country which is not a Member State is considered as a safe third country for the applicant, pursuant to Article 38.'[79] Moreover, the Directive allows Member States to undertake no, or no full examination of the application for international protection and of the safety of the applicant in his or her particular circumstances shall take place in cases where a competent authority has established, on the basis of the facts, that the applicant is seeking to enter or has entered illegally into its territory from a European safe country.[80] The new asylum procedures Directive thus confirms the practice of deflection of asylum seekers from the territory of the European Union

---

[72] Article 31(8)(h) and (i).

[73] Article 31(8)(d).

[74] Article 31(8)(c).

[75] Article 31(8)(j).

[76] Preamble, recital 42. Emphasis added.

[77] Case C-69/10, *Diouf*, Judgment of 28.7.2011. For a commentary, see Reneman (2014).

[78] Article 33.

[79] Article 33(2)(c).

[80] Article 39(1). On the criteria for a country to be considered as such see Article 39(2). The country: has ratified and observes the provisions of the Geneva Convention without geographical limitations; has in place an asylum procedure prescribed by law; and has ratified the ECHR and observes its provisions, including the standards relating to effective remedies. According to the Preamble to the Directive, these countries observe 'particularly high human rights and refugee protection standards' (recital 45).

via the use of the concept of safe third countries.[81] The procedural use of the safe third countries concepts in the procedures Directive mirrors the system put forward by the Dublin Regulation: asylum seekers are being transferred to third countries (this time outside the European Union) quasi-automatically on the basis of generalised presumptions of safety. The new procedures Directive has taken a number of steps to address the human rights and rule of law concerns that this automaticity entails. New Article 34 of the procedures Directive introduces special rules on the admissibility review regarding inadmissible applications, including those related to safe third countries. It requires Member States to allow applicants to present their views with regard to the application of the grounds referred to in Article 33 *in their particular circumstances* before the determining authority decides on the admissibility of an application for international protection adding that to that end Member State must conduct a personal interview on the admissibility of the application.[82] Moreover, the application of the concept of a safe third country is subject to a series of rules laid down in national law including inter alia rules requiring a connection with the third country and rules in accordance with international law *allowing an individual examination of whether the third country concerned is safe for a particular applicant*, which as a minimum shall permit the applicant to challenge the application of the safe third country concept on the grounds that the third country is not safe *in his or her particular circumstances.*[83] The move from generalised to individual assessments of safety is also confirmed in the Preamble to the Directive, according to which Member States should only proceed on that basis where that particular applicant would be safe in the third country concerned.[84]

A similar focus on the provision of remedies to the asylum applicant to challenge the applicability of the safe third country concept in his or her individual circumstances arises in the context of European safe countries. According to new Article 39(3), the applicant must be allowed to challenge the application of the concept of European safe third country on the grounds that the third country concerned is not safe in his or her particular circumstances. These developments are coupled with the general Directive provisions on remedies: the right to an effective remedy applies to both categories of safe third country concepts[85] with new stronger rules allowing applicants to remain in the territory of Member States until the time limit within which to exercise their right to an effective remedy has expired and, when such a right has been exercised within the time limit, pending the outcome of the remedy[86] and, in the case of European safe countries, giving the power to courts to rule under

---

[81] For an analysis of the potential impact of the 2005 asylum procedures Directive in this context, see Costello (2005).

[82] Article 34(1).

[83] Article 38(2), emphasis added. Under a new provision introduced in the 2013 procedures Directive, the applicant must also be allowed to challenge the existence of a connection between him or her and the third country-Ibid.

[84] Preamble, recital 44.

[85] Article 46(1)(a)(ii) and (iv) respectively.

[86] Article 46(5).

certain conditions whether or not the applicant may remain on the territory of the Member State.[87] The strengthening of the Directive's provisions on remedies is coupled by calls to Member States to take into account information provided by expert bodies such as the European Asylum Support Office and the UNHCR when applying safe country concepts on a case-by-case basis or designating countries as safe.[88] This move reflects to some extent the evidence-based approach introduced by European courts in *M.S.S.*, *N.S.* and *Hirsi.* These judgments are extremely important in the development and interpretation of safe third country concepts in European asylum law. Human rights concerns arising from the transfer of asylum seekers within the European Union under the Dublin system are equally, if not more, valid in the context of the transfer of asylum seekers in third, non-EU countries. Developments in European case-law have put an end to automaticity in the transfer of asylum seekers to third countries on the basis of generalised presumptions of safety. Not only must Member States' authorities consider the situation of individual applicants on a case-by-case basis when called to apply the safe third country criteria, but any decision not to examine an asylum application in the jurisdiction of an EU Member State must be based on a detailed assessment of the full and on the ground compliance of the third state in question with European human rights and international and European refugee law.

4.3 Detention, Removal and the Management of Risk Under the Returns Directive

4.3.1 The Returns Directive: Background and Content

The removal of migrants from the territory of the European Union has always been a priority for Member States, either by signing (bilaterally or at EU level) readmission agreements with third states[89] or by applying the principle of mutual recognition to expulsion decisions.[90] However, no EU measure is more emblematic of the priority to deport migrants from the territory of the European Union than the Returns Directive, which constitutes a major development of the European Union *acquis* in relation to immigration enforcement. Two features of the Directive are key in contextualising and analysing its impact on immigration detention in EU law: the first feature is the achievement by the Directive of a high level of

---

87 Article 46(6)(d).

88 Preamble, recital 46.

89 For an analysis see N. Coleman, *European Readmission Policy,* Nijhoff, 2008. On the relationship between re-admission agreements concluded by Member States and EU law, see Panizzon (2012).

90 Council Directive 2001/40/EC on the mutual recognition of expulsion decisions of third-country nationals, OJ L149/34, 2.6.2001.

harmonisation of aspects of immigration enforcement at EU level; and the second feature is that the Directive contributes to the criminalisation of migration at EU level, in particular by including specific legal provisions on immigration detention. The high level of harmonisation is evidenced by the very title of the measure in question, a Directive 'on common standards and procedures in Member States for returning illegally staying third-country nationals'[91] and is confirmed by the opening Article of the Directive according to which it sets out common standards and procedures to be applied in Member States for returning illegally staying third country nationals, in accordance with fundamental rights as general principles of Community law as well as international law, including refugee protection and human rights obligations.[92] Unlike EU measures in the field of granting rights to migrants and in particular asylum seekers, where EU action has taken initially the form of minimum standards, the Returns Directive thus reflects a consensus by EU institutions on the need to adopt common rules on immigration enforcement. This consensus is the outcome of different priorities by the different EU institutions involved in the legislative process leading to the adoption of the Returns Directive. Member States have been traditionally keen to adopt at EU level strong standards on immigration enforcement. In the heavily securitised Hague Programme of 2004, the European Council 'called for the establishment of an effective removal and repatriation policy based on common standards for persons to be returned in a humane manner and with full respect for their human rights and dignity' and for the start of Council discussions on minimum standards for return procedures including minimum standards to support effective national removal efforts taking into account special concerns with regard to safeguarding public order and security.[93]

The securitised approach on returns by Member States is here evident, and it is noteworthy that the EU legislative outcome has surpassed the initial Council ambition for the adoption of mere minimum standards in the field. The achievement of a high level of harmonisation has been facilitated by the integrationist ambitions of the European Commission and the European Parliament, which acted as a co-legislator in the adoption of the returns Directive.[94] The Commission in its proposal for the returns Directive justified the adoption of common standards by arguing that co-operation among Member States is likely to be successful if it is based on a common understanding on key issues and that common standards should be set in order to facilitate the work of the authorities involved and to allow enhanced co-operation among Member States. According to the Commission, in the long term such standards will provide the ground for adequate and similar treatment of illegally staying third-country nationals, regardless of the Member State which carries

[91] Directive 2008/115/EC of the European Parliament and of the Council of 16 December 2008 on common standards and procedures in Member States for returning illegally staying third-country nationals, OJ L348/98, 24.12.2008.

[92] Article 1.

[93] The Hague Programme: Strengthening Freedom, Security and Justice in the European Union, OJ C53/1, 3.3.2005, para 1.6.4. See also recital 2 in the Preamble of the returns Directive.

[94] See Acosta (2009).

out the return procedure.[95] While the common standards set out by the Returns Directive reflect on a number of occasions a draconian policy towards migrants, they can, as will be seen below, act as a limit to further criminalisation of migration by providing clear limits to Member State enforcement action.

Negotiations leading to the adoption of the Directive have proven to be controversial, in view of the different views of the EU institutions involved as regards the content of the Directive and the significant potential consequences of the Directive for the protection of fundamental rights.[96] At the heart of the Directive lies Chap. II which is entitled 'termination of illegal stay' and contains detailed provisions on the return decision, voluntary departure and removal, detention and the relevant safeguards. There are two main areas which underline the criminalisation of migration in the Returns Directive: the combination of a return decision with a re-entry ban, and allowing Member States to detain migrants pending their return. A very broadly worded re-entry ban is set out in Article 11 of the Directive, according to which such a ban is compulsory if no period for voluntary departure has been granted, or if the obligation to return has not been complied with—but Member States may also impose such a ban in other cases.[97] The length of such a ban is also prohibitive and arguably disproportionate—it will in principle not exceed 5 years but this time limit is not absolute—it can exceed 5 years if the third-country national represents a serious threat to public policy, public security or national security.[98] There is a relaxation of the ban under certain conditions for victims of trafficking who co-operate with the authorities under Directive 2004/81/EC[99]and an obligation to apply the provisions on the re-entry ban without prejudice to the right of international protection under EU asylum law.[100] As regards immigrant detention, the key provision signalling the criminalisation of migration is Article 15 of the Directive which confirms detention as an accepted means of enforcing the return of irregular migrants.

However, it must be noted that the Returns Directive places Member States' detention powers under a series of limits. Detention is allowed only for the purposes of removal[101] and only if other sufficient but less coercive measures cannot be applied

---

[95] COM (2005) 391 final, Brussels, 1.9.2005.

[96] For an analysis see Baldaccini (2009a), Acosta *call-out.*

[97] Article 11(1).

[98] Article 11(2).

[99] Article 11(3).

[100] Article 11(5).

[101] According to Article 15(1) of the Directive, Member States may only keep in detention a third-country national who is the subject of return procedures in order to prepare the return and/or carry out the removal process—in particular when:

(a) there is a risk of absconding or
(b) the third-country national concerned avoids or hampers the preparation of return or the removal process.

effectively in a specific case.[102] Most importantly, any detention shall be for as short a period as possible and *only maintained as long as removal arrangements are in progress and executed with due diligence.*[103] The requirement for the existence of a link between detention and a prospect of removal is confirmed by Article 15(4) of the Directive according to which when it appears that a reasonable prospect of removal no longer exists for legal or other considerations or the conditions laid down in Article 15 (1) of the Directive no longer exist, detention ceases to be justified and the person concerned shall be released immediately. These limits to Member States' power to detain are watered down significantly by the length of detention allowed by the Directive. According to Article 15(5), detention will be maintained for as long a period as the conditions laid down in Article 15(1) are fulfilled and it is necessary to ensure successful removal for a period which may not exceed 6 months. The Directive allows Member States to extend this period for a limited period not exceeding a further 12 months in accordance with national law in cases where regardless of all their reasonable efforts the removal operation is likely to last longer owing to a lack of cooperation by the third-country national concerned, or delays in obtaining the necessary documentation from third countries.[104] The Returns Directive allows thus Member States to detain immigrants for the sole purpose of removal for a period up to 18 months.[105] The limits that this lengthy period of detention places upon the proportionality requirement for detention have been noted[106] and the approach of the Directive on the length of detention has been heavily criticised.[107] Further criticism of the Directive has been voiced by the United Nations Special Rapporteur on the rights of migrants, Francois Crépeau, according to whom the systematic detention of irregular migrants has come to be viewed as a legitimate tool in the context of EU migration management, despite the lack of any evidence that detention serves as a deterrent, adding that the Directive can be said to have institutionalised detention within the European Union as a viable tool of migration management.[108] The Returns Directive has indeed normalised the detention of irregular migrants and in this manner constitutes another clear example of the criminalisation of migration. However, as will be seen below, safeguards included in the Directive such as the establishment of a clear

---

102 Ibid.

103 Ibid. Emphasis added.

104 Article 15(6).

105 The Directive has attempted to introduce common standards in a highly diverse field, with some Member States having established clearly determined and limited periods of detention under their national law, while others not having laid down any maximum time limit for pre-removal detention in their national law—see European Union Agency for Fundamental Rights (2011).

106 Cornelisse (2012).

107 Baldaccini (2009b). As Baldaccini eloquently notes, this is an extremely long period for depriving irregular migrants of their liberty for the sole reason of facilitating their removal and preventing them from absconding in the meantime.

108 United Nations General Assembly, Report of the Special Rapporteur on the human rights of migrants, Francois Crépeau: *Regional Study: Management of the External Borders of the European Union and its impact on the human rights of migrants,* 24 April 2013, para 47.

link between detention and a prospect of removal on the one hand, and the setting out of maximum—albeit lengthy—periods of detention on the other, have proven to be instrumental towards the limitation of national criminalisation practices in the interpretation of the Directive by the Court of Justice.

4.3.2 *Detention and Risk Under the Returns Directive—the Case of Kadzoev*

The Court of Justice has now had a number of opportunities to clarify the relationship between immigration detention and European Union law in the context of litigation concerning the implementation of the Returns Directive. A key ruling in this context has been the Court's judgment in Kadzoev.[109] The case concerned the prolonged detention in Bulgaria of Mr Kadzoev, who was eventually declared by the Bulgarian authorities to be a stateless person. According to the order for reference, the help centre for survivors of torture, the office of the United Nations High Commissioner for Refugees and Amnesty International found it credible that Mr Kadzoev was the victim of torture and inhuman and degrading treatment in his country of origin. Moreover, and despite the efforts of the Bulgarian authorities, several non-governmental organisations and Mr Kadzoev himself to find a safe third country which could receive him, no agreement was reached, and he had not as yet obtained any travel documents.[110] The reference by the Administrativen sad Sofia-grad has led to the Court of Justice clarifying a number of aspects of the Returns Directive related to immigration detention. Firstly, the Court confirmed that the period of detention completed by the person concerned during the procedure in which the lawfulness of the removal decision is the subject of judicial review must be taken into account for calculating the maximum duration of detention laid down in Article 15(5) and (6) of the Returns Directive. The Court held that, if it were otherwise, the duration of detention for the purpose of removal could vary, sometimes considerably, from case to case within a Member State or from one Member State to another because of the particular features and circumstances peculiar to national judicial procedures, which would run counter to the objective pursued by Article 15(5) and (6) of the Returns Directive, *namely to ensure a maximum duration of detention common to the Member States*.[111] The Court distinguished the maximum period of detention from the situation concerning suspensive appeals in asylum law, stating that the maximum periods laid down in Article 15(5) and (6) of the Returns Directive *serve the purpose of limiting the deprivation of a person's liberty*.[112] This maximum detention limit also applies

[109] C-357/09 PPU, *Said Shamilovich Kadzoev (Huchbarov)*.

[110] Paragraphs 22–24.

[111] Paragraphs 53–54, emphasis added.

[112] Paragraph 56, emphasis added.

when the affected individual was deemed to be high risk by state authorities. The referring Court asked whether Article 15(4) and (6) of the Returns Directive allow the person concerned not to be released immediately, even though the maximum period of detention provided for by that directive has expired, on the grounds that he is not in possession of valid documents, his conduct is aggressive, and he has no means of supporting himself and no accommodation or means supplied by the Member State for that purpose.[113] To this the Court reiterated that Article 15(6) of the Returns Directive in no case authorises the maximum period defined in that provision to be exceeded and that the possibility of detaining a person on grounds of public order and public safety cannot be based on the Directive.[114]

The Court stressed further the requirement for immigration detention under the Returns Directive to be linked with a reasonable prospect of removal. According to the Court, it is clear that, where the maximum duration of detention provided for in Article 15(6) of the Directive has been reached, the question whether there is no longer a 'reasonable prospect of removal' within the meaning of Article 15(4) does not arise. In such a case the person concerned must in any event be released immediately. Article 15(4) of the Directive can thus only apply if the maximum periods of detention laid down in Article 15(5) and (6) of the directive have not expired.[115] The Court added that under Article 15(4) of the Returns Directive, detention ceases to be justified and the person concerned must be released immediately when it appears that, for legal or other considerations, a reasonable prospect of removal no longer exists.[116] As is apparent from Article 15(1) and (5) of the Directive, the detention of a person for the purpose of removal *may only be maintained as long as the removal arrangements are in progress and must be executed with due diligence, provided that it is necessary to ensure successful removal.*[117] It must therefore be apparent, at the time of the national court's review of the lawfulness of detention, that a real prospect exists that the removal can be carried out successfully, having regard to the periods laid down in Article 15(5) and (6) of the Directive, for it to be possible to consider that there is a 'reasonable prospect of removal' within the meaning of Article 15(4) of that directive.[118] A reasonable prospect of removal does not exist where it appears unlikely that the person concerned will be admitted to a third country, having regard to those periods.[119]

Kadzoev is an important judgment as it confirms the limits of detention under the Returns Directive and reiterates the key principles which govern its interpretation. As regards the length of detention, the Court links the achievement of a high level of harmonisation via the adoption of common standards with the imposition of a

[113] Paragraph 68.

[114] Paragraphs 69–70.

[115] Paragraphs 60–61.

[116] Paragraph 63.

[117] Paragraph 64. Emphasis added.

[118] Paragraph 65.

[119] Paragraph 66.

non-negotiable, maximum duration of immigration detention for the purposes of the Directive. Member States are prohibited by EU law to extend immigration detention beyond the time limits set out by the Returns Directive, even in cases where the individual under detention is deemed to be a risk to public order. This restrictive interpretation is inextricably linked with the teleological interpretation espoused by the Court in relation to the objectives of the Directive. In *Kadzoev*, the Court stresses that detention can be justified only if there is a reasonable prospect of removal and if Member States exercise due diligence in relation to the returns procedure. As in its case-law in the *El Dridi* type cases analysed above, the Court emphasises again here that detention is only justified if it serves the key objective of the Returns Directive which is the removal of irregular migrants. What *Kadzoev* also confirms is that the requirements of the existence of a reasonable prospect of removal and of the exercise of due diligence by States exist throughout the returns process and underpin the legality of immigrant detention. This has been confirmed recently by the European Court on Human Rights in its ruling on *Amie v Bulgaria.*[120] The Court avoided to rule specifically on the compatibility of domestic law with the Returns Directive and the maximum detention periods prescribed therein.[121] However, the Court found a breach of Article 5(1)(f) ECHR as it found that the grounds for the first applicant's detention—action taken with a view to his deportation—did not remain valid for the whole period of his detention due to *the lack of a realistic prospect of his expulsion and the domestic authorities' failure to conduct the proceedings with due diligence.*[122] The Court also confirmed that the length of detention should not exceed that reasonably required for the purpose pursued.[123]

4.3.3 Detention and Asylum Under the Returns Directive—the Case of *Arslan*

If *Kadzoev* can be read as a judgment setting limits to risk-based immigration detention, the Court's approach to risk in the context of immigration detention appears to be more nuanced in its more recent ruling in *Arslan.*[124] The case involved a request for a preliminary ruling by the Czech Supreme Administrative Court in proceedings between Mr Arslan, a Turkish national arrested and detained in the Czech Republic with a view to his administrative removal who, during his

[120] Application No 58149/08.

[121] Paragraphs 74–75.

[122] Paragraph 79, emphasis added.

[123] Paragraph 72. The Court noted that a similar point was recently made by the ECJ in relation to Article 15 of the returns directive. It should however be pointed out that unlike that provision Article 5(1)(f) ECHR does not lay down maximum time-limits: the question whether the length of deportation proceedings could affect the lawfulness of detention under this provision thus depends solely on the particular circumstances of each case.

[124] Case C-534/11, judgment of 30 May 2013.

detention has made an application for international protection and the Czech police. Mr Arslan's detention was extended notwithstanding his lodging of an asylum application as it was deemed that the extension was necessary for preparing for the enforcement of the decision to remove him in view of the fact that the asylum procedure was still ongoing and it was not possible to enforce the removal decision while the asylum application was being considered. The Czech authorities also stated that the application for international protection had been made with the intention of hindering enforcement of the removal decision.[125] In the light of the above facts, the Czech Court asked Luxembourg whether the Returns Directive does not apply to a third country national who has lodged an application for international protection within the meaning of the asylum procedures Directive, and whether, if the Returns Directive does not apply, the detention of a foreigner for the purpose of return must be terminated if he applies for international protection and there are no other reasons to keep him in detention.

The Luxembourg Court appeared to concur in principle with the referring court in finding that the Returns Directive does not apply to a third-country national who has applied for international protection within the meaning of the asylum procedures Directive during the period from the making of the application to the adoption of the decision at first instance on that application or until the outcome of any action brought against that decision is known.[126] However, this prima facie exclusion of the applicability of the Returns Directive does not result in an unqualified protection of the asylum seeker from detention. In answering the second question, the Court of Justice—rather than applying directly the Returns Directive—used this Directive in order to interpret European asylum law. The Court noted that European asylum law (and in particular Article 7(3) of the reception conditions Directive and Article 18 of the asylum procedures Directive) allows Member States to confine an applicant to a particular place in accordance with their national law.[127] The Court further noted that neither the reception conditions nor the procedures Directive carries out currently a harmonisation of the grounds on which the detention of asylum seekers may be ordered —therefore, for the time being it is for Member States to establish, in full compliance with their obligations under international and EU law, the grounds on which an asylum seeker may be detained or kept in detention.[128] According to the Court,

> As regards a situation such as that at issue in the main proceedings, in which, firstly, the third-country national was detained on the basis of Article 15 of Directive 2008/115 on the ground that his conduct gave rise to the concern that, if not detained, he would abscond and frustrate his removal, and, secondly, the application for asylum seems to have been made with the sole intention of delaying or even jeopardising enforcement of the return decision taken against him, such circumstances can indeed justify that national being kept in detention *even after an application for asylum has been made.*[129]

---

[125] Paragraph 25.

[126] Paragraphs 40–49.

[127] Paragraphs 53 and 54 respectively.

[128] Paragraphs 55–56.

[129] Paragraph 57, emphasis added.

The Court has thus combined the limited harmonisation in European asylum law with the use of the Returns Directive, interpreted in a highly securitised, risk-based approach, in order to justify Member Sates' discretion to detain asylum seeker s for extensive periods of time. The Court justified this approach further by arguing that a national provision which allows, in such circumstances, the detention of an asylum seeker is compatible with Article 18(1) of the asylum procedures Directive, since that detention does not result from the making of the application for asylum but from circumstances characterising the individual behaviour of the applicant before and during the making of that application.[130] Detention under Article 15 of the Returns Directive acts thus as a factor justifying the detention of asylum seekers under European asylum law, based on the pre-supposition that the asylum seeker in question is a high-risk individual. The objectives of the Returns Directive (the effective return of third country nationals) are used here not to protect third country nationals, but to extend detention under this risk-based approach.[131] However, this approach sits uneasily with the Court's constant finding that detention for the purposes of removal governed by the Returns Directive and detention of asylum seekers under the reception and procedures Directives and national law fall under different legal rules.[132] It also results in the criminalisation of asylum seekers, by allowing their extensive detention under national law which is interpreted in the light of the Returns Directive, which provides a high degree of harmonisation on enforcement. Immigration enforcement law is thus also applied in asylum law, although the objectives and scope of these two areas of law are markedly different. This approach, which is based heavily on the acceptance by the Court of governmental perceptions of risk, leads to clearly disproportionate outcomes for the asylum seekers involved. In the case of *Arslan,* the Court's ruling means that the effects of detention are intensified rather than alleviated by the fact that the third country national in question has lodged an asylum application.

4.3.4 Detention and Undocumented Migrants Under the Returns Directive—the Case of Mahdi

The Court of Justice was called to rule on the limits of detention under the Returns Directive with regard to undocumented migrants in the case of *Mahdi.*[133] The Court was asked to assess inter alia whether Article 15(1) and (6) of the Returns Directive must be interpreted as precluding national legislation under which an initial 6-month period of detention may be extended solely because the third country

[130] Paragraph 58.

[131] Paragraph 60.

[132] *Arslan,* para 52. *Kadzoev,* para 45.

[133] Case C-146/14 PPU, *Mahdi*, judgment of 5 June 2014.

national concerned has no identity documents and, accordingly, there is a risk of him absconding.[134] The Court found that the fact that the third-country national concerned has no identity documents cannot, on its own, be a ground for extending detention under Article 15(6) of the Directive.[135] The Court noted firstly that the concept of 'risk of absconding' is defined in Article 3(7) of the Directive as the existence of reasons in an individual case which are based on objective criteria defined by law to believe that a third country national who is the subject of return procedures may abscond.[136] Secondly, the Court reiterated its finding that Article 15(1) of the Directive makes clear that recourse may be had to detention only when other sufficient but less coercive measures cannot be applied effectively in a specific case.[137] The Court went on to reiterate that the extension of detention under Article 15(6) of the Directive may be ordered only if the removal operation is likely to last longer owing either to a lack of cooperation by the third-country national concerned or to delays in obtaining the necessary documentation from third countries, no mention being made of the fact that the person concerned has no identity documents.[138] Any decision to extend detention must be preceded by a re-examination of the substantive conditions which formed the basis for the initial decision to detain the third-country national concerned. That calls for an assessment by the judicial authority, in the course of the examination required under the second sentence of Article 15(3) of the directive, of the circumstances which gave rise to the initial finding that there was a risk of the third-country national absconding.[139] In this context, the Court stressed that any assessment relating to the risk of the person concerned absconding must be based on an individual examination of that person's case and that decisions taken under the directive should be adopted on a case-by-case basis and based on objective criteria.[140]

The application of a proportionality test combined with the emphasis on procedural safeguards and a facts-based assessment on a case-by-case basis[141] have thus led the Court to reject the automatic extension of detention on the basis of a presumption of risk on the sole ground that a third-country national has no identity documents. The Court has further circumscribed the extension of detention by interpreting Article 15(6)(a) of the Returns Directive as meaning that a third-country national who has not obtained an identity document which would have made it possible for him to be removed from the Member State concerned may be regarded as having demonstrated a 'lack of cooperation' within the meaning of that provision only if an examination of his conduct during the period of detention

134 Paragraph 65.

135 Paragraph 73.

136 Paragraph 66.

137 Paragraph 67.

138 Paragraph 68, and reference to para 58.

139 Paragraph 69, and reference to para 61.

140 Paragraph 70.

141 See also para 64 of the judgment.

shows that he has not cooperated in the implementation of the removal operation and that it is likely that that operation lasts longer than anticipated *because of that conduct*, a matter which falls to be determined by the referring court.[142] Extension of detention can thus take place only if national courts establish a direct and exclusive causal link between the non-cooperative conduct of the third-country national and the lengthening of the removal operation. As the Court has noted, if such removal is taking longer than anticipated for another reason, no causal link may be established between the latter's conduct and the duration of the operation in question and therefore no lack of cooperation on the part of the third country national can be established.[143] The Court's finding here echoes its' findings concerning the requirement for Member States to contribute to the effective implementation of the returns Directive by respecting the time-limits it has established. However, the Court has stopped short of linking the release of third-country nationals following the expiry of the detention deadlines in the Returns Directive with the granting of residence rights. According to the Court, a Member State cannot be obliged to issue an autonomous residence permit, or other authorisation conferring a right to stay, to a third-country national who has no identity documents and has not obtained such documentation from his country of origin, after a national court has released the person concerned on the ground that there is no longer a reasonable prospect of removal within the meaning of Article 15(4) of the Returns Directive—a mere written confirmation of the third-country national's situation is required.[144] This ruling leaves affected migrants in a legal limbo, the consequences of which will have to be addressed in litigation before national and European courts.

4.3.5 Detention and Defence Rights Under the Returns Directive—the Case of M.G.

Another recent judgment which is informed by a restrictive, law enforcement approach is the Court's ruling in *M.G.*[145] In this case, the Court of Justice was asked to examine the impact of a breach of the rights of the defence by a decision by a national authority to prolong detention to the actual detention decision. The Court found that irregularities in the exercise of the rights of the defendant do not trigger automatically the release of the third country national in detention.[146] It is for the national judge to ascertain whether such irregularity could lead to a different

[142] Paragraph 85, emphasis added.

[143] Paragraph 82.

[144] Paragraph 89.

[145] Case C-383/13 PPU, *M.G. and N.R. v Staatsecretaris van Veligheid en Justitie,* judgment of 10 September 2013.

[146] Paragraph 39.

result for the third country national.[147] According to the Court, not recognising a margin of appreciation in this context to the national judge, and ruling that any violation of rights would lead automatically to the annulment of the decision prolonging detention would risk to undermine the effectiveness of the Returns Directive.[148] The Court added that coercive measures taken under the Directive are not only subject to the principle of proportionality, but also to the principle of effectiveness[149] and reiterated that the return of irregularly staying third country nationals is a priority for Member States under the Directive.[150] In this manner, the principle of effectiveness is used here by the Court to strengthen coercive action by the state under the Returns Directive and to nuance the protection of fundamental rights. The Court has thus used effectiveness in the field of procedural law in a markedly different manner to its approach in the *El Dridi* type cases involving criminalisation under substantive national criminal law. The ruling in *M.G.* is also another nod of the Court in favour of state sovereignty in the field of immigration control, most notably by stressing the discretion that national authorities, including courts, have in assessing aspects of the compliance of implementing action with the Returns Directive and EU constitutional law more broadly.

4.3.6 Detention and Imprisonment Under the Returns Directive—the Cases of Thi Ly Pham and Brero and Bouzalmate

In what has been perhaps the most blatant manifestation of the link between detention of migrants for the purposes of return and the criminalisation of migration, the Court of Justice was called to rule on two cases involving questions from German Courts on whether it is acceptable for migrants to be detained together with ordinary prisoners in prison accommodation. In the case of *Thi Ly Pham,*[151] the Court rejected firmly such a prospect. The Court noted that it is clear from the wording of Article 16(1) of the Returns Directive that it lays down an unconditional obligation requiring illegally staying third-country nationals to be kept separated from ordinary prisoners when a Member State cannot provide accommodation for those third-country nationals in specialised detention facilities.[152] This obligation is not coupled with any exception and *constitutes a guarantee of observance of the rights* which have been expressly accorded by the EU legislature to those third-country nationals in the context of the conditions relating to detention in prison

---

[147] Paragraph 40.

[148] Paragraph 41.

[149] Paragraph 42.

[150] Paragraph 44.

[151] Case C-474/13, *Thi Ly Pham*, judgment of 17 July 2014.

[152] Paragraph 17.

accommodation for the purpose of removal.[153] The Court added that the obligation requiring illegally staying third-country nationals to be kept separated from ordinary prisoners, laid down in the second sentence of Article 16(1), is more than just a specific procedural rule for carrying out the detention of third country nationals in prison accommodation and *constitutes a substantive condition for that detention, without observance of which the latter would, in principle, not be consistent with the directive.*[154] Such is the strength of this finding that the Court ruled that the second sentence of Article 16(1) of the Returns Directive must be interpreted as not permitting a Member State to detain a third-country national for the purpose of removal in prison accommodation together with ordinary prisoners even if the third-country national consents thereto.[155] In a further judgment issued on the same day, the Court rejected the justification by Germany of the detention of migrants for the purposes of return in prisons on the basis of the particularities of the German federal system.[156] The Court stated unequivocally that Article 16(1) of the Returns Directive must be interpreted as requiring a Member State, as a rule, to detain illegally staying third-country nationals for the purpose of removal in a specialised detention facility of that State even if the Member State has a federal structure and the federated state competent to decide upon and carry out such detention under national law does not have such a detention facility.[157] The Court has thus sent a clear signal against the legality of the criminalisation of migration in Europe when this takes the form of the imprisonment of migrants for the purposes of removal. Immigration detention is not a criminal penalty. There is a clear separation between immigration law and criminal law. As Advocate General Bot stated in his powerful Opinion in *Bero and Bouzalmate,* by referring to the Court's earlier ruling in *El Dridi*[158]:

> …detention does not constitute a penalty imposed following the commission of a criminal offence and its objective is not to correct the behaviour of the person concerned so that he can, in due course, be reintegrated into society. Any idea of penalising behaviour is, moreover, missing from the rationale forming the legal basis of the detention measure. It must not be overlooked that, at that stage, a migrant awaiting removal is not caught by any criminal statute, or be forgotten that, even in the member state concerned classifies, as the Court recognises it has a legitimate right to do, the act of unlawfully entering its territory as a 'criminal offence', the Court has also held that the potentially criminal nature of that conduct must yield to the priority that must be given to removal.[159]

---

[153] Paragraph 19. Emphasis added.

[154] Paragraph 21. Emphasis added.

[155] Paragraph 23.

[156] Joined Cases C-473/13 and C-514/13, *Brero and Bouzamate*, judgment of 17 July 2014.

[157] Paragraph 34.

[158] For an analysis of *El Dridi* see Chap. 3.

[159] Opinion of Advocate General Bot delivered on 30.4.2014, Joined Cases C-473/13 and C-514/13, *Brero and Bouzalmate,* para 92.

4.4 Conclusion

The chapter demonstrated how European Union law has resorted to the criminalisation if migrants after their entry onto the European Union by focusing on their exclusion from the jurisdiction of EU Member States and their removal from EU territory, backed up by a series of provisions on detention. As regards asylum-seekers, the evolution of the Common European Asylum System has maintained provisions on exclusion from refugee status and systems whereby EU Member States absolve themselves from the responsibility of examining or examining fully asylum applications by justifying the removal of asylum seekers to other states within the European Union (under the Dublin system) or outside the Union (applying largely concepts of safe third countries). In both these cases, removal of asylum-seekers to third states is justified largely on presumptions of safety and human rights compliance of these states, and was envisaged to take place quasi-automatically if these presumptions were deemed to apply. In parallel to the evolution of European asylum law, the European Union legislator has continued to place emphasis on measures ensuring the removal of irregular migrants from the territory of the European Union. Removing migrants from the territory of the European Union has perhaps unsurprisingly been a high political priority for EU Member States and governments wishing to be seen to have control over their borders.[160] Nowhere else has this political priority to exclude and remove migrants from the European Union been reflected more clearly than with the adoption of the Returns Directive, which aims at ensuring speedy removal while at the same time legitimises the criminalisation of migration by allowing Member States to detain migrants.

However, as with the instances of criminalisation of migration discussed in the previous chapters of this book, the law in these instances has not remained static. The Court of Justice has again intervened to address the human rights challenges arising from EU legislation in the field. The Court's case-law has introduced a paradigm change in European asylum law: in addition to strong rulings on remedies with regard to the refugee qualification and asylum procedures Directives, the Court has put an end to the automaticity inherent in the Dublin system by affirming first that national authorities are obliged to examine the individual circumstances of each case and the impact of removal for the asylum-seeker concerned and second that the Dublin Regulation will be suspended and removal will not take place if removal will lead to serious human rights violations. Not only is the Court's ruling in *N.S.* applicable in the safe country system established in the asylum procedures Directive, but as has been seen above it has led already to law reform within the EU, with the Court's case-law incorporated within the new Dublin Regulation. The Court of Justice has also made a significant contribution towards upholding fundamental rights in the context of the application of the Returns Directive. In addition to the use of the Directive to place limits on national criminalisation powers examined in

[160] On the symbolic and political functions of removal, see Cornelisse (2010).

Chap. 3, in a series of cases the Court has placed clear limits to the detention of migrants in Member States. It is hoped that the Court's case-law will have a real impact on Member States' practice and implementation of the detention provisions of the Returns Directive, which according to the latest Commission implementation Report shows great variation.[161] The Court of Justice has made decisive steps towards decriminalising migration by emphasising the requirement for a link between detention and a real prospect of removal and by distinguishing clearly between imprisonment and immigration detention.

References

Acosta, D. (2009). The good, the bad and the ugly in EU migration law: Is the European Parliament becoming bad and ugly? (The Adoption of Directive 2008/15: The Returns Directive). *European Journal of Migration and Law, 1*(1), 19–39.

Baldaccini, A. (2009a). The EU directive on return: Principles and protests. *Refugee Survey Quarterly, 28*(4), 114–138.

Baldaccini, A. (2009b). The return and removal of irregular migrants under EU law: An analysis of the returns directive. *European Journal of Migration and Law, 11*(1), 1–17.

Blake, N. (2001). The Dublin convention and rights of asylum seekers in the European Union. In E. Guild & C. Harlow (Eds.), *Implementing Amsterdam* (pp. 95–115). Oxford: Hart Publishing.

Cornelisse, G. (2010). Immigration detention and the territoriality of human rights. In N. de Genova & N. Peutz (Eds.), *The deportation regime. Sovereignty, space, and the freedom of movement* (pp. 101–122). Durham: Duke University Press.

Cornelisse, G. (2012). Detention of foreigners. In E. Guild & P. Minderhoud (Eds.), *The first decade of EU migration and asylum law* (pp. 207–228). Leiden, Boston: Nijhoff.

Costello, C. (2005). The asylum procedures directive and the proliferation of third country practices. *European Journal of Migration and Law, 7*, 35–70.

Drywood, E. (2014). Who's in and who's out? The court's emerging case law on the definition of a refugee. *Common Market Law Review, 51*, 1093–1124.

European Union Agency for Fundamental Rights. (2011). *Detention of third-country nationals in return procedures*, pp. 31–36.

Goodwin-Gill, G. (2008). Forced migration: Refugees, rights and security. In J. McAdam (Ed.), *Forced migration, human rights and security* (pp. 1–18). Oxford: Hart Publishing.

Guild, E. (2004). Seeking asylum: Storm clouds between international commitments and EU legislative measures. *European Law Review, 29*, 198–218.

Guild, E., & Garlick, M. (2011). Refugee protection counter-terrorism and exclusion in the European Union. *Refugee Survey Quarterly, 29*, 63–82.

Labayle, H. (2011). Le Droit Européen de 'Asile devant ses Juges: précisions ou remise en question? *RFDA*:273.

Mathew, P. (2008). Resolution 1373—A call to Pre-empt asylum seekers? In J. McAdam (Ed.), *Forced migration, human rights and security* (pp. 19–62). Oxford: Hart Publishing.

Mitsilegas, V. (2006). The constitutional implications of mutual recognition in criminal matters in the EU. *Common Market Law Review, 43*, 1277–1311.

[161] European Commission, *Communication from the Commission to the Council and the European Parliament on EU Return Policy*, COM (2014) 99 final, Brussels, 28.3.2014.

Mitsilegas, V. (2012). The limits of mutual trust in Europe's area of freedom, security and justice. From automatic interstate cooperation to the slow emergence of the individual. *Yearbook of European Law, 31*, 319–372.

Moreno-Lax, V. (2012). Dismantling the Dublin system: M.S.S. v. Belgium and Greece. *European Journal of Migration and Law, 14*, 1–31.

Nicolaidis, K. (2007). Trusting the poles? Constructing Europe through mutual recognition. *Journal of European Public Policy, 14*, 682–698.

Panizzon, M. (2012). Readmission agreements of EU member states: A case for EU subsidiarity or Dualism? *Refugee Survey Quarterly, 31*, 101–133.

Reneman, M. (2014). Speedy asylum procedures in the EU: Striking a fair balance between the need to process asylum cases efficiently and the asylum applicant's EU right to an effective remedy. *International Journal of Refugee Law, 25*, 717–748.

Chapter 5
Decriminalising Migration in EU Law: Upholding Human Rights and the Rule of Law After Lisbon

This book has demonstrated the extent to which European Union law has in recent years led to the increase of state power in immigration control based to a great extent on the proliferation of legal avenues for the criminalisation of migration. A key element in this move towards the criminalisation of migration has been the emphasis on prevention. The increase in extraterritorial immigration control has been accompanied by the extension of the arm of the state via the delegation of power to both the private sector (land and air carriers) and to European Union agencies (FRONTEX). Moreover, the legal expression of the nexus between prevention, immigration control and security has led to the development of a far-reaching EU framework of pre-emptive surveillance, consisting of the collection and transfer of every day personal immigration data *en masse* to law enforcement authorities, the establishment of large-scale EU databases (such as the Visa Information System) and surveillance systems (such as EUROSUR), the normalisation of the use of sensitive personal data for immigration control purposes such as biometrics and the relaxation of purpose limitation requirements by allowing law enforcement authorities to have access to personal data collected for immigration control purposes. The main aim of this multi-layered system of prevention has been on the one hand to stop migrants from reaching the external border of the European Union, and on the other hand to shield the European Union and its Member States from legal responsibility towards migrants by conducting immigration control outside of EU territory. The rule of law challenges this approach entails (via the creation of gaps in the law) are coupled with real risks of human rights violations, in particular as regards the right to seek asylum and the rights to non-discrimination, privacy and data protection. Towards this seemingly relentless evolution of the preventive paradigm of the criminalisation of migration, it is courts who have provided answers and limitations. The European Court of Human Rights in Strasbourg in its landmark ruling in *Hirsi* has sent the strongest message possible with regard to the requirement for both fundamental rights and the rule of law to be upheld in instances of extraterritorial immigration control. What is crucial to note in this context is that the Court's ruling has generated concrete instances of law reform

V. Mitsilegas, *The Criminalisation of Migration in Europe*,
SpringerBriefs in Law, DOI 10.1007/978-3-319-12658-6_5

at EU level as regards standards on FRONTEX and Member States' operations and search and rescue at sea. A similar pattern may emerge as regards the securitisation of migration in the form of pre-emptive surveillance, with both the Strasbourg and the Luxembourg Courts having delivered a number of important judgments which limit the retention of sensitive personal data by the state in cases involving individuals not convicted of a criminal offence (*Marper*) and prohibiting the generalised, *en masse* retention of every day personal data by the private sector (*Digital Rights Ireland*). The Strasbourg and Luxembourg Courts have thus challenged radically the paradigm of the preventive criminalisation of migration and have made the re-thinking of this paradigm and ensuing law reform a matter of urgency.

This transformative power of the European judiciary has also been visible as regards the criminalisation of migration after entry into EU territory. With regard to the use of substantive criminal law to regulate migration, it must be reminded that while EU law has aligned itself with the global securitised criminalisation initiatives as regards human trafficking and smuggling, it has not as such imposed criminal sanctions on migrants themselves. Not only that, but EU law has acted as a limit to the introduction of such criminalisation by Member States via the intervention of the Court of Justice. What is significant in the landmark ruling of the Court of Justice in *El-Dridi* and its aftermath, is that the Court used here primarily general principles of EU law (in particular the principle of effectiveness) in order to limit criminalisation. Effectiveness in this context, together with proportionality, may back up human rights obligations and serve in the future as further limits to the criminalisation of migration at both national and EU levels. At the stage of removal, the Court of Justice (following the landmark Strasbourg *M.S.S.* ruling) introduced in *N.S.* a paradigm change as regards the automaticity of exclusion inherent in the Dublin system. As in the case of *Hirsi,* judicial intervention has led here to concrete law reform to address human rights concerns. The Court of Justice has also been active in cases concerning the interpretation of the detention provisions of the Returns Directive, where it has sent strong messages against indefinite detention on the grounds that an individual constitutes a security risk, confirming the necessity of a link between detention and a real prospect of removal, and affirming the distinction between immigration detention and imprisonment. In all three levels of criminalisation, it has thus been the judiciary which has rebalanced the system to take into account rule of law and human rights concerns. This will remain an ongoing process with Courts facing growing litigation following the development of the various strands of EU legislation in the field. The growing synergy between the Strasbourg and Luxembourg Courts, the requirement of compliance with the ECHR not only by EU Member States but also by EU institutions after the accession of the EU to the ECHR and the increasing importance of the Charter of Fundamental Rights in interpreting EU law and its implementation render the further reconfiguration of the current paradigm of criminalisation of migration in EU law in favour of upholding human rights and the rule of law highly probable. In the meantime, current judicial developments render the need to revisit highly invasive EU surveillance systems including in the field of immigration control a matter of urgency.

MIX
Papier aus verantwortungsvollen Quellen
Paper from responsible sources
FSC® C105338

If you have any concerns about our products,
you can contact us on
ProductSafety@springernature.com

In case Publisher is established outside the EU,
the EU authorized representative is:
Springer Nature Customer Service Center GmbH
Europaplatz 3, 69115 Heidelberg, Germany

Printed by Libri Plureos GmbH
in Hamburg, Germany

LIBRARY

ASTRONOMY AND ASTROPHYSICS LIBRARY

Springer-Verlag Berlin Heidelberg GmbH

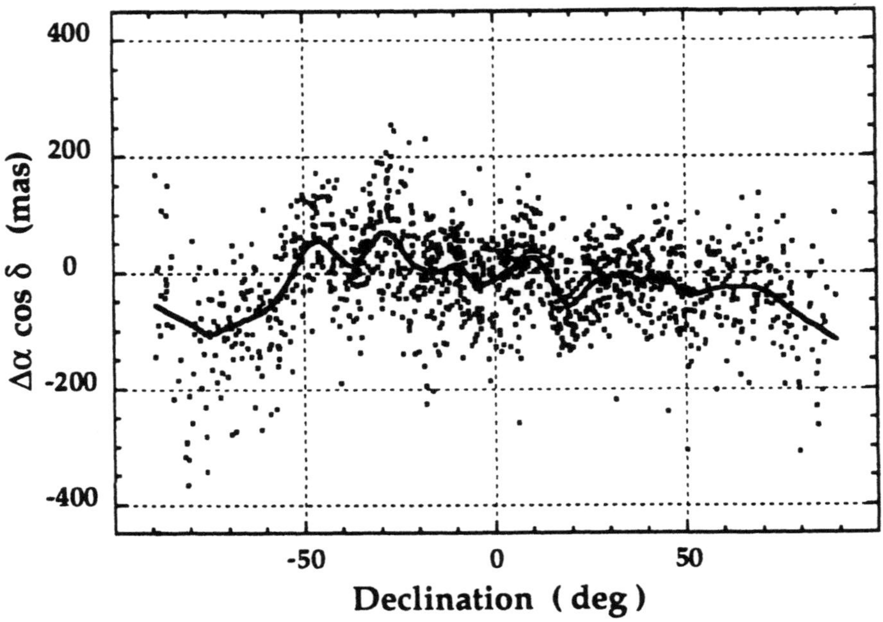

Differences in right ascension between the FK5 and the Hipparcos Catalogue at epoch J1991.25; the plotted points are FK5 minus Hipparcos right ascensions. [After ESA (1997), Vol. 3, p. 419]

Hans G. Walter   Ojars J. Sovers

Astrometry of Fundamental Catalogues

The Evolution from Optical to Radio Reference Frames

With 29 Figures

Springer

Professor Dr. Hans G. Walter
Astronomisches Rechen-Institut
Mönchhofstrasse 12-14
69120 Heidelberg
Germany

Dr. Ojars J. Sovers
Caltech/Jet Propulsion Laboratory
4800 Oak Grove Drive
Pasadena, CA 91109-8099, USA
Present address:
Remote Sensing Analysis Systems
2235 N. Lake Avenue
Altadena, CA 91001, USA

Cover picture: This planar equal-area projection of the sky shows all 608 International Celestial Reference Frame radio sources: the 212 'defining' sources as well as the 396 sources in the other two categories. The ecliptic and galactic planes are indicated in green and orange, respectively. Right ascension increases from right to left, and declination increases from bottom to top. The sources are colour coded acccording to their declination accuracies: positional uncertainties decrease from cool to warm colours. Red represents the best-known sources: σ<0.5 mas, yellow: 0.5<σ<1.0, green: 1.0<σ<2.0, and blue: σ>2.0 mas. (Picture by H.G. Walter and O.J. Sovers)

ISSN 0941-7834
ISBN 978-3-642-63158-0 ISBN 978-3-642-57260-9 (eBook)
DOI 10.1007/978-3-642-57260-9

Library of Congress Cataloging-in-Publication Data. Walter, Hans G. (Hans Georg), 1928- Astrometry of fundamental catalogues : the evolution from optical to radio reference frames / Hans G. Walter, Ojars J. Sovers. p.cm. – (Astronomy and astrophysics library, ISSN 0941-7834) Includes bibliographical references and index. ISBN 3540674365 (alk. paper) 1. Astrometry. I. Sovers, Ojars J. (Ojars Juris), 1937- II. Title. III. Series. QB807.W35 2000 522–dc21 00-030753

Originally published by Springer-Verlag Berlin Heidelberg New York in 2000
Softcover reprint of the hardcover 1st edition 2000

Typesetting: Camera ready by the authors using a Springer TEX Macro package
Cover design: *design & production* GmbH, Heidelberg

Printed on acid-free paper SPIN: 10533924 55/3141/di - 5 4 3 2 1 0

Prologue

Why does the force of one's spiritual and mental associations act to inspire and revive? Because when reading a work of one's colleagues and friends one feels himself repeatedly in touch with all the valuable discoveries the authors of the work have enjoyed themselves, especially in the vast domain of Astronomy. As it had been remarked by the great Frenchman, François Arago, Astronomy does not need any decorations, being ornamented by the innumerable stars above one's head. And, lo! that head succeeds in deciphering the everlasting kinematical and dynamical wonders of the Heavens, in spite of being itself like an incomparably tiny particle next to the immense sizes of the heavenly objects and the distances separating them, not to mention the enigmatic flow of Time, flowing since for ever and ever. Truly, one could exclaim "Stolze Demuth" with another great man, Karl Schwarzschild, simply illustrating the sense of insignificance of a human being living in the vast Universe and his pride in himself at being able to discover, using his tiny brain, some of the Laws governing the dynamics and evolution of this Universe around him.

These associations become more profound when one takes into his hands the book "Astrometry of Fundamental Catalogues – The Evolution from Optical to Radio Reference Frames" written by two outstanding scholars in the field – Drs. Hans G. Walter and Ojars J. Sovers. They have succeeded in presenting the entire multifaceted history of astrometric research against a background of the technique development, and its brilliant achievements shining throughout like preciously encrusted milestones along the bumpy roads of scientific pursuit. Even the epigraph chosen by the authors from the immortal William Shakespeare's "Hamlet", if combined with "Hamlet's Mill", written by Giorgio de Santillana brings one onto a plane of analogies between the contemporary and most advanced scientific achievements in studies on Space and Time and the wise, although not perfect conclusions of the Ancients in the same knowledge categories derived just from the ad hominem appeal and based on their naked-eye observations of the apparent movements of stars and planets.

Putting aside other, sometimes terrible and horrifying, things that we have lived through in the 20th century, our generation is very lucky to be eyewitness to the vast harvest in Astrometry gathered with new, powerful instruments never seen before, working with enigmatic invisible rays, and providing a researcher with new observables. The fruits of the progress in Mathematics, Radio Physics, and Astrodynamics are incorporated in a series of new star catalogues constituting the most reliable and precise basis for contemporary astronomical research, and have recently been adopted by the International Astronomical Union as the International Celestial Reference Frame. Therefore, the book by Walter and Sovers, revealing the fundamentals and principles of the art of Fundamental Catalogue construction on the basis of processing optical observations of stars and radio measurements of extragalactic sources, is a timely manual of long-lasting value for everybody who is practically engaged in the field of Astrometry.

The authors describe the difficult and complicated historic path trodden to arrive at the most reliable approximations to the inertial system of reference by various approaches based on astrometric and dynamical procedures. Having taken several detailed steps towards explaining the dramatic changes over many decades in the instruments used, observation reductions, and catalogue compilation, they arrive at the most progressive astrometric achievement crowned by the coupling of Radio Astrometry with Space Astrometry, while also providing clues to understanding the development of the methods and results of each partner and of their family as a whole.

One should note that the authors never underestimate the results of the work of foregoing generations of astrometrists, observers and theoreticians, and give proper and detailed consideration to classical methods and theories in the field, some of which may seem obsolete, or even of no meaning nowadays to someone apt to cast a superficial glance on profound things. This feature is expressed with the utmost clarity in the particular case of the Hipparcos Catalogue tie with the International Celestial Reference Frame and with other conventional reference frames.

As nothing of real value, especially in the Science of Astronomy, may completely be accomplished for eternity, the authors dedicate the final pages of their excellent oeuvre to their view of optimistic future prospects of creating new observational techniques and space missions and of establishing new fundamental catalogues (the FK6 among them!). Both roads should lead to new, highly refined celestial reference frames which are the eternal goals of Astrometry and its servants, who were called by Professor Paul Couteau "ces Astronomes fous du Ciel".

Dr. Victor K. Abalakin
Associate Member of the Russian Academy of Sciences
and
Director of Pulkovo Observatory

Preface

There are more things in heaven and earth, Horatio,
than are dreamt of in your philosophy.

Hamlet, Act I, Scene V

Even in the early history of astronomy, the compilation of catalogues of star positions was important. This is easily traced back to the times of Hipparchus (190–120 BC) and his predecessors, Timocharis and Aristillos, who lived approximately 150 years earlier. Their cataloguing of star positions enabled Hipparchus to compare them with current observations and thus to discover the phenomenon of the precession of the Earth's axis of rotation. Since these early times, star catalogues have never ceased to serve as reference maps in studies of the motions of celestial bodies. Refinements in astrometric techniques were instrumental in improving the precision of star positions from about 1500 arcsec at the time of Hipparchus to 0.2 arcsec or better by around 1980. The development of star catalogues of positions and, after the discovery of stellar motions, of lists of positions and proper motions culminated in the fifth fundamental catalogue, FK5 (FK being the German abbreviation of 'Fundamental-Katalog'). The FK5 was constructed in accordance with the recommendations contained in resolutions that the International Astronomical Union (IAU) approved in 1976.

Over the last two decades, new astrometric techniques, particularly radio interferometry and space astrometry as, for instance, performed by the Hipparcos project at optical wavelengths, improved the precision of positions to as good as 0.001 arcsec. (Hipparcos is an acronym standing for HIgh Precision PARallax COllecting Satellite.) This enormous improvement in precision suggested a reconsideration of the concept of fundamental catalogues. In contrast to radio techniques, Hipparcos provides only differential astrometry, and therefore the new approach to fundamental catalogues has been guided by the methods of radio interferometry. For the first time in the history of astronomy it was possible, with the aid of radio interferometry, to choose extragalactic sources with negligible motion with respect to the Universe as reference objects for astrometry. On this basis, a resolution was submitted to IAU in 1991 (IAU 1992) recommending that selected extragalactic radio sources should play the role of the fiducial points in the future celestial reference frame. Accordingly, the establishment of a fundamental catalogue of positions of extragalactic radio sources was suggested for defining this frame. Access to the frame at visual wavelengths is secured by the mathematical interconnection of this catalogue of extragalactic radio sources and the best catalogues of star positions, in particular the FK5 and the Hipparcos Catalogue.

Our goal in writing this book is twofold: First, we wish it to be understood as a self-contained guide to the current celestial reference systems and the concomitant modern fundamental catalogues for applications in astronomy, geodesy and geodynamics. It is this class of catalogues that forms the conventional basis for the orientation on the celestial sphere as a function of time. We intend to give the general astronomer and geodesist an overview of the process of construction of conventional reference frames by presenting the basic principles of such work. This occasionally involves very detailed explanations, and leads to some quite lengthy expositions. With this end in view, we discuss the construction of fundamental catalogues, starting from first principles and building on the observations, theoretical concepts and models, passing through the intermediate steps to the final catalogues. The various stages are treated to the extent possible in generally intelligible terms, such that the discussion may be followed by a reader with some elementary astronomical training. Developments are not always given at the level of detail necessary for full comprehension. When such is the case we attempt to provide key references, trusting that modern bibliographic services can easily provide the full story. Second, we address the watershed event that involved the transition from the traditional fundamental catalogue of stellar positions and proper motions (FK5) to the fundamental catalogue of positions of extragalactic radio sources defining the International Celestial Reference Frame (ICRF) in 1998. In this context we delve into methods of modern astrometry which, on the one hand, pave the way to the establishment of the extragalactic celestial radio reference frame represented by a catalogue at the positional precision level of 0.001 arcsec and, on the other hand, to the construction of internally coherent differential star catalogues of a comparable precision level at visual wavelengths. To ensure utmost preservation of the high internal accuracy of the two types of catalogues, much attention is paid to the connection of the two reference frames so that the unavoidable systematic errors are minimized.

Preparations for the transition to the extragalactic frame began in the 1980s and are manifested in the IAU resolution on the celestial reference frame. This resolution became effective in 1991 and is based on recommendations from the IAU Working Group on Reference Systems (IAU 1992). The official replacement of the FK5 frame by the extragalactic frame took place at the beginning of 1998. At this critical juncture, the comprehensive treatment of both the classical construction of the FK5 and the modern construction of the ICRF is intended to facilitate full understanding of both the former and the present scenarios. The order of the subject matter does not follow its historical evolution, but is rather grouped into the two broad categories that correspond to the spectral regions: optical and radio wavelengths.

In clarification, some basic terminology and definitions are set out concerning fundamental catalogues, reference frames and reference systems. This is briefly done in Chap. 1, which continues with a recapitulation of two subjects that are inseparable from fundamental catalogues: precession of the Earth and the approaches pursued to establish inertial frames. The chapter ends with general remarks on conventional stellar, as well as conventional extragalactic, reference systems, and elaborates on the respective peculiarities of both types of systems. Chapter 2 documents the principles, main tools and procedures employed for the establishment of the FK5. Considerable details concerning the FK5 work are presented, in anticipation that this history might serve as a guide during the future evolution of the Hipparcos and ICRF catalogues. Additional high-precision observations are likely to lead to problems similar to those encountered during the development of the FK5.

The IAU resolution on the celestial radio reference frame calls for accessibility to astrometry at both visual and radio wavelengths. By extending the radio source catalogue to visual wavelengths with the aid of the Hipparcos catalogue, the original radio frame becomes accessible to optical astrometry. Therefore, the Hipparcos catalogue plays an important role in the overall concept of the new frame. For this reason, Chap. 3 treats the essential steps leading to the positions and proper motions of the intermediate Hipparcos catalogue, still with provisional zero points of the position and proper motion scales.

As radio interferometry is the observational tool for obtaining radio source positions of high astrometric standards, Chap. 4 is devoted to astrometry with radio interferometers, emphasizing the process of deriving source coordinates from the signals received at the antennas, thus ultimately providing the material for the catalogues of extragalactic radio sources. Methods of construction of these types of catalogues are the subject of Chaps. 5 and 6, where Chap. 6 is devoted entirely to the construction of the ICRF. It also takes account of the rapidly accumulating observations of celestial objects and demonstrates their exploitation for the benefit of maintenance, refinement and densification of the new radio/optical reference frame that came into being by the amalgamation of the ICRF and Hipparcos catalogues.

As shown in Chap. 7, the inertial character of the official Hipparcos catalogue is substantiated by connecting it with the IAU approved radio reference frame known as ICRF. Estimates of possible link improvements are based on radio star positions that have become available since the ICRF/Hipparcos link establishment. Finally, Chap. 8 concludes the book with an outlook for the interconnections between astrometry and fundamental catalogues. Without claim of completeness, we briefly describe the prospects of some promising future astrometric missions, and discuss their anticipated repercussions on the construction of celestial reference frames.

The bottom margins of the pages of the main text contain data concerning the 212 defining ICRF sources. For familiarity's sake, each source is identified by its old B1950 name. Right ascension and declination are given together with their error estimates, where the latter refer to the last decimal digits of the coordinates. Each entry is terminated with an indication of the type of object and its red shift, if known. Here Q symbolizes quasar, G = galaxy, L = BL Lac object, S = galaxy with a Seyfert spectrum, and ? = type unknown. We trust that this abbreviated compilation will be useful in providing an overview of the ICRF sources in a convenient way.

This book would never have been completed without the kind and competent help of numerous friends and colleagues. We have benefitted from thorough readings by, and subsequent stimulating discussions with a number of associates during the process of preparing this work. These contributors included P. Charlot, C. de Vegt, E. Groten, C.S. Jacobs, J.H. Lieske, C. Ma and H. Schwan. We greatly appreciate their expenditure of considerable amounts of time, and regard the manuscript to be substantially improved as a direct result of our consultations. They all read critically through the whole manuscript or specific chapters, and gave us much valuable advice. Perhaps we may not have always followed their suggestions, but it is a pleasure to record our gratitude to all of them for the efforts they have made, sometimes working with incomplete drafts. By no means should our colleagues be held jointly accountable for remaining errors and shortcomings of the text: that responsibility is totally ours.

One of us (H.G.W.) owes a very considerable debt to the Astronomisches Rechen-Institut, Heidelberg, for the opportunity to prepare the manuscript and for assistance during that period. Likewise O.J.S. is grateful to J.L. Fanselow of RSA Systems and G.M. Resch of NASA's Jet Propulsion Laboratory for their encouragement and support of this task. We wish to thank the staff of Springer-Verlag for their judicious and helpful cooperation.

Finally, we are particularly thankful for the support given and the forbearance shown by our families.

Heidelberg and Pasadena,
April 2000

Hans G. Walter
Ojars J. Sovers

Table of Contents

1. Fundamental Catalogues

1.1 Introductory Remarks

Prior to the establishment of a fundamental catalogue of positions, it is necessary to define the reference system which postulates the basic principles to be followed in order to arrive at the star coordinates of the fundamental catalogue. Usually, these principles include the concept of an inertial system defined such that in the framework of Newtonian mechanics the differential equations of motion can be written without terms involving linear and rotational accelerations. These principles also comprise the models and constants employed for deriving the coordinates. In the original terminology a *fundamental catalogue of positions* consists of star places, which are inferred from absolute observations of the equatorial coordinates, right ascension and declination. These observations are made with one single instrument, a transit or meridian circle, for instance, and without reference to previously determined positions of stars. The right ascensions of stars in such an instrumental or individual catalogue of absolute observations are obtained by comparing the transits of stars across the local meridian with those of objects of the solar system, predominantly the Sun, whose ephemerides are a realization of the celestial reference system that is defined by the solar system. A sidereal clock is required for recording these transit times. It is one of the most delicate tasks of meridian circle astrometry to determine the clock corrections in order to provide the correct sidereal time (Sect. 2.3.2). As an alternative, the so-called equatorial clock-stars may serve as a 'sidereal clock' (Sect. 1.7). The determination of absolute declinations of stars is made from observations at upper and/or lower culminations at transit time, but use is made of celestial pole determinations from observations of circumpolar stars at upper and lower culminations. Often, these observations are supplemented by observations of solar system objects to determine the position of the equator from their declinations in relation to the ephemerides. These types of catalogues are usually designated *individual absolute observation catalogues* to distinguish them from the more customary present-day definition of fundamental catalogues given below.

The term *fundamental catalogue* is also applied to a combination of several instrumental catalogues of absolute observations provided that they are built on the same reference system. Occasionally such combined catalogues are also designated general fundamental catalogues. For example, the FK5 (Fricke et al. 1988), where FK stands for 'Fundamental-Katalog', is a (general) fundamental catalogue whose underlying system is based on 85 absolute and quasi-absolute catalogues. A quasi-absolute catalogue is the same as an absolute catalogue except for the omission of solar system objects from the observation programme. Consequently, characteristic of quasi-absolute catalogues are absolute declinations but only absolute right ascension differences instead of absolute right ascensions, thus requiring the adoption of the right ascension zero point from external sources. Absolute right ascension differences result from observing campaigns if the right ascension measurements are all made relative to one chosen object. A small subset of fundamental catalogues have fundamental proper motions added that are consistent with the system of the fundamental catalogue of positions. Ideally, two fundamental catalogues of positions, which are given at different epochs and are free from systematic errors, would be sufficient to provide a fundamental system of proper motions. Since, in practice, the assumption of absence of systematic errors is inadmissible, the system of proper motions is defined by a wealth of fundamental catalogues of positions, whose epochs are distributed over several decades. A fundamental catalogue supplemented by fundamental proper motions is also known as a *fundamental catalogue of positions and proper motions*. Again, FK5 provides an example of this catalogue type.

We extend the term fundamental catalogue to frequency ranges other than the optical spectrum. For instance, with the inception of radio astronomy, it became possible to set up position catalogues by means of radio interferometry. Since useful radio observations of solar system bodies are generally not available to define the origin of right ascensions (see Sect. 5.4.5), a fundamental catalogue of radio sources normally provides absolute right ascension differences and absolute declinations by analogy with the above definition of quasi-absolute catalogues. The objects eligible for a fundamental catalogue of radio sources are at present almost exclusively extragalactic radio sources, because the majority of the astrometrically suitable galactic objects (the radio stars) are too faint to be reliably detected by current receivers, and are often variable in intensity and sporadically distributed on the sky. In contrast to optical observations, experiments in the radio frequency range can cover a larger fraction of the celestial sphere visible to a given network within a 24-hour period, especially if high-speed steerable antennas are used. As in the optical case, radio observations yield 'instrumental' fundamental catalogues referring to a specific network of antennas, and combined fundamental catalogues, which are composed of several instrumental catalogues.

In going one step further, we may add to the category of fundamental catalogues the Hipparcos instrumental or intermediate catalogues in the form as they resulted from the FAST and NDAC data reduction consortia (Kovalevsky et al. 1992; Lindegren et al. 1992). Hipparcos is an acronym for a space mission of the European Space Agency (ESA) standing for HIgh

```
0007+106     00 10 31.005888±32  +10 58 29.50412±68     S  0.090
```

Precision PARallax COllecting Satellite. This mission performed optical astrometry in space (see Chap. 3). FAST is the abbreviation of 'Fundamental Astrometry by Space Techniques' and NDAC stands for 'Northern Data Analysis Consortium'. Clearly, the amalgamation of the two catalogues belongs to this category as well (Arenou 1996; ESA 1997, Vol. 3, p. 369). As a matter of fact the Hipparcos observations, collected on an orbital platform, provide absolute right ascension and declination differences, as well as proper motions on a rigid sphere independently of previously determined stellar positions. What is missing for satisfying, in the strict sense, the criteria for a fundamental catalogue is the rotation of this rigid sphere to conventional zero points of right ascension and declination, thus providing quasi-absolute right ascensions and declinations. Because of the method of construction, these catalogues are loosely tied to the FK5 catalogue of positions and proper motions (see Chap. 3). If, for instance, the intermediate catalogues had been tied to FK5 by adopting its zero points of right ascension and declination for the orientation of the system at some epoch and stopping possible angular velocities of the coordinate frame by adjusting to the proper motions of FK5, then the Hipparcos instrumental catalogues could be considered as quasi-fundamental catalogues that are extensions of the FK5. Actually, the zero points have been adopted from the extragalactic radio reference frame (see Sect. 1.8; Chap. 4), whose system reflects the features of a kinematic definition.

Later in this chapter we dwell upon the notions and concepts that have been quite abruptly introduced here to provide the setting for the essential topics treated in the subsequent chapters. This discussion will include the subjects *inertial frame* and *precession of the Earth's axis of rotation*, which are two inseparable items in establishing fundamental catalogues.

As outlined in the foregoing, the establishment of a fundamental catalogue requires intensive use of the diverse and complex tools of spherical astronomy and astrometry treated in textbooks such as Woolard & Clemence (1966), Eichhorn (1974), Green (1985), Kovalevsky (1995b) and Schödlbauer (2000). These tools are referred to in the following chapters whenever the need arises.

1.2 Objectives of Fundamental Catalogues

A brief narrative survey of astrometry may be helpful at this point. This discipline, also known as positional astronomy, comprises the activities which deal with the determination of positions of celestial bodies in a variety of spectral regions (e.g., optical, radio, X-ray and infrared wavelengths). Motions of the celestial bodies are derived from their positions given as a function of time, and the determination of parallaxes is likewise based on time-varying positions. When speaking of parallaxes, we refer here to the annual parallax which is defined as the angular difference between the heliocentric and geo-

0007+171 00 10 33.990619±21 +17 24 18.76135±35 Q 1.601

centric direction of an object outside the solar system. Typical applications of astrometry are:

1) the establishment of the local inertial frame of rest,
2) the determination of proper motions of stars for the purpose of investigating stellar kinematics,
3) the unique identification of celestial objects observed in different spectral regions for a reliable interpretation of superimposed structures at different wavelengths,
4) studies of the motions of extragalactic objects relating to cosmological research.

The Earth, the planets, the stars and the Galaxy are all in relative motion. Astrometric observations are prerequisites of studies of such motions which, however, can be exactly described only with respect to some 'absolute' reference. For this reason fundamental catalogues are established with the intention that the catalogue objects represent as closely as possible fiducial points which are free from linear and rotational accelerations. Paradoxically, the catalogue construction also relies on extensive and repeated astrometric observations of objects in motion such as members of the planetary system, stars and extragalactic objects. Once a fundamental catalogue is constructed, it serves as a basis for further research in celestial mechanics as well as kinematics and dynamics of the Galaxy. As a whole, astrometric observations provide the empirical material for fundamental catalogues. In fact, these catalogues arise out of an iterative process which contributes to knowledge concerning the motions of celestial bodies and the determination of astronomical constants on the one hand, and the improvement of the fundamental catalogues on the other.

Fundamental catalogues are conceivable for all frequency bands that contain objects which are amenable to absolute observations by suitable techniques. Often it may be desirable to devise the means for a tie between the observations made in different bands. When considering astrometric observations, one is tempted to think of all frequencies of the electromagnetic spectrum, in particular of the radio, infra-red, optical and X-ray frequencies. An ideal catalogue would consist of point-like objects radiating in all frequencies of the spectrum and thus provide a simple relationship between the positions determined at different frequencies. In reality, catalogues at different frequencies are generally built up from different objects. First, the number of objects radiating intensely in two or more frequency bands is rather small and, second, at the currently common astrometric accuracy level of some milliarcseconds (mas), it cannot be taken for granted that the various emission centres coincide. Therefore, the accurate relation of catalogues based on different frequencies easily grows into a delicate and time-consuming task. For example, the establishment of the final Hipparcos catalogue was confronted with such intricacies, as will be discussed in some detail in Sect. 7.1. Another problem is normally posed by the limited dynamical range of the observing techniques. For example, it may be necessary to partition an optical catalogue as a consequence of different magnitude ranges accessible to photographic and meridian circle astrometry. Similarly, the flux densities of radio sources ranging from a few tenths of a millijansky to several jansky (see Sect. 4.1.3) require an adaptation of the observing techniques to the fluxes, thus complicating the merging of all objects into one single catalogue.

1.2.1 Optical Catalogues

More than 3000 years have passed since historical records for the first time indicated the role of stars and members of the solar system as fiducial points for local and temporal orientation on the Earth. During this entire period the visible light emanating from the celestial bodies was observed and used for position determination at sites dedicated to such measurements. This activity marks the birth of optical astrometric catalogues. In the course of time the positional accuracy evolved from approximately half a degree around the time of Hipparchus to 3×10^{-7} degrees or 1 milliarcsec (mas) at the end of the 20th century. The evolution of the observational error as a function of time is shown in Fig. 1.1.

Triggered by the chronology of Fig. 1.1, an abbreviated narrative of the history of astrometry may be of interest:

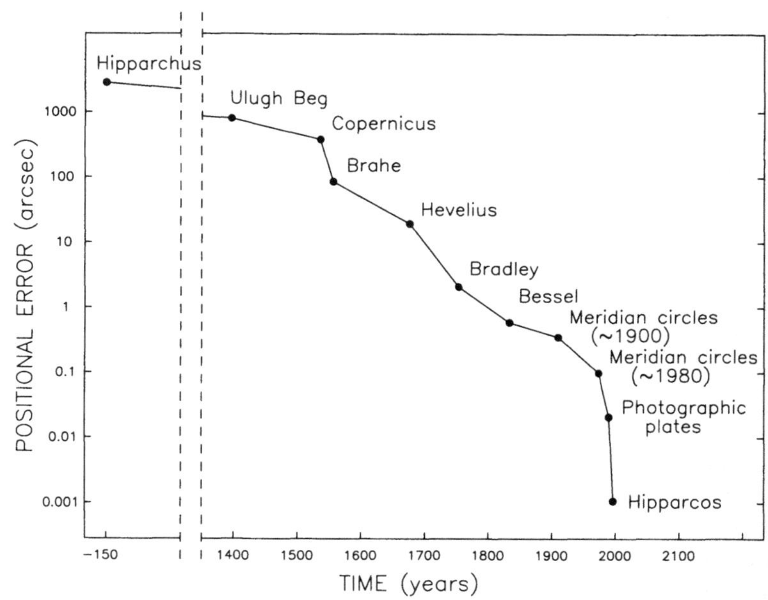

Fig. 1.1. The decrease in the observational error of position measurements of celestial bodies from the time of Hipparchus until the present (After Schmeidler 1980)

Astrometry made little progress during the millenium after Hipparchus (190–125 BC) and Claudius Ptolemaeus (around 150 AD), and this was even more true during the Dark Ages, when the doctrine of scholasticism predominated between the 9th and 15th centuries. The Dark Ages of the western civilization blocked the dissemination of the astrometric results obtained by the ruler of the Tatars, Ulugh Beg (1394–1449), who established a position catalogue of 1018 stars using the 48-metre sextant of his observatory at Samarkand in Uzbekistan. Remarkably enough, this was the first independent catalogue since the time of Hipparchus and the objects selected for observation were essentially those of the ptolemaic catalogue of fixed stars. Ulugh Beg's work was in conflict with contemporary occidental religious teachings, and it is conjectured that he was murdered for this reason.

Copernicus (1471–1543) is renowned for his promulgation of the heliocentric concept rather than for having measured substantial numbers of stellar positions. His other lasting achievement is the method of equinox determination, which provided the zero point for his longitude and right ascension measurements. Brahe (1546–1601) is also known for the development of a refined method of equinox determination. Predominantly, however, he deserves credit for carrying out long series of observations during the second half of the 16th century using his famous brass azimuth quadrant. These observations paved the way to Kepler's laws of planetary motion.

In 1609 the optical telescope was invented and, after about half a century had elapsed, astrometry started to capitalize on this instrument. Hevelius (1611–1687) stands as a representative of this epoch. Further, in 1657 the pendulum clock was developed by Huygens (1629–1695), and soon afterwards, in 1704, the first meridian circle was set up by Rømer (1644–1710) in his *Observatorium Tusculanum* near Copenhagen. But only after another fifty years were meridian circles regularly applied to astrometric observations (see Sects. 2.3.1 and 2.3.2). Since approximately that time, one may say that, in principle, the contemporary instrumental tools used for the measurement of fundamental stellar positions from the surface of the Earth were available.

Advantage has been taken of these tools for astrometric observations made during the eras of Bradley (1692–1762), Lalande (1732–1807) and Bessel (1784–1846) until well into the 20th century. The observations so obtained formed the basis of the series of fundamental star catalogues that manifest a new start in the second half of the 19th century.

Soon after the introduction of dry emulsion plates, the maturation of the photographic camera gave yet another impulse to astrometry around 1880. A number of pioneering projects demonstrated the potential of photographic methods for obtaining accurate star positions and trigonometric parallaxes. Steadily increasing precision of star positions was documented in a series of fundamental optical catalogues throughout the 20th century. This work culminated in the introduction of the methods of space astrometry (Chap. 3) during the 1990s.

Until recently, the Fifth Fundamental Catalogue, FK5 (Fricke et al. 1988), was the most advanced representative of a stellar fundamental catalogue of positions and proper motions that has been constructed to fulfill the objectives of fundamental catalogues (Sect. 1.2). The FK5 contains positions and proper motions of 1535 stars brighter than $m_v = 7.5$. Depending on the epoch, the average mean position errors lie between 30 and 40 mas. For another 3117 stars brighter than $m_v = 11.0$ the positions and proper motions are compiled in the FK5 Extension (Fricke et al. 1991).

According to the 1991 IAU resolution (IAU 1992) the FK5 positions and proper motions, which constituted the IAU-recommended coordinate system up to 1998, have now been replaced (IAU 1999) by the fundamental catalogue of positions of extragalactic radio sources known as ICRF (International Celestial Reference Frame).

1.2.2 Radio Source Catalogues

With the discovery of quasars in the early 1960s and with the advent of radio interferometry shortly afterwards (Cohen et al. 1968), the construction of catalogues of extragalactic radio sources with a theoretical position accuracy better than 1 milliarcsecond came within reach. This fact shifted attention from optical positional catalogues to radio catalogues. As a concomitant of this evolution it became possible to venture into establishment of a reference frame based on distant extragalactic objects. Actually, the idea was born much earlier, when it was proposed to use galaxies as reference objects in astrometric research (Herschel 1785; also Wright 1950, Deutsch 1954). At the time of Herschel, galaxies had to be excluded from optical fundamental observations for positional astronomy due to their faintness. Galaxies, however, became suitable reference objects for the determination of absolute proper motions of stars by photographic or equivalent techniques.

The radio emitting quasars and the technique of radio interferometry revolutionized the scene radically, to the extent that radio frequencies now dominate in the field of fundamental catalogues. Since the late 1960s the technique of Very Long Baseline Interferometry (VLBI) is employed for position measurements of extragalactic radio sources as described, for instance, in the pioneering work by Cohen & Shaffer (1971). Initially the positional accuracies were typically 1 to 3 arcseconds, although theoretical estimates predicted precisions of one milliarcsecond. Refinements in the early 1980s moved the precision nearer to the theoretical value. Especially the modernized data recording system known as bandwidth synthesis (Rogers 1970) contributed immensely to the upgrading of the VLBI technique. Its implementation allowed position determinations of extragalactic radio sources accurate to better than 3 mas (Johnston et al. 1995), with a potential for even better accuracies. As a byproduct, VLBI confirmed the theoretically predicted resolving power and demonstrated the existence of pointlike objects at the milliarcsecond level.

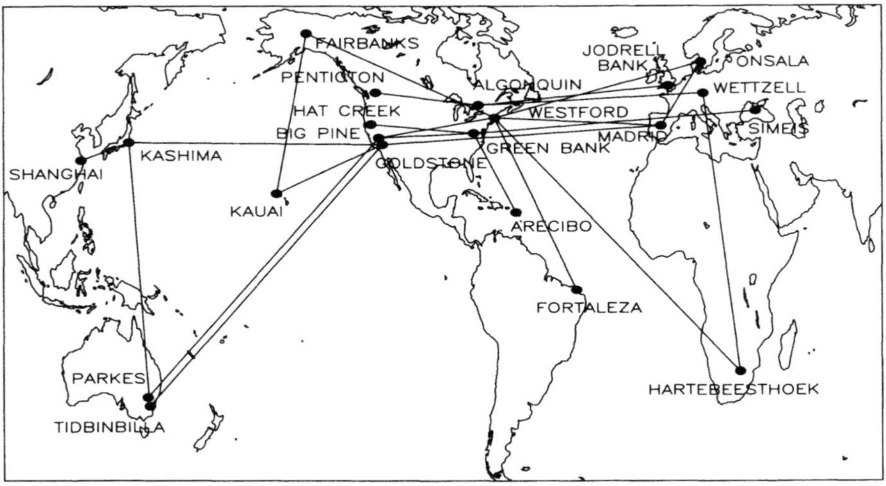

Fig. 1.2. Map showing some of the interferometer stations and baselines used for radio astrometry of galactic and extragalactic sources. Not all stations could be conveniently shown; the selection includes historically important stations, as well as those contributing heavily to the celestial reference frame and recent geographical extensions

During the same period additional and modernized continental and intercontinental VLBI networks were installed, providing baseline lengths of up to 10 000 km (see Figs. 1.2 and 1.3). In the northern hemisphere the number of radio antennas available for linking to a network is impressive, but the southern hemisphere also contributes to the new technique through stations in Australia, South America and South Africa.

For a detailed treatment of the catalogue construction from radio measurements we refer to Chap. 5. Initially, some 600 objects were selected as potential candidates for the fundamental catalogue of extragalactic radio sources (Kovalevsky 1995a). They were recommended for regular observations by VLBI networks. In this context individual position catalogues were generated at regular intervals by several analysis centres. From half a dozen of these catalogues the International Earth Rotation Service (IERS) compiled annually a combination catalogue representing a quasi-absolute general fundamental catalogue at radio frequencies (e.g., IERS 1994a). These catalogues, in principle, are paralleled by the fundamental catalogue FK5 at optical frequencies, but their precision is approximately two orders of magnitude better than that of the FK5.

More recently, the construction of combined catalogues was replaced by a monolithic analysis of the original VLBI observables (time delay and fringe rate), acquired from August 1979 through July 1995. This led to a fundamental catalogue of 608 extragalactic radio sources (Ma et al. 1998). The catalogue was established under IERS and IAU responsibilities and is the re-

0109+224 01 12 05.824718±27 +22 44 38.78619±49 L ...

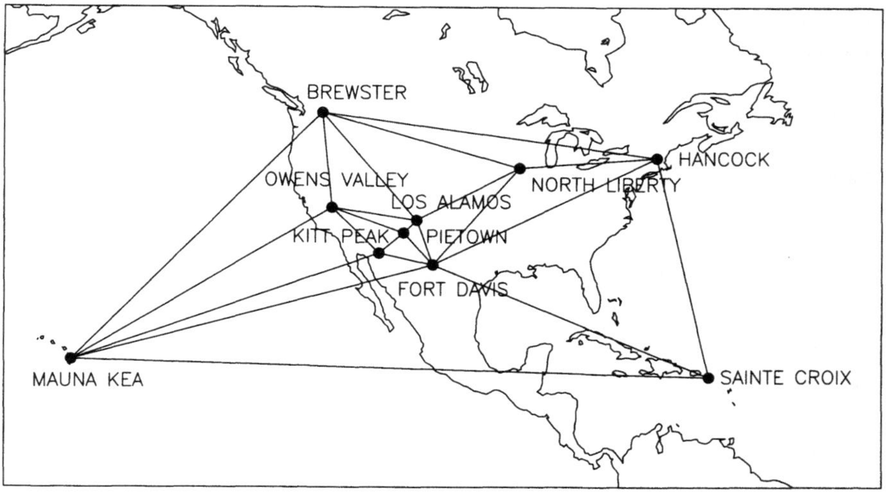

Fig. 1.3. Very long baseline array (VLBA) in the United States: locations of the 10 antennas forming the network. Only selected baselines are shown in order to delineate the network extent

alization of the International Celestial Reference System (ICRS). It has been adopted by the 1997 IAU General Assembly as the official conventional celestial reference frame in astronomy becoming effective on 1998 Jan. 1 (IAU 1999).

1.2.3 Unification of Optical and Radio Catalogues

In view of the comparatively small number of extragalactic radio sources whose precise positions are presently known, a densification of the ICRF catalogue (e.g., IERS 1996a) is highly desirable. The densification at visible wavelengths is offered by the positions and proper motions of some 118 000 stars of the Hipparcos Catalogue (ESA 1997) comprising stars brighter than $m_v = 12$ and having positional precisions comparable with the ICRF catalogue, i.e. at the milliarcsecond level. At the same time this method of densification facilitates access of optical astrometry to the properties of the ICRF catalogue. The connection of the two catalogues is a complex task: differences in the physical properties of the objects, in the observation methods and wavelengths, and in the concepts of compilation of the ICRF on the one hand, which is essentially based on quasi-absolute observations, and the intermediate Hipparcos Catalogue on the other (based on differential observations), necessitate the development of special methods of linking catalogues. This was one of the crucial procedures in the establishment of the final Hipparcos Catalogue (see Chap. 7).

0123+257 01 26 42.792631±30 +25 59 01.30079±54 Q 2.353

1.3 Background of Conventional Fundamental Catalogues

1.3.1 Various Aspects of Catalogue Compilation

Since we deal here with the present-day catalogues known as FK5, Hipparcos Catalogue and the catalogue of the ICRF, some introductory remarks concern obvious analogies and differences between the construction of compilation catalogues based on observations obtained from

- Earth-based optical astrometry
- Space astrometry at optical wavelengths
- Earth-based radio astrometry.

Earth-based optical astrometry. A prerequisite for constructing a celestial reference frame is the ability to relate the positions of objects separated by large angles or, in other words, to measure large angles. The typical instrument for such measurements is the transit or meridian circle with the Earth rotation as the intermediary of large angles (Sect. 2.3.1). Observations made by any such instrument cover a certain declination zone whose upper and lower limits depend essentially on the instrument's geographical latitude. These observations, however, cover all right ascensions during one year. Therefore, several instruments adequately distributed over the surface of the Earth are needed to survey the whole sky and to provide some desirable overlap of the declination zones. Assuming that each such instrument provides an individual observation catalogue, the question arises of how to piece together these usually heterogeneous catalogues. In general, the latter result from different instrumental systems, each with its own intrinsic systematic errors. Chapter 2 discusses this problem and its resolution.

Space astrometry at optical wavelengths. Contrary to ground-based astrometry, it is possible to attain full sky coverage by means of telescopes mounted on a space platform orbiting about the Earth as demonstrated by, e.g., the astrometry satellite Hipparcos (Chap. 3). By analogy with meridian circles, the measurements of large angles are provided by the controlled rotation of the telescope about a selected axis as well as by a calibrated angular standard (Sect. 3.3). A single telescope served the Hipparcos observation campaign that yielded multiple full sky coverage during a mission lasting approximately three years. Such an approach eliminates the problems arising in combining heterogeneous catalogues from multiple instruments, which complicates meridian circle astrometry.

Of course, ventures into space are also encumbered with drawbacks. For instance, a telescope in space is susceptible to irregular changes of the orientation. To gain control of this phenomenon requires the installation of costly devices for attitude determination. Among the other technical complications it is worth mentioning that operation and maintenance of the spacecraft payload depends entirely on remote control, and that data acquisition is an expensive undertaking.

Earth-based radio astrometry. Keeping in mind the establishment of celestial reference frames, we are obliged to make measurements that allow relating the positions of objects separated by large angles. In the radio domain, the most appropriate for this purpose are astrometric observations by means of the technique of radio interferometry discussed in Chap. 4. As in the case of meridian circles the large angles between the objects under observation are provided by the rotation of the Earth. Indeed, there is a close analogy between a two-element radio interferometer with a baseline oriented east-west and a meridian circle. While the latter measures the transit time when the projection of the horizontal axis of the instrument on the line of sight to the optical object is zero, the radio interferometer measures the projection of the baseline on the line of sight to the radio source (Murray 1976).

By means of an Earth-based radio interferometer only a limited declination zone can be covered, but all right ascensions are visited during 24 hours. In the early days of radio geodetic and astrometric measurements, interferometers were formed by a limited number of participating network stations. Each such network produced its individual observation catalogue of positions in right ascension and declination derived from the original radio observations. Since each installation introduces its own intrinsic systematic errors, the fundamental question recurs: how to merge these individual catalogues for the benefit of a global catalogue. One approach suggests the determination of the small-angle rotations of the coordinate axes of the respective catalogue relative to the triad of a master catalogue as outlined for the IERS combination catalogues in Sect. 5.5.3. Through this procedure possible systematic differences between the orientations of the individual triads are removed, but likely regional irregularities are not properly eliminated. With the more recent evolution of computing power, it has become possible to analyse simultaneously long spans of observations from all available networks. The original observations, i.e. the group delays and phase delay rates, allow access to the full information content of these observations, which is contained in the covariance matrix (Sect. 5.5.2). The realization of the catalogue is then the result of a single analysis of a large set of relative positions based on the original observations (Ma et al. 1998).

1.3.2 Terminology and Definitions

For clarification we introduce some specific terminology that is widely used in catalogue work and provides the setting for describing the scope of conventional fundamental catalogues. Present-day examples of such catalogues are the FK5 catalogue of star positions and proper motions, and the more recent ICRF catalogue of positions of extragalactic radio sources that has now taken the place of the FK5. Since these catalogues have been adopted by the international astronomical community, they are also known as 'conventional' fundamental catalogues to distinguish them from ordinary fundamental catalogues. Note that a conventional fundamental catalogue inevitably implies the existence of a conventional celestial reference frame and the definition of a conventional celestial reference system. Because there is some arbitrariness in defining a celestial reference system, actual practice dictates the adoption of one or another convention. This is another aspect explaining the term 'conventional', in addition to the fact that the catalogue is intended for general use. Section 2.3 exemplifies why certain conventions are appropriate.

The notation and definitions employed in the following paragraphs are essentially taken from Kovalevsky & Mueller (1989). We have decided in favour of these, although slightly diverging but equally expedient definitions are introduced elsewhere (e.g., Wilkins 1990). A brief but broad and complete review of the present state of astronomical reference frames was recently published by Johnston & de Vegt (1999).

Let us begin with the concrete and materialized subject known as the *fundamental catalogue* and investigate its conceptual background that is characterized by the *reference frame* and the *reference system*. In this context the terms *coordinate frame* and *coordinate system* are employed and therefore defined first:

- A coordinate frame is synonymous with a triad of rectangular coordinate axes or, equivalently, with any other geometrical configuration defined to such an extent that a direction or the position of a point may be specified by a set of coordinates with respect to the triad or equivalent. For example, a spheroid may be such a geometrical configuration apart from the customary triads.
- A coordinate system comprises the theoretical concept that allows the specification of a direction or the position of a point with respect to a particular coordinate frame, i.e. one adopts a method of allocation of coordinates given the geometrical configuration of the frame. The directions and positions may be specified by linear, spherical, ellipsoidal etc. coordinates.

Catalogue, frame and system are interrelated in the following ways:

- A conventional fundamental catalogue is a set of adopted coordinates of reference points and, if applicable, of adopted rates of change of these reference points. For specifying rates it is customary to adopt expressions for calculating the coordinates as a function of time. Through this procedure the time scale becomes part of the catalogue.
  The coordinates as functions of time are used for the representation of a conventional reference frame at some chosen epoch.
- A conventional celestial reference frame consists of the (time dependent) coordinates of the reference points in the fundamental catalogue or of a subset thereof that serve the establishment of a particular coordinate frame by defining its axes with respect to actual objects, e.g., a triad of rectangular

coordinate axes. The coordinates of the reference points and their variations with time form the set of intermediaries to which new points may be referred by differential measures.
A conventional reference frame is the materialization of a conventional reference system.

- A conventional celestial reference system comprises the theoretical concepts needed to define the frame in which a point may be described unambiguously by its coordinates. Thus, an integral part of the system is the set of models, procedures, equations of motion, parameters and constants that are required to determine the coordinates of the reference points from observations and to provide the reference frame associated with the system.

Guided by the above definitions of catalogue, frame and system the view may be taken that the system's realization is provided by the frame through some operational steps: Given the theoretical concept of the system including the accessories such as models, procedures, parameters and astronomical constants etc., selected reference points are subjected to fundamental observations by suitable instruments. On reducing the observed quantities by taking account of the system accessories, it is possible to ascribe coordinates to the reference points. Normally, the reference points show measurable motions. If so, the latter are determined from fundamental observations at different epochs yielding the variation of the coordinates with time. The coordinates of the reference points and, if applicable, their variations, form the catalogue. Finally, the frame is defined at any arbitrary epoch by the catalogue entries.

The theoretical concepts make up the centrepiece of a reference system. Usually the level of the concepts ranks high among the possible choices, since it is dictated by the desirable properties of the system's realization, i.e. the frame which, among other things, claims the capability of describing precisely the positions and motions of celestial bodies. We may call such a choice an ideal system, admitting at the outset the possibility that the concepts of an ideal system may risk demanding too much and, therefore, may not be directly usable in practical situations. In circumstances like this, one concedes one or another relaxation of the system concepts. For instance, the requirement of a global non-rotating system cannot be met in the framework of General Relativity unless the spatial distribution of mass is known. One way out of this complexity is to model the relativistic effects in the local frame and to apply corrections to the results of Newton's mechanics.

In simplified terms, a conventional celestial reference system may be seen as the collection of tools for the assignment of coordinates to fiducial points, whose physical counterparts have been observed with the intention of determining these coordinates. Theories, models, procedures involving astronomical and geophysical constants, environmental parameters etc. form part of these tools, and indicate that a system is a scientific artifact based on conventions and, moreover, a snapshot of the current knowledge of the subject.

There is no absolute unique reference system; instead, a reference system adapts in the best possible way to the contemporary experience and progress in observation techniques, physical models and computational methods.

One characteristic item common to the concepts of ideal reference systems is the requirement that the system has the property of being 'inertial' or 'non-rotating', which is a prerequisite for measuring absolute motions. Therefore, a digression into the subject of inertial systems seems appropriate and, consequently, likewise into the phenomenon 'precession' that is unavoidably encountered, in one way or another, during attempts to construct non-rotating systems.

The subsequent chapters resume the definition of conventional reference systems in the framework of the definition of the individual systems that are related to the two conventional fundamental catalogues known as the FK5 star catalogue and the ICRF catalogue of extragalactic radio sources.

1.4 Inertial Reference Systems and Frames

Since the study of absolute motions of celestial bodies is one of the main fields of fundamental astrometry, we desire to have a conventional reference system which is to be regarded, in Newtonian mechanics, as non-rotating. We further strengthen this request by requiring an inertial system. One reason for this additional requirement is suggested by the practice to relate, for consistency, the observations of solar system bodies also to this desirable reference system, in order to provide a solid basis for the study of their motions. As a matter of fact, these motions follow theoretically the laws of Newtonian mechanics only on the assumption that the positions are referred to an inertial system. In principle, Newtonian mechanics is based on the three laws of motion which postulate, 1) inertia: a body not subject to any external force moves with constant velocity and, therefore, in a straight line; 2) definition of force: the rate of change of momentum of any body is equal to the force applied externally to that body; 3) action-reaction: action and reaction are equal and opposite. The relationship of the inertial reference system with Newtonian mechanics explains that 'inertia' is a property of this desirable reference system. Also, this relationship expresses that, in the strict sense, an inertial reference system has a dynamical definition although the term 'inertial reference system' is used in a broader sense for systems not defined dynamically but, for instance, defined kinematically, and when account is taken of the influence by the theories of Special and General Relativity. In these cases it is more appropriate to speak of 'quasi-inertial reference systems' or 'non-rotating reference systems'.

In the same way as the property of inertia may be characteristic of a reference system, it is inherent in the corresponding reference frame that materializes the inertial reference system or quasi-inertial reference system, as the case may be. Several definitions of inertial frames are in use, and some of them are given below for later reference when the opportunity arises.

1) A frame is said to be inertial if, in this frame, the motion of a body obeys Newton's first and second laws of motion in the absence of inertial forces such as Coriolis forces and centrifugal forces.

For illustration, this definition of an inertial frame is translated into the field of motion in the solar system. There, the forces are generated by Newton's inverse square law of gravitation. The accelerations in the equations of motion result merely from gravitational attraction of masses, and no other terms of linear or rotational accelerations are required for describing the motion.

In these circumstances certain planes and directions within the solar system are invariant, apart from computable secular perturbations. These planes and directions can be employed for the establishment of a coordinate frame associated with an inertial reference frame that is defined dynamically. The solar system may be regarded as representing a local inertial reference frame of dynamical definition. More details follow in Sect. 2.2 in relation with the definition of the FK5 system.

2) An inertial frame of reference is non-rotating with respect to the rest of the Universe. This definition relates to Mach's principle (Mach 1893, pp. 229–238), according to which the inertia of a body is caused by the distribution of the rest of the material in the Universe. This statement is substantiated by the following consideration: inertia is the measure of the resistance of a body against any kind of acceleration with respect to absolute space. Consequently, the absolute space, i.e. the distribution of mass in the Universe effects inertia. If Mach's principle is valid, it would follow that an inertial frame cannot be rotating with respect to the rest of the Universe as a whole; further, the principle would postulate a non-rotating Universe.

Intuitively, the frame represented by the directions to distant extragalactic objects complies with this definition of an inertial frame. It is notable that the extragalactic objects provide an inertial frame with no need for any dynamical analysis. The definition of this frame is also known as a 'kinematic' or 'static' definition because of the apparent absence of transverse motions of the objects. As substantiated in Sect. 1.8, the transverse motions of the extragalactic objects produce relative shifts below the level of the measurement accuracy of current observation techniques.

3) In terms of the General Theory of Relativity an inertial frame of reference is a coordinate frame in which the metric for the square of the element of interval $\mathrm{d}s^2$ takes the form

$$\mathrm{d}s^2 = c^2\mathrm{d}\tau^2 = c^2\mathrm{d}t^2 - \mathrm{d}\boldsymbol{x}^2 \tag{1.1}$$

at infinite distance from the origin and in a region far removed from any masses (e.g., Murray 1983, p. 7). Here c is the velocity of light, τ and t are the proper and coordinate times, respectively, and $ct, \boldsymbol{x} = (x^1, x^2, x^3)$ are the four space-time coordinates.

An interesting question raised by definitions 1) and 2) concerns the equivalence of the inertial frames represented by the solar system on the one hand and by distant extragalactic objects on the other. For a deeper discussion of the problem we refer to Bondi (1960), pp. 27–33.

As inferrable from definition 3), the General Theory of Relativity casts new light on the question of inertial frames. Because of the distribution of matter we cannot expect the existence of a unique global inertial frame, but only quasi-inertial frames for finite regions. This follows from Einstein's principle of equivalence which states the possibility of constructing local inertial frames at any point in a gravitational field, see, e.g., Murray (1983) and Soffel (1989).

The effects of General Relativity on particles moving about the Sun are of the order $(v/c)^2$, where c is the speed of light and v is a typical velocity within the solar system. In other words, the differential equations of motion expressed in the space-time metric differ by one part in 10^8 from the equations written in terms of Newtonian mechanics. In practice, these differences are taken into account by small corrections in the formulations of classical mechanics.

A more pragmatic definition of an inertial frame has been proposed by Clemence (1966) and seems to be better suited to the discussions in the following chapters. His definition reads:

4) An inertial frame of reference is defined as a frame that is free from linear and rotational accelerations.

Clearly, definition 4) encompasses definitions 1) and 2) provided that, in case 1) agreement is demonstrated of the ephemerides (which result from solving the differential equations of motion) with the observed positions of solar system objects, and, in case 2) evidence of the non-rotating Universe is proven. Definition 4) hints at the employment of mechanical devices for testing the inertial properties of a frame. From a purely theoretical point of view one may think of using gyroscopes to determine the rate of rotation of a frame at the site of the gyroscope. Given the uncertainty of the luni-solar precession, we conclude that acceleration measurements accurate to 10^{-8} yr^{-2} are required to check the inertial property of current reference frames, we cannot rely on the present generation of ring laser gyroscopes which provide acceleration measurements accurate only to approximately 10^{-6} yr^{-2}. A new generation of ring laser gyroscopes of higher sensitivity is under development (Schreiber et al. 1999). For the time being, however, we have to consider other available precise mechanical systems that relate the motions of their members to an inertial frame. In order of increasing size, the more popular among such devices are:

`0153+744    01 57 34.964908±91   +74 42 43.22998±31    Q  2.338`

- The solar system, represented by the motions of its members about the barycentre of the solar system.
- The stellar system in the vicinity of the Sun, represented by the motions of the stars inside a sphere of about 500 pc radius centred at the Sun. Radio emitting stars are included in the ensemble of system members.
- The galactic system, represented by the motion of the stars about the galactic centre.
- The extragalactic system, represented by the kinematics of extragalactic radio sources.

In the sense of definition 4) the validation of an inertial system requires the measurement of absolute acceleration on Earth, which is a highly theoretical question. The definition implies an empirical process for the establishment of an inertial frame: With the aid of the available instruments one measures the detectable accelerations and, after having made allowance for these, an improved inertial reference frame is provided. In a subsequent process, using improved models and techniques, this frame undergoes iterative refinements over the course of time. The instruments that are used leave their imprint on the reference frame. Therefore, independent observational means, such as meridian circles and radio interferometers, normally give rise to different but compatible frames within the observational errors. Contemporary examples of such frames are the stellar reference frame represented by the FK5 (Fricke et al. 1988), and the extragalactic reference frame represented by the ICRF catalogue (Ma et al. 1998).

At least in the 'dynamical definition' of an inertial frame, a trace of contradiction is discernible: Initially, we accept by experience that Newton's law of gravity governs the motion of masses in the Universe, and particularly in the solar system. Subsequently we search for the inertial frame relative to which the observed motions of the masses are expressed by the law of gravity. Making the observations, however, already presupposes the existence of this inertial frame. The logical flaw may be compensated by iterative improvements of the frame (e.g., Fricke 1982) and by amending the Newtonian equations of motion by adding correcting terms that account for the motion of the perihelia predicted by the General Theory of Relativity (Bauschinger 1922). In this respect the FK5, having a largely dynamically defined system, can be expected to be a better approximation to an inertial frame than its predecessors.

1.5 Precession and Nutation

As long as observations are made from the surface of the Earth, the instantaneous coordinates of a stellar object are affected by the complex motions of the Earth as described by the Earth orientation parameters (IERS 1996b). With the exception of the effects of the gravitational forces exerted on the

Earth by the Moon, Sun, and planets, these motions are best regarded as a motion of the Earth about its axis of rotation and not as a motion of the axis in space. On the other hand, the gravitational couples between the Moon and the Earth and between the Sun and the Earth cause torques on the Earth, because it is a finite body and, furthermore, its mass distribution deviates from spherical homogeneity. Consequently, the individual mass elements move in different potentials of the gravity field, leading to different attractive forces that cause the phenomena of precession and nutation. A simplified discussion of luni-solar precession follows, using the physical model illustrated in Fig. 1.4. A more thorough and causal treatment of the luni-solar precession is given by Danjon 1980, p. 82, and, in terms of the Eulerian equations of motion of a rotating triaxial ellipsoid, by, e.g., Blanco & McCuskey (1961), p. 206, and Smart (1953), p. 343 ff.

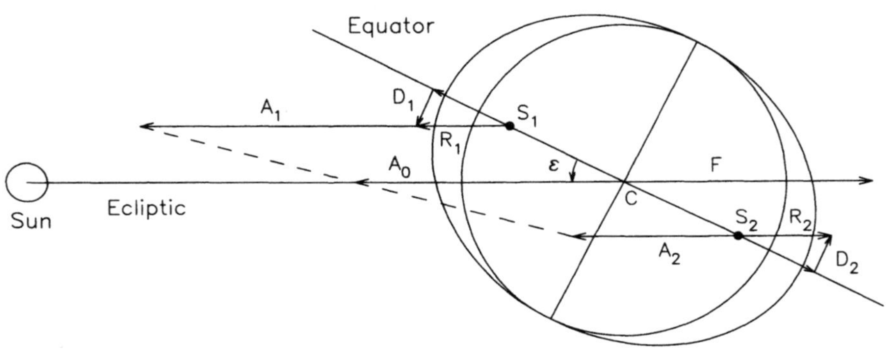

Fig. 1.4. Forces acting upon the Earth and producing the torques that cause the luni-solar precession. For notation see the text

The torques affect the orientation of the Earth's axis of rotation in space and, thus, also that of the celestial equator (Fig. 1.5). These orientation-changing effects are known as luni-solar precession and nutation. The former is a long-period effect, while the latter is a shorter-period effect, both acting on the mean equator. Although the separation into two parts is artificial, it is at least convenient for the work with catalogues, where the coordinates are referred to the mean equator to render applications more economical. The existence of these torques on the Earth make it important to determine precession, which process is discussed below in full. The orders of magnitude of precession and nutation are 50 arcsec/yr and 17 arcsec, respectively. For a detailed discussion on nutation we refer to textbooks on spherical astronomy and to the specialists' literature (e.g. Kinoshita & Souchay 1990). Here, we merely remark that the astronomical nutation has its root causes in the variation of the torques as a function of time. Indeed, the torques exerted on the Earth by the Moon and the Sun point in slightly different directions with

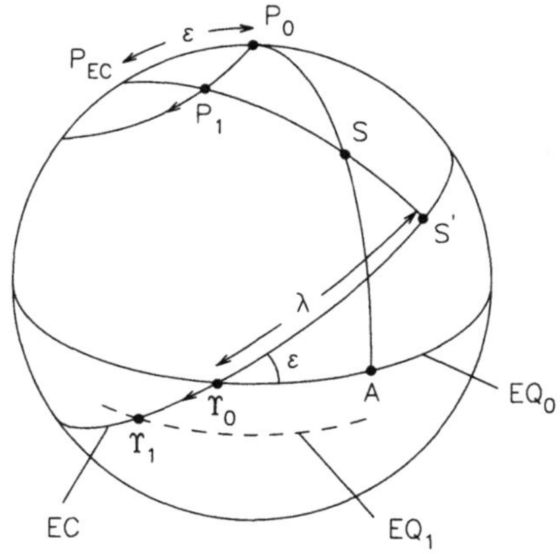

Fig. 1.5. The motion of the equator under the influence of luni-solar precession. P_0, P_1: north poles of the equators EQ_0 and EQ_1 at times t_0 and t_1, respectively, $t_1 > t_0$, P_{EC}: north pole of the fixed ecliptic, EC, ε: obliquity of the ecliptic, Υ: vernal equinox, λ: ecliptic longitude, S: star position, A, S′: its projections on the equator and ecliptic, respectively

respect to the ecliptic, and change slowly due to the relative motions of the three bodies.

In elaborating the causes of precession and nutation we consider, for simplicity, the Earth as a homogeneous sphere with the equatorial bulge resting on the sphere between the poles. If we had to cope only with the underlying perfect sphere, the members of the solar system could not exert any torques on the Earth for reasons of symmetry with respect to the attracting bodies. Therefore, in what follows we may disregard the sphere and concentrate on the bulge, which is responsible for the precession as illustrated in Fig. 1.4, where the Earth is cut into two halves perpendicular to the equatorial plane. Let S_1 and S_2 be the centres of gravity of the two halves, and ε the obliquity of the ecliptic. As the gravitational forces of the Moon and Sun act on these points, they produce the lunar and solar torques that now will be treated in turn, beginning with the Sun.

Since the Earth–Moon system is in dynamical equilibrium in the gravity field of the Sun, the gravitational force of the Sun, $\boldsymbol{A_0}$, and the centrifugal force, $\boldsymbol{F}$, exerted on the centre of gravity, C, are equal but of opposite direction. The gravitational force is proportional to the inverse square of the distance and, therefore, larger at S_1 than S_2. Because of the smallness of the distance Δs between S_1 and S_2 compared with the distance to the Sun, the differences between the attractive forces, $\boldsymbol{A_0}$, $\boldsymbol{A_1}$ and $\boldsymbol{A_2}$, may be approximated by linear functions of Δs. Ignoring the rotation of the Earth, the centrifugal forces, $\boldsymbol{F}$, acting on the mass elements of the bulge are identical for each element. Adding $\boldsymbol{F}$ to $\boldsymbol{A_1} = \boldsymbol{A_0} + \Delta\boldsymbol{A}$ and $\boldsymbol{A_2} = \boldsymbol{A_0} - \Delta\boldsymbol{A}$,

0215+015 02 17 48.954740±22 +01 44 49.69909±39 Q 1.715

and considering that $\boldsymbol{A_0} = -\boldsymbol{F}$, the two remaining forces, $\boldsymbol{R_1} = \Delta\boldsymbol{A}$ and $\boldsymbol{R_2} = -\Delta\boldsymbol{A}$, are in opposite directions: $\boldsymbol{R_1} = -\boldsymbol{R_2}$. Decomposition parallel and perpendicular to the equatorial plane yields the 'perpendicular' vector components $\boldsymbol{D_1}$ and $\boldsymbol{D_2}$, of equal magnitude but opposite in direction, that cause the solar torque on the Earth trying to tilt the Earth's equator towards the plane of the ecliptic.

By analogy to the Sun one may find the torque caused by the Moon. With reference to a coordinate frame fixed to the Moon, the gravitational force exerted by the Moon on the Earth and the centrifugal force of the Earth in its relative motion about the Moon act upon S_1 and S_2, thus producing the lunar torque on the Earth. This torque tries to tilt the equatorial plane to the plane of the lunar orbit. Because the latter is only slightly inclined to the ecliptic, the lunar torque acts in essentially the same direction as that of the Sun.

Since the Earth rotates about its axis, the luni-solar precession, resulting from the lunar and solar torques, is explained by the gyroscopic theory. Accordingly, the Earth's axis of rotation describes the surface of a circular cone about the direction to the north pole of the ecliptic, with an aperture equal to twice the size of the obliquity of the ecliptic, and with a period of approximately 25 800 years. The ecliptic remains fixed and the vernal equinox moves along it in a direction such that the ecliptic longitudes of celestial objects increase. Note that the plane of the ecliptic is defined by the orbital motion of the Earth–Moon system about the Sun, and the vernal equinox is defined as that point on the line of intersection of the equatorial and ecliptic planes where the apparent path of the Sun crosses the celestial equator from south to north. The celestial equator is the fundamental circle whose points have the declination 0°, or the north polar distance 90°. In the case of nutation a smaller motion, periodic and superimposed on the precession, is obtained, which moves the equinox ahead and behind its mean position with a principal period of 18.6 years. Both luni-solar precession and nutation leave the pole of the ecliptic unchanged; therefore, the ecliptic latitudes of fixed points remain unchanged to a first approximation. What is changed are the axes of the equatorial coordinate frame, whose fundamental plane is normal to the Earth's axis of rotation.

A further precession effect caused by the gravitational torques between the centres of mass of the Earth and the planets is the planetary precession, which produces a progressive motion of the equinox eastward along the equator.

The provision of the correct value of the luni-solar precession is an indispensable task for astrometry. An erroneous value would introduce fictitious shifts in ecliptic longitudes as illustrated by the following thought experiment: Let us start out from a set of extragalactic radio sources that constitute an inertial frame (see Sect. 1.4). We observe these objects at epochs t_i and reduce the observations to the equator and equinox of the frame objects at the some common epoch t_0 using, for instance, the precession adopted by IAU

(1977). One must not forget that this precession value is the result of an empirical approach, since it is based on proper motions obtained from observations of stars without convincing knowledge of the true value of precession. The frame associated with this precession may be called an empirical inertial frame. Assuming an imperfect luni-solar precession, the comparison of the ecliptic longitudes derived from the observations with those of the frame at epoch t_0 would give rise to a rotation of the observed objects about the polar axis of the ecliptic. We conclude from this thought experiment that, in principle, corrections to the luni-solar precession may be determined from observations of extragalactic radio sources over some interval of time. Recently Charlot et al. (1995) and Walter & Sovers (1996) worked along these lines, and arrived at a correction of the luni-solar precession of approximately −3 mas/yr to the 1976 IAU value.

The above thought experiment is also applicable to the dynamical inertial system defined by the motions of the planets. If the observations of planets are reduced by means of an imperfect value of precession, the comparison between the observed positions and those derived from the equations of planetary motion would predict a theoretical rotation about the axis perpendicular to the ecliptic plane. While theoretical planetary ephemerides are accurate to better than 5 mas for the major planets (Standish & Newhall 1996), the currently inadequate accuracies of optical observations of planets preclude an immediate detection of the shift.

1.6 Determination of the Luni-solar Precession

Having paid tribute to the importance of the luni-solar precession for establishing inertial frames, we now delve into some of the customary methods of its determination. In this context, it may be worthwhile to include also methods that suggest themselves convincingly from a theoretical viewpoint, but turn out to be impracticable for whatever barriers. The mechanical method using the torques acting on the Earth and the dynamical method using observations of planets belong to this category. We have omitted the analysis of stellar proper motions with respect to galaxies because of controversial numerical precession values obtained from these experiments (e.g., Fatchikhin 1970; Vasilevskis & Klemola 1971).

1.6.1 Luni-solar Precession from Lunar and Solar Torques

Generally speaking, the luni-solar precession originates from gravitational attraction of the Moon and Sun for the equatorial bulge of the Earth. In principle, therefore, the determination of luni-solar precession is primarily a matter concerning these three bodies of the solar system. Complex torques

0220−349 02 22 56.401625±50 −34 41 28.73011±44 Q 1.490

by the Moon and Sun acting on the aspherical and rotating Earth with an irregular distribution of mass in its interior make it difficult to treat the precession as a phenomenon of the gyroscopic theory. To set up at least an approximate model of the luni-solar precession based on torques the following assumptions are made:

- The distribution of the mass in the interior of the Earth is radially symmetric.
- The Earth has the shape of an ellipsoid of revolution.

With these simplifications the analytical formulation for the rate of change of the retrograde shift of the equinox, i.e. the luni-solar precession, ψ, becomes (Smart 1953, p. 352)

$$\psi = -\frac{1}{C\omega \sin\varepsilon}\,\frac{\partial U}{\partial \varepsilon}\,, \tag{1.2}$$

where, on neglecting the eccentricity of the orbits of the Moon and Sun, the force function U is

$$U = -\frac{3}{2}\,(C - A)\left(GM_{\rm m}\,\frac{\sin^2\delta_{\rm m}}{a_{\rm m}^3} + GM_{\rm s}\,\frac{\sin^2\delta_{\rm s}}{a_{\rm s}^3}\right) \tag{1.3}$$

with the following designations:

ω:	angular velocity of the Earth about its spin axis;
ε:	obliquity of the ecliptic;
C:	moment of inertia with respect to the rotation axis of the Earth;
A:	moment of inertia with respect to any axis in the equatorial plane of the Earth;
$\dfrac{C-A}{C}$:	mechanical ellipticity of the Earth (dynamical flattening);
G:	gravitational constant;
$M_{\rm m}$, $M_{\rm s}$:	masses of Moon and Sun, respectively;
$a_{\rm m}$, $a_{\rm s}$:	radii of the (circular) orbits of Moon and Sun, respectively;
$\delta_{\rm m}$, $\delta_{\rm s}$:	declinations of Moon and Sun, respectively.

On averaging the declinations over a full period of 18.6 years corresponding to one revolution of the lunar node along the ecliptic, one gets

$$\psi = -\frac{3G}{2\omega}\,\frac{C-A}{C}\left(\frac{M_{\rm m}\cos i_{\rm m}}{a_{\rm m}^3} + \frac{M_{\rm s}\cos i_{\rm s}}{a_{\rm s}^3}\right), \tag{1.4}$$

where $i_{\rm m}$ and $i_{\rm s} = \varepsilon$ denote the inclination of the orbits of Moon and Sun with respect to the Earth's equator, respectively.

The last equation shows the relationship between the luni-solar precession and the mechanical ellipticity of the Earth. Due to the simplifications introduced in deriving expression (1.4) and mainly because of insufficient knowledge of the mechanical ellipticity as a consequence of the Earth not being in hydrostatic equilibrium, this method determines the luni-solar precession with a relative error not better than 1%. It cannot compete with empirical methods based on stellar proper motions or apparent motions of extragalactic objects, some of which are now approaching an accuracy level of 0.0002% or 0.1 mas/yr (e.g., Charlot et al. 1995).

1.6.2 Dynamical Determination of the Luni-solar Precession

To briefly state the principle of the dynamical determination of precession we proceed from the scenario in which each solar system body is established in the fundamental reference frame through observations of the object's position as well as through the gravitational theories, including planetary perturbations. On the assumption of a continual rotation of this reference frame due to an imperfect value of precession, the observations will directly reflect this phenomenon by showing disagreement with the positions predicted by the gravitational theory of planetary motion. Then, corrections to precession are inferrable from the functional relationship between the unknown excess rotation and the empirically determined and predicted observations. It is therefore plausible to determine the luni-solar precession from observations of planets and the Moon, provided that their theoretical ephemerides represent the dynamically defined inertial frame, in which the motions of the planetary objects are completely described by Newton's law of gravity.

Since this approach is somewhat involved, a few details may be in order: As shown previously, the plane of the ecliptic is invariant under the influence of luni-solar precession, whereas this precession is responsible for a rotation of the Earth's orbit within the plane of the ecliptic simply because of the change of the longitude, e.g., the longitudes of the nodes and the perihelion. When observed from the Earth, this rotational effect is visible in the nodes and perihelia of planets. In addition, the orbit of each planet rotates in its own plane at a rate depending upon the masses of other planets that disturb its motion. To investigate this possibility of precession determination more deeply we consider, at different epochs, the longitude of the perihelion, $\tilde{\omega}$, and the longitude of the ascending node, Ω, of a planet given with respect to the ecliptic coordinate frame (see Fig. 1.6). Both longitudes are subject to change due to the luni-solar precession. In principle, these longitudes are observable from the Earth, and such observations are referred to the equinox which is moving due to precession. On the other hand, longitudes are also inferrable from the ephemerides. Any discrepancy between the observed and calculated longitudes is largely a consequence of the luni-solar precession or, more precisely, of the general precession in longitude which also contains the planetary precession.

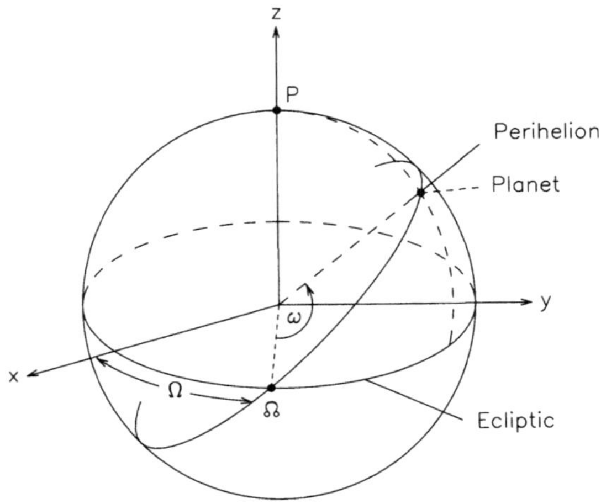

Fig. 1.6. The orbital elements of a planet, Ω and $\tilde{\omega}$, that are subject to change by precession. Ω: longitude of the ascending node, ω: argument of the perihelion, $\tilde{\omega} = \Omega + \omega$: longitude of the perihelion

The application of the dynamical method to the determination of precession is not quite as simple as the general outlines above may suggest. Indeed, the observed rotations of the longitudes of the perihelion and ascending node are composed of one part due to precession, and a second part that is a rotation along the ecliptic caused by the masses of the disturbing planets. If these masses are known, the perturbations of the longitudes are calculable resulting in exact planetary ephemerides. Then, any difference between the observed and calculated rotations would have to be ascribed to the general precession in longitude or eventually to the luni-solar precession, provided that the value of the planetary precession may be assumed.

An essential drawback of the dynamical method is the insufficient knowledge of the disturbing masses. It prevents estimation of a reliable value of the luni-solar precession. From observations of Mercury, Venus and the Sun, Laubscher (1976a) has determined a correction to the Newcomb (1898a) luni-solar precession of +1.12 arcsec per Julian century, in striking agreement with the value inferred from proper motions of the fundamental stars (Fricke 1972), but with an uncertainty as large as the quantity itself. Using observations of Mars the same good agreement was achieved with, however, a smaller uncertainty (Laubscher 1976b).

For the time being optical astrometry of solar system bodies does not yield a value of the luni-solar precession that competes with the value derived from stellar proper motions or, all the more, with the value obtained from the analysis of VLBI observations of extragalactic objects and lunar laser ranging data (LLR). Future improvements of the observational techniques and a better knowledge of the masses of planets may encourage the reapplication of the dynamical method.

1.6.3 Luni-solar Precession Derived from Stellar Proper Motions

In the past the value of precession has been derived by analyzing the proper motions of fundamental stars, taking into account the fact that in the solar neighbourhood the stars themselves are revolving about the centre of the galaxy (Fricke 1967). Using the revised (IAU 1977) precession value, Lieske et al. (1977) developed the formulae for the rigorous calculations of the effects of precession. When, however, the general precession in longitude is studied in relation to stellar proper motions, it may be more appropriate to describe the speed of precession in terms of the general precession in right ascension and declination. The discussion below follows this custom.

Access to the speed of precession is provided by the stars' observed motions relative to a coordinate frame rotating due to the precession of the Earth's axis. The determination of precession is equivalent to the determination of the absolute speed of rotation of the reference frame used for the observations of the stars. Once the precession is known, the stellar proper motions in right ascension (μ_α) and declination (μ_δ) are derived from the observed total motion by subtracting the speed of precession giving

$$\mu_\alpha = \frac{\mathrm{d}\alpha}{\mathrm{d}t} - (m + n\sin\alpha\tan\delta)\,, \tag{1.5}$$

$$\mu_\delta = \frac{\mathrm{d}\delta}{\mathrm{d}t} - n\cos\alpha \tag{1.6}$$

with the following meaning of the notation:

$\frac{\mathrm{d}\alpha}{\mathrm{d}t}, \frac{\mathrm{d}\delta}{\mathrm{d}t}$ are the stellar motions derived from absolute observations covering some interval of time, and referring to a rotating coordinate frame defined by the mean equator and equinox at the observation epochs,

m, n are the rates of general precession in right ascension and declination, respectively:

$$m = \psi\cos\varepsilon - \chi\,, \tag{1.7}$$

$$n = \psi\sin\varepsilon\,, \tag{1.8}$$

where ε is the instantaneous obliquity of the ecliptic, ψ the luni-solar precession and χ the planetary precession. The complete expressions for m and n are not needed in this analysis; they may be found in Lieske et al. (1977). On the right sides of (1.5) and (1.6) we have combined, for simplicity, the various contributions to the proper motions, which are detailed in (1.9).

0239+108 02 42 29.170847±18 +11 01 00.72823±30 Q ...

To be precise, the astrometrically determined quantity ψ is the actual luni-solar precession, ψ_0, diminished by the geodesic precession, ψ_g:

$$\psi = \psi_0 - \psi_g \, .$$

The geodesic precession is a relativistic motion of the equinox in the direction opposite to the motion due to the luni-solar precession. It is an effect of the General Theory of Relativity caused by the slow rotation of the coordinate frame in the neighbourhood of the orbiting Earth with respect to the barycentric inertial frame. A model of geodesic precession is given by de Sitter & Brouwer(1938) as

$$\psi_g = 3/2 \; k^2 (1 - e_\oplus) \, n_\oplus \, ,$$

where k is the constant of aberration (in radians), $e_\oplus$ the eccentricity of the Earth and $n_\oplus$ the mean angular orbital motion of the Earth (in arcsec/cy). Both the luni-solar precession and geodesic precession are motions of the equinox along the ecliptic and, therefore, not separable in an astrometrical treatment of precession determination. The value $\psi_g = 1.''92$ per century has been adopted for the geodesic precession (Lieske et al. 1977). It is based on the IAU (1976) System of Astronomical Constants.

Equations (1.5) to (1.8) show how an erroneous value of the luni-solar precession propagates into the proper motions. Thus, by analyzing proper motions of a sufficient number of stars having a uniform distribution over the sky, it is possible to determine the luni-solar precession from (1.5) to (1.8). This is known as the method of stellar kinematics for precession determination.

This approach is also beset with difficulties, which are mainly ascribed to the entanglement of true stellar proper motions with precession. In attempting to separate the precessional part from the proper motions, one is faced with a frame centred on the Sun because the proper motion of a star depends on its velocity relative to the Sun. The Sun, however, has its own peculiar velocity with respect to the Local Standard of Rest (LSR) which is defined by the mean motion of the stars in the solar neighbourhood. The LSR rotates about the galactic centre; its velocity is estimated from the adopted model of galactic kinematics and is given by Oort's constants (e.g van de Kamp 1967; Kerr & Lynden-Bell 1986). This implies that the velocity of the LSR and the peculiar velocity of the Sun, also known as local solar motion, are both present in the proper motion of every star. Two corrections, therefore, need to be applied to remove external effects from the proper motions: a correction for the differential rotation of the galaxy, and a correction for the motion of the Sun with respect to the LSR. These adjustments are evidence of the kinematic features that have been carried over to the definition of stellar celestial reference systems via this approach to precession determination.

Among the varied methods of determining precession (Lieske 1985) the method of stellar kinematics has been the most frequently used in the past.

It was last applied extensively by Fricke (1967) in the attempt of delineating an inertial system through the analysis of proper motions, and yielded the luni-solar precession with an uncertainty of ± 0.15 arcsec per Julian century, corresponding to a relative or fractional error of 10^{-5}. We outline in more detail the method of stellar kinematics below with a focus on the principle, but also in order to demonstrate that it has surmounted the former objections, in which the assumption of a Gaussian distribution of the proper motions was criticized in the treatment of the observational equations resulting from (1.5) and (1.6) by least squares techniques.

At the outset of Fricke's determination of the luni-solar precession stand the fundamental proper motions of stars. They are composed of several parts emanating from different origins (Fricke 1977):

- A parallactic motion $(\mu_\alpha)_\odot$, $(\mu_\delta)_\odot$ of each star due to the solar motion with respect to the stars.
- A rotation $(\mu_\alpha)_{\rm rot}$, $(\mu_\delta)_{\rm rot}$ due to, first, precessional errors and, second, the rotation of the assembly of stars considered. One part of the latter rotation is a uniform rotation about the axis of the Galaxy at a rate given by Oort's constant B. (Concerning B see, e.g., van de Kamp (1967), p. 62.) Another part of this rotation is known as the equinox motion Δe. It is interpreted as a fictitious motion along the equator originating from erroneous determinations of the equinox. As a consequence the fundamental proper motions in right ascension derived from right ascensions in absolute catalogues might be systematically in error by a common amount Δe.
- A motion $(\mu_\alpha)_{\rm shear}$, $(\mu_\delta)_{\rm shear}$ caused by galactic shearing or differential galactic rotation leading to a deformation of the velocity field of the stars. The effect is described by Oort's constant A. (Concerning A see, e.g., van de Kamp (1967), p. 62.)
- A residual motion $(\mu_\alpha)_{\rm res}$, $(\mu_\delta)_{\rm res}$ due to the peculiar or intrinsic motion of the stars and internal errors of the motions.

The first three types of motion constitute the systematic components of the proper motions while the last type is a random quantity. Disregarding less immediately pertinent motions such as the motion of stars with respect to the cosmic microwave background, the above list is complete and free from assumptions. Any such motion produces effects so small that they do not affect the proper motions used in this method of precession determination, which are accurate to a few mas/yr. Omitting possible systematic errors, the observed stellar motions, therefore, are composed to a good approximation of four portions, i.e.

$$\frac{{\rm d}\alpha}{{\rm d}t} = (\mu_\alpha)_\odot + (\mu_\alpha)_{\rm rot} + (\mu_\alpha)_{\rm shear} + (\mu_\alpha)_{\rm res}\,, \tag{1.9}$$

and an analogous expression for ${\rm d}\delta/{\rm d}t$. These observed quantities are analysed in the rectangular equatorial coordinate frame with its origin at the solar system barycentre, and with its x, y and z axes directed to ($\alpha = 0°$, $\delta = 0°$),

0256+075 02 59 27.076633±21 +07 47 39.64323±35 Q 0.893

($\alpha = 90°$, $\delta = 0°$) and the celestial pole ($\delta = 90°$), respectively, to derive the value of precession and the other parameters appearing in (1.9). Typical of this approach is the resolution of the rotational parts of stellar motion, i.e. $(\mu_\alpha)_{\text{rot}}$ and $(\mu_\delta)_{\text{rot}}$, into rotations about the three axes of the rectangular coordinate frame defined above, giving the components ω_1, ω_2 and ω_3 of the total angular velocity vector about the x, y and z axes. With these components in mind, the hypothesis is made of interpreting them as the combined effects of three rotations having their origins in

- the luni-solar precession, which is explained by a rotation about the axis pointing to the pole of the ecliptic,
- the planetary precession and the equinox motion, which give rise to a rotation about the axis pointing to the celestial pole,
- the galactic rotation, which takes place about the axis pointing to the galactic pole.

Denoting the inclination of the galactic plane to the equator by i, and the right ascension of the ascending node on the equator by Ω, the components of the total angular velocity vector become (Fricke 1977)

$$\omega_1 = B/47.4 \ \sin\Omega \sin i \tag{1.10}$$

$$\omega_2 = B/47.4 \ \cos\Omega \sin i \ - \Delta n \tag{1.11}$$

$$\omega_3 = B/47.4 \ \cos i + \Delta k, \tag{1.12}$$

where by applying (1.7) and (1.8)

$$\Delta k = \Delta m - \Delta e = \Delta n \operatorname{cotan} \varepsilon - (\Delta\chi + \Delta e) \tag{1.13}$$

and Δe stands for the motion of the equinox. The relationship between the rates of rotation about the three rectangular axes and the variations of the rotational motion of the stars in spherical coordinates is formally given by the standard expressions

$$\left(\frac{\mathrm{d}\alpha}{\mathrm{d}t}\cos\delta\right)_{\text{rot}} = \omega_1 \sin\delta\cos\alpha + \omega_2 \sin\delta\sin\alpha - \omega_3\cos\delta \tag{1.14}$$

$$\left(\frac{\mathrm{d}\delta}{\mathrm{d}t}\right)_{\text{rot}} = -\omega_1 \sin\alpha + \omega_2\cos\alpha. \tag{1.15}$$

The way these equations are written implies a rotation from the inertial frame, which one strives for, into the frame used as the reference for the measurement of the stellar motions.

If the combined rotational effects on the left-hand sides of (1.14) and (1.15) were known, it would be possible to estimate the components of the angular velocity vector and, hence, Oort's constant B and the precessional quantities Δn and Δk. Unless the correction of the planetary precession is adopted from external sources, Δe cannot be singled out immediately from the rightmost part of Δk in (1.13). In fact the adoption of an independent

0302−623 03 03 50.631333±47 −62 11 25.54983±33 Q ...

correction to the planetary precession is suggested since it has been determined with high accuracy solely from the revised system of planetary masses (Laubscher 1972).

In addition to the rotational effects, there are the solar motion with respect to the stars, known as parallactic motion of the Sun, and the deformation of the velocity field due to the differential galactic rotation. Both of them contribute to the stellar motions:
The parallactic motion may be expressed by

$$\begin{aligned} \left(\frac{\mathrm{d}\alpha}{\mathrm{d}t}\cos\delta\right)_{\odot} &= F_{\alpha}\left(f, X, Y, \alpha\right) , \\ \left(\frac{\mathrm{d}\delta}{\mathrm{d}t}\right)_{\odot} &= F_{\delta}\left(f, X, Y, Z, \alpha, \delta\right) \end{aligned}$$

with the unknowns X, Y and Z denoting the solar motion components along the x, y and z axes of the equatorial coordinate frame. The parallax factor, f, is inversely proportional to the distance of the star.
The proper motion part ascribed to the differential galactic rotation is

$$\begin{aligned} \left(\frac{\mathrm{d}\alpha}{\mathrm{d}t}\cos\delta\right)_{\text{shear}} &= G_{\alpha}\left(A, l, b, \Phi\right) , \\ \left(\frac{\mathrm{d}\delta}{\mathrm{d}t}\right)_{\text{shear}} &= G_{\delta}\left(A, l, b, \Phi\right) \end{aligned}$$

with Oort's constant A as unknown, (l, b) denoting the galactic coordinates of a star, and Φ the parallactic angle at the star's position in the galactic and equatorial coordinate frames.

Having modelled the contributions to the fundamental proper motions caused by the rotational effects, parallactic motion and deformation of the velocity field, we arrive at the observational equations of one star on summing up the above three models in accordance with (1.9):

$$\frac{\mathrm{d}\alpha}{\mathrm{d}t}\cos\delta = H_{\alpha}\left(\omega_1, \omega_2, \omega_3; X, Y; A; \alpha, \delta\right) , \tag{1.16}$$

$$\frac{\mathrm{d}\delta}{\mathrm{d}t} = H_{\delta}\left(\omega_1, \omega_2, \omega_3; X, Y, Z; A; \alpha, \delta\right) . \tag{1.17}$$

The functions H_{α} and H_{δ} are linear in the unknowns listed as arguments. For an assembly of stars we obtain a set of observational equations to estimate the unknowns by the method of least squares. Then on substituting ω_i into (1.10) to (1.12) the estimation of Oort's constant B and of the quantities Δn, Δk is straightforward. This last step terminates the determination of the luni-solar precession from stellar kinematics.

Several assumptions are made in this context:

1) reality of the decomposition of the angular velocity vector into three rotational effects,

0306+102 03 09 03.623523±23 +10 29 16.34082±42 Q 0.863

2) applicability of the Oort-Lindblad model (Oort 1927) as a sufficient approximation to the galactic rotation,
3) acceptability of the interpretation of the equinox motion,
4) fulfillment of the conditions for employing the least squares procedure.

Evidence has been given by Fricke (1981) that these assumptions are justified. Concerning the least squares procedure, the residuals of the proper motions after the elimination of the systematic effects caused by a combined rotational effect, the solar motion and the deformation of the velocity field, are free from systematic parts, a fact which supports the application of least squares techniques. It was found that the residuals are somewhat larger than the errors of the observed fundamental proper motions, indicating potential presence of systematic errors. Also, one cannot rule out the possibility that the peculiar motions dominate the other effects because of increasing measurement accuracy. These suspected traces of systematic residual effects diminish, however, when the data of more distant fundamental stars are included (Fricke 1967).

These results speak in favour of the parameter estimation that presupposes a normal distribution of the data and a maximum of the likelihood function. If one had dispensed with Gaussian distribution of the residuals and, instead, aimed at an estimation constrained to minimum variances of the parameters, identical results would have been obtained. The two approaches are equivalent, leading via different conditions to the most probable parameters. In the absence of normal distribution the validity of the results is not limited since the method of least squares is also successfully applicable when positive and negative errors of equal order of magnitude appear among the data with about the same frequency, yielding unknowns with smallest mean errors. Should even this assumption be infringed, the least squares method holds the advantage of providing unique values of the unknowns and their errors by applying minimum corrections and, at the same time, by limiting the computational effort to a tolerable scale (Grossmann 1969).

1.6.4 Luni-solar Precession Derived from Positions of Extragalactic Objects

The kinematics of extragalactic objects at large distances from the Earth represent a special case inasmuch as the objects may be considered at rest. In fact, as substantiated in Sect. 1.8 no systematic motion is detectable with the aid of the current high precision observing techniques. Thus, these objects are suitable as fiducial points fixed in space. Under the influence of precession, however, the celestial equator moves and, consequently, the instantaneous equatorial coordinates of the fiducial points change their values with time. In the absence of any measurable motion of the object and on the assumption that any effects causing apparent motions exclusive of precession are perfectly modelled, these changes of coordinates may be unambiguously ascribed to precession.

`0308−611     03 09 56.099167±38   −60 58 39.05628±29     Q   ...`

To illustrate the principle of precession determination from observations of extragalactic objects, we model the observable, l, of an object using a model of precession, P, and a combination model, X, standing for a variety of astronomical, geophysical and geodetic effects that are assumed to be correctly known. Formally, the modelled observable at time t can be expressed by the function F, giving

$$l_{\mathrm{mod}} = l_{\mathrm{mod}}(t) = F\left(\boldsymbol{r_0}, P(t, t_0, \zeta, z, \Theta); X\right), \tag{1.18}$$

where $\boldsymbol{r_0}$ is the position vector of the object referring to a rectangular coordinate frame at some fixed equator and equinox, e.g., J2000.0, and, for model P, the precession matrix is taken which transforms $\boldsymbol{r_0}$ into $\boldsymbol{r}$ referring to the mean equator and equinox of date; i.e. $\boldsymbol{r} = P\boldsymbol{r_0}$. The quantities ζ, z and Θ are the equatorial precession parameters (Lieske 1979).

If the model of precession is correct, only statistical differences within the observation accuracy appear between the actual observations, l_{obs}, and the modelled ones, l_{mod}, made during a sufficiently long time span. Otherwise, systematic differences are expected, and therefore it is possible to fit the precession model to the observations of a sample of extragalactic objects and thus to estimate the equatorial precession parameters from the observational equations of the following formal type using linearization and least squares adjustment:

$$l_{\mathrm{obs}} = F'(\boldsymbol{r_0}, P(t, t_0, \zeta + \Delta\zeta, z + \Delta z, \Theta + \Delta\Theta); X)\ . \tag{1.19}$$

The determination of corrections $\Delta\zeta$, Δz and $\Delta\Theta$ is a lengthy procedure since the matrix P is composed of elements consisting of sums of products of trigonometric functions of ζ, z and Θ, thus complicating the calculation of the partial derivatives of F in (1.19) for the purpose of linearization.

In reality, many more unknowns are simultaneously estimated including, e.g., the source positions, Earth orientation parameters, station coordinates, environmental parameters, etc. So, in the extreme, an estimation process builds up for many thousands of unknowns. In combining data from Very Long Baseline Interferometry (VLBI) and Lunar Laser Ranging (LLR), Charlot et al. (1995) found a correction of $-3.00\pm$ 0.20 mas/yr to the IAU adopted luni-solar precession (IAU 1977).

1.7 Conventional Stellar Celestial Reference Systems

Absolute astrometry of stars was traditionally intimately connected with observations using meridian circles or transit circles and, therefore, it should not be surprising that the equator plays a dominant role as the fundamental plane. This is all the more true since other instruments such as vertical circles, transit instruments and astrolabes, contributing widely to astrometry, also give preference to the equator. Consequently, there seems to be every reason to choose the Earth's equator, defined by the instantaneous axis of the Earth's rotation, as the fundamental plane of the stellar reference system. The Earth's rotation axis along with the vernal equinox constitute the two fundamental directions of the stellar reference system. For its realization, absolute right ascensions and declinations of stars and members of the planetary system have to be determined. Declinations are reckoned from the equatorial plane, and the vernal equinox serves as the origin for reckoning right ascensions. This natural choice of fundamental directions, however, imposes some drawbacks that are associated with the motion of the Earth's axis of rotation due to luni-solar precession and nutation, with the motion of the ecliptic due to planetary precession, and with the orbital motion of the Earth causing annual aberration. The system established in this way is a rotating reference system because of precession and nutation, and it is centred on the Earth.

When meridian circles or their equivalents are used for making fundamental observations, there is, in principle, no need for geophysical modelling of purely terrestrial effects such as polar motion, plate tectonics, Earth tides etc., as long as these effects have periods longer than a few hours. In these circumstances the astronomical latitude of the observing station is of no disturbing influence as it is 'instantaneously' derived from the zenith distances of circumpolar stars. Then, the declinations of the stars to be observed are found from the zenith distances at upper and lower culminations along with the daily redetermined station latitude, and any effects due to variations of the Earth's crust can be eliminated with sufficient care. The same considerations are applicable to right ascension measurements, requiring a time interval during which stars and objects of the planetary system are observable. When, however, the periods of crustal variations are shorter than one night's observing session, some monitoring of the observation sites would be appropriate provided that the effects are comparable with the measurement accuracy of modern meridian circles, which reaches about 1 m on the Earth's surface, equivalent to ≈ 0.03 arcsec.

Both the equinox and the equator are required for measuring right ascensions and declinations. In the practical realization of a stellar reference system, equinox and equator are determined from observations of the Sun and members of the solar system. For instance, in order to provide absolute stellar right ascensions with the aid of the Sun, absolute right ascensions of the Sun are determined from absolute declination measurements according to (2.2). Then, that solar ephemeris is used to whose right ascension zero point the stellar right ascensions were initially referred during observations. By comparing the observed solar right ascensions with those predicted by the ephemeris, an offset $\Delta\alpha$ is determined that is added to the initial stellar right ascensions to yield the absolute right ascensions, now related to the actual position of the Sun and independent of any presumed positions (see Sect. 2.2.2). By analogy an offset $\Delta\delta$ is derived and, however, added only to the decli-

`0342+147    03 45 06.416546±21   +14 53 49.55818±32    ?   ...`

nations of the equatorial zone; for higher declinations, northern or southern, usually the corresponding correction proportional to $\cos\delta$ is applied. The recourse to the Sun and planets ties the equinox and equator determination to the solar system, known to be an inertial system of dynamical definition, since the motions of these bodies are to a sufficient approximation described by Newton's inverse square law of gravitation (see Sect. 1.4).

In the practical procedure for determining absolute right ascensions, it is common to use a set of selected stars well distributed in the equatorial zone, $-30° < \delta < +30°$. These stars, called clock-stars, stand out because of their accurately known right ascensions. Their continual improvement is an indispensable task that is achieved along the following lines:

1) measuring the right ascension differences between clock-stars;
2) analyzing these differences to separate systematic parts, $\Delta\alpha_{sys}$, from random parts, $\Delta\alpha_{ran}$;
3) correcting the clock-star system by constraining $\sum \Delta\alpha_{sys}$ to zero by, e.g., the closed loop method;
4) differential observations of clock-stars with respect to the Sun;
5) absolute observations of the Sun.

Improved right ascensions of the clock-stars are obtained through this procedure. The clock-star system greatly simplifies the determination of absolute right ascensions of other objects as they need only to be observed relative to clock-stars.

To arrive at a non-rotating system, independent of time, it is necessary to refer the rotating system to a fixed equator and equinox at some standard epoch. This procedure requires the transformation of coordinates by applying models of precession, nutation, stellar aberration and parallax as exactly as possible. The transformation is based on *conventions* inherent to these and other models employed, which makes it possible to speak of a non-rotating barycentric system bearing the designation *conventional celestial reference system*. The models comprise the following phenomena: luni-solar precession (including geodesic precession), planetary precession and nutation to compensate for the effects of the rotation of the Earth's axis, and, also, annual aberration to account for effects caused by the orbiting Earth. On using these models for the transformation, the generation of coordinates of a non-rotating system is expected which, however, is centred on the Earth at some epoch. With the aid of the conventional stellar parallaxes, the conventional stellar celestial reference system is completely defined as a barycentric, non-rotating and time-independent system.

Since the stars are in motion, the rigorous transformation to some standard epoch requires values of the stellar proper motions. Repeated absolute observations of the same stars at different epochs are necessary for determining such proper motions. In principle, two fundamental catalogues of positions suffice to set up a system of fundamental proper motions. Each set of absolute observations provides the instantaneous equator and equinox as reference directions at the chosen epoch. If precession, nutation and aberration are properly applied to the observations in transforming them to the equator and equinox at some standard epoch, differences of positions show up as functions of the epochs. These variations allow the determination of fundamental proper motions of the stars with respect to the fixed equatorial plane and equinox.

In constructing the fundamental catalogue associated with the system, it is customary to combine observations of stars covering several decades and originating from different observatories. Mean places of the stars and their proper motions are derived with the aid of sophisticated methods as exemplified in Chap. 2. The core of the fundamental catalogue is made up of these mean places at a given epoch, plus the proper motions. Consequently, the frame is defined primarily by the catalogue positions at the reference epoch. Further, it can be extended to other epochs through the proper motions. In practice, the catalogued star positions also define implicitly the mean equator and equinox, which are not directly observable.

Among the above-mentioned conventional models the luni-solar precession plays the most crucial part in constructing a stellar reference frame defined by a non-rotating system. With the true value of the luni-solar precession available, the speed and the direction of the equinox are given so that the coordinates of stars may be reduced from any epoch to the equator and equinox at some standard epoch. From then on these coordinates represent a frame with invariant directions in space, i.e. a non-rotating frame. Planetary precession, geodesic precession, nutation and aberration are assumed to be known to the accuracy required for the transformation within the observational errors. Any imperfection of the luni-solar precession would be manifested as a rotation of the frame about the polar axis of the ecliptic plane. In other words, the realization of an inertial stellar reference system is crucially dependent on determining the exact value of the luni-solar precession.

1.8 Conventional Extragalactic Celestial Reference Systems

As discussed in Sect. 1.4, a characteristic of the dynamical definition of an inertial reference system is the existence of a coordinate frame relative to which the differential equations of motion of system members are expressed solely with the aid of Newton's law of gravity, i.e. terms involving linear and rotational accelerations are absent. If we are to refer to the solar system as a dynamically defined inertial system, it becomes clear that increasing measurement accuracies inevitably require the consideration of the General Theory of Relativity in formulating the equations of motion. Within the solar system relativistic effects give rise to relative errors of the order of $(v/c)^2$ amounting to 10^{-8} for a typical velocity v of the system's member,

0406+121 04 09 22.008740±21 +12 17 39.84750±33 L 1.020

and the speed of light, c. Comprehensive accounting for these effects and the presence of masses complicate the dynamical definition of the inertial system. Moreover, the requirement for a non-rotating frame which reflects, in the best possible way, the present state with regard to theories, models and observing techniques, suggests the reconsideration of the current definition of the stellar celestial reference system.

To comply with general relativity and to endeavour to provide an optimum approximation to a non-rotating celestial frame of reference, the International Astronomical Union urged in Resolution A4, Recommendations I to IX (IAU 1992) the establishment of an inertial system quite different from the dynamical one that is represented by the solar system. These nine recommendations introduce explicitly the General Theory of Relativity as the theoretical background for the definition of the celestial space-time reference system. They also make use of an isotropic model of the Universe, which is suggested by the observational evidence of the distribution of distant galaxies, and by the predominantly spherically symmetric 3K microwave background radiation. The new reference system materializes through a frame that is fixed with respect to the non-rotating Universe. This definition of an inertial system is of the static type, occasionally also called an inertial system (Sect. 1.4, item 2) of kinematic definition (Hohenkerk et al. 1992), since it depends on the kinematic behaviour of very distant objects that are assumed to be free from systematic motions (Kovalevsky & Mueller 1989).

Extragalactic radio sources at great distances exceeding 10 megaparsecs are regarded as suitable objects for defining the frame that realizes the system, because they exhibit non-measurable proper motions when referred to an inertial frame. Indeed, on the hypothesis of an isotropic model of the Universe the apparent transverse motion of a distant extragalactic object (EGO) is extremely small (see Sect. 4.1.2). If, for instance, on making the most pessimistic assumption, the transverse velocities of EGOs are assumed to be as large as their radial velocities, an upper bound of the proper motions of EGOs can be estimated by means of the Hubble constant. Taking $H_0 = 75\,\mathrm{km\,s^{-1}\,Mpc^{-1}}$, the proper motions at a typical EGO distance of 0.1 Gpc do not exceed 0.02 mas/yr and, thus, are just below the borderline of detectability with current observing techniques. On the same hypothesis, it is predictable that the rotation of the Universe as a whole is a negligible quantity.

Many of the EGOs are radio emitters, for which position determination with milliarcsecond precision by means of radio interferometry has become routine. Undoubtedly, this procedure is more efficient than position determination of those solar system bodies that form the backbone of an inertial system of dynamical type (Sect. 1.7). At present, even powerful optical telescopes are not capable of reaching such unprecedented precisions from the ground. There is a possibility that optical interferometry may compete with radio interferometry early in the 21st century (Shao & Colavita 1992). For the

0414−189 04 16 36.544466±51 −18 51 08.34012±48 Q 1.536

time being, however, the extragalactic celestial reference frame is becoming a reality only through the radio interferometric positions of selected quasars or active nuclei of galaxies. From this point of view distant EGOs provide the basis for inertial reference systems of kinematic definition. Chapters 4 and 5 attend to the position determination of extragalactic radio sources and the construction of extragalactic reference frames.

0422−380 04 24 42.243727±33 −37 56 20.78423±119 Q 0.782

2. The Conventional Fundamental Catalogue FK5

A stellar fundamental catalogue compiled from absolute and differential observations of stellar positions at various epochs is the practical realization of a fundamental system of positions and proper motions of the stars. Utmost efforts are made to arrive at a catalogue of star positions that represents an inertial frame. The immediate purpose of the catalogue is to serve as the reference frame of positional astronomy. It should also fulfill the requirements of astronomical research in general, and of celestial mechanics, galactic and extragalactic research in particular. Until 1998 the FK5 constituted the IAU-sanctioned fundamental reference catalogue designed for meeting the aforementioned requirements. The following sections are intended to provide some insight into the lengthy process of constructing this catalogue. Nowadays, applications of stellar fundamental catalogues to the time and latitude service stay in the background, as is the case for geodesy and navigation, since radio interferometric and satellite laser techniques provide results far superior to the classical optical methods. A turning point in favour of optical methods may have been reached by the extension of the extragalactic reference frame to the optical wavelengths with the aid of the Hipparcos catalogue. Although the positions and proper motions of the Hipparcos stars were originally derived from differential astrometry, the connection of these positions and proper motions to the extragalactic reference frame (see Chaps. 6 and 7) promotes the status of the Hipparcos catalogue to that of a quasi-fundamental catalogue. Nevertheless, it is worth considering the principles of the FK5 construction.

2.1 Historical Review

During the course of the 19th and 20th century, quite a number of fundamental catalogues have been established. One of the motivating forces of these efforts aimed at the construction of fundamental catalogues that represent approximations to inertial systems in the best possible way, in order to satisfy the needs for studying absolute motions, as first pointed out by celestial mechanics and later by galactic research. Another motivation arose from the plans for astrometric mapping of the whole sky, subdivided inevitably into zones corresponding to the stars' visibility from selected observatories. It was realized that the consistency of the planned all-sky catalogue would profit from the availability of a fundamental catalogue of reference stars to which the stars of the individual zones can be uniformly referred.

In principle, there exist two types of fundamental optical catalogues: the American and the German series of fundamental catalogues. Starting with Newcomb's Catalogue of Fundamental Stars (Newcomb 1898b), containing 1297 stars, the American series culminated with the 'General Catalogue of 33342 Stars for the Epoch 1950' (GC) by Boss (1937) and the 'Catalog of 5268 Standard Stars, 1950.0, Based on the Normal System N 30' (N 30) by Morgan (1952). The German series of fundamental catalogues, sometimes abbreviated as the FK series where FK stands for 'Fundamental-Katalog', begins with the 'Fundamental-Catalog' (FC) published by Auwers in two parts: one for the northern hemisphere (Auwers 1879) and one for the southern hemisphere (Auwers 1883) comprising 539 and 83 stars, respectively. It is followed by the 'Neuer Fundamental Katalog' (NFK) compiled by Peters (1907). Positions and proper motions of 925 stars are contained in the NFK. It was suggested in the 1920s to repeat the photographic mapping of the northern sky on the basis of a unique reference system. The need for a revision of the NFK was immediately recognized because the catalogue positions had deteriorated in the intervening years due to the poor accuracy of the proper motions listed in the NFK. This fact gave impetus to the formation of the 'Third Fundamental Catalogue' known as FK3. This catalogue gives the positions and proper motions of the NFK stars diminished by 52 double stars that were eliminated because of their unsuitability as fiducial points (Kopff 1937), and of a supplement of 662 stars (Kopff 1938) containing positions and proper motions with respect to improved systems of right ascension and declination.

The subsequent discovery of systematic errors in the system of the FK3 and the imminent plans for a new photographic project of sky mapping by means of wide-angle astrographs initiated the construction of the 'Fourth Fundamental Catalogue' (FK4) issued by Fricke & Kopff (1963). This catalogue contains 1535 stars for the equinoxes and epochs of 1950.0 and 1975.0; it is accompanied by the compilation of 1987 supplementary stars (ARI 1963), whose positions and proper motions are tied to the FK4 frame but have not contributed to the construction of this system.

An extensive description of the American series of fundamental catalogues is given by Eichhorn (1974). Likewise, the German series is described there up to and including the FK4. The approach of the German series is characterized by uniformity and continuity of the applied construction methods, while its selectivity of the observational material and its reliance on personal judgment have occasionally been criticized.

Soon after the completion of the FK4 a considerable number of new observation catalogues of stars were produced covering both hemispheres. The new data revealed imperfections of the FK4 catalogue and, thus, called for rectifications. In essence, systematic and random errors of the positions and proper motions could be identified by comparing the more recent observation catalogues with the FK4. Furthermore, an adjustment of the right ascension offset was required, which had its origin in the difference between the catalogue equinox and the dynamical equinox. The former is defined as the equatorial zero point for right ascension, and the latter is the point of intersection of the Earth's instantaneous orbit with the celestial equator. Hence it is defined by solar system dynamics and plays the role of the authentic zero point of right ascension. Last but not least the introduction of a new system of astronomical constants was imminent (IAU 1977), together with conventions for the reference frame at the standard epoch J2000.0. Thus the time seemed to be ripe for revisions of the fundamental catalogue taking full account of newly acquired data and the international agreements. Procedures for catalogue development were set up aiming towards an impersonal treatment of the observations by statistical methods and, at the same time, an extension to more fundamental stars and a fainter magnitude limit, using as far as possible all the available old and modern observation catalogues (Fricke & Gliese 1968). Guided by the above considerations the work on the FK5 began in the early 1970s. Because of the departure from the traditional methods employed for construction of the German series of fundamental catalogues, and because of the role that the FK5 played as the conventional reference catalogue near the close of the 20th century, we present below the principles of its construction.

2.2 The FK5 Celestial Reference System

What has generally been said in Sect. 1.7 about conventional stellar reference systems applies of course to the FK5 system, and will now be detailed and tailored to the requirements of the FK5 catalogue. As do its predecessors, the FK5 relies mainly on transit circle observations, with the consequence that the instantaneous celestial equator is one of the two reference points in the system's definition. The vernal equinox is adopted as the second reference point. In this framework a transit circle produces positions relative to the instantaneous equator and the chosen equinox.

As discussed in Sect. 1.7, the equator and equinox are determined from observations of members of the solar system and, ultimately, the right ascensions and declinations of stars are tied to the solar system, known from Sect. 1.4 to be a potentially inertial system. For this reason the solar system plays a distinct role in the FK5 system definition. Attention is drawn to some facts that corroborate the inertial property of the solar system:

1) There is ample evidence that the motions of members of the solar system result solely from the internal gravitational forces acting between these members. Their motions obey the laws of mechanics. The absence of forces

0426−380 04 28 40.424306±36 −37 56 19.58031±47 L 1.030

originating outside the solar system is supported by investigations of the precessional motion of the invariable plane of the solar system with respect to the galactic plane (van Woerkom 1943). Significant effects on the orbital angular momentum of the solar system could not be found, thus underlining the assumption that the solar system is an isolated dynamical system, at least within the accuracy of meridian circle measurements.

In the solar system the barycentre may be treated as the origin of an inertial coordinate frame. Indeed, despite the revolution of the Sun about the galactic centre, the acceleration of the barycentre is quite small and not detectable by means of contemporary position and radial velocity measurements. Assuming that the Sun is moving in a circular orbit of radius $r = 8.5$ kpc with a period $T = 250 \times 10^6$ yr, an approximation of the solar acceleration, a, follows from the conventional treatment of circular motion:

$$a = r\,\omega^2 = r\,(2\pi/T)^2 \approx 2 \times 10^{-8}\,\mathrm{cm\,s^{-2}}\,.$$

Since this acceleration is presently undetectable, it is tolerable to consider the barycentric celestial sphere combined with a fixed equator and equinox as an inertial reference frame.

2) If the equations of motion for members of the solar system are formulated by including the mutual forces acting according to Newton's law of gravitation between the bodies of the solar system, one realizes that, by integration of the equations of motion, quantities are determined such as orbital planes, directions and orbital elements of orientation. They are mechanically defined and are fixed apart from the computable secular perturbations (e.g., Fricke 1981). The quantities so defined are immediately usable for an inertial coordinate system. One of these quantities is the plane of the ecliptic, which is chosen as one of the fundamental planes of the inertial system of the FK5.

The above-mentioned properties of the solar system are akin to the first definition of inertial systems listed in Sect. 1.4, and give the FK5 system the character of a dynamically defined inertial system.

As a consequence of choosing the ecliptic as the inertial plane, and because of the fact that the observations refer to the equator, the problem of equator and equinox determination arises (see also Sect. 1.7). It may therefore be instructive to comment briefly here on the procedure of the equator and equinox determination: The positions of solar system members obtained from observations relative to provisional star positions at some epoch are compared with the corresponding quantities taken from the theoretical ephemerides based on Newtonian dynamics. From the position differences, averaged over several years, follow the corrections $\Delta\alpha$ and $\Delta\delta$ to the equinox and equator. Their application to the provisional right ascensions and declinations of the stars links the latter to the solar system, thus preparing the ground for the dynamical definition of the FK5 system, and the equator and equinox determination. Section 2.2.2 discusses the link with the solar system in some detail.

0437−454 04 39 00.854714±57 −45 22 22.56260±78 ? ...

The reduction of observations and the transformation of positions to a common equator and equinox, as required for the link to the solar system and elsewhere in the compilation of the FK5, necessitate the treatment of refraction of light, annual aberration, light deflection, precession and nutation. All these phenomena, therefore, form part of the FK5 system definition. Also involved in these reductions and transformations are time scales which are attended to in Sect. 2.2.3.

2.2.1 Definition of the FK5 System

Recalling that a celestial reference system comprises the theoretical concepts, procedures, models, parameters and astronomical constants required to establish a reference frame, we now summarize those essential elements contained in the definition of the conventional celestial reference system of the FK5.

Theoretical concept:

- The fundamental directions of the reference system are marked by the orbital motion of the Earth–Moon system about the Sun, which defines the plane of the ecliptic, by the direction of the Earth's axis of rotation, which defines the plane of the celestial equator, and by the intersection of the two planes, which defines the equinoctial points.
- The target is the establishment of an inertial system.
- A star catalogue is the realization of the system.

Procedures:

- Algorithms for the reduction from geocentric apparent places to barycentric places, i.e. transformation of proper directions to barycentric directions.

Models:

- The motions of solar system members.
- Precession and nutation.
- Stellar galactic kinematics.
- Annual aberration.
- Refraction of light.
- Light deflection.

Parameters and constants:

- Stellar parallaxes.
- Stellar proper motions.
- Luni-solar precession.
- Planetary precession.

- Geodesic precession.
- Coefficients of nutation in longitude and obliquity.
- Obliquity of the ecliptic.
- Miscellaneous parameters appearing in the procedures and models for observation reduction.

One of the methods of determining precession takes advantage of stellar kinematics (see Sect. 1.6.3). By applying this method that value of precession was determined which eventually entered the FK5 (Fricke 1967). Consequently, models of stellar kinematics of the Galaxy participated in generating the FK5 proper motions which, therefore, constitute a system of proper motions on a kinematic basis. Nevertheless, in its original design the FK5 system is dynamically defined because of the link to the solar system (see Sect. 2.2 above, and Sect. 2.2.2). Only through the transformation to coordinates at J2000.0 with the aid of precession and proper motions did kinematic features find their way into the catalogued positions. In summary, one can say that the FK5 system as realized by the FK5 catalogue of positions and proper motions at the standard epoch J2000.0 has a hybrid definition. This means it is a system of primarily dynamical definition, supplemented by some ancillary kinematic definition. Because the precession is determined from observed proper motions, one speaks also of the empirically defined inertial system of the FK5. If, on the other hand, the precession had been determined from the dynamics of planets, the FK5 system could claim to be of an entirely dynamic definition.

2.2.2 Link Between FK5 and the Solar System

Let us start out from the ephemerides of members of the solar system that are the solutions of differential equations of motion taking account of gravitational forces only. For the determination of corrections to the equator and equinox one considers fundamental observations of the Sun. Meridian circle observations yield the Sun's absolute declination

$$\delta_\odot = \varphi - z_\odot\,, \tag{2.1}$$

while its absolute right ascension is derived from the absolute declination measurements via the following expression of spherical trigonometry:

$$\sin\alpha_\odot = \tan\delta_\odot \, \mathrm{cotan}\, \varepsilon. \tag{2.2}$$

Here, ε denotes the obliquity of the ecliptic, φ the latitude of the observing site, which must be determined simultaneously with the absolute observations, and z is the zenith distance. This method is not free from complications as it also must address the problem of equinox motion. A comprehensive treatment may be found in Eichhorn (1974), p. 55, and Fricke (1985).

`0446+112     04 49 07.671119±24   +11 21 28.59662±51     G  ...`

From the offsets

$$\Delta\alpha = (\alpha_\odot)_{\mathrm{obs}} - (\alpha_\odot)_{\mathrm{eph}}\,, \quad \Delta\delta = (\delta_\odot)_{\mathrm{obs}} - (\delta_\odot)_{\mathrm{eph}} \tag{2.3}$$

between the observed coordinates and those predicted by the solar ephemeris one finds the equinox and equator corrections, $-E$ and $-D$, respectively, by averaging over at least one year. As discussed in Sect. 1.7, these offsets are applied to the right ascensions and declinations of the stars observed with respect to the initially chosen equator and equinox, yielding absolute star positions that can then be claimed to represent a dynamically defined inertial reference system.

When, however, the accuracy of the ephemeris is called into question due to the initial conditions and imperfect models, it is also possible to improve the ephemeris with the aid of the observations as outlined below. For this purpose a procedure is employed that calculates simultaneously the equinox and equator corrections along with the corrections of the orbital elements from a set of conditional equations for $\Delta\alpha$ and $\Delta\delta$. In the case of the Sun these equations read:

$$\begin{aligned}\Delta\alpha &= -E + \cos\varepsilon\,\sec^2\delta\,\Delta\lambda - \cos\alpha\tan\delta\,\Delta\varepsilon \\ &\quad +2\sin\alpha\,\sec\,\delta\,\Delta h - 2\cos\alpha\,\sec\,\delta\cos\varepsilon\,\Delta k\,,\end{aligned} \tag{2.4}$$

$$\begin{aligned}\Delta\delta &= -D + \cos\alpha\sin\varepsilon\,\Delta\lambda + \sin\alpha\,\Delta\varepsilon \\ &\quad +2\sin\delta\cos\alpha\,\Delta h - 2\cos^2\!\alpha\cos\delta\sin\varepsilon\,\Delta k\,,\end{aligned} \tag{2.5}$$

where $h = e\cos\pi$, $k = e\sin\pi$, and the orbital elements of the Earth are given by the heliocentric longitude (λ), the longitude of the pericentre (π), the obliquity of the ecliptic (ε) and the orbital eccentricity (e). No attempt is made here to improve the semimajor axis since superior methods exist to make this correction.

When observations of planets are treated in a similar way to those of the Sun, values for D and E are again inferrable from the analogues of (2.4) and (2.5), but now by using the observed planetary coordinates and the coordinates predicted from the planetary ephemerides. For the inner and outer planets the corresponding conditional equations are given in Schmeidler (1965) and Hughes & Scott (1982). Occasionally, asteroids play the role of planets in determining D and E. A survey of this approach to equator and equinox corrections is given in Fricke (1972).

In summary, the celestial reference system of the FK5 is related to the observations of objects of the solar system: the Sun, planets, and asteroids. As the suitable solar system bodies are few in number and their precise observation is not free from problems, limits are put on the realization of a dynamical reference system based on the solar system. How a purely kinematic definition of the reference system obviates these drawbacks, has been outlined earlier in Sect. 1.8 and will be resumed in Chap. 6.

Incidentally, the approach practiced with the FK5 illustrates that setting up an inertial system follows an iterative procedure, encompassing first of all the astronomical constants, but also parameters, physical models, mathematical methods and a time scale. The constants, parameters and models are not independent of one another, and may be considered to constitute the space-time frame of the reference system.

To demonstrate the iterative approach inherent in the establishment of an inertial frame, we choose, as the departure point, the integration of the differential equations of planetary motion using approximate initial conditions, since the exact ones are normally not available. The resulting theoretical positions are compared with observations based on the current set of astronomical constants by referring to the immediate frame of reference defined by an adopted equator and equinox. What follows is their proper correction and that of the star coordinates in the fundamental catalogue representing this immediate frame. In a further step, all or some of the astronomical constants may be improved on the basis of corrected stellar coordinates, refined models and theories. Likewise, the initial conditions of planetary motion may have profitted from the comparison of observed and predicted planetary positions, as will normally be the case when D and E corrections are determined simultaneously with the orbital elements.

Now we assume that the catalogue stars are reobserved by employing the results of the first iterative loop. Then, by starting again the integration of the equations of motion, the second iterative loop commences, in principle following the above scheme. All in all, the establishment of an inertial frame is a continuous combination of theoretical and empirical findings, leading over extended intervals of time to increasing exactness.

2.2.3 Time and Time Scales

Ultimately, the stellar coordinates in the FK5 refer to the standard epoch J2000.0 which is 2000 January $1.^{\mathrm{d}}5$ equivalent to the Julian date JD 2451545.0, and the standard equinox corresponds to this instant. Instants of time different from the standard epoch are expressed in Julian epochs. Most of the individual catalogues that contribute to the FK5 construction contain observations in terms of Besselian epochs. These observations are transformed to Julian epochs by means of the following formulae giving the relationship between the Besselian or Julian epochs and the Julian date (JD) (e.g., Green 1985, p. 251):

$$\begin{aligned} \text{Besselian epoch} &= \text{B1900.0} + (\text{JD} - 2415020.31352)/\text{yr}_{\text{trop}}\,, \\ \text{Julian epoch} &= \text{J2000.0} + (\text{JD} - 2451545.0)/\text{yr}_{\text{Jul}} \end{aligned}$$

where $\text{yr}_{\text{trop}} = 365.^{\mathrm{d}}242198781$ and $\text{yr}_{\text{Jul}} = 365.^{\mathrm{d}}25$. The Besselian year is fixed at the length of the tropical year, yr_{trop}, at B1900.0 equivalent to JD 2415020.31352.

The unit of time used in the formulae for epoch transformation and calculation of precession is the Julian century of 36525 days, and the unit of time of the time-scale Julian century is the day of 86400 SI seconds.

Planetary ephemerides play a role in defining the FK5 system and, therefore, the time involved in the ephemerides deserves attention. The time scale of these ephemerides is a dynamical time, which is the independent variable of the equations of motion of the bodies of the solar system. The independent variable of an apparent geocentric ephemeris is known as a terrestrial dynamical time. Specifically, it was chosen by the IAU to be a unique time scale independent of various forms of relativistic theories, and designated Terrestrial Dynamical Time (Temps Dynamique Terrestre, TDT). Commonly, the equations of motion refer to the barycentre of the solar system. In this case the independent variable is designated Barycentric Dynamical Time (Temps Dynamique Barycentrique, TDB). The two time scales, TDB and TDT, are offset with respect to each other by small periodic variations.

Since the standard epoch J2000.0 is on Barycentric Dynamical Time, the notation J2000.0, strictly speaking, refers to an instant expressed in terms of TDB, i.e. 2000 January $1.^{d}5$ TDB = JD 2451545.0 TDB.

Julian dates can be expressed either in universal time (UT) or dynamical time. The two times differ by ΔT in the sense ΔT = TDT−UT, and ΔT is determined from observations of the Moon and planets on condition that, for any preceding epoch, the differences caused by variations of the Earth's rotation vanish between the observed positions and those calculated by the dynamical theory. Within the accuracy of the FK5 no need arises to distinguish between JD TDT and JD UT.

Though of no direct concern to FK5, we mention in view of modern astrometry that the IAU has defined in 1991 new time scales to clarify the relationships between space-time coordinates (IAU 1992). These time scales are TCB (Barycentric Coordinate Time), TCG (Geocentric Coordinate Time) and TT (Terrestrial Time), where the latter can be considered equivalent to the TDT defined above. The definitions of the new time scales and the interconnections with the former ones (TDB, TDT) are formulated in the framework of the General Theory of Relativity (e.g. Seidelmann et al. 1992).

Since the adoption of International Atomic Time (TAI) in 1972 with the SI second as its fundamental unit, the observation time is measured in terrestrial time (TT) and preserved in the reduction process. The terrestrial time TT is related to TAI through

$$\mathrm{TT(TAI)} \quad = \quad \mathrm{TAI} + 32.184\ \mathrm{s}\,.$$

Prior to 1972, it was customary to give observation times in terms of universal time, especially UT1. For details see Seidelmann et al. (1992).

0458+138 05 01 45.270840±37 +13 56 07.22063±64 ? ...

2.3 First Principles of Compiling the FK5

At the root of the FK5 compilation stands the conceptual definition of the FK5 system. One of the ideally desirable properties of a celestial system is that it be inertial. As were its predecessors, the FK5 system is primarily defined by the instantaneous Earth's equatorial plane and the vernal equinox. As such the system is rotating due to precession and nutation, with the consequences that the axis perpendicular to the equatorial plane rotates about the pole of the ecliptic, and the ecliptic plane is also in motion. In order to obtain a non-rotating reference system, the equator and equinox must be fixed at some standard epoch, e.g., J2000.0. It is this equatorial plane and equinox which define the FK5 reference system. Eventually, it is represented by the right ascensions and declinations of selected stars at the standard epoch. It can also be extended to other epochs provided that fundamental proper motions of these stars are available.

So far, the system definition of the FK5 is of purely theoretical wording although, in principle, the polar distance of the instantaneous equator may be obtained from circle readings of meridian circles, and the equinox from circle and clock readings. To bridge the gap between the theoretical conceptual definition of the reference system and its physical construction, some modelling is needed of the motions (concerning, e.g., precession and nutation) and, further, environmental parameters have to be adopted (concerning, e.g., masses of planets, aberration, atmospheric refraction). All in all, there is some freedom in these choices, suggesting that they should be based upon conventional agreements. The FK5 system, therefore, is known as the FK5 conventional celestial reference system. For its practical structure we return to first principles in order to demonstrate that the ideal definition goals (see Sect. 2.2.1) are indeed attainable to an excellent degree of approximation. At the same time, these first principles provide the key to the construction of the FK5 catalogue of star positions and proper motions that represent the system. Note that, in accordance with common practice, we speak occasionally of the system of star positions and proper motions of the FK5. This terminology refers to the set of stars of the FK5 catalogue representing the FK5 reference system, and should not be confused with the definition of the FK5 conventional celestial reference system.

The first principles are understood as a collection of the following basic items:

- Theory of the motion of the Sun and of members of the solar system.
- Model of the motion of the celestial pole giving the precession and nutation parameters, which describe the motion of the Earth's axis of rotation.
- Knowledge of the obliquity of the ecliptic and its variation in time.
- Realization of the coordinate system by the Earth's equatorial plane of date, to which declinations are referred, and by the equinox of date, from which right ascensions are reckoned.

`0502+049 05 05 23.184723±37 +04 59 42.72448±60 Q 0.954`

- Procurement of observations of right ascension and declination of stars and planetary bodies, referring to the coordinate system delineated in the previous item. Reobservation of these objects at other epochs.
- Transformation of the instantaneous stellar coordinates of right ascension and declination at epoch to a common equator and equinox at some standard epoch, and shifting the origin of the frame to the barycentre of the solar system.

Below we comment in turn on the fulfillment of the these first principles at the time of the FK5 compilation.

Motion in the solar system. Aiming at a dynamical definition of the FK5 reference system, it seems sensible to link the Earth's equatorial plane, which is the fundamental plane of the system, to members of the solar system. Indeed, in terms of classical mechanics the solar system dynamics is described by the differential equations of motion based entirely on Newton's law of gravitation. The coordinates obtained by integrating the differential equations provide an inertial frame, since these equations are formulated in accordance with Newton's laws of motion (see Sect. 1.4). At this point, a stage is reached where the ephemerides of the Sun, the major planets and selected minor planets are available with respect to an inertial dynamical system. Observation of these objects in conjunction with stars is a prerequisite for the determination of absolute right ascensions of stars. Moreover, these observations reveal possible differences between the catalogue equinox, realized by the right ascensions of stars in the reference frame, and the true dynamical equinox, defined by solar system dynamics, thus leading finally to a correction of the catalogue equinox.

Celestial pole. During the preparatory stages of work on the FK5, the motion of the celestial pole in the space-fixed frame was modelled by Newcomb's value of precession (Newcomb 1898a) and Woolard's theory of nutation (Woolard 1953). In the framework of the IAU 1976 Astronomical Constants (IAU 1977) a revised value of precession was proposed. This change, however, does not alter the principles of catalogue compilation; it does influence the adaptation of the proper motions of the FK5 stars to the equator and equinox at the standard epoch J2000.0 in accordance with the new IAU conventions (e.g., USNO 1981).

Although the 1977 value of precession involves hypotheses of stellar kinematics (see Sect. 1.6.3) by adopting a model of galactic rotation, it is nevertheless correct to consider the FK5 system primarily as a system having a dynamical definition. This arises from the relation of the star positions to those of members of the solar system. Elements of a kinematic definition have also entered through the interrelation between proper motions and the value of precession derived from stellar proper motions.

Ecliptic. The fundamental plane of the FK5 reference system is the Earth's equatorial plane whereas, originally, luni-solar precession and nutation are

0506−612 05 06 43.988739±47 −61 09 40.99328±35 Q 1.093

measured on the ecliptic plane. To account for these effects in the equatorial plane, a value of the obliquity of the ecliptic is required as a basic quantity. It is either adopted from astronomical conventions (such as those recently compiled by IERS 1996b), or it can also be determined from absolute observations of the Sun's declination at two successive solstices (see Sect. 2.2.2).

Realization of the coordinate system. It is not immediately obvious how to realize the equatorial coordinate system by means of an observing instrument. In pursuing this goal we resort to using the horizontal coordinate system, since its axes can be oriented toward points on the surface of the Earth. Furthermore, we assume that a theodolite-like instrument is available allowing rotations about two perpendicular axes, thus providing angular measurements of azimuth (A) and zenith distance (Z). On these grounds, Sect. 2.3.1 shows that meridian circles are capable of realizing the equatorial coordinate system by determining right ascensions and declinations of celestial bodies.

Provision of observations of right ascension and declination. Two types of observations are customary in establishing fundamental catalogues: absolute observations, which are made without any a priori knowledge about stellar coordinates, and differential observations, which make use of known coordinates of other stars. Due to the need for instrument calibration, determination of geographical latitude, and consideration of atmospheric refraction, the observation of absolute right ascensions and declinations is a time-consuming and complex task. Making differential observations is quicker and simpler but, nevertheless, it is also an involved undertaking. In catalogue work these observations serve to densify the fundamental reference frame, whose construction rests upon absolute observations. The procedures for both types of observations are treated in great detail by, e.g., Podobed (1965). In recognition of the importance of absolute observations we sketch in Sect. 2.3.2 the basic steps leading to their generation.

Observations of the same stars repeated at different epochs offer the opportunity to improve the positional precision and, above all, to determine stellar proper motions.

Transformation of instantaneous stellar coordinates. Clearly, a compilation catalogue is made up of a limited set of stars; in the case of the FK5 the set consists of 1535 stars. For each star several dozen absolute and differential observations are usually available, taken at many observatories over an extended period, and with reference to an adopted epoch for the equator and equinox. A prerequisite for inclusion in a catalogue is the reduction of the individual instantaneous stellar coordinates to a common epoch and to a common mean equator and equinox, with the origin of the coordinates at the barycentre of the solar system. On the assumption that the original observed topocentric positions have been transformed into geocentric apparent positions (places), the standard task remains (after reduction to a common mean equator and equinox): to calculate barycentric positions from geocentric apparent positions. In performing this reduction a number of steps must be carried out, involving astronomical constants and stellar parameters (see e.g., Hohenkerk et al. (1992), pp. 152–155). The shift to the solar system barycentre serves the purpose of providing a system of stellar coordinates that is independent of observation times and locations.

As shown by the items discussed above, there exists an empirical relationship between the physical structure of the reference system on the one hand, and astronomical constants and stellar parameters on the other. To the latter group, for instance, belong stellar proper motions and parallaxes. The determination of some of these quantities requires the existence of an inertial reference system on the basis of which they can be reliably determined from observations. Due to these empirical elements, the construction of a conventional celestial reference system is an iterative and evolving process, reflecting the progress in observational techniques and modelling of the theoretical system's concepts. Consequently, the quality of a compilation catalogue improves with the accuracy of astronomical constants and stellar parameters. A great deal of effort, therefore, has been invested in making sure that optimum values of these quantities are employed in constructing the FK5.

2.3.1 Installation and Operation of Meridian Circles

The horizontal coordinate system is of fundamental importance to the anchoring of a meridian circle. First, the perpendicularity of the vertical axis of the theodolite-like instrument to the local geoid is examined and corrected if necessary and, second, the vertical circle is adjusted by pointing the telescope to the zenith. When this procedure is finished, one of the fundamental directions, the z_h axis, is fixed by orientation to the zenith with the sole aid of a spirit level attached to the vertical circle. The z_h axis, being the normal to the tangential plane at the location of the spirit level, defines the horizon as the fundamental plane. The basic geometry of meridian circle measurements is illustrated in Fig. 2.1, where the horizontal rectangular coordinate frame $(x_\mathrm{h}, y_\mathrm{h}, z_\mathrm{h})$ and the equatorial rectangular coordinate frame $(x_\mathrm{eq}, y_\mathrm{eq}, z_\mathrm{eq})$ are introduced along with the respective spherical coordinates azimuth, zenith distance (A, Z) and hour angle, declination (t, δ).

Next, the direction of the x_h axis in this fundamental plane is needed. Let the azimuth (A) be reckoned from the north; the $-x_\mathrm{h}$ axis, by convention, points to the south lying in the plane of the vertical circle known as the meridian. The diurnal motion of stars helps to determine the meridian, which is the location where the stars attain their smallest zenith distance (Z), i.e.

$$\frac{\mathrm{d}Z}{\mathrm{d}t} = 0 \qquad \text{for} \quad A = 180^\circ \,.$$

As outlined below, stars are suitable for fixing the meridian, since they fulfill the condition of constant declination during the process of meridian determination (Schaub 1950, p. 179). Use is made of the transformation formula for

0507+179   05 10 02.369122±20   +18 00 41.58171±30   ?   . . .

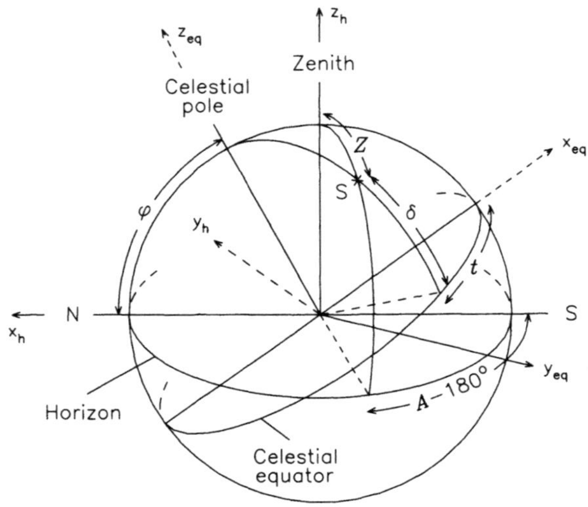

Fig. 2.1. Relationship between azimuth, zenith distance (A, Z) and hour angle, declination (t, δ) of a star S observed from a site of geographical latitude φ

the position vector, $\boldsymbol{s}$, from the frame of horizontal coordinates (A,Z) to the frame of hour angle and declination (t,δ) given as

$$\boldsymbol{s}_{A,Z} \quad = \quad \mathbf{M_2} \cdot \mathbf{M_1} \ \boldsymbol{s}_{t,\delta} \ , \tag{2.6}$$

where $\mathbf{M_1}$ rotates the left-handed (t, δ) coordinate frame about the $y_{\rm eq}$ axis by $90° - \varphi$ in the clockwise sense, and $\mathbf{M_2}$ rotates this frame about the $z_{\rm eq}$ axis by 180°. The angle φ denotes the geographical latitude of the observing site. For completeness, the rotation matrices are given:

$$\mathbf{M_1} = \begin{pmatrix} \sin\varphi & 0 & -\cos\varphi \\ 0 & 1 & 0 \\ \cos\varphi & 0 & \sin\varphi \end{pmatrix} , \qquad \mathbf{M_2} = \begin{pmatrix} -1 & 0 & 0 \\ 0 & -1 & 0 \\ 0 & 0 & 1 \end{pmatrix} .$$

Expressing the position vectors by their components in spherical coordinates and regarding Z and δ as the variables, differentiation of the third component of (2.6) yields

$$-\sin Z \ \frac{\mathrm{d}Z}{\mathrm{d}t} \quad = \quad (-\cos\varphi\sin\delta\cos t + \sin\varphi\cos\delta) \ \frac{\mathrm{d}\delta}{\mathrm{d}t} \quad - \quad \cos\varphi\cos\delta\sin t \, .$$

Let t_0 be the hour angle at which $\mathrm{d}Z/\mathrm{d}t = 0$. Then

$$\sin t_0 \quad = \quad (-\tan\delta\cos t_0 + \tan\varphi) \ \frac{\mathrm{d}\delta}{\mathrm{d}t} \ ,$$

and the second component of (2.6) gives

```
0516−621     05 16 44.926178±48   −62 07 05.38930±42     ?   ...
```

$$\sin A_0 = (-\tan\delta\cos t_0 + \tan\varphi)\,\frac{\cos\delta}{\sin Z_0}\,\frac{\mathrm{d}\delta}{\mathrm{d}t}\,,$$

which demonstrates that the smallest zenith distance is reached in the meridian, $t = 0$ and $A = 180°$, only for objects with constant declinations. It is for this reason that stars are used for fixing the meridian in contrast to solar system bodies.

Direct measurement of the variation of the zenith distance is impractical because of its smallness near the meridian. Instead one takes advantage of the third component of (2.6) stating that for constant declination the zenith distance is equal at the hour angles $-t$ and t before and after the meridian passage. On forming the average of the readings on the horizontal circle at identical zenith distances, the direction is obtained to the southern point, i.e. the direction of the $-x_h$ axis, and may be fixed by means of meridian marks, also known as mires.

2.3.2 Generation of Absolute Observations by Meridian Circles

After instrument calibrations and azimuth checking of the meridian circle with the help of meridian marks the instrument is operational for making absolute observations. The zenith distance of a celestial body is directly measurable with reference to the instrument's astronomical zenith. Given the astronomical latitude (φ) of the instrument site and counting the zenith distance always positive, the following relations hold between zenith distance and declination in the northern hemisphere ($\varphi > 0$):

$$Z_\mathrm{u}^\mathrm{s} = \varphi - \delta \quad \text{for stars at upper culmination south of the zenith,} \tag{2.7}$$

$$Z_\mathrm{u}^\mathrm{n} = \delta - \varphi \quad \text{for stars at upper culmination north of the zenith between the zenith and the pole,} \tag{2.8}$$

$$Z_\mathrm{l} = 180° - \delta - \varphi \quad \text{for stars at lower culmination.} \tag{2.9}$$

The corresponding expressions for the southern hemisphere ($\varphi < 0$) read:

$$Z_\mathrm{u}^\mathrm{s} = \varphi - \delta \quad \text{for stars at upper culmination south of the zenith between the zenith and the pole,} \tag{2.10}$$

$$Z_\mathrm{u}^\mathrm{n} = \delta - \varphi \quad \text{for stars at upper culmination north of the zenith,} \tag{2.11}$$

$$Z_\mathrm{l} = 180° + \delta + \varphi \quad \text{for stars at lower culmination.} \tag{2.12}$$

We note that the expressions for the zenith distances at upper culmination south of the zenith are identical in both hemispheres and, likewise, for those north of the zenith.

The zenith distance is the only angle measurable by meridian circles without the aid of other means. Before zenith distances are usable as absolute astrometric quantities, however, it is required that the disturbing effects caused by atmospheric refraction be eliminated. Correction for refraction is performed by a lengthy process: for its treatment we refer to Podobed (1965). Yet another step is required for deriving absolute declinations from zenith distances. This is the determination of the instrument's geographical latitude. We explain briefly how circumpolar stars serve this purpose.

From the zenith distances of a circumpolar star at upper and lower culmination there follows from (2.8) and (2.9)

$$\varphi = \tfrac{1}{2}\left[180^\circ - (Z_\mathrm{l} + Z_\mathrm{u})\right]. \tag{2.13}$$

Given the zenith distances and the astronomical latitude, absolute declinations follow from (2.7 to 2.12).

Nowadays radio interferometry and methods of satellite geodesy provide accurate station coordinates. For instance they are given in the annual reports and technical notes of the IERS (e.g., IERS 1996c; IERS 1998). The astronomical latitude of the site of a meridian circle is inferrable from these coordinates by means of collocation methods.

In contrast to measurement of declinations, right ascension measurements require the use of a clock, since the right ascension (α) of an object is defined by the sidereal time (θ), i.e. the hour angle of the vernal equinox, according to the standard expression

$$\theta = \alpha + t,$$

which becomes

$$\theta = \alpha \tag{2.14}$$

at upper meridian passage, i.e. at hour angle $t = 0$, thus yielding the right ascension from reading a clock that gives sidereal time. The determination of absolute right ascension is therefore equivalent to the determination of absolute sidereal time, which is identical with the determination of the vernal equinox. Note that the right ascension is reckoned from the vernal equinox eastward to the hour circle of the object under observation.

In the absence of an ideal sidereal clock we may assume a clock that runs nearly synchronously with the Earth's rotation, approximating more or less sidereal time but leaving an offset ΔC of the clock readings C. At transit we get

$$\theta = \alpha = C + \Delta C. \tag{2.15}$$

The task of determining absolute sidereal time reduces to the determination of the clock offset. For this purpose we take advantage of the path of the Sun along the ecliptic and of the fact that, at vernal equinox, $\alpha_\odot = \delta_\odot = 0$. From the right-angled spherical triangle formed by the equinox, the Sun's position in the ecliptic and the Sun's right ascension follows the relation

$$\sin \alpha_{\odot} = \tan \delta_{\odot} \operatorname{cotan} \varepsilon , \tag{2.16}$$

where ε is the obliquity of the ecliptic. For its independent determination see below.

From the measurement of absolute declinations of the Sun by meridian circles, as outlined above, it is possible to determine the position of the vernal equinox from (2.16) by interpolating the values of $\alpha_{\odot}$. To find the clock offset we apply (2.15) to the Sun giving

$$\Delta C = \alpha_{\odot} - C_{\odot} ,$$

where $\alpha_{\odot}$ follows from (2.16) and $C_{\odot}$ is the clock reading at solar transit. Knowing ΔC, one obtains absolute right ascensions of any star by substituting the clock reading at transit into (2.15).

Concerning the determination of the obliquity, we now apply (2.16) to the instances when the Sun passes two successive solstices. Absolute declination measurements yield $\varepsilon = \pm\delta_{\odot}$. For a complete discussion of the determination of the obliquity we refer to Podobed (1965), and to modern techniques that make use of lunar laser ranging data (Standish 1982a) and of pulsar astrometry. In the latter case position determination of pulsars is performed in the ecliptic celestial coordinate frame by means of pulse timing on the one hand, and in the equatorial celestial coordinate frame by means of VLBI on the other (Backer et al. 1985, Bartel et al. 1996). More recently, it became common practice to employ those values of astronomical and geophysical constants and parameters that are based on international efforts to determine optimal values from proven theoretical and experimental methods. A typical example of this approach is the application of the 1996 IERS Conventions (IERS 1996b).

2.4 Scope of the FK5 Work

Resolutions adopted by the IAU in 1973 (IAU 1974, p. 84) urged work on the improvement of the fundamental catalogue FK4 and its extension to fainter magnitudes to be finished by the mid-1980s. The driving forces for replacing FK4 after only a short lifetime were threefold: First, the mean epochs of the right ascension and declination systems of the FK4 lie as far back as 1925 and 1935, respectively. As time passes, the position errors at an advanced epoch grow due to the errors in proper motion and because of imperfections of astronomical constants. Eventually, these errors no longer meet the requirements of astronomy. Second, modernized meridian circles and automated observation techniques have led to important gains in data yield and accuracy. As a consequence, there is a strong requirement that the recent

0530−727 05 29 30.042235±73 −72 45 28.50731±35 ? . . .

high accuracy observations should help to shape the fundamental catalogue. Third, many fields of astronomy and astrophysics engage in the study of faint objects. Since the early 1970s photoelectric meridian circles have been able to measure stars down to magnitude 10 with accuracies comparable with those of the brighter stars. In the wake of these achievements it became desirable and possible to extend the fundamental catalogue to fainter stars. Basically, these three points of view sketch the essential rationales for the establishment of the FK5. One may add that observations with Danjon astrolabes were initiated in the 1970s, and merit inclusion in the new fundamental catalogue as differential observations (Billaud et al. 1978).

In considering the motivations for an update of the current fundamental catalogue in conjunction with the first principles referred to in Sect. 2.3, Fricke (1974) has given a survey of the main tasks related to the establishment of the FK5. These tasks are briefly discussed below and some subtasks added, which arose during catalogue construction:

1) Collection and study of the available observation catalogues in view of the techniques of observation and the methods of reduction that have been applied. The potential of the catalogues is twofold: They contribute to the improvement of the systematic and individual accuracy but also to the extension to stars fainter than visual magnitude 7.5, which is the upper limit of the visual magnitudes of FK4 stars.

2) Choice of B1950.0 as starting point of the FK5 development. Preparatory work on the FK5 began already in the early 1970s at a time when the IAU 1976 resolutions, which have a strong bearing on the future conventional fundamental catalogue FK5, had not yet been released (IAU 1977). These resolutions deal with the introduction of a new system of astronomical constants, new time scales and a new standard epoch. Most important for the FK5 is that part of the resolutions which adopts a new value of the general precession in longitude, and recommends the redetermination of the equinox and the elimination of a suspected non-precessional motion of the equinox. It proved to be appropriate, therefore, to develop the FK5 initially in the framework of the mean equator and equinox of B1950.0 and the conventions in use then. Further, it was decided to develop the FK5 by improving and extending the FK4. In pursuing this goal great care was exercised to avoid piling correction upon correction. As a matter of fact, all available data between 1900 and 1980 had been reanalysed and subjected to largely objective selection criteria. As soon as the IAU 1976 resolution had taken effect, the improved FK4 version was treated accordingly, thus generating FK5 at the standard epoch J2000.0.

3) Determination of the FK5 system from corrections of the FK4 system of stellar coordinates and proper motions. This action strives for the elimination of large-scale inhomogeneities in all regions of the sky by using the absolute and quasi-absolute observations available in the catalogues between 1900 and 1980. Since the determination of systematic corrections is an intricate task

of different facets, we discuss the principles separately in Sects. 2.4.1 and 2.4.2. Altogether, 85 absolute and quasi-absolute catalogues retrieved from the literature proved to be suitable for determining the systematic corrections FK5 – FK4. To be precise, nearly 70 catalogues served to derive corrections in right ascension, and some 50 catalogues contributed to corrections in declination.

4) Derivation of individual corrections to the positions and proper motions in the FK4 from absolute and differential observations in those catalogues which are not yet included in the FK4. About 90 catalogues were available for this purpose, not counting some 200 catalogues already embodied in the FK4. By the elimination of the systematic differences, (Catalogue minus FK4), these additional catalogues had been consistently reduced to the FK4 system. The resulting positional residuals enter the usual conditional equations, from which the corrections to the FK4 positions and proper motions are derived by weighted least squares adjustment. Weighting of catalogues followed a method developed by Bien (1987). As soon as these corrections are added to the corresponding FK4 quantities, after the application of system corrections, one obtains improved positions and proper motions in a preliminary system of the FK5, but still with reference to the B1950.0 standard epoch. A further step deals with the transformation of the positions and proper motions to the FK5 system at J2000.0 (Sect. 2.5).

5) Improvement of the value of general precession in longitude. We reiterate that in this context the determination of precession is equivalent to establishing an inertial frame of reference. Constructing a fundamental catalogue requires utmost care concerning the correctness of the value of precession because of its intimate interconnection with proper motions. The FK5 is based on an improved value of precession that has been derived from corrections to Newcomb's value of the luni-solar precession (see Sect. 1.6.3) amounting to $\Delta\psi = +1.''10/\mathrm{cy}$ (Fricke 1967) and from a correction $\Delta\chi = -0.''029/\mathrm{cy}$ to the planetary precession (Lieske et al. 1977). These recommended changes of the luni-solar and planetary precessions (IAU 1977) entail corrections of the FK4 proper motions. Using the notation introduced earlier in Sect. 1.6.3, one gets the following quantities that must be added to the FK4 proper motions in order to be consistent with the new precession values:

$$\begin{aligned} \Delta\mu_\alpha \cos\delta &= -\Delta k \cos\delta - \Delta n \sin\alpha \sin\delta \, , \\ \Delta\mu_\delta &= -\Delta n \cos\alpha \, . \end{aligned}$$

6) Determination of the equinox and the equator of the FK5. Typical of the definition of the FK5 reference system is the Earth's equator as the fundamental plane, from which declinations are reckoned, and the vernal equinox as the zero point of right ascension. Observations of the Sun, Moon and other members of the planetary system have been used for determining both the equator and the dynamical equinox. Plotted in Fig. 2.2 are the zero point corrections derived from independent observations of objects in

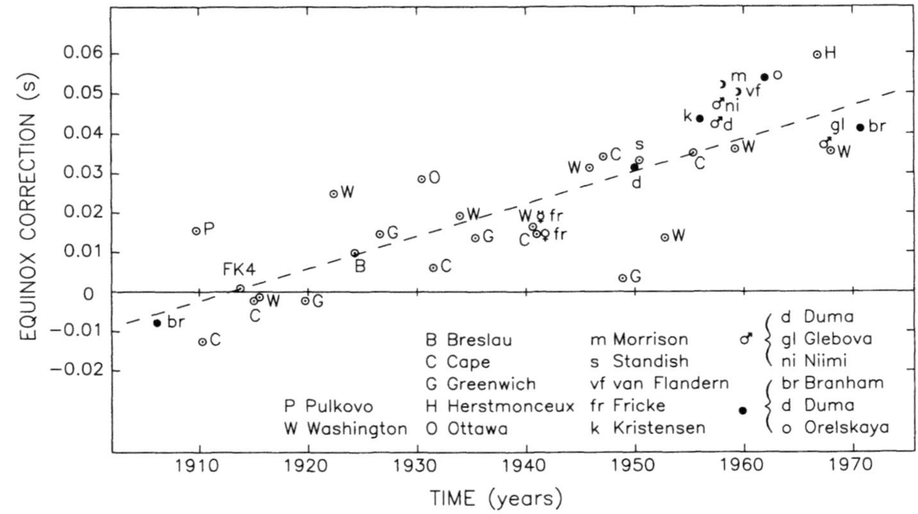

Fig. 2.2. Correction of the right ascension zero point of the FK4 versus time, derived from observations of the Sun, the planets and planetoids, and lunar occultations of stars (After Fricke 1985)

the planetary system made between 1900 and 1970. The broken line represents $E(T)$ obtained by smoothing (Fricke 1985). All but one of the equinox corrections prior to 1950 rest upon daylight observations, whereas the more recent determinations result form a reasonably unbiased mixture of objects and observation methods. Therefore, a more reliable equinox correction is expected from post-1950 data. Using only the individual equinox corrections from 1950 onwards a weighted least squares estimate (Fricke 1982) yielded the correction $E(T)$ to the FK4 zero point of right ascension for the epoch of observation T measured in Julian centuries:

$$E(T) \quad = \quad +0\overset{s}{.}035 + 0\overset{s}{.}085\,(T - 19.50)\,. \tag{2.17}$$

It is the value of $E = +0\overset{s}{.}035$, by which the right ascensions of the FK4 have to be increased in order to refer them to the dynamical equinox. This means

$$\alpha(\mathrm{FK4}) + 0\overset{s}{.}035 \quad = \quad \alpha(\mathrm{FK5}) \text{ at B1950.0}\,.$$

The equator of the FK5 coincides with that of FK4, since the analysis of the observations suitable for the determination of the equator did not reveal any significant correction.

A full report on the method of equinox and equator determination from observations of the Sun has been given by Fricke (1985). Incidentally, this procedure for equinox and equator determination is also relevant to the question concerning the dynamical definition of the FK5 system (see Sect. 2.2.2).

0538+498 05 42 36.137916±53 +49 51 07.23356±54 Q 0.545

7) Removal of the non-precessional motion of the equinox. This type of motion became obvious in the course of the determination of the luni-solar precession from proper motions of stars in fundamental catalogues (Fricke 1977). Further, it was identified in the analysis of lunar occultation observations (Martin & van Flandern 1970) and in investigations of the motions of Mars (Laubscher 1976b). The equinox motion, Δe, is equivalent to the time-dependent term in (2.17), i.e.

$$\Delta e \;=\; \dot{E} \;=\; 0\overset{\mathrm{s}}{.}085 \pm 0\overset{\mathrm{s}}{.}010 \;/\; \mathrm{cy}$$

and has been derived from 35 individual equinox corrections. By analogy to the right ascensions, the centennial proper motions of the FK4 stars require the correction Δe to account for the shift of the zero point of proper motions. This means

$$\mu_\alpha(\mathrm{FK4}) + 0\overset{\mathrm{s}}{.}085 \;=\; \mu_\alpha(\mathrm{FK5}) \;\; \text{at B1950.0}\,.$$

Independent determinations of the secular variation $\dot{E}$ of the equinox have also been made from proper motions of FK4 stars and lunar occultations of celestial bodies, resulting in values close to the one given above. Indeed, $\dot{E} = 0\overset{\mathrm{s}}{.}085/\mathrm{cy}$ may be taken as the mean of the values derived from individual equinox corrections, proper motions of stars and lunar occultations. A not-yet-explained minor inconsistency of $\dot{E}$ is reported by Morrison (1982).

8) Extension of the fundamental catalogue into both the faint and bright magnitude ranges. A pool of faint stars in the visual magnitude range of 6.5 to 9.2 is made available by the stars known as International Reference Stars (IRS), whose positions are compiled in the catalogues AGK3R (Smith 1980) for the northern hemisphere and SRS (Smith et al. 1990) for the southern hemisphere. In either case several observatories have contributed to these catalogues with observations relative to FK4. The magnitude limit of 9.2 is essentially set by the dependence of positional observations on the apparent magnitude, which has the consequence that bright stars refer to a magnitude system different from that of faint stars. Therefore, on reducing a catalogue to the FK4, an inconsistency may be introduced into the positions of bright and faint stars unless the catalogue has been observed with screens, which help to avoid a 'magnitude equation' as much as possible because these screens are able to bridge a gap of about 5 magnitudes.

Broadly speaking, the selection of faint stars from the IRS pool proceeded as follows: First, those individual stars which are found in absolute and differential catalogues of meridian circle observations made after 1890, were identified with the corresponding objects in the pool to get an idea of the observing history of the respective stars. Second, a criterion for the suitability of the catalogue under consideration is the size of the intersection of catalogue and the pool augmented by the FK4 stars. Both the faint and FK4 stars must be represented in sufficient numbers to make the catalogue eligible for the extension. The presence of FK4 stars is required because of the need to

0544+273 05 47 34.148941±32 +27 21 56.84240±43 ? ...

reduce the observation catalogue to the FK4 system. This procedure, however, is restricted to catalogues observed with screens, and it does not work at all if the catalogue contains only faint stars. As a preparatory measure, therefore, an auxiliary system of mean positions and proper motions has been established for AGK3R stars by reducing to FK4 all those catalogues that have been observed with screens and that are comprised of FK4 and faint stars in sufficient number (Corbin 1974). This stellar system is known as the northern base system. It contains a total of 5590 stars and is defined for declinations north of −30°.

The base system provided the possibility of treating catalogues containing faint stars only. Catalogues not observed with screens could be reduced to this system, yielding results which, in principle, are equivalent with a direct reduction to (bright) FK4 stars.

In the southern hemisphere the establishment of a base system was more complicated because of the lack of catalogues observed with screens. Instead, the southern catalogues observed by using moving wire micrometers, which provide declination-independent magnitude errors, offered the opportunity to reduce to the northern base system those unrefined southern catalogues that cover also the zone between −30° declination and the equator. Since the magnitude error does not vary with declination, it is permissible to apply any detected magnitude equation to the catalogue stars south of −30°. Seven catalogues have been reduced to the FK4 in this manner. They constitute (together with the FK4 stars) the southern base system containing mean positions and proper motions of 4708 stars. Some 75 southern catalogues have been reduced to this base system, whose observations were obtained using moving-wire micrometers (Corbin 1985, Corbin & Urban 1990).

The extension to bright stars of magnitude 5 to 7 was simplified by the existence of the FK4 Supplement (ARI 1963). The stars of this catalogue had been selected from absolute and quasi-absolute observation catalogues that contain a sufficient number of FK4 stars needed for the reduction of the catalogues to the FK4.

On choosing stars for the faint and bright extensions certain selection criteria have been applied as guidelines. Fulfillment of these criteria was striven for in the best possible way:

a) uniform distribution of the stars in the final catalogue over the whole sky with respect to position, apparent magnitude and spectral type;
b) acceptance only of stars with an excellent observation history. This state is normally attained as soon as the observations of a star are made at several epochs spread out in time, and are free from magnitude errors;
c) evidence that the positions in the observation catalogues have been reduced by accounting for polar motion, which is usually true for observations after 1900;
d) avoidance of visual binaries and nearby stars.

0556+238 05 59 32.033133±22 +23 53 53.92690±32 ? . . .

2.4.1 Systematic Catalogue Differences

As outlined in item 3) above the system of the FK5 has been determined from systematic corrections to the FK4. Here we give details of the procedure that is based on the guideline to adopt the FK4 as the reference, from which the FK5 systems of positions and proper motions are developed. Ultimately, by catalogue comparison the absolute and quasi-absolute observation catalogues (Cat), suitable for system development, were reduced to the system of the FK4 for the calculation of systematic differences Cat – FK4 at the mean epoch of the observation catalogue and for the FK4 equinox. For this purpose the analytical method was used as described by Bien et al. (1978). Given therein are also two numerical methods for the calculation of catalogue differences. The numerical methods were applied for checking purposes, and showed generally excellent agreement with the analytical method. The latter is favoured because of its more impersonal style, implying objective statistical criteria to discriminate between the systematic and random parts of the catalogue differences. In addition, the analytical method takes account of the dependence of the differences in right ascension (RA) and declination (Dec) on the stars' RAs as well as Decs. We present the principles of this method below.

Let $\Delta\alpha \cos\delta$ and $\Delta\delta$ be the differences between the star positions of two catalogues, $\mathrm{Cat}_1, \mathrm{Cat}_2$, e.g., in the sense $\mathrm{Cat}_2 - \mathrm{Cat}_1$. For illustration we imagine a plot of N such differences on the celestial sphere, thus generating on the sphere one surface each for the RA and Dec differences. As a common notation for the surfaces we choose

$$\Delta = f(\alpha, \delta) + \varepsilon \,. \tag{2.18}$$

The first and second terms on the right-hand side express the systematic and random parts of the position differences, respectively, and Δ takes the values

$$\Delta_i = \left\{ \begin{array}{l} \Delta\alpha_i \cos\delta_i \\ \text{or} \\ \Delta\delta_i \end{array} \right\}, \; i = 1, ..., N \,.$$

In general, the differences also depend on the apparent magnitudes of the stars. Therefore, it is common practice to include the magnitude as a third parameter in the systematic part. Sophisticated treatments of catalogue comparison even pay attention to the influence of the spectral types.

Disregarding lengthy details, the basic idea for determining the systematic part of the catalogue differences reduces to the development of $f(\alpha, \delta)$ into a series of surface spherical harmonics, and retention of only those terms that decrease significantly the dispersion of the random part, ε (Brosche 1966).

The surface spherical harmonic of n-th degree is defined by

$$Y_n(\alpha, \delta) = \sum_{m=0}^{n} (a_{nm} \cos m\alpha + b_{nm} \sin m\alpha) P_{nm}(\delta),$$

where the quantities a_{nm}, b_{nm} are constant coefficients, while $P_{nm}(\delta)$ stands for the associated Legendre function of degree n and order m. The surface spherical harmonics form a complete system of orthogonal functions suitable to represent the catalogue differences on the surface of the sphere by series expansion, i.e.,

$$\Delta_i = \sum_{s=0}^{l} A_s Y_s(\alpha_i, \delta_i) + \varepsilon_i,\ i = 1, ..., N. \tag{2.19}$$

In each application one decides from case to case on the size of the upper summation limit.

From experience with test cases, this method has been refined in order to improve the smoothing process of differences by series expansion, and also to include effects of stellar magnitudes. As a result, the catalogue differences are expressed formally by

$$\Delta_i = \sum_{s=0}^{l} A_s Y_s(\alpha_i, x(\delta_i), y(m_i)) + \varepsilon_i,\ i = 1, \ldots, N, \tag{2.20}$$

where l denotes the order of approximation, N refers to the number of stars considered, and the functions Y_s are products of Fourier terms, Legendre polynomials and Hermite polynomials with α, $x(\delta)$ and $y(m)$ as independent variables, respectively (Schwan 1977, Bien et al. 1978, Schwan 1983). These products form a complete, orthogonal and normalized system of functions for $0 \leq \alpha \leq 2\pi$, $-1 \leq x \leq +1$, $-\infty < y < +\infty$. It is for this reason that the catalogue declinations and magnitudes had to undergo an appropriate transformation. In turn, these functions are representative of smoothing the catalogue differences: The Fourier terms cope with the systematic differences of the right ascensions, the Legendre polynomials with the systematic differences of the declinations, and the Hermite polynomials with the systematic differences of the apparent magnitudes. Characteristic quantities of the catalogue differences are the coefficients A_s whose values are numerically determined by least squares methods. Since, in (2.19) and (2.20), the position differences in α and δ are treated independently of one another, one speaks also of the 'scalar harmonics method' as opposed to the 'vectorial harmonics method' referred to in Sect. 7.3.1.

A crucial point in the application of this analytical method is the distinction between the part of the systematic differences, described by the order l of the series expansion in (2.20), and the part of the random differences, expressed by ε_i. To avoid personal judgment of the data in the best possible way, a statistical test is employed to distinguish between the systematic and random parts (Brosche 1966). Once the order l of the optimum approximation of Δ_i is known, it is possible to estimate the standard deviation σ of the random part as may be inferred from the following facts: The order l and standard deviation σ are interrelated insofar as l is determined to the extent that the coefficients A_s are significantly different from zero for $s < l$.

The determination of the order l is outlined below. For details we refer to Brosche (1966) and Schwan (1977). If σ of the random part is known, the optimum order of the series expansion is statistically defined by the expected χ^2 distribution of $\sum(\varepsilon_i/\sigma)^2$. Usually, however, σ is unknown, and l is determined by trial and error proceeding along these lines: The residuals O − C, formed by the differences of Δ_i, which are the observed quantities (O), and the values of the series expansion, which are the computed quantities (C), are inspected for random distribution. Basically, this amounts to a variance test of the residuals O − C. A typical variance test is, e.g., the F-test or variance ratio test (van der Waerden 1965, Sachs 1972) combined with some choice of significance level. The principle of this test is as follows: Given are two populations of normal distributions with standard deviations, σ_1 and σ_2, and the test function $F = \sigma_1^2/\sigma_2^2$. The hypothesis $\sigma_1 = \sigma_2$ is tested by comparing the ratio σ_1^2/σ_2^2 with the (tabulated) theoretical value F_0 that depends on the prescribed significance level and the degrees of freedom, under which σ_1 and σ_2 had been derived. If σ_1^2/σ_2^2 is greater than F_0, the hypothesis is rejected with an error probability according to the significance level.

On applying this test to the determination of the order l of approximation, one assumes at first that all coefficients A_s in (2.20) vanish for $s \geq l$. Starting with $l = 0$, one estimates on each level of l the standard deviations of the random part, $\sigma_1 = \sigma_1(l)$ on the one hand, and $\sigma_2 = \sigma_2(l)$ on the other, thus preparing the usage of the F-test. The process continues, step by step, with $l = 1, 2, \ldots$ until for some value of l, e.g., $l_{\max}$, the hypothesis $\sigma_1(l_{\max}) = \sigma_2(l_{\max})$ is no longer rejected by the test.

One estimate, $\sigma_1(l)$, of the standard deviation of the random part of the Δ_i's, with one degree of freedom, is derived from the mean error of the unknown A_l, whose value was originally assumed to have vanished. Therefore, it is permissible to interpret the value $A_l \neq 0$, resulting from the least squares estimate, as an estimate of the mean error of A_l, i.e. $\sigma(A(l)$. In fact, the least squares estimate provides this error in the form

$$\sigma(A_l) = \sigma_1 \sqrt{\mathrm{cov}_{ll}}\,, \tag{2.21}$$

where σ_1 is the error of unit weight of the random part, and cov_{ll} is the l-th main diagonal element of the covariance matrix, which is equal to the inverse of the normal matrix of the least squares fit.

0629−418 06 31 11.998059±86 −41 54 26.94611±95 Q 1.416

Another estimate, σ_2, of the standard deviation of the random part, with $N-l$ degrees of freedom, is given by the post-fit mean error of the observation of unit weight, i.e.

$$\sigma_2 = \sqrt{\sum_{i=1}^{N} \varepsilon_i^2/(N-l)}\,. \tag{2.22}$$

Now the data are available for applying the F-test to σ_1 and σ_2. The rejection of the hypothesis of equal standard deviations indicates with high probability that the coefficient A_l is significantly different from zero. Thus, the inclusion of the term associated with Y_l is required, otherwise one rejects it. Afterwards one proceeds to the order $l+1$ of approximation, and so forth. The order of the approximations l is typically found to lie between $l \leq 5$ and $l = 20-25$ depending on the type of catalogue (absolute or differential) and the sky coverage of the catalogue under investigation. Small declination zones generally give rise to low values of l, while l tends to approach the upper limit for catalogues with full sky coverage.

2.4.2 System Improvement

At this stage we know the systematic differences, reduced to the FK4 zero points, between observation catalogues and the FK4 at the epoch of the observation catalogue, and for the equinox B1950.0. The improvement of the position and proper motion systems makes use of these differences by adhering to the following scheme: Let Cat_k, $k = 1, \ldots, K$ be absolute or quasi-absolute observation catalogues for which the systematic right ascension and declination differences have been determined according to (2.20) for those regions of the sky that are covered by the respective catalogues. Further, it is assumed that the catalogues span a sufficiently large range of epochs of 50 to 100 years to allow estimates of the proper motion system.

To state briefly the principle of system improvement, the observation catalogues are ordered by the catalogue mean epochs. Those catalogues of approximately equal mean epochs are grouped, and the mean epoch, t_g, of each group, g, of catalogues is formed. Next, the mean value of the systematic part of the catalogue differences $\mathrm{Cat}_k - \mathrm{FK4}$ is determined for the n_g catalogues of each group. These mean values, designated as $\Delta p(\mathrm{Cat}(g), \mathrm{FK4})$, form a function of time and are interpreted as the systematic errors of the positions, $\Delta p(\mathrm{FK4})$, and proper motions, $\Delta \mu_p(\mathrm{FK4})$ of the FK4 system. This situation suggests the fitting of a linear function of time to the mean values of the various groups. In these circumstances, each group provides a conditional equation which may be written as follows:

$$\Delta p(\mathrm{Cat}(g), \mathrm{FK4}) \quad = \quad \Delta p(\mathrm{FK4}) \;+\; (t_g - t_0)\, \Delta \mu_p(\mathrm{FK4}), \tag{2.23}$$

where t_0 denotes the mean epoch of the FK4 system of position; p stands for α and δ as functions of α or δ. In general, four types of systems of conditional equations of the form of (2.23) are available for the determination of systematic corrections Δp and $\Delta\mu_p$ to the FK4 positions and proper motions at epoch t_0. After allocation of weights to the conditional equations, each of the sets is solved yielding for the respective domain the systematic corrections to the FK4 in terms of α_δ, $(\mu_\alpha)_\delta$, δ_δ, $(\mu_\delta)_\delta$ and α_α, $(\mu_\alpha)_\alpha$, δ_α, $(\mu_\delta)_\alpha$. Finally, the corrections are tabulated and added to the corresponding positions and proper motions of the FK4.

Loosely speaking, this stage of system improvement may be regarded as the FK5 system at B1950.0, and this catalogue, FK5(B1950), would have reached its completion here as soon as the individual corrections to the positions and proper motions in the FK4 were added (see the beginning of Sect. 2.4). A number of conditions imposed on the FK5 by the IAU necessitated, however, the working procedure treated in Sect. 2.5.

Here follow the essential details of the actual construction of the systems of positions and proper motions of the FK5 in agreement with the principal steps of system improvement mentioned above. Contrary to the customary numerical methods employed for the FK4 and its predecessors, the FK5 system has been generated with the aid of the analytical method developed by Schwan (1983). Weights were assigned to the observation catalogues according to the deviation of the individual system of each observation catalogue from the mean system of all catalogues (Fricke et al. 1988).

At this stage we have left the level of coordinate differences (Δ_i) of stars in an individual catalogue but deal exclusively with the systematic parts of the catalogue differences of K catalogues. For each of these catalogues the left-hand side of (2.23) is furnished with the systematic part obtained by means of the analytical method for calculating systematic catalogue differences as described in Sect. 2.4.1. Denoting this systematic part by Δ_k, the systematic differences of the catalogues Cat_k may be written:

$$\Delta_k = \sum_{s=0}^{l_k} A_{sk} Y_{sk}\left(\alpha, x_k(\delta), y_k(m)\right), \quad k = 1, \ldots, K, \tag{2.24}$$

$$0 \le \alpha \le 2\pi, \quad -1 \le x_k \le +1, \quad -\infty < y_k < +\infty.$$

All differences are assumed to be related to the equator and equinox B1950.0; they are valid for the mean epoch of the catalogue Cat_k. Note that the series expansions Δ_k normally differ from catalogue to catalogue in the coefficients A_{sk} and the effective set of orthogonal functions Y_{sk}.

From now on we consider the systematic differences Δ_k as errors of the FK4 system and try to correct the system by averaging the systematic differences of all catalogues. The lines of thought of the analytical treatment described below follow the procedures developed by Schwan (1983):

Some preparations precede the analytical treatment of the system corrections. First of all, it must be ensured that the systematic differences Δ_k, valid for the mean epoch T_k of Cat$_k$, are related to the same equinox and equator, for which B1950.0 has been stipulated. To fulfill this condition, the Δ_k's were referred to the FK4 zero points of right ascension and declination. Despite the suspicion that the zero points may be subject to change, the reduction had to be performed at this stage in order to generate systematic differences free from possible zero point errors in right ascension and declination. At a later stage, the separately determined corrections to the FK4 equinox and equator (Fricke 1982) were added to the updated intermediate systems of positions and proper motions (see Sect. 2.5).

Other preparations deal with the averaging of the Δ_k's given in (2.24) that are not only catalogue- and epoch-dependent, but also depend on the variables x_k, y_k, which refer to different ranges of declination and apparent magnitude of the K catalogues. Let G_0 be the domain common to the catalogues Cat$_k$, as described by the respective ranges of declination and magnitude. To create the intervals in which the properties of orthogonality and normalization are ensured of the Legendre and Hermite polynomials composing Y_{sk}, suitable transformations have to be made so that $0 \leq \alpha \leq 2\pi$, $-1 \leq x_0(\delta) \leq +1$, $-\infty < y_0(m) < +\infty$. As soon as the various catalogue comparisons have been homogenized with regard to the independent variables of the common domain, we obtain the following formal representation of Δ_k:

$$\Delta_k \quad = \quad \sum_{s=0}^{l_k} A_{sk} Z_{sk}(\alpha, x_0, y_0) \,, \tag{2.25}$$

where Z_{sk} is the product of a polynomial in x_0, a polynomial in y_0 and Fourier terms. This expression is the result of the substitution of linear functions of $\sin\delta$ and m into Y_{sk}, which itself is the normalized product of Legendre polynomials, Hermite polynomials and Fourier terms.

The systematic difference Δ_k is typical of Cat$_k$ with mean epoch T_k. The Δ_k's form the data for the correction of the FK4 systems of positions and proper motions. For this purpose a straight line is fitted to the Δ_k's taking account of the different mean epochs of the Cat$_k$'s. The functional dependence, suitable for smoothing the systematic differences, may be expressed simply as a linear function of time, i.e.,

$$\Delta_k \quad = \quad A + (T_k - T_0)\, B + \varepsilon_k \;, \; k = 1, \ldots, K \,. \tag{2.26}$$

While T_k is the mean epoch of Cat$_k$, T_0 refers to the mean epoch of the system S defined by the K catalogues Cat$_k$; $\varepsilon_k = \varepsilon_k(\alpha, x_0, y_0)$ denotes the deviation of Δ_k from the model. On the left-hand side of (2.26) stands the analytical representation of the systematic differences between Cat$_k$ and FK4 in the region G_0 valid for the epoch T_k. A possible approach to the estimation of the unknown expressions, A and B, is offered by their expansion in series of orthogonal functions Y_s, which are products of Legendre polynomials, Hermite polynomials and Fourier terms by analogy to the representation of catalogue differences, Δ_i, in (2.20); i.e.,

$$A(\alpha, x_0, y_0) = \sum_{s=1}^{l_b} b_s Y_s(\alpha, x_0, y_0) , \tag{2.27}$$

$$B(\alpha, x_0, y_0) = \sum_{s=1}^{l_c} c_s Y_s(\alpha, x_0, y_0) .$$

Herein l_b and l_c indicate the number of functions Y_s used for the analytical representation of A and B, respectively. The coefficients b_s and c_s are estimated by weighted least squares adjustment starting from the condition

$$W = \sum_{k=1}^{K} w_k \iiint \left[\varepsilon_k^2(\alpha, x_0, y_0)\varrho(y_0)\right] \mathrm{d}\alpha\, \mathrm{d}x_0\, \mathrm{d}y_0 = \text{minimum} ;$$

w_k denotes the individual catalogue weights and $\varrho(y_0)$ is the weighting function of the Hermite polynomials.

The least squares process applied to (2.26) results in averaging of the coefficients A_{sk} $(k = 1, \ldots, K)$, over the region G_0. Considering (2.27), this average can be expressed as

$$\Delta(\alpha, \delta, m, T) = \sum_{s=1}^{l_b} b_s Y_s + (T - T_0) \sum_{s=1}^{l_c} c_s Y_s , \tag{2.28}$$

where the left-hand side signifies the correction to the FK4 that yields the improved system $S = \mathrm{FK4} + \Delta$ at the mean epoch T_0, which is the weighted mean of the catalogue epochs. On the right-hand side of (2.28) the first and second sums represent the corrections to the position and the proper motion systems, respectively.

2.5 Transition to the Standard Epoch J2000.0

Starting from the FK4 on the equinox and epoch B1950.0, briefly denoted FK4(B1950), and after having carried out the tasks 1) to 8) described in Sect. 2.4, the way is paved for the construction of the FK5. To comply with resolutions of the International Astronomical Union (IAU 1977) additional conditions were imposed on the new fundamental catalogue FK5. These resolutions required, inter alia, the introduction of the adopted IAU (1976) System of Astronomical Constants on 1984 January 1, the introduction of J2000.0 as the new standard epoch, and the elimination of elliptic aberration. This posed problems concerning the transition from B1950.0 to J2000.0, which, in the framework of the FK5 construction, were solved according to a two-step procedure given by Aoki et al. (1983) using 1984 January 1 as a turning point. It was generally known that the new system of astronomical constants and the equinox corrections (offset and drift) have repercussions on the formulation of the functional relationship between UT1 and mean sidereal time. For this purpose Aoki et al. (1982) reexamined the definition of UT1, which was modified so that on 1984 January 1 no discontinuity of UT1 occurred either in value or rate. Alternate procedures for the transition from B1950.0 to J2000.0 are mentioned at the end of this Section.

In the two-step transition from B1950.0 to J2000.0 via 1984 January 1, the change of the general precession in longitude and the elimination of the equinox motion deserve special attention with regard to the calculation of positions and, especially, proper motions for the equinoxes and epochs concerned. The effects of the corrections to precession and equinox are quantified under the tasks 5), 6) and 7) in Sect. 2.4.

Generally speaking, after the elimination of the effects of elliptic aberration (E-terms), step 1 transforms the FK4(B1950) to FK4 on the mean equinox and epoch of 1984 January 1 using the values of general precession related to Newcomb's results (Newcomb 1898a). At the end of step 1 the Julian century is introduced as unit of time, replacing the tropical century, and the correction to the equinox is applied to the right ascensions of the stars. Further, the stellar proper motions are corrected as a consequence of the improved value of precession and the detected equinox motion, and, finally, the FK4 systematic corrections are added to the instantaneous positions and proper motions. Step 2 then transforms the resulting positions and proper motions to the mean equinox and epoch J2000.0 using the precessional quantities adopted in the IAU (1976) System of Astronomical Constants. The end product is known as the Fifth Fundamental Catalogue, FK5(J2000), or simply FK5.

In performing steps 1 and 2, it is emphasized that the transformation from one equinox to another requires the precession of the proper motion components along with that of the position components. Also, in transforming from one epoch to another, the effects of the star's motion on the components of the mean position and proper motion need to be taken into account. This is achieved by the inclusion of a foreshortening term or, more generally, by basing the transformation on the star's space motion. Full reports on the transformation of positions and proper motions of stars from the equinox and epoch B1950.0 to the equinox and epoch J2000.0 with due account of the resolutions adopted by the IAU in 1976 (IAU 1977) are found in, for example, Standish (1982b), Aoki et al. (1983), Lederle & Schwan (1984) and Smith et al. (1989). Controversial opinions have been put forward by the various authors as discussed by Murray (1989). Despite the differences no significant errors are committed as far as the FK5 range of accuracy is concerned.

2.6 Organization of the FK5

Up to this point we dealt with the principles of the FK5 construction, and there was no need to distinguish between the classical 1535 fundamental stars of the FK5 carried over from the FK4, and the 3117 new fundamental stars added to the classical stars for densification of the catalogue. For technical reasons, related to the very different observation histories of the two categories of stars, a distinction was suggested to such an extent that the classical stars form Part I of the Fifth Fundamental Catalogue (FK5) known as 'The Basic Fundamental Stars' (Fricke et al. 1988), while the supplementary stars form Part II, known as 'The FK5 Extension – New Fundamental Stars' (Fricke et al. 1991). Part I is also referred to as the 'Basic FK5' and Part II as the 'FK5 Extension'. Both parts are representatives of the FK5 reference frame.

The great attention paid to the stars of the Basic FK5 during the past decades is reflected in the high frequency of observations, resulting in positions and proper motions of much better accuracies than those of the FK5 Extension. In particular, the faint stars of the Extension having magnitudes between 6.4 and 9.2 suffer from poor observation histories compared with stars of the Basic FK5. A further complication was introduced by the presence of a magnitude equation, which becomes effective when making the attempt to tie faint stars to the system of brighter ones. As auxiliary measures sufficiently large base systems had to be constructed first, taking advantage of faint star catalogues observed by means of screens or moving wire micrometers as outlined in Sect. 2.4, item 8).

For comparison, Table 2.1 shows mean epochs and average precisions of positions and proper motions referring to the Basic FK5 and the FK5 Extension. Despite the inhomogeneities of the FK5 Extension with regard to distribution of stars and their observation histories (Corbin & Schwan 1991), the procedure proved successful in tying the stars of the Extension in a first

Table 2.1. Average precisions of the Basic FK5 and the FK5 Extension

	Mean epoch		$\sigma_\alpha \cos\delta$	$\sigma_{\mu_\alpha} \cos\delta$	σ_δ	σ_{μ_δ}
	α	δ	[arcsec]	[arcsec/cy]	[arcsec]	[arcsec/cy]
Basic FK5						
$-30° < \delta \leq +90°$	1953	1943	0.014	0.056	0.019	0.064
$-90° \leq \delta \leq -30°$	1958	1947	0.024	0.101	0.032	0.107
FK5 Extension						
$-90° \leq \delta \leq +90°$	1946	1942	0.051	0.243	0.059	0.267

0716+714   07 21 53.448459±58   +71 20 36.36339±28   L   ...

step to the FK4, and subsequently applying the systematic differences FK5 – FK4 determined with the aid of the stars of the Basic FK5. The aim was to make both sets of stars, the Basic FK5 comprising 1535 stars and the FK5 Extension comprising 3117 objects, refer to the same system. In view of the different methods employed in the construction of the systems of the Basic FK5 and the FK5 Extension, one cannot exclude possible differences between these two systems. Apart from a few exceptions, however, no systematic differences could be identified (Schwan 1993).

0722+145	07 25 16.807752±23	+14 25 13.74684±46	?	...

3. Contributions of Space Astrometry to Fundamental Catalogues

3.1 Astrometric Space Missions

At the close of the 20th century, considerable improvement of astrometric precision was obtained by transferring the telescope site into Earth orbit and by employing space techniques for the observation of celestial objects. Instead of observing from the ground, space astrometry is performed from an observing platform beyond the perturbing atmosphere resulting in minimized refraction, better astronomical 'seeing' and, ultimately, in images with well defined diffraction patterns. The price of going into space is the loss of the stable telescope site provided by the motion of the Earth in space, which is very complex but minutely recorded on the ground. In contrast, the spacecraft carrying the instruments is subject to numerous perturbations, sometimes affecting the spatial orientation in unpredictable ways. At first glance, therefore, highly precise positions of individual objects are not expected. Practically, however, it is found that extremely precise angular distances between objects are indeed determinable in space. Subsequently, these differential observations are related to a conventional celestial reference frame of milliarcsecond precision to yield individual object positions of the same order of magnitude (Chap. 7).

To date, two space missions have delivered considerable astrometric results: The Hubble Space Telescope (HST) launched by the National Aeronautics and Space Administration (NASA) in 1990 carrying instruments for both astrophysical and astrometric research, and the Hipparcos satellite launched by the European Space Agency (ESA) in 1989 with purely astrometric mission objectives. Detailed views of the HST project are given by Longair (1979) and Hall (1982). Since the Hipparcos project contributes extensively to astrometric catalogues and reference frames, some of its specific aspects are discussed in the following sections.

3.2 The Astrometry Satellite Hipparcos

The Hipparcos satellite, designed and operated by ESA, is a mission fully dedicated to space astrometry (Perryman et al. 1992; Kovalevsky 1995b; ESA

`0723−008    07 25 50.639953±19   −00 54 56.54438±34    L  0.127`

1997, Vol. 1). It was launched as the lower passenger in the piggy-back mode by an Ariane 4 rocket on 8 August 1989. Due to failure of the apogee motor the satellite did not reach the specified geosynchronous orbit but stayed in the elliptic transfer orbit of about 500 km perigee and 36 500 km apogee height. Nevertheless, after a somewhat prolonged commissioning phase the payload instruments acquired high-quality scientific data between November 1989 and March 1993 with the exception of a few gaps. Ultimately, the successful data acquisition covered a total of 37 months. The project designation 'Hipparcos' is an acronym standing for HIgh Precision PARallax COllecting Satellite pointing at one of the project's main goals of determining stellar parallaxes. It also honours the Greek astronomer Hipparchus for his critical analysis of star positions that led him to the discovery of the Earth's precession.

Immediate advantages of such a space mission are the all-sky visibility by one single instrument, its circumvention of the atmospheric refraction problem, the freedom from gravitational flexure and, to a large extent, the absence of unmodelled thermal fluctuations. Two major astrometric catalogues have been produced by the Hipparcos mission: The Hipparcos Catalogue comprising 118 218 stars, and the Tycho Catalogue containing 1 058 332 stars including 6301 stars of the Hipparcos Catalogue. The primary objective of the mission was the development of the Hipparcos Catalogue which provides positions, annual proper motions and absolute trigonometric parallaxes of the stars free from regional distortions and with errors at the level of 1 milliarcsec (mas). These astrometric results are compiled in the Hipparcos Catalogue (ESA 1997) along with ancillary stellar data of astrophysical significance. This seventeen-volume document also presents a comprehensive treatment of the spacecraft design, operation and data analysis.

In contrast to the lower-accuracy Tycho Catalogue, the positional precisions of the Hipparcos Catalogue nearly match those of the extragalactic objects of the International Celestial Reference Frame (ICRF) treated in Chap. 6. The Hipparcos star positions, therefore, provide ideal conditions for a precise connection of the Hipparcos Catalogue to the ICRF. Further, the similarity of precisions makes it possible to densify the fundamental catalogue of extragalactic radio sources by merging it with an equivalent optical catalogue, thus extending the quasi-inertial radio frame to the optical domain. As a result we obtain an optical reference frame that profits from the properties of the radio reference frame, but is accessible to optical astrometry and sufficiently dense, with 2 to 3 stars per square degree on the average. How the two frames are connected will be shown in Chap. 7. Hence, from the viewpoint of fundamental astrometry the Hipparcos catalogue plays a key role in expanding the ICRF to visible wavelengths, and for this reason the Hipparcos catalogue construction is studied below in some detail.

0723−008 07 26 11.735177±97 +79 11 31.01624±27 L 0.127

3.2.1 Overview of the Instrument Payload

In the compendium 'The Hipparcos Mission', the satellite and its payload are described in great detail (ESA 1989, Vol. I, p. 57 ff.). We confine the discussion here to the main features of the telescope optics and the transmission of light to gain familiarity with the observing principle.

The payload is built around an all-reflective Schmidt telescope having an entrance pupil of 290 mm diameter and a focal length of 1400 mm. Three mirrors form the telescope: the beam-combining mirror, the flat-folding mirror and the spherical mirror. Figure 3.1 shows the configuration of the telescope instrumentation. One of the main functions of the beam-combiner is the mapping, one above the other, of the two fields of view separated in the sky by the basic angle (see Sect. 3.3). In addition, the beam-combining mirror performs corrections of the aberrations of the spherical mirror. The flat folding mirror folds the optical beam to provide a more compact configuration, and the spherical mirror reflects the beams to the modulating grid, which is located at the telescope's focal surface. The modulating grid or main grid is imaged onto the photo cathode of the image dissector tube by means of a set of folding mirrors and relay lenses. The instantaneous field of view of the image dissector tube is circular with a diameter of 38 arcsec, and can be directed to any point of the grid by varying the currents applied to the deflection coils. At the end of this main detection chain, a photomultiplier receives the photons emitted from a star crossing the grid and being tracked by the instantaneous field of view of the image dissector tube.

There is a second detection chain that is part of the payload. It includes the star mappers, whose primary function is the procurement of data allowing the determination of the telescope orientation or, in technical terms, the

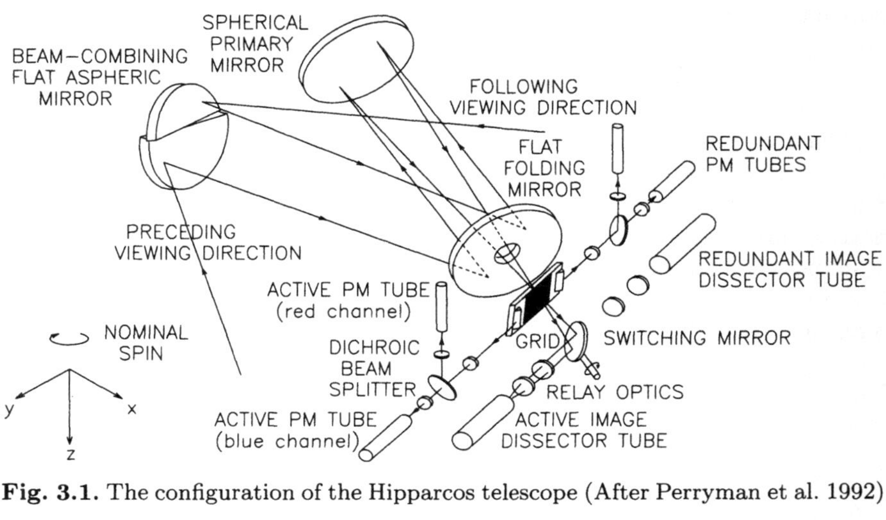

Fig. 3.1. The configuration of the Hipparcos telescope (After Perryman et al. 1992)

0733−174 07 35 45.812508±61 −17 35 48.50131±138 ? ...

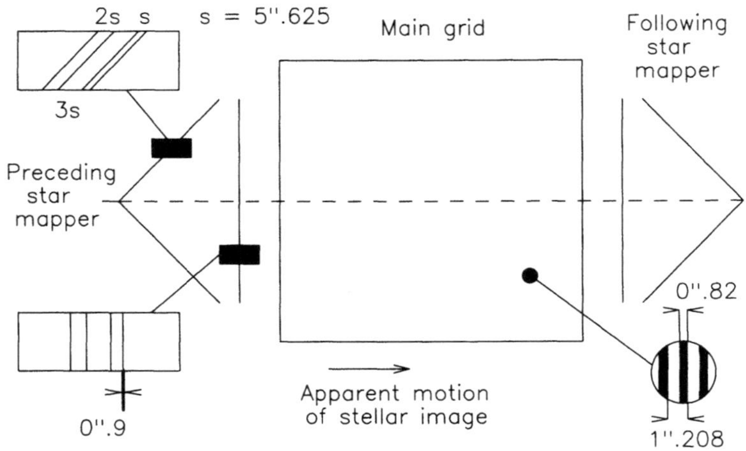

Fig. 3.2. The structure of the modulating grid and of the star mapper. The quantity s denotes the smallest distance between two successive slits

reconstitution of the triaxial satellite attitude in real time on board, as well as on the ground in the course of the analysis of the gathered data. The star mapper grids are located on either side of the modulating grid (Fig. 3.2). Two photomultipliers measure the light transmitted by the star mapper grid in one of two different spectral bands, enabling in this way two-colour photometric measurements from the Tycho data.

3.2.2 Attitude Control

A 'scanning law' has been devised that permits scanning the whole sky and maximizing the number of observations of a star. It takes into account the observational constraints imposed by the stray light of the Sun and the sensitivity of parallax measurements as a function of the inclination of the scanning circle on the ecliptic.

The rotation of the satellite dictated by the nominal scanning law is subject to many perturbing torques caused by, e.g., the radiation pressure of the Sun and Earth, variations of the Earth's gravity gradient, terrestrial magnetism and atmospheric drag. Any departure from the path of the nominal scanning law is recorded by the on-board attitude determination equipment, based on the star mapper readings. Whenever the actual and nominal scanning directions differ by more than 10 arcmin, the attitude control system reacts by activating gas jets to counteract the motion straying from the specified path.

3.3 Observing Principle

Because fundamental astrometry was the driving force of the Hipparcos mission, the instrumental design concentrated on the precise measurement of large angles in the sky. Wide-angle measurements are a prerequisite of fundamental or global astrometry in order to relate distant parts of the celestial sphere in a homogeneous way. Two principal methods have been employed for this purpose in the past. The first measures large angles by an exactly known rotation thus, in practical execution, shifting the problem to the measurement of time which is presently one of the most precise techniques of metrology. An example is the measurement of the right ascension of celestial bodies by means of a transit instrument or meridian circle by taking advantage of the rotation of the Earth, which is nowadays monitored with high precision by VLBI, GPS, and laser ranging techniques. Indeed, the measure of the Earth's rotation is the sidereal time, and the universal time, UT1, is derived from sidereal time accurate to 0.2 mas in angular units. Note that sidereal time, by definition, measures the rotation of the Earth with respect to its instantaneous rotation axis. Radio interferometry also takes advantage of precisely the same method for measuring large angles (see Chap. 4). The second principal method for large-angle measurements compares the angles with a calibrated angular standard that, for instance, is represented by a divided circle. Declinations are obtained in that manner by meridian circles. It is also typical of astrolabes to rely on built-in instrumental angular standards allowing the measurement of declinations between $\varphi + Z$ and $\varphi - Z$, where φ and Z denote the geographical latitude and zenith distance, respectively. In the case of the Danjon prism astrolabe (Danjon 1960) Z is equal to 30°, corresponding to the calibrated angular standard of a prism with the vertical angle $2\,Z$, and permitting measurements of angular distances between stars separated by angles less than or equal to $2\,Z$. Observations at other zenith distances are also possible, e.g., by means of the photoelectric astrolabe (Billaud 1986).

In order to measure large angles the Hipparcos telescope takes advantage of both the method of angular standards and the method of rotation (Fig. 3.3).

The angular standard is realized by the angle $\gamma/2$, where $\gamma = 58°$ is the nominal angle of separation of the two superimposed fields in the sky (see Fig. 3.4), and is also known as basic angle. Its value results from a compromise between scientific requirements and technical limitations:

- From the point of view of scientific applications the basic angle should be of the order of 50° to 100° in order to, first, improve the rigidity of the system of positions and proper motions by linking widely separated regions of the sky, and second, to obtain absolute parallaxes by directly comparing very different parallax factors, which are due to the varying angles between the Sun and the stars during any one scan lasting only a fraction of a day.

0738+313 07 41 10.703308±22 +31 12 00.22862±29 S 0.630

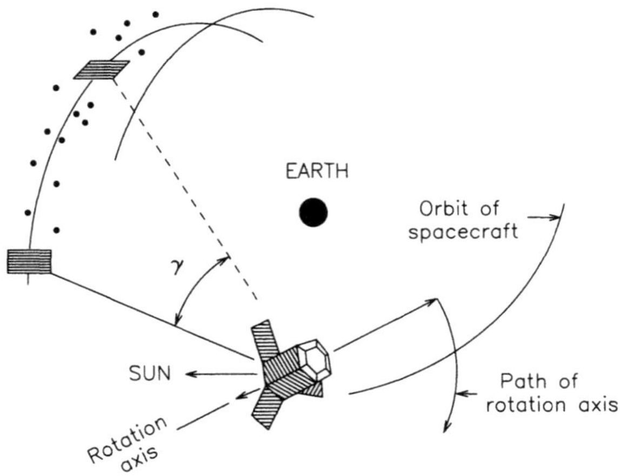

Fig. 3.3. Hipparcos measurement of large angles between stars with the aid of tilted halves of the mirror subtending the angle $\gamma/2$, and by the rotation of the telescope about the indicated axis

To avoid unwanted correlations of measurements on successive scans the basic angle should not be an integer divisor of 360°.

- On the technical side, a small basic angle, though desirable from the viewpoint of spacecraft construction, is ruled out because it would increase the tolerable length of the telescope, and the limit of a larger angle is dictated by the Schmidt correcting surface at the level of the beam-combining mirror.

During the mission the basic angle, γ, is calibrated to provide its instantaneous value for data reduction. The angle is formed by the beam-combining

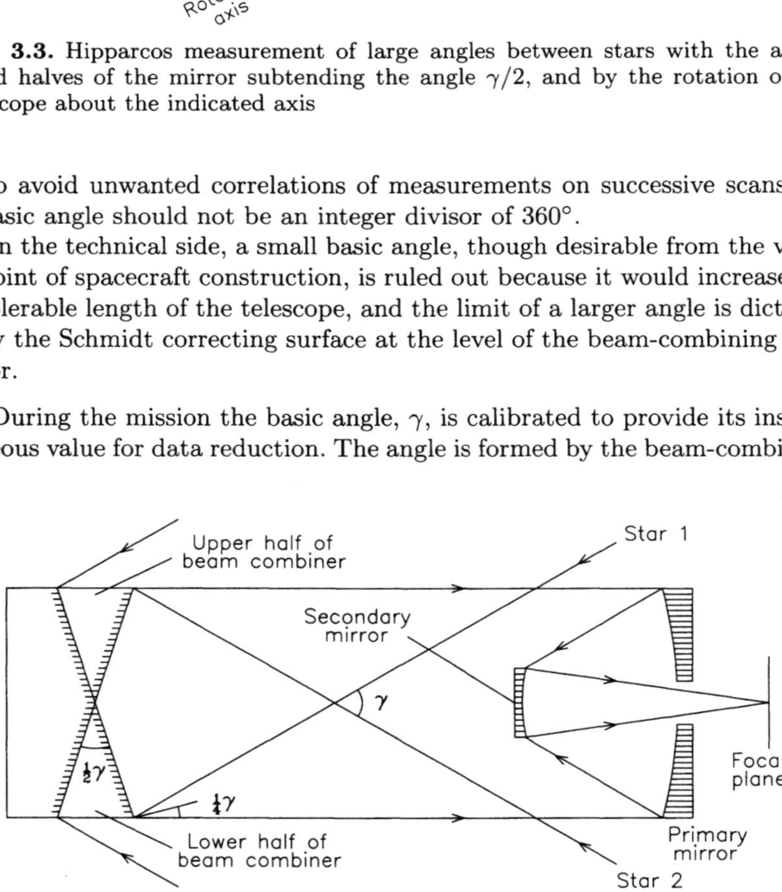

Fig. 3.4. Schematic representation of the light paths originating from two regions of the sky separated by the angle γ and reflected into the telescope optics by the beam-combining mirror

0743+259 07 46 25.874166±33 +25 49 02.13488±66 ? ...

mirror having two halves glued together in such a way that the normals of the surfaces subtend the angle $\gamma/2$. Both halves reflect the light to a common focal plane, thus combining the images of stars in two different fields with an angular separation of γ, and allowing the measurement of relative positions in the focal plane. As the telescope rotates about an axis perpendicular to the plane formed by the directions to the centres of the two stellar fields, it scans a circle in the sky. Because of this rotation about an axis, the orientation of which is known from spacecraft attitude determination, and by analogy to the meridian circle method, large angles can also be measured along each scan circle between stars that are not simultaneously visible in the focal plane. Finally, to cover the whole sky the telescope rotation axis is steadily reoriented by the adopted program of attitude control known as the scanning law.

3.4 Organization of the Data Reduction

The preceding summary of the instrument payload gives the clue that the Hipparcos telescope is not a customary imaging instrument but measures the positions of celestial objects in its instantaneous field of view. Indeed, the telescope cannot 'see' an object but only 'sense' its presence after moving the instantaneous field of view to the object's approximate position. An inventory, therefore, is required comprising the targets with their approximate coordinates enabling the telescope to point to the desired directions. It was the chief objective of the Hipparcos Input Catalogue Consortium (INCA) to provide this inventory known as the Hipparcos Input Catalogue (ESA 1992; Jahreiss et al. 1992).

The Hipparcos data reduction has been performed along two independent processing chains designed by the consortia NDAC (Northern Data Analysis Consortium) and FAST (Fundamental Astrometry by Space Techniques), respectively. An all-embracing treatment of the Hipparcos data reduction is documented in the Hipparcos catalogue (ESA 1997), and by Lindegren et al. (1992) for NDAC and Kovalevsky et al. (1992) for FAST. We, therefore, introduce here only those key functions of the Hipparcos data reduction that are essential for a general insight into the derivation of the quasi-absolute positions and proper motions, and absolute parallaxes. The starting point, which suggests itself for this insight, is marked by the original optical signals from the stars:

From any star (i) the photon counts are registered at the time instants t_k in accordance with the scanning law of the sky. These photon counts, P_{ik}, contain information on the position and velocity vectors of the star, $\boldsymbol{s}_i$ and $\dot{\boldsymbol{s}}_i$, on the instantaneous attitude of the telescope, A_k. Auxiliary parameters, H_k, describe the state of the instrument as a function of time. Thus, in general terms, the photon counts are expressed as

$$P_{ik} \quad = \quad F\left(\boldsymbol{s}_i, \dot{\boldsymbol{s}}_i, t_0, A_k, H_k\right) . \tag{3.1}$$

Given the photon counts, the ultimate goal of the data reduction is the estimation of the position and velocity vectors of the stars at some selected time t_0, also known as the astrometric parameters at epoch t_0. In parallel, those angles are estimated that describe the attitude of the telescope, as well as those parameters which allow supervising the state of the on-board instruments under space conditions.

Considering that the Hipparcos data acquisition covers approximately 37 months and that the sampling frequency was 1200 s^{-1}, about 10^{11} functional relations of the form of (3.1) have accumulated. Because of this immense data yield the idea of a single direct parameter estimation fell outside the practicable software and hardware resources at the time of the mission design around 1980. Therefore, the task had to be segmented into three principal steps which are known as 'determination of the grid coordinates of a star from photon counts', 'determination of the star abscissae on reference great-circles from grid coordinates' and 'determination of the astrometric parameters from the abscissae'. Note that a reference great-circle is the fundamental plane of an intermediate spherical coordinate frame. The third step deals with global astrometry and is also known as the 'sphere solution'. Data compression is common to all three tasks in the sense that the respective input data streams are reduced during the passage through each of the segments.

The FAST data reduction has adopted the basic principles of the NDAC data reduction method (Lindegren 1991) as far as the aforementioned segmentation is concerned. Essentially, the reduction comprises the following subtasks: 1) determination of the spatial orientation of the instrument, 2) extraction of the positional information of stars from photon counts, 3) abscissa determination on reference great-circles, 4) determination of astrometric parameters in a differential mode and 5) connection of the new stellar frame to a conventional celestial reference frame.

One of the authors was a member of the FAST consortium, and is therefore more intimately familiar with this consortium's approach. Hence, the treatment given below reflects primarily the FAST analysis. It concentrates on those facets of the data reduction that are prerequisite to follow the evolution from photon counts to star positions.

3.5 From Photons to Grid Coordinates

Hipparcos observes the sky by a rotating telescope with aperture $D = 290$ mm and focal length $F = 1400$ mm that collects the photons originating from two fields of the sky separated by the angle γ. A flat mirror divided into two halves subtending the angle $\gamma/2$ combines the two light beams and reflects them onto the focal plane. There, the image of the two fields is obtained on a quadratic grid containing 2688 parallel and equidistant slits with a spatial grid periodicity of 8.2 μm corresponding to a slit width of $s = 1.208$ arcsec on the sky for the above focal length (Fig. 3.1). Thus, the angular size of the grid is a square field of $0^\circ\!.9 \times 0^\circ\!.9$. Only 39 % of each slit is transparent to light. This is a concession to the detectability of double and multiple stars.

Since the instrument rotates about an axis parallel to the slits with the nominal period of 128 min there are 140 slits moving across the star images per second; consequently their intensities are modulated with the fundamental frequency of $\nu = 140$ Hz. Given the grid periodicity of 8.2 μm the fundamental frequency of the grid becomes $1/(8.2\ \mu\text{m}) = 1.2 \times 10^5\ \text{m}^{-1}$. Comparison of this value with the maximum spatial frequency $D/(F\lambda_{\text{min}}) = 5.2 \times 10^5\ \text{m}^{-1}$ ($\lambda_{\text{min}} = 400$ nm) of the diffraction image of the telescope gives evidence that the Fourier representation of the intensity modulation behind the grid is made up of at most four harmonics. Of these only the fundamental and first harmonics are of significant importance because of the designed ratio of the dark and transparent portions of the slit. Therefore, the modulation may be seen as a periodic function of the position of the image along its path perpendicular to the grid slits, and the signal intensity corresponding to the photon counts of a single star is modelled by a Fourier expansion consisting of two harmonics:

$$I_k = I_b + I_s + I_s\left[M_1 \cos g(t_k) + M_2 \cos(2g(t_k) + v)\right]. \qquad (3.2)$$

The symbols have the meanings listed below:

- I_k is the photon count at the instant t_k. Recall that the sampling period is 1/1200 s and that an elementary observation frame consists of 2560 samples, equivalent to 2.133 s during which the selected stars are scanned on the grid. Accordingly, k runs from 1 to 2560 in an observation frame whose central instant, the frame mid-time, is taken as the origin $t = 0$ of the frame time. In statistical terms I_k may be considered as an expectation value $E(N_k)$ for the following reason: The photons collected behind the grid constitute a random signal of extremely rare occurrence compared with the large number of samples during one frame. In other words, we have to deal with rare events, a fact which suggests the hypothesis of a Poisson distribution for modelling the sequence of photon counts. The probability that the number of counts, i.e. the number of occurrences (X) of the event, is exactly N_k in the k-th sample is given by the probability function of the Poisson distribution

$$P(X = N_k) = \frac{\mu^{N_k}}{N_k!}\mathrm{e}^{-\mu}$$

  with $\mu = E(N_k)$. This distribution function is employed for estimating the unknown parameters in (3.2).
- I_b and I_s are the intensities of the background and the averaged intensity of the observed stars in counts per sample, respectively; both quantities are not modelled by the grid but add to the total acquisition of photons.

- In the case of the single star model M_1, M_2 and v are instrumental constants which, however, vary slightly as a function of time, position in the field of view, and star colour. The instantaneous values of these optical transfer function parameters are derived from instrument calibration.
- $g(t_k)$ is the grid modulation phase or simply modulation phase of the image in the k-th sample.

We will show that the modulation phase contains the positional information of the image on the grid and provides the key to the determination of the grid coordinates with reference to a local zero point on the grid. The problem of obtaining the required positional information will be solved by estimating the modulation phase at frame mid-time, $g(0)$, for each star in a frame.

While a star traverses the grid the modulation phase increases with time as a function of the instrument spin rate. This phase may be interpreted as an image coordinate measured perpendicular to the slits and expressed as

$$g(t) = 2\pi n_0 + d. \tag{3.3}$$

Here, n_0 is an integer lying between 1 and 2688 according to the number of slits on the grid, and d lies in the range $[-\pi, +\pi]$. The model of (3.2), being invariant to n_0, is therefore confined to estimating only the fractional part, d, of the total phase, while some a priori knowledge of the star position, which is expected to be accurate to better than $s/2$, supplies the integer part. So, at the early stage of data reduction, the analysis profits from the accuracy of the Hipparcos Input Catalogue (Sect. 3.4).

Within a frame the modulation phase may be written

$$g(t_k) = g(0) + p_k, \tag{3.4}$$

with p_k denoting the instrumental phase due to the motion of the image from frame mid-time ($t = 0$) to the time t_k of the k-th sample, $-1280 \le k \le +1280$. Disregarding disturbing effects the instrumental phase is completely defined by the fundamental frequency ν of the grid, and is given by

$$p_k = 2\pi\nu t_k, \quad \nu = \omega/s\,,$$

where ω is the angular velocity in arcseconds per second of the instrument rotating about an axis parallel to the slits. In practice, the computation of p_k takes account of deviations of the grid frequency caused by irregularities in the actual scanning speed ω and the grid period s.

Substituting (3.4) into (3.2) results in an expression for the photon counts which is known as the ‘three parameter model’ valid for single stars:

$$\begin{aligned} E(N_k) \equiv I_k &= I_b + I_s + I_s\,[M_1\cos(g(0) + p_k) \\ &\quad + M_2\cos(2g(0) + 2p_k + v)]\,. \end{aligned} \tag{3.5}$$

The unknowns are I_b, I_s and $g(0)$ that are estimated from a second-order Fourier analysis. With the grid phase $g(0)$ known, the grid coordinate of the image at mid-time of the frame becomes $G = g(0)/2\pi$.

Due to superimposing of the two fields of observation there are, on average, five programme stars resident on the grid. They share the 2560 samples collected during one frame period. To give an idea of the extent of data compression during this step, some 500 samples are exploited for the determination of the grid coordinate per frame and star.

Applying the angle-sum relations of trigonometric functions to (3.5) the signal converts into

$$E(N_k) \equiv I_k = b_1 + b_2 \cos p_k + b_3 \sin p_k + b_4 \cos 2p_k + b_5 \sin 2p_k \qquad (3.6)$$

with b_1 to b_5 as unknowns. In routine operations the estimation is based on this more general expression known as the 'five-parameter model'. The generalization is justified because the 'three parameter model' is confined to actual single stars while, in reality, many objects are double or multiple stars, or have other complex structures producing signals that are superpositions of functions like (3.5), and can be combined to an expression of the form of (3.6). In contrast to single stars, however, the optical transfer function parameters, M_1 and M_2, are more complicated in the generalized model. This means that it is no longer possible to consider these parameters as quantities known from calibrations, a fact that explains the two additional unknowns.

For single stars one finds the relationship between the unknowns of the 'five-parameter model' and the 'three parameter model' simply from comparing (3.5) with (3.6) yielding

$$\begin{aligned} I_b + I_s &= b_1 \\ I_s M_1 &= \sqrt{b_2^2 + b_3^2} \\ g(0) &= \arctan\left(-b_3/b_2\right) \mod 2\pi\,, \end{aligned}$$

where $g(0)$ is unambiguously determined apart from the 2π multiplicity. By comparing (3.5) and (3.6) we get for checking purposes

$$\begin{aligned} I_s M_2 &= \sqrt{b_4^2 + b_5^2}, \\ g^*(0) &= \frac{1}{2}\left[\arctan\left(-b_5/b_4\right) - v\right] \mod \pi\,. \end{aligned}$$

For a single star one expects $g^*(0) - \frac{1}{2}v = g(0)$ within the uncertainty of the estimate. Violations of this equality are an indication that the star may have complex structure, suggesting giving preference to the application of the 'five-parameter model'.

A full exposition of the principles of estimation of the unknowns in the case of the 'five-parameter solution' is given in ESA (1989) Vol. III, pp. 33–49 and ESA (1997), Vol. 3.

0805+410 08 08 56.652038±23 +40 52 44.88889±27 Q 1.420

3.6 Reduction to Reference Great Circles

The scanning algorithm guides the rotating telescope smoothly across the whole sky. During one rotation of about 2 hours and 8 minutes' duration, the scanned area of the sky is approximated by an instantaneous great circle which is only slightly distorted by the rate of variation of the scanning direction. Grid coordinates of stars are derived from batches of observation frames of 2.13 s duration of photon counts collected along a great circle. The grid coordinates are defined with respect to the modulating grid which is related to a rotating local coordinate frame of the instrument as shown in Fig. 3.5. The apparent direction to a star in this rotating instrument coordinate frame is expressed by the so-called field angles or field coordinates. Because of the instrument rotation there is, at first, a need to transform the grid coordinates into abscissae of a fixed coordinate frame, which accounts for the orientation of the satellite in space. This is the main objective of the great-circle reduction that combines the observations on the grid, obtained from the objects during a time interval of a few hours, into a set of one-dimensional coordinates, known as abscissae, defined along a designated reference great circle. These abscissae are the main input to the subsequent sphere solution, which derives the astrometric parameters of the stars.

Apart from a few high-proper-motion stars, it can be assumed that the star coordinates remain constant during some 5 successive revolutions of the telescope corresponding to a time interval of about 10 hours. It is, therefore, possible to combine the measurements during this limited time interval into one reference great circle, and to derive for each star a single angular coordinate, known as the star abscissa on a reference great circle (RGC). The RGC is chosen roughly in the middle of the band on the celestial sphere scanned by the telescope during the revolutions that belong to this reference great

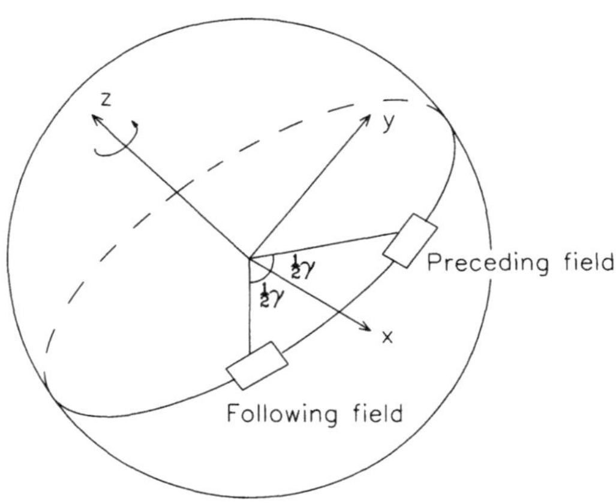

Fig. 3.5. Definition of the rotating instrument coordinate frame (x,y,z), in which x is directed along the optical axis of the telescope

0812+367 08 15 25.944824±31 +36 35 15.14830±46 Q 1.025

circle, and the RGC is the fundamental plane of an intermediate celestial reference frame. In this plane an arbitrary origin is chosen from which the abscissae are reckoned. The ecliptic longitude of the ascending node of the RGC and its inclination with respect to the plane of the ecliptic define the orientation of the RGC in space. Figure 3.6 along with Sect. 3.6.1 illustrate the projection of a star position from an instantaneous great circle (IGC) to the corresponding reference great circle.

3.6.1 The Model of Abscissa Estimation

The great-circle reduction is treated as a parameter adjustment process with grid coordinates as the observations. In performing this task, the abscissae are estimated from the object coordinates on the main grid by using the satellite attitude determined for each observation frame from the star mapper data. Only the measurements made on the main grid are capable of providing positional precision at the level of milliarcseconds. It is the purpose of the great-circle reduction to establish, at the mid-time of the RGC duration, the relationship between the position of an object referring to the fixed great-circle frame and the object's position referring to the rotating frame linked to the instrument.

At this point Terrestrial Time (TT) is introduced into the data reduction, i.e., the mid-time of an RGC is given in TT and, hence, the abscissae representing the individual observations of the stars refer to TT. Consequently, the astrometric parameters, derived subsequently from the abscissae, are also given in TT. Note that prior to the abscissa determination the data reduction steps were controlled by the on-board time, which derives its signal from a crystal controlled oscillator. The on-board time is related to Universal Time Coordinated (UTC) available at the telemetry ground stations through broadcast time signals. In associating the on-board time with UTC, account is taken of corrections for delay times between satellite and ground station. UTC differs from TAI (International Atomic Time) by an integer number of seconds and, to close the sequence of time transformations, we point out the relationship between TT and TAI as stated in Sect. 2.2.3.

Let v (abscissa) and r (ordinate) be the spherical coordinates of a star or member of the solar system with respect to the RGC frame, and η, θ the corresponding pair of local coordinates, also known as field coordinates, with reference to the respective IGC. The coordinates v_i and r_i of a star i are associated with the grid coordinate, $G_{i,k}$, that is obtained by observing star i at the instant of frame k. This association of coordinates takes place in three steps with due consideration of the different types of positions involved.

First, the geometric direction given by v_i and r_i is transformed into the proper direction or apparent position at the time of observation and with respect to the fixed RGC frame using the known orientation of the RGC in space. Note that, for the Hipparcos reductions, isotropic coordinates were used, assuming a spherically symmetric, heliocentric metric. The geometric direction referred to above takes account of parallax and proper motion effects, and is equivalent to the isotropic coordinate direction at the time of observation (ESA 1997, Vol. 3, p. 225).

Second, the star's proper direction with respect to the RGC frame (X, Y, Z) is transformed into the rotating instrument reference frame yielding the field coordinates, $\eta_{i,k}$ and $\theta_{i,k}$, for frame k. The principal plane of the instrument reference frame is defined by the optical axes of the two fields of view, with the x axis bisecting the angle γ. The z axis is perpendicular to the principal plane and coincides nominally with the rotation axis of the satellite, so that it is identical with the normal of the instantaneous great circle (IGC); finally, $\boldsymbol{y} = (\boldsymbol{x} \times \boldsymbol{z})$, see Fig. 3.6. For example, this transformation may be composed of three rotations through the angles Ω_k, ζ_k and ξ_k, which are known from the attitude determination of the telescope at the instant k. The angles ζ and ξ describe rotations about the X and Y axes, and the angle Ω means a rotation about the Z axis of the RGC frame. Denoting the vector to the star by $\boldsymbol{S}_{\mathrm{TEL}}$ and $\boldsymbol{S}_{\mathrm{RGC}}$ in the telescope and RGC frames, respectively, this transformation is described by

$$\boldsymbol{S}_{\mathrm{TEL}} = \mathbf{R_1}(\zeta_k)\mathbf{R_2}(\xi_k)\mathbf{R_3}(\Omega_k)\boldsymbol{S}_{\mathrm{RGC}}\,, \tag{3.7}$$

where $\mathbf{R}_\nu(\varepsilon)$, $\nu = 1, 2, 3$, signifies, in turn, a rotation by angle ε about the X, Y and Z axes.

To complete the transformation to grid coordinates, a distinction must be made between observations in the preceding and following fields of view.

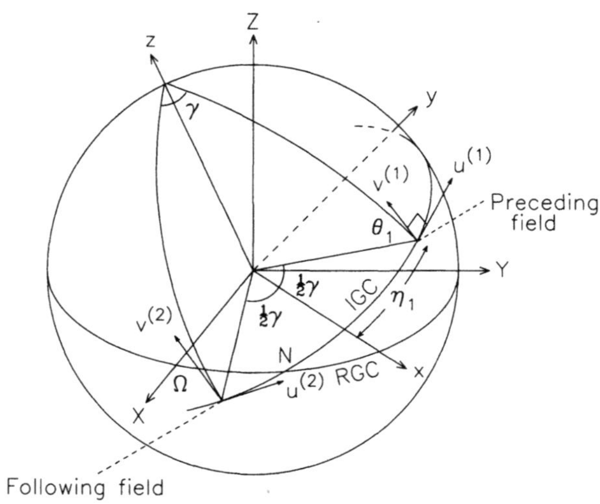

Fig. 3.6. Geometry of great-circle reduction: transformation of field angles referring to the rotating instrument coordinate frame (x, y, z) and to the fixed RGC coordinate frame (X, Y, Z) by taking account of the satellite's orientation

Let $u^{(1)}, v^{(1)}$ and $u^{(2)}, v^{(2)}$ be local spherical coordinates of a star, which are centred at the preceding and following field, with u measured in the plane of the IGC and v in the perpendicular direction of the z axis. Then we obtain:

$$\begin{aligned} \text{Preceding field :} \quad & \eta_{i,k} = +\gamma/2 + u_{i,k}^{(1)}, \quad \theta_{i,k} = v_{i,k}^{(1)} \\ \text{Following field :} \quad & \eta_{i,k} = -\gamma/2 + u_{i,k}^{(2)}, \quad \theta_{i,k} = v_{i,k}^{(2)} . \end{aligned}$$

In other words, one passes from the field coordinates over to the local spherical coordinates by rotating the telescope frame about the z axis by $-\gamma/2$ in case of the preceding and $+\gamma/2$ in case of the following field of view (Fig. 3.6).

Third, the field coordinates are related to the grid coordinates, $G_{i,k}$. This procedure is called the field-to-grid transformation (ESA 1997, Vol. 3, p. 175). It also monitors the evolution of designated instrumental parameters, especially geometric distortions of the modulating grid and the basic angle, γ, of the beam-combining mirror.

After these preliminaries, the relationship between the grid coordinate and the geometric position of star i may be formally written as

$$G_{ik} = G\left(v_i, r_i, \Omega_k, \zeta_k, \xi_k, \boldsymbol{d}\right) + \eta'_{ik} \tag{3.8}$$

with η' denoting the photon noise effect on the grid coordinates, and the vector $\boldsymbol{d}$ denoting the instrument parameters, which are respectively part of the transformation from field to grid coordinates, and effects of telescope variations with time. Details on the background of (3.8) are found in van der Marel & Petersen (1992).

3.6.2 The Procedure of Abscissa Estimation

The model for the grid coordinates given in (3.8) is instrumental in estimating the abscissae. It should be recalled that the abscissae are defined in terms of isotropic coordinate directions, while the grid coordinates reflect proper directions. Since the model takes account of this fact by duly including stellar aberration and light bending by the Sun and Earth, the abscissae are free from these effects and, hence, directly usable for deriving barycentric coordinate directions.

It is a characteristic of Hipparcos that the measurements in the main grid contain only information along the scanning direction. As a consequence, the abscissa v_i and the along-scan attitude component Ω_k are determinable from (3.8), while the ordinate r_i and the transverse attitude components ζ_k and ξ_k cannot be estimated to the required accuracy. As a matter of fact, all three attitude components are predetermined by the attitude reconstitution proper with, however, the low precision of 100–150 mas. This is sufficient for the transverse components because of the small inclination of the instantaneous scanning circles with respect to the RGC, but entirely unsatisfactory in the along-scan direction, where a final precision at the milliarcsecond level is required. It is therefore imperative to improve the along-scan attitude component in the course of the great-circle reduction.

Least squares adjustment is applied to solve for the abscissae, along-scan attitude, and instrumental parameters. The observation equations follow from (3.8) by linearization:

$$\Delta G_{ik} = \frac{\partial G_{ik}}{\partial v_i}\,\Delta v_i + \frac{\partial G_{ik}}{\partial \Omega_k}\,\Delta\Omega_k + \left(\frac{\partial G_{ik}}{\partial \boldsymbol{d}}\right)^{\mathrm{T}} \Delta\boldsymbol{d} + \eta'_{ik} \tag{3.9}$$

with $\Delta G_{ik} = G_{ik}^{\mathrm{obs}} - G_{ik}^{\mathrm{calc}}$, and η'_{ik} representing the measurement noise. Here G_{ik}^{obs} is the observed grid coordinate at time t_k, and G_{ik}^{calc} is its value computed by using approximations of the parameters appearing in the model for calculating grid coordinates. Especially for ζ_k, ξ_k and r_i, which are not amenable to estimation, approximate values are taken from the attitude reconstitution and from external star catalogues, respectively. Unknowns in the least squares adjustment are the quantities Δv_i, $\Delta\Omega_k$ and $\Delta\boldsymbol{d}$. The latter signifies corrections to the above-mentioned instrumental parameters.

The effect of parameter approximations is progressively eliminated in the course of iterated great-circle reductions based on improved star positions resulting from the sphere solution and astrometric parameter determination that comprise the final step of the data reduction chain. On average a great-circle reduction yields the spherical coordinates of roughly 1800 stars referred to the intermediate reference frame defined by the plane of the RGC and a zero point in this plane. At this stage the zero point is arbitrary due to the differential observations made on the main grid. Consequently, the design and normal matrices of the least squares adjustment are encumbered with a rank defect of 1 under normal circumstances. A simple method of removing this rank defect sets the abscissa of one selected star, the so-called base star, equal to zero. From this special choice of a star, however, ensues a zero variance that contradicts the reality of the observation practice. For statistical reasons, therefore, the great-circle solution and the concomitant covariance matrix are transformed into a minimum norm solution, yielding non-zero variances by constraining to zero the sum of the abscissa corrections of the RGC stars.

By analogy to the construction of a general catalogue of positions from individual catalogues of ground-based observations, we may consider the set of coordinates of the stars belonging to an RGC as an individual observation catalogue. Combination of all of these observation catalogues, each of which is associated with one RGC, makes it possible to compile the provisional Hipparcos catalogue covering the whole sky and referring to an intermediate but, nonetheless, well-defined system. How this is achieved falls under the topic ‘global astrometry’ and is treated in Sect. 3.7.

3.6.3 The Astrometric Information Content of the Abscissae

The abscissa of a star fixes the position of this star on the respective RGC at its mid-time or, in other words, at the epoch of the observation catalogue which comprises the star abscissae of the corresponding RGC. Under normal circumstances, a star belongs to a number of RGCs distributed over the entire mission duration of about three years. Therefore, the extraction of information on stellar position and proper motion from the abscissae is plausible. On the other hand, it may be interesting to identify that information hidden in the abscissa measurements, which concerns parallaxes. As will be demonstrated, this information has the potential to determine, in principle, absolute annual trigonometric stellar parallaxes as a result of the wide-angle measuring capability of the Hipparcos instrument. In fact, during the scanning period of an RGC, lasting a few hours, the angular distances between many stars with different angular separations from the Sun are measured, providing the key to parallax determination. What cannot be excluded, however, is a small global shift of the parallax zero point caused by a thermal effect due to the varying aspect angle of solar irradiation while the satellite is rotating about its axis. Since this shift is independent of star position, magnitude and colour, it can be easily calibrated by means of a set of programme stars which have extremely small parallaxes so that, finally, absolute parallaxes have been obtained (ESA 1997, Vol. 3, p. 353 and p. 441).

The annual parallax of a star denotes the change in the observed geometric position due to the orbital motion of the Earth. As seen from the Hipparcos satellite the geometric position of the star is displaced from the heliocentric position toward the satellite-centric position of the Sun, in the plane of the Sun ($\odot$), the satellite (H), and the star (S). Figure 3.7 illustrates this parallactic displacement measured in the scan direction along the great circle through $\odot$ and S.

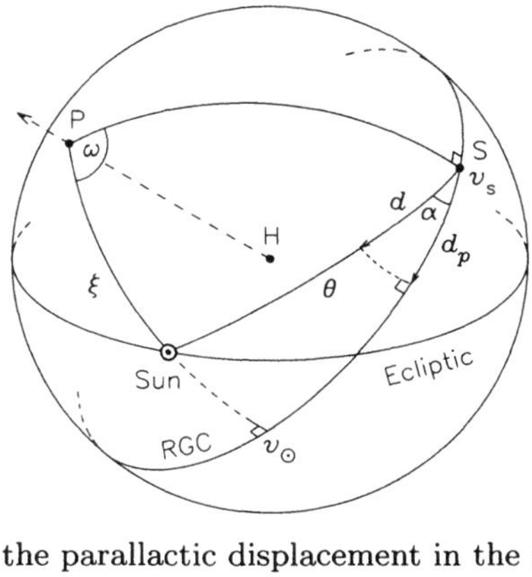

Fig. 3.7. The share of the parallactic displacement in the abscissa of a star S. For notation see text

0829+046 08 31 48.876955±26 +04 29 39.08534±53 L 0.180

By definition, the parallactic displacement of a star at a distance r from the Sun is

$$d = \frac{R \sin\theta}{r}, \tag{3.10}$$

where R and θ denote the distance of the observing site, H, from the Sun, and the angular separation between star and Sun, respectively. If the unit of R is the astronomical unit and r is measured in parsec, then d is given in arcsec. From spherical trigonometry applied to the triangle P⊙S follows with the notation of Fig. 3.7

$$\sin\theta = \frac{\sin\omega}{\cos\alpha} \sin\xi . \tag{3.11}$$

Here P refers to the pole of the RGC; ω is equal to $v_{\odot} - v_S$, which is the difference between the abscissae of the Sun and the star; α denotes the angle between the RGC and the great circle through ⊙ and S containing the parallactic displacement, and ξ is the angular distance of the telescope spin axis from the Sun having the value 43°.

Accordingly, with (3.10) and (3.11), the projection of the parallactic displacement onto the RGC becomes

$$d \cos\alpha = d_{\mathrm{p}} = R\,\pi \sin\xi \sin\omega , \tag{3.12}$$

and π is the trigonometric parallax in arcsec. Recalling that ξ is constant and different from zero, d_{p} is a sinusoidal function of ω that describes the parallax information embedded in the star abscissae.

To show how the parallax ensues from the projected parallactic displacements on RGCs, we fall back on the measured abscissa differences between pairs of stars. From these differences relative abscissae are derived by adopting the position of a selected base star on the RGC as zero point from which the other abscissae are measured (Sect. 3.6.2). Two cases may be distinguished:

1) the base star has a negligible parallax ($\pi = 0$), then the relative abscissae of the stars on the RGC are free from any parallactic displacement of the base star, but may be affected by the choice of its nominal position;
2) if the base star has a parallax $\pi > 0$, but unknown, the relative abscissae of the stars on the RGC reflect a change by the parallactic displacement of the base star in addition to the possible shift due to the choice of the base star position.

Both cases give rise to a constant offset in each of all the abscissae pertaining to an individual RGC. This fact, however, does not pose a serious problem because the offsets are constant per RGC and, therefore, can be estimated in a simultaneous solution together with the astrometric parameters, including the parallaxes of all primary stars, i.e. also those of negligible parallaxes. This estimation process uses the abscissae of the entire set of RGCs. Since all

RGCs are involved one speaks of a global solution at whose completion the constant offsets are known. In anticipating the global solution, these offsets may be eliminated from the abscissae, yielding reduced abscissae that reflect the genuine astrometrically relevant information on stellar position, motion and parallactic displacement, which is the input for astrometric parameter determination that provides absolute parallaxes as one specific result. Section 3.7 discusses the global solution and parameter determination.

3.7 Sphere Solution

3.7.1 Conceptual Background

One-dimensional measurements along the scanning direction of the telescope yielded the abscissae of the stars on the respective RGCs. On average a star appeared on 28 RGCs during the 37 months of data acquisition from the satellite. Altogether there are 2281 RGCs, with each of these forming a specific spherical reference frame defined by the fundamental plane of the RGC containing a zero point. The distance between any two stars projected onto an RGC is invariant to changes of the zero point.

It is the aim of the 'Sphere Solution' to derive a two-dimensional solution of spherical stellar coordinates from the one-dimensional abscissae measured on RGCs with different poles, and to embed these coordinates into a coherent net on the sphere. The last requirement necessitates the solution of the problem on a global basis rather than on a star-by-star basis.

First let us consider an idealized thought experiment to focus on the crucial points of the sphere solution. We assume fixed positions in ecliptic longitude (λ) and latitude (β) of the stars during the observation campaign. Further, the abscissae for star i are given on K RGCs by the arcs between the ascending node of the RGC on the ecliptic and the projection of the star on this RGC. The directions $\boldsymbol{r}_k$ of the RGC poles are assumed to be known. Then, the abscissa v_{ik} of star i on RGC k is modelled as a random variable by

$$v_{ik} = F\left(\lambda_i, \beta_i, \boldsymbol{r}_k, t_k\right), \; k = 1, ..., K, \tag{3.13}$$

where t_k is the central time of RGC k. The abscissae play the role of the observations, and the stellar coordinates are the only unknowns. Their efficient estimation by least squares methods does not encounter any problems because good initial approximations of the unknowns are available, as well as redundant observational equations.

In practice, however, the abscissae are measured from an arbitrary zero point on the RGC, $Z_1, Z_2, \ldots$, since its ascending node on the ecliptic is not known (see Fig. 3.8). To get coherent abscissae for star i we introduce the shift c_k, $k = 1, ..., K$ on the k-th RGC. Note that the abscissa differences between any pair of stars on the same RGC is invariant to this procedure,

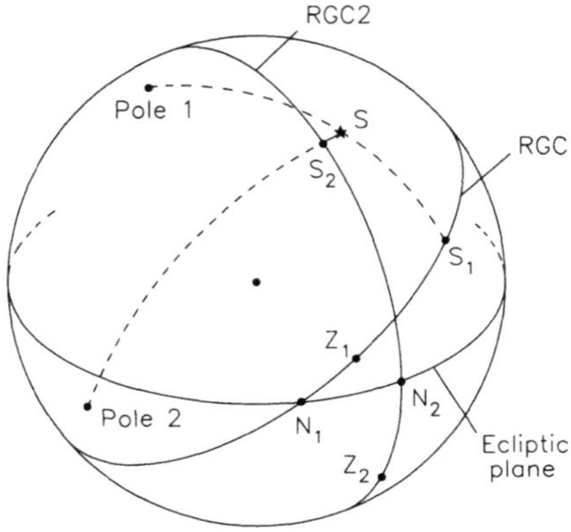

Fig. 3.8. Embedding the abscissae Z_1S_1, Z_2S_2 etc. of star S into a coherent net on the sphere by adjusting the arbitrary zero points Z_1, Z_2 etc. together with those of the other stars so that abscissa compatibility is accomplished on the sphere

but the relative shifts are added as further unknowns. One concludes from (3.13)

$$v_{ik} = F(\lambda_i, \beta_i, \boldsymbol{r}_k, t_k) - c_k,\ k = 1, ..., K\,. \tag{3.14}$$

There are K equations for $K+2$ unknowns λ_i, β_i and c_k, thus leaving two origins undefined. We may choose another star whose abscissae appear on RGCs that contain those two hitherto undefined origins, but which can now be determined from (3.14) after tailoring it to the additional star. On choosing enough stars well distributed on the sphere, it is possible to determine the shifts for all RGCs and to solve for coherent abscissae in an optimum statistical sense. Once the coherence shifts are applied to the abscissae, two of them, in principle, are sufficient to extract the spherical coordinates of a star, and to achieve the transition from one-dimensional abscissae to two-dimensional star places.

In reality, the stars are in motion and, therefore, the abscissae are functions of this motion as schematically depicted in Fig. 3.9. The displacements on the sphere of a star's geometrical position are caused by stellar proper motion, possible gravitational influences by companions in double or multiple systems, and parallactic displacements due to the orbital motion of the Earth. To determine coherent shifts of the abscissa origins, account is taken of these displacements during the entire observation period covering several years. The model providing the geometrical positions of stars throughout the course of the mission assumes rectilinear stellar motion of uniform velocity. With respect to the solar system barycentre, this motion is defined for some epoch t_0 by the vectors of position and velocity. In ecliptic coordinates, this is equivalent to the star's longitude, latitude and parallax (π) on the one hand, and proper motions in longitude (μ_λ) and latitude (μ_β), and the radial velocity (V) on the other. Since the Hipparcos measurements are relatively

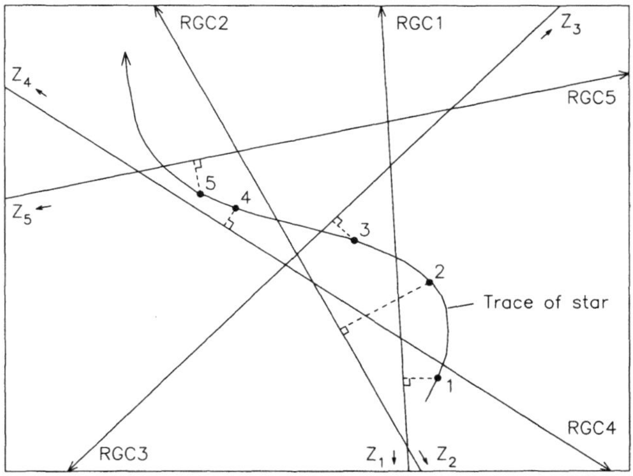

Fig. 3.9. On the sphere the stellar motion traces a curved line of the star's geometric positions that provide the abscissae by projection onto the associated RGCs at the central time of the respective circle. The zero points of the RGCs are indicated by Z_i $(i = 1, \ldots, 5)$

insensitive to radial velocities, values precisely determined by spectroscopic means are taken whenever radial velocities are needed to calculate geometric positions of stars. Using this generalized model, the star abscissa may be expressed as

$$v_{ik} = F\left(\lambda_i, \beta_i, \mu_{\lambda_i}, \mu_{\beta_i}, \pi_i, V_i, t_0, \boldsymbol{r}_k, t_k\right) - c_k + \boldsymbol{d}\,. \tag{3.15}$$

The unknowns are the five astrometric parameters, $\lambda, \beta, \mu_\lambda, \mu_\beta, \pi$, the zero point corrections (c_k), and $\boldsymbol{d}$, where the latter item characterizes a group of general parameters that can only be estimated at the level of the sphere solution. These additional parameters represent different kinds of large scale distortions of the abscissae caused by instrumental effects as well as by deficient models used in the data reduction. An extensive treatment of the abscissa modelling and parameter solution is given by Lindegren et al. (1992).

3.7.2 Observation Equations and Estimation of Unknowns

Approximately 40 000 so-called primary stars have been selected for the sphere solution by the FAST consortium (Kovalevsky et al. 1992). This selection was guided mainly by the requirement that the establishment of the provisional Hipparcos frame should only use those stars that behave closely in accordance with the generalized star model introduced at the end of Sect. 3.7.1. For example, those stars have been avoided as primary stars that revealed features of strong variability and unmodelled motions, as is typical of double and multiple star systems. The observation equations follow from linearizing (3.15) about the current values of the unknowns yielding

$$\begin{aligned} \Delta v_{ik} &= \frac{\partial v_{ik}}{\partial \lambda_i \cos \beta_i} \Delta\lambda_i \cos \beta_i + \frac{\partial v_{ik}}{\partial \beta_i} \Delta\beta_i \\ &+ \frac{\partial v_{ik}}{\partial \mu_{\lambda_i} \cos \beta_i} \Delta\mu_{\lambda_i} \cos \beta_i + \frac{\partial v_{ik}}{\partial \mu_{\beta_i}} \Delta\mu_{\beta_i} + \frac{\partial v_{ik}}{\partial \pi_i} \Delta\pi_i \\ &+ \frac{\partial v_{ik}}{\partial c_k} \Delta c_k + \frac{\partial v_{ik}}{\partial \boldsymbol{d}} \Delta \boldsymbol{d}\,. \end{aligned} \tag{3.16}$$

In the mean each star gives rise to 28 observation equations corresponding to the average number of RGCs per star. The zero point correction of a specific RGC appears in all those observation equations which deal with the reference great circle set of that RGC. On average 1800 stars belong to each such set. Finally, the general parameters extend over all stars and great circle sets. To convey an idea of the size of the task: the number of unknowns is composed of $40\,000\times5$ astrometric parameters, about 2300 zero point corrections and a dozen general parameters. There are approximately $40\,000\times28\approx1.2\times10^6$ observation equations.

The least squares problem of (3.16) is solved by means of the Cholesky factorisation algorithm (Lawson & Hanson 1974), yielding the abscissa shifts of the RGCs, the general parameters and, most importantly, the differential corrections to the astrometric parameters of the primary stars.

Still missing are the astrometric parameters of the roughly 80 000 remaining programme stars or secondary stars of the observing programme (see Sect. 3.4). For the determination of the positions of secondary stars one takes advantage of the zero point corrections of the abscissae and the general parameters known at this stage. By substituting these quantities into (3.15) we obtain the model that, after linearization, allows the determination of the five astrometric parameters star by star by means of least squares adjustment. Compared with the primary stars, each system of observational equations contains only five unknowns and consists on average of 28 equations. Mathematically the procedure is simple; its application to 80 000 stars constitutes the bulk of the task. On the other hand, this procedure offers some flexibility by enlarging the set of astrometric parameters to be fitted to the observed abscissae. For example, the star-by-star processing comes to fruition in the double star treatment, when the rates of proper motion, star separations and position angles or even orbital parameters suggest the estimation of additional unknowns. Concerning double star parameter determination we refer to Söderhjelm et al. (1992), Mignard et al. (1992) and ESA (1997), Vol. 3, p. 233.

3.8 Construction of the Hipparcos Catalogue

In the last section we have outlined how the astrometric parameters of the stars of the Hipparcos catalogue project are produced. Prior to finalization of the catalogue, however, a few specific points typical of the Hipparcos data reduction need to be considered. They concern the quality and consistency of the results. In detail these are:

1) the solution of the normal equations for the primary stars bearing in mind that, by definition, the stars form a system of mass points with six degrees of freedom,
2) the iteration of parts of the data reduction chain in order to arrive at parameter precisions that approach the limit of 1–2 mas set by the photon noise,
3) the merging of the two catalogues established independently by the FAST and NDAC consortia into one single Hipparcos catalogue representing a defined but still provisional system.

The following sections attend briefly to these apparently minor subjects which, however, are essential for a complete overview of the data analysis.

3.8.1 Rank Deficiency

Let us consider a rigid sphere whose centre coincides with the origin of a space-fixed coordinate frame. This sphere has three degrees of freedom corresponding to its undefined orientation which, for example, may be defined by the three Eulerian angles at some epoch. In generalizing the rigid body motion we assume that the sphere rotates uniformly about an axis through the origin. This rotation also has three degrees of freedom, corresponding to the undefined rotation rates about the three coordinate axes. Fixing, for example, the rates of change of the Eulerian angles defines the rotation of the rigid body. The sphere solution, aiming at estimating the astrometric parameters, then faces the problem posed by these six degrees of freedom, because the observed abscissae do not measure the positions in any absolute frame due to the arbitrarily chosen zero points. Consequently, one expects a rank deficiency of six inherent in the normal matrix of the least squares adjustment of the primary stars.

Theoretically, the least squares solution is indefinite with respect to three undefined angles of orientation and their rates of change. These six quantities eventually define the absolute orientation and rotation of the system of positions and proper motions. In practice this rank deficiency did not manifest itself seriously, so that the normal equations could be solved without constraints. A possible explanation of this unexpected behaviour is given by the procedure by means of which the individual RGC frames are transformed into a global frame. In constructing this global frame one would expect rotations about the three axes of the RGC frame because of the three degrees of freedom of a system of positions. Instead, in applying the transformation procedure, only one rotation is performed about the axis to the pole of the RGC, as described above in the course of the zero point correction of the abscissae (see Sect. 3.6). Throughout the data reduction, constant values were assigned to the pole coordinates, with the consequence that some absolute positional orientation is introduced, and this is apparently sufficient to provide the normal matrix with the full rank.

It has been demonstrated that the distortion of the abscissae may reach 2 mas if the poles are kept fixed (Lattanzi et al. 1990). The effect, however, is not serious, since it is remedied in the course of the iteration of the attitude determination, great-circle reduction and sphere solution. Indeed, the procedures applied to great-circle reduction and sphere solution resemble the block relaxation technique with successive iterations where, in several stages, some of the unknowns are estimated, while the remainder are kept fixed. In this kind of approach the reasons may be seen why there is no serious question of rank deficiency and why overconstraining by fixing some 2300 RGC pole directions is not detrimental to the numerical solution (van Daalen et al. 1987). This problem has been reanalysed in the framework of the actual global solutions, and a mathematical quantification was given of the only weakly ill-conditioned equations for the sphere solution (ESA 1997, Vol. 3, p. 215).

3.8.2 Iterative Data Reduction

Iterations of the reduction results are required first of all because the final precision of astrometric parameters predicted from simulations cannot be reached in one cycle. This is mainly due to the unsatisfactory precision of the starting values of the parameters taken from the Hipparcos Input Catalogue (ESA 1992), which is the initial reference catalogue. Its average positional precisions are more than two orders of magnitude worse than the potential inherent in the design of the Hipparcos mission. In the FAST consortium, the Input Catalogue supplied the starting values for the processing of the first 18 months of observed data. Updated parameter values were obtained from this operation. Next, a new reference catalogue was constructed from these results, and then an iteration of the same 18 months of data performed. Subsequently, this new reference catalogue was used to process the first 30 months of observed data, yielding up to 50 % improvement of the precisions compared with the iterated 18-month solution (Kovalevsky et al. 1995). Again, these results became the basis for a further reference catalogue and an iterated 30-month solution. Finally, the complete set of observations covering 37 months was treated with the reference catalogue obtained from the 30-month iterated solution.

At the very end of the iterations stand the iterated 37-month solutions, which provided the reference catalogues for the last and definitive solutions of the FAST (F) and NDAC (N) consortia, known as F37.3 and N37.5. Table 3.1

Table 3.1. Averaged formal standard errors of the successive FAST (F) and NDAC (N) astrometric parameter solutions for data sets consisting of single or at least nonproblematic stars. The standard errors of position (σ_{pos}), proper motion (σ_μ) and parallax (σ_π) are given by the respective median values, i.e. half of individual standard deviations are less than the median value and half are greater. The individual standard deviations of positions and proper motions are defined by $\sigma_{\mathrm{pos}} = [1/2((\sigma_\alpha \cos\delta)^2 + \sigma_\delta^2)]^{1/2}$ and $\sigma_\mu = [1/2((\sigma_{\mu_\alpha} \cos\delta)^2 + \sigma_{\mu_\delta}^2)]^{1/2}$, respectively

Data sets Fmm and Nmm (mm stands for the interval of data acquisition in months)	Epoch	Number of stars included in the statistics	Standard errors σ_{pos} [mas]	σ_μ [mas/yr]	σ_π [mas]
F18 (Hip. Input Catalogue as reference catalogue)	1990.70	≈ 80000	1.4	3.4	2.1
F18 (iterated 18-month reference catalogue)	1990.70	88922	1.3	3.1	1.8
N18 (instantaneous best reference catalogue)	1990.70	94210	1.5	3.4	2.0
F30 (iterated 18-month reference catalogue)	1991.15	95025	1.0	1.4	1.3
N30 (instantaneous best reference catalogue)	1991.15	96881	1.1	1.6	1.5
F37.3 (iterated 37-month reference catalogue)	1991.25	101189	1.0	1.2	1.3
N37.5 (instantaneous best reference catalogue)	1991.25	101071	0.9	1.1	1.3

shows the evolution of the formal standard errors of the astrometric parameters as obtained in successive iterative steps by the two consortia (ESA 1997, Vol. 3, pp. 341–342; Kovalevsky et al. 1995).

3.8.3 Merging of the Provisional Hipparcos Catalogues

Although the FAST and NDAC consortia process identical streams of photons for the purpose of catalogue compilation, they arrive in practice at slightly different results at the submilliarcsecond level. The physical models and mathematical methods adopted for data reduction are the most probable reasons for such differences. The organization of the data, the segmentation of the data flow, and the computer hardware and software are also likely to contribute to the differences. Merging the two provisional catalogues, therefore, is an indispensable step towards optimum numerical and statistical values of the astrometric parameters, and must be performed by taking due account of possible correlations between the two provisional catalogue results. Con-

0912+297 09 15 52.401620±32 +29 33 24.04274±57 L ...

cerning the need for proper treatment of correlations, some analogy may be drawn with the combination method of VLBI catalogues (Sect. 5.5.3).

Theoretically, the correlations between the astrometric results of the consortia are equal to 1 if the photon noise of the original measurements is the sole error source. In these circumstances one could simply provide the combined solution as the weighted mean of the astrometric parameters estimated by the consortia. Correlation coefficients different from 1, however, are expected between FAST and NDAC results because of differences in the models and procedures adopted for data processing. In fact, the correlation coefficient between the astrometric results of the two consortia turned out to be about 0.7 on average. Therefore, when merging the catalogues, it makes sense to take into consideration the correlations of the individual catalogue data, since this procedure promises statistical improvement of the astrometric parameters. For this purpose catalogue merging was performed at the level of the great circle reduction, aiming at a least squares estimate of the astrometric parameters that is based on correlated abscissae, which are derived from the abscissae provided by the two consortia. This approach yields the astrometric parameters and the associated covariance matrix, but now for a set of correlated abscissae as input in contrast to the parameter estimation described in Sect. 3.7.2. The derivation of the correlations between the abscissae provided by the individual consortia is an involved process whose details are presented in ESA (1997), Vol. 3, p. 369, and which is only summarized here.

The departure points of the correlation study are the independent provisional Hipparcos catalogues F37.3 and N37.5 of the FAST (F) and NDAC (N) consortia, respectively. These catalogues comprise the total of data acquisition during the 37 months of satellite observations and have reached their final stages in the course of iterative data reduction. Below we delineate briefly the train of thought for combining the FAST and NDAC abscissae:

1) The FAST and NDAC astrometric parameters are transformed to a common reference frame which in the mean is aligned with the frame of the FK5 catalogue. Further, the FAST abscissae given with respect to the ascending node of the reference great circle on the ecliptic are transformed with the aid of spherical trigonometry so that they refer to the ascending node of the reference great circle on the equator, in order to conform to the NDAC abscissa convention. From this procedure result the F and N abscissa residuals referring to a common frame:

$$\begin{aligned} \Delta v_{\mathrm{F}}(\boldsymbol{a}_{\mathrm{F}}) &= v_{\mathrm{F}}^{\mathrm{obs}} - v_{\mathrm{F}}^{\mathrm{calc}}(\boldsymbol{a}_{\mathrm{F}}), \\ \Delta v_{\mathrm{N}}(\boldsymbol{a}_{\mathrm{N}}) &= v_{\mathrm{N}}^{\mathrm{obs}} - v_{\mathrm{N}}^{\mathrm{calc}}(\boldsymbol{a}_{\mathrm{N}}), \end{aligned}$$

where the $\boldsymbol{a}_{\mathrm{F}}$ and $\boldsymbol{a}_{\mathrm{N}}$ stand for the respective sets of astrometric parameters. To allow direct comparison and averaging of residuals, a set of average parameters is introduced by forming

$$\boldsymbol{a}_{\mathrm{H}} = (\boldsymbol{a}_{\mathrm{F}} + \boldsymbol{a}_{\mathrm{N}})/2.$$

In the course of successive merged solutions $\boldsymbol{a}_{\rm H}$ is replaced by improved values. Substituting $\boldsymbol{a}_{\rm H}$ into the F and N abscissa residuals, they take the form

$$\Delta v_{\rm F}(\boldsymbol{a}_{\rm H}) = \Delta v_{\rm F}(\boldsymbol{a}_{\rm F}) - \sum_{i=1}^{5} \frac{\partial v_{\rm F}}{\partial a^i} \left(a^i_{\rm H} - a^i_{\rm F}\right), \quad (3.17)$$

$$\Delta v_{\rm N}(\boldsymbol{a}_{\rm H}) = \Delta v_{\rm N}(\boldsymbol{a}_{\rm N}) - \sum_{i=1}^{5} \frac{\partial v_{\rm N}}{\partial a^i} \left(a^i_{\rm H} - a^i_{\rm N}\right). \quad (3.18)$$

Along with the residuals in (3.17) and (3.18) the formal errors $\sigma_{\rm F}$ and $\sigma_{\rm N}$ are supplied with reference to the common set of average astrometric parameters, $\boldsymbol{a}_{\rm H}$. The partial derivatives in the above expressions are known from the respective sphere solutions of the two consortia.

2) Prior to the assessment of correlations some scaling is applied to $\sigma_{\rm F}$ and $\sigma_{\rm N}$, reflecting the unit weight errors of the abscissa residuals and the stellar magnitudes. These calibrations are required to smooth the variations of the unit weight errors and to ensure that the formal standard errors are unbiased. Afterwards, the correlation coefficient, ϱ, of the abscissa residuals, defined by

$$\varrho = \frac{\mathrm{cov}\,(\Delta v_{\rm F}, \Delta v_{\rm N})}{\sigma_{\rm F}\ \sigma_{\rm N}},$$

is determined by making use of the variance of the difference of the F- and N-type abscissa residuals, given by $\sigma^2(\Delta v_{\rm F} - \Delta v_{\rm N}) = \sigma^2(\Delta v_{\rm F}) + \sigma^2(\Delta v_{\rm N}) - 2\,\mathrm{cov}(\Delta v_{\rm F}, \Delta v_{\rm N})$, where cov stands for the covariance. Thus,

$$\varrho\,(\Delta v_{\rm F}, \Delta v_{\rm N}) = \frac{\sigma^2_{\rm F} + \sigma^2_{\rm N} - \sigma^2\,(\Delta v_{\rm F} - \Delta v_{\rm N})}{2\,\sigma_{\rm F}\ \sigma_{\rm N}}. \quad (3.19)$$

Using the available standard errors and the variance of the residual difference derived from (3.17) and (3.18), the correlations are computed after placing $\sigma_{\rm F}$ and $\sigma_{\rm N}$ into 0.1×0.1 mas bins. The resulting correlation coefficients are shown in Fig. 3.10, and exhibit a ridge at $\sigma_{\rm F} \approx \sigma_{\rm N}$. The approximate behaviour of the correlations follows from (3.19) on the assumption of $\sigma_{\rm F} = \sigma_{\rm N}$, yielding $\varrho \approx 1 - \mathrm{const}/(\sigma_{\rm F}\sigma_{\rm N})$.

A more refined analysis of the correlations given by (3.19) as a two-dimensional function necessitated the empirical calibration of the standard errors, $\sigma_{\rm F}$ and $\sigma_{\rm N}$, of the abscissae. Moreover, a magnitude effect and a dependence on the mission duration had to be corrected by fitting a third order polynomial for each. Finally, the adopted correlation coefficient is represented by a rather complicated function of the standard errors reported by the consortia, the stellar magnitude and the observation time.

3) After the execution of the aforementioned preparatory steps each FAST and NDAC abscissa is associated with the respective standard error and a

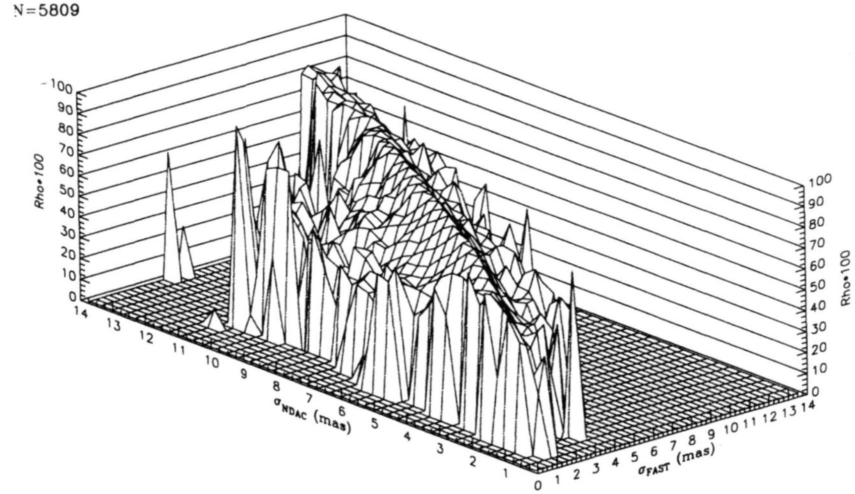

Fig. 3.10. Correlation coefficient ϱ between the FAST (F) and NDAC (N) abscissae, calculated for N=5809 bins of 0.1 mas by 0.1 mas in σ_F and σ_N (ESA 1997, Vol. 3, p. 369)

correlation coefficient allowing the construction of the covariance matrix required for a least squares estimate of the astrometric parameters using correlated abscissae as 'observations'. In principle, the parameters are estimated as described in Sect. 3.7.2. Without loss of generality the abscissae may be grouped by pairs of FAST and NDAC abscissae. In these circumstances and since correlations between RGCs are neglected, the covariance matrix consists essentially of two column sub-matrices arranged along the main diagonal, being structured as

$$\begin{pmatrix} \sigma^2_{\mathrm{F}i} & \varrho_i\sigma_{\mathrm{F}i}\sigma_{\mathrm{N}i} \\ \varrho_i\sigma_{\mathrm{F}i}\sigma_{\mathrm{N}i} & \sigma^2_{\mathrm{N}i} \end{pmatrix}$$

for the i-th FAST and NDAC abscissae.

From the iterated sphere solution based on the merged abscissae and the respective standard errors and correlations ensue the best estimates of the astrometric parameters together with the accompanying covariance matrix. These parameters constitute the optimum but still provisional Hipparcos catalogue, H37C, that refers to a reference frame defined by the sphere solution. At this stage, therefore, one must not exclude a coordinate frame which is slowly spinning with respect to extragalactic objects, and an undefined orientation of the axes at a given epoch. In a final step this provisional catalogue is tied into the extragalactic radio reference frame (see Chap. 7), thus producing the official Hipparcos Catalogue that extends the radio reference frame established in Chap. 6 to optical wavelengths.

3.8.4 Differences of Principle Between the Construction of the FK5 and Hipparcos Catalogues

Chapters 2 and 3 convey insight into the construction of the FK5 and Hipparcos Catalogues. There are a few fundamental differences of catalogue development that we recapitulate below to provide an easily comprehensible comparison. Some of the more essential design properties have been selected and are enumerated in turn for FK5 and Hipparcos:

1) a) The FK5 materializes basically a dynamical reference system whose inertiality is based on the validity of Newton's laws of motion for the objects of the solar system (Sect. 1.4).

b) Through its link to the ICRF (Chaps. 6 and 7) the Hipparcos system acquires the properties of a kinematic system that is based on the positions of extragalactic objects at rest or, in other words, in motion which is not measurable with current observing techniques (Sect. 1.8).

2) a) For the FK5 construction a model of precession is needed since the instantaneous equator is adopted as the fundamental plane for the observation of celestial bodies (Sect. 1.7), and this plane is precessing about the pole of the ecliptic. If this precession model is based on stellar proper motions, additional models of solar motion with respect to the stars, galactic rotation and galactic shearing are required (Sect. 1.6.3).

b) The differential measurements leading to the provisional Hipparcos Catalogue (Sect. 3.8.3) are unaffected by the complex motion of the Earth, and this freedom from the Earth's motion is preserved for the final Hipparcos Catalogue as a consequence of the link to the ICRF (Chap. 7). Actually, in establishing the ICRF immense efforts have been made to minimize the influence of the motion of the Earth caused by the ground-based VLBI observations. Needless to say, this link is one of the key points of the Hipparcos Catalogue compilation, demanding utmost care to avoid unwelcome distortions.

3) a) The FK5 Catalogue is compiled from ground-based observations obtained essentially by a variety of meridian circles, each of them covering only part of the sky, usually some declination zone. After reduction of the heterogeneous raw observations, which involve a whole host of conventions concerning different standards, each meridian circle gives rise to an individual catalogue of stellar positions that is characteristic of the respective instrumental system of the observing equipment. Therefore, one of the first steps of the FK5 compilation deals with the harmonization of the individual catalogues. This is a procedure not fully deterministic, but does leave room for averaging statistical effects (Sects. 2.4.1 and 2.4.2).

b) The Hipparcos Catalogue profits from space-based observations by one single instrument that provides total coverage of the sky. Thus the costly methods for harmonizing catalogues belonging to different instrumental systems are eliminated at this stage, and the reduction of the raw data takes place along the guidelines of one standard set of conventions. Additionally, the reduction of the data acquired in space is relieved of the burden of atmospheric refraction.

When, in the course of future years, data should become available from several Hipparcos-like astrometric missions, it may be possible, under certain circumstances, to merge the raw observations of the respective missions. A global catalogue could then be derived from one large homogeneous data set, circumventing the complex comparison of the individual catalogues from each mission. Otherwise the arduous avenue of catalogue comparison (Sect. 2.4.1) with all its shortcomings remains as an alternative.

4. Astrometry with Radio Interferometers

This chapter summarizes the principles and tools of radio astronomy that ultimately lead to the establishment of a fundamental catalogue via application of the technique of radio interferometry to the measurement of positions of sources at cosmological distances. With this target in mind we briefly introduce the scope of radio astronomy, followed by a short outline concerning the basic terms and concepts of radio interferometry. We discuss the signal reduction from the observables of radio interferometry to astrometric quantities in some detail and, finally, consider the requirements for astrometry. At this point the stage is set for the establishment of a fundamental catalogue for use in astronomy and geodesy.

Radio astronomy plays a complementary role in the astrometry of extragalactic objects. Immediately following the discovery of quasi-stellar objects at cosmological distances in 1963, the potential of extragalactic objects was realized for forming a reference frame, which eventually materialized through a catalogue of positions of radio sources. In numerous observation campaigns the precise optical positions of many of these objects were determined soon after their discovery. Around the same time, radio astronomy also developed the ability to provide positional information from electromagnetic radiation in a spectral range other than the optical. Both types of positions immediately raise questions about the identity of the emission centres and therefore the equivalence of fundamental catalogues derived from observations made in independent frequency ranges. Moreover, astrophysical interpretation is desirable for sources, both optical and radio, that show spatial structure.

Satisfactory answers to these kinds of questions are expected from precise optical and radio astrometry of selected objects that qualify as candidates for fundamental catalogues. Once the optical and radio catalogues are projected onto each other, for instance by rigid rotations, systematic differences between the catalogues can for the most part be eliminated, and the way is prepared for studies of spatial structures with respect to coordinates in the unified optical and radio frames. At this stage it will also be possible to decide on the coincidence of the optical and radio emission centres at the milliarcsecond (mas) level. Because of the complexities of both the catalogue construction and connection of catalogues, an iterative treatment seems indispensable in order to identify sources with negligible structure, which is a necessary condition for meaningful comparisons in the optical and radio domains.

Extensive introductions to radio astronomy are given, e.g., in the textbooks by Rohlfs & Wilson (2000) and Christiansen & Högbom (1985). The technique of radio interferometry, its theoretical background and practical applications are treated in compendia and textbooks such as those of Marton (1976), Thompson et al. (1991), Wohlleben et al. (1991) and Takahashi et al. (2000).

4.1 Radio Astronomy

4.1.1 Historical Review

Observations of celestial bodies made with the naked eye during thousands of years produced evidence that the members of the solar system and the stars are distant objects obeying defined laws of motion. Approximately 400 years ago the invention of the telescope opened up the study of extended structures; progress in this field was further accelerated by the construction of large telescopes and spectrographs. Our knowledge of the Universe is thus almost exclusively based on electromagnetic radiation, since only very little information is obtained from the transport of matter. Planck announced his revolutionary radiation formula in 1902, and in consequence the electromagnetic wave theory postulated radiation of stars spanning the range from X-ray waves to radio waves. The latter are important to astronomy, since they open a new window to the celestial sphere from the surface of the Earth, and this window is complementary to the optical one. Owing to the fact that radio waves have wavelengths 10^6 times longer than those of optical radiation, the resolving power of a radio telescope is relatively low. Efficient radio astronomical devices, such as interferometers, compensate for this drawback to the extent that astrometry with radio interferometers can easily compete with high-precision optical astrometry, as will be shown further below.

Until the beginning of the 20th century only visible light could be used to gain astronomical information from the radiation penetrating down to the Earth's surface. By 1930 the observable spectral region was marginally extended to ultraviolet and near infrared wavelengths (Rohlfs & Wilson 2000, p. 1), thus covering wavelengths in the range $0.35\,\mu\text{m} < \lambda < 1\mu\text{m}$. At that time there was no possibility of observing at other wavelengths, for reasons of either atmospheric opacity or unavailability of suitable detectors.

Radio-frequency radiation from extraterrestrial sources was first reported by Karl Jansky in 1931. At the Bell Telephone Laboratories he detected radio noise using a rotational antenna at 20.5 MHz (wavelength of 14.6 m). The signals came from a direction that rotated through nearly 360° in 24 hours and was close to the galactic centre. In 1937, Grote Reber, an American radio engineer living in the state of Illinois, successfully resumed Jansky's observations at the higher frequency of 160 MHz (1.87 m). He noticed strong indications of radiation at this wavelength along the galactic equator that appeared to be most pronounced at the galactic centre. Over the years Reber undertook a systematic survey of the sky at 160 MHz and, by means of his publications, paved the way to the active phases of radio astronomy starting in the second half of this century. Vigorous research in radio astronomy was stimulated by World War II. Only then was radio radiation from the Sun detected, almost ten years after Jansky and Reber had given evidence of radio emission from the galactic centre. A recent reanalysis of Jansky's observations demonstrated the correctness of their interpretation (Sullivan 1978).

The radio window extends from $\lambda = 20\,\mathrm{m}$ (15 MHz) to $\lambda = 1\,\mathrm{mm}$ (300 GHz). The limits are not sharply marked, since they depend on the geographical latitude and the instantaneous state of the atmosphere and ionosphere, the latter being correlated with solar activity.

The cutoff at high frequencies is caused by molecular resonances of water vapour, oxygen and ozone in the troposphere. A consequence of these resonances is atmospheric attenuation usually extending over regions beyond the resonance frequency. Absorption by the H_2O molecule takes place around 22.2 GHz and 184 GHz, whereas the O_2 molecule shows strong absorption in the vicinity of 60 GHz and 118 GHz.

Absorption bands of other molecules in the atmosphere, such as N_2 and CO_2, are found at frequencies much higher than 300 GHz, where the atmosphere is opaque anyway. The atmospheric attenuation at very high frequencies has a negative effect on the applicability of radio astronomy because of the numerous emission and absorption lines of interstellar molecules that fall in this range.

At the lower end of the range of radio frequencies, electromagnetic radiation is subject to another absorption mechanism in the ionosphere. This is caused by the collision of electrons with ions and neutral particles. The free electrons in the ionosphere tend to absorb the radio radiation if its frequency is smaller than the critical or plasma frequency ν_p. In general, the plasma frequency is a phenomenon of wave propagation in an ionized medium depending on the number, charges and masses of the particles, and the permittivity of vacuum (Kraus 1966). For electrons the plasma frequency can be approximated by

$$\nu_\mathrm{p} = 9\sqrt{N_\mathrm{e}}, \tag{4.1}$$

where ν_p is given in hertz and N_e is the number of electrons per m^3. During normal solar activity typical values of the maximum electron density at nighttime and daytime are $2.5 \times 10^{11}\,\mathrm{m}^{-3}$ and $1.5 \times 10^{12}\,\mathrm{m}^{-3}$, respectively. The plasma frequency, therefore, varies roughly between 4.5 MHz at night and 11.0 MHz during the day. A necessary condition for eliminating ionospheric attenuation is the choice of an observing frequency well above these limits.

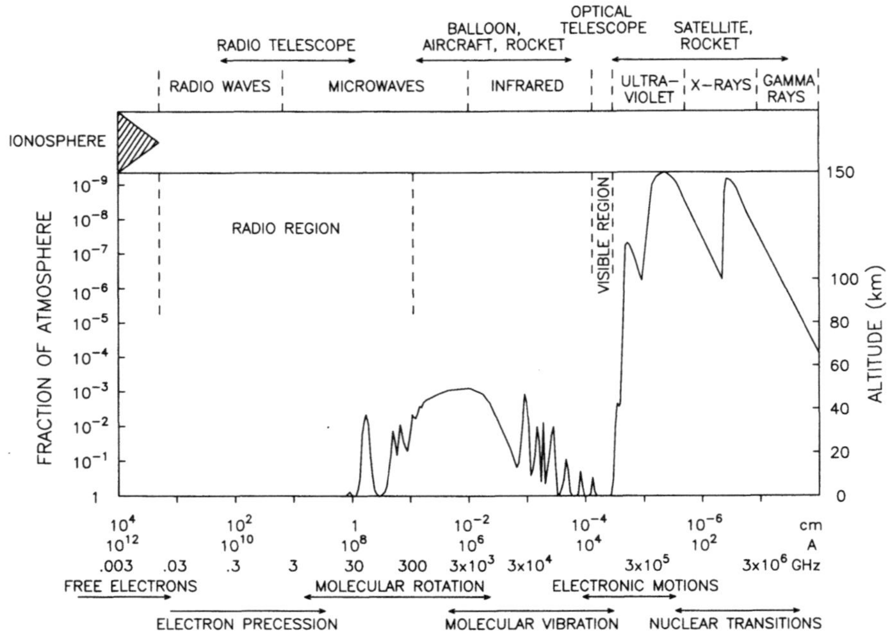

Fig. 4.1. Transparency of the Earth's atmosphere to electromagnetic radiation showing the radio and visible regions. The diagram gives the height of the atmosphere at which the intensity of radiation is attenuated by a factor of 2 (After Rohlfs & Wilson 2000)

Figure 4.1 shows the transparency of the Earth's atmosphere to electromagnetic radiation.

4.1.2 Quasars

Surprising objects have been discovered to emit within the radio window. Among them are solar system bodies, interstellar clouds, masers, pulsars, radio stars and the extravagant radio sources known as quasars, to mention only a few. Their existence became fact with the inception of the new discipline of radio astronomy and has stimulated the development of new theories and the design of mechanisms to explain the detected phenomena. A typical example is the radiation mechanism of quasars, which shows an energy distribution decreasing with increasing radiation frequency. In contrast to the customary thermal emission of optical astrophysics, the radio emission of quasars is of non-thermal origin.

The designation 'quasar' has a long history: It was initially shown in 1953 that the radio source Cygnus A was associated with a remote galaxy (Baade & Minkowski 1954). This fact immediately implied the assumption that some peculiar galaxies might be detectable by radio techniques even

1020+400 10 23 11.565623±29 +39 48 15.38539±36 Q 1.254

if they were so far away that the integrated light from the galaxy failed to register optically. Successful attempts to discover the optical counterparts of radio sources led in 1963 to the recognition that the Universe contained a new class of objects which looked like ordinary stars on photographic plates (Matthews & Sandage 1963; Schmidt 1963). Their spectra displayed emission lines with large red shifts which were indicative of the light's extragalactic origin. For an object of this new class the designation 'quasar' was chosen as a contraction of 'quasi-stellar radio source'. Nowadays, the term quasar is commonly used to describe the entire class of compact extragalactic objects which look like point sources of light, irrespective of existing radio emission.

With the intention of establishing a fundamental catalogue of radio sources we single out radio-emitting quasars from the variety of radio objects. Only a small fraction of the quasars is associated with a powerful and also compact radio source (Kellermann & Owen 1988). It is this subclass that is of interest here, because radio quasars have the potential to provide fiducial points for an extragalactic radio reference frame. Equally important is the availability of the technique of radio interferometry, allowing the determination of the directions to these points accurate to a fraction of a milliarcsecond.

Let us first deal with the nomenclature of quasars. Like those of most celestial bodies, their positions are given in spherical coordinates of right ascension (RA) and declination (Dec). These coordinates became the basis of the international system of nomenclature for quasars (IAU 1974, p. 142). Accordingly, the designation consists of a string of eight characters containing the right ascension and declination with reference to the mean equator and equinox of the Besselian epoch 1950 (B1950.0). The first four characters give the hours and minutes of right ascension, the fifth the sign of the declination, and the remaining three the degrees and truncated tenths of a degree of declination. Prior to the adoption of this IAU nomenclature, i.e. during the pioneering time of radio astronomy and early quasar observations, a multitude of designations for the same object were put into circulation or, simply, the former designation of the New General Catalogue of Nebulae and Clusters of Stars (NGC) was adopted after identification of the object. This early nomenclature still persists for quite a number of sources.

Recently the *Task Group on Astronomical Designations of IAU Commission 5* contemplated a modification of the international system of nomenclature. The new proposal retains the former character string consisting of RA and Dec, but it imposes the condition to refer the spherical coordinates to the mean equator and equinox at the Julian epoch 2000 (J2000.0) and to mark the string by a preceding 'J', standing for 'Julian'. A further condition is to extend the character string in order to accommodate the augmented observation accuracy and to better discriminate objects of small separation (e.g., Lortet et al. 1994 and updates).

In the following examples a variety of designations refer to the same radio source: 0316+413 is equal to 3C 84 indicating source number 84 in the third Cambridge catalogue (Edge et al. 1959); furthermore, it is identical with NGC 1275 and the radio source Perseus A. In the recommended IAU nomenclature the designation of this object reads J031948.16+413042.1, where J relates to the standard Julian epoch J2000.0 followed by hours, minutes, seconds of time and truncated hundredths of seconds of right ascension. The next character gives the sign of the declination followed by degrees, minutes, seconds of arc and truncated tenths of seconds of declination. Another example is 1958−179 equal to OV−198 of the Ohio surveys (Kraus 1977) and also equal to PKS 1958−179 of the Parkes surveys (Bolton et al. 1975) as well as J200057.09−174857.7 in terms of the recommended IAU nomenclature. In both examples the designations given in the new system are based on the coordinates at J2000.0 listed in Kovalevsky (1995a) and Ma et al. (1998).

Strong theoretical reasons speak in favour of using radio emitting quasars as distinguished astrometric objects for a fundamental catalogue. On the hypothesis of an isotropic model of the expanding Universe, as inferred from the 3 K microwave background radiation, the global rotation of the Universe is less than 10^{-9} mas/yr and, therefore, a negligible quantity (Collins & Hawking 1973). The radial velocities increase systematically with distance, while the transverse velocities are randomly distributed about zero and are independent of the distance. Thus, if the speed of light is assumed as the maximum transverse velocity, objects at large distances of approximately 0.1 Gpc, which is typical of a sizeable subset of quasars and distant galaxies, reach at most random motions of 0.6 mas/yr. Using more realistic estimates the upper limit of these motions reduces to 10^{-2} mas/yr (Sect. 1.8). Motions of such magnitude are normally not detectable by current observation techniques and may, therefore, be disregarded. Since there is no evidence of any systematic motion that could be identified with a background rotation, it is natural to define a static (or kinematic) reference system on the hypothesis that distant extragalactic radio objects, mostly quasars, are at rest.

While the absence of a global rotation of the Universe is based on the assumption of isotropy and on some observational evidence excluding the existence of strong anisotropies in the 3 K background radiation, the smallness of random motions of quasars is demonstrated by actual observations. Shapiro et al. (1979) measured the relative coordinates of 3C 345 and NRAO 512 with an uncertainty of about 0.3 mas, and placed an upper bound of 0.5 mas/yr on the relative proper motion of the centres of brightness of the two sources. Likewise, Guirado et al. (1995) determined the position difference of the radio sources 1928+738 and 2007+777 accurate to 0.2 mas, which again suggests that quasar proper motions are of the order of small fractions of milliarcseconds per year. Other recent studies of morphological changes in galaxies between different epochs are indicative of extremely small angular motions of the blobs within the quasar boundaries, probably less than 0.3 mas/yr for a source distance of nearly 100 Mpc (Giovannini et al. 1998). On the hypothesis of the blob velocities having a systematic direction, one

1032−199 10 35 02.155274±50 −20 11 34.35975±48 Q 2.198

may venture to identify the systematic part of the blob angular velocities with a proper motion of the quasar. A quite different approach to estimating the random transverse velocities is provided by the Sun's own velocity with respect to the background of the Universe. As inferred from studies of the microwave background radiation the Sun's velocity is about 400 km/s. If the Sun's velocity is typical of transverse velocities of all bodies in the Universe, the corresponding proper motion would be 10^{-3} mas/yr for objects as distant as 0.1 Gpc.

The above-mentioned kinematical points of view favour quasars as ideal reference objects for astrometry. But also from an observational point of view the quasars are ideal reference objects inasmuch as they represent point-like sources. To illustrate this property we consider the subclass of quasars of variable luminosity, known as BL Lacertae objects, the light curves of which vary substantially over periods of several weeks (Stein et al., 1976). The train of thought is as follows: Physical laws suggest that the mechanism leading to the change of luminosity involves the entire object. In these circumstances, the time needed for completing the process is equal to the difference between the times associated with the minimum and maximum intensity levels. The order of magnitude of this time difference is inferred in practice from the sign changes of the luminosity derivative. Taking 100 Mpc as a typical distance of a quasar and a time difference of a few days, one calculates an angular source diameter well below 1 mas, indicating a point-like structure that is resolvable neither in the optical nor in the radio domain with current observing techniques.

In addition to point-like sources among BL Lacertae objects, sources having this property are also found among the broader class of quasars. Indeed, structure studies have confirmed a substantial number of point-like sources among quasars by using the techniques of radio astronomy (e.g., Pearson et al. 1985; Kellermann et al. 1994; Fey & Charlot 1997, 2000). Thousands of extragalactic objects have been identified in the course of radio surveys. They form a data base of potential candidates for a fundamental catalogue. In early experiments, the images of a class of quasars could not be resolved even on the longest baselines. Many hundreds are now known to exhibit structure at the milliarcsecond level. Nevertheless, the time and frequency variation of most of their internal structures is gentle enough to permit their use as fiducial marks in establishing radio frequency reference frames of sub-mas accuracy (IERS 1994a; Johnston et al. 1995; Ma et al. 1998).

4.1.3 Some Basic Terms and Definitions

With the advancement of radio astronomy it became quite natural to observe discrete sources at different frequencies within the radio window. One of the characteristic quantities obtained by the measurements is the strength of the radio signal received from a source. This is known as the spectral flux density,

```
1038+064     10 41 17.162504±20  +06 10 16.92378±35     Q  1.265
```

flux density or, simply, flux (S), and is measured in watts per square meter per hertz. A convenient unit of flux density is the jansky (Jy):

$$1\,\mathrm{Jy} = 10^{-26}\,\mathrm{W m^{-2}\,Hz^{-1}}\ .$$

Only a small minority of quasars exceed the flux density of a few tenths of Jy. For example, those sources selected for the new IAU fundamental reference frame belong to this minority, showing a median flux density just under 1 Jy at frequencies between 2 and 8 GHz. But even a flux of 1 Jy produces a signal of only 10^{-15} W if a bandwidth of $\Delta\nu = 20$ MHz and an aperture of $5 \times 10^3\,\mathrm{m}^2$ are assumed, corresponding to a telescope of 100 m diameter. At present, a conservative figure for the lower limit of measurable flux is 0.1 millijansky, which, for the above telescope, would mean a detection limit of 10^{-18} W. In comparison, optical telescopes on the surface of the Earth register signals as small as 3×10^{-17} W originating from the faintest objects of magnitude $m = 22$.

Observations at different frequencies reveal a spectral characteristic of radio sources, called the radio spectrum, which shows the dependence of flux density on frequency. The radio spectrum provides a means of distinguishing between sources of thermal and non-thermal radiation. For the first kind of sources the flux density increases with increasing frequency, while for the second kind the flux falls with increasing frequency (Fig. 4.2). As can be seen in Fig. 4.2, the radio spectra of some sources show piecewise power-law dependence on frequency. These can be decomposed into pieces of the form

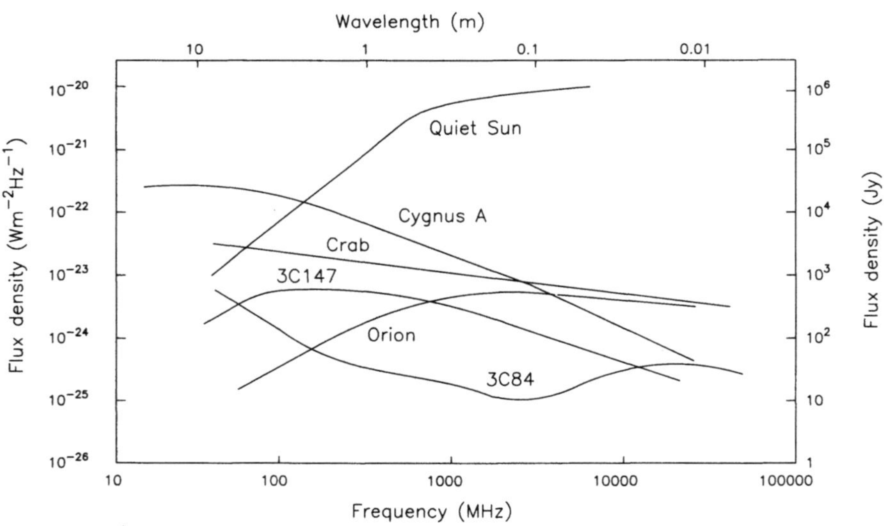

Fig. 4.2. Radio spectra of some prominent radio sources. The quiet Sun and the Orion nebula are thermal sources. The non-thermal sources include a supernova remnant (the Crab nebula), a quasar (3C 147) and two radio galaxies, Cygnus A and 3C 84 (After Christiansen and Högbom 1985)

1038+064 10 41 46.781639±29 +52 33 28.23127±28 Q 1.265

$S \propto \nu^{\alpha}$, where α is the spectral index. In the case of thermal radiation from a black body, the spectral index is 2 as follows from the Rayleigh–Jeans approximation of the radiation law, applied to the lower frequencies encountered in radio astronomy. Examples of thermal radiators are the Moon and the quiet Sun. Their radio emissions originate from regions of a hot medium. The Orion nebula also exhibits thermal radiation caused by the collision of free electrons in the electric field of ions. For this reason, the radiation mechanism is called thermal bremsstrahlung, as opposed to synchrotron emission or magnetic bremsstrahlung. This mechanism is ascribed to the radiation of extragalactic sources and would explain the extremely high radio brightness. Synchrotron emission occurs as a result of the acceleration of relativistic electrons spiralling in magnetic fields. Characteristic of non-thermal radiation is the predominance of negative spectral indices in the radio spectra, as exemplified in Fig. 4.2 by the Crab nebula, which is a supernova remnant, the quasar 3C 147 = 0538+498, and the radio galaxy 3C 84 = 0316+413. The two latter objects are representatives of the class of quasars and distant galaxies that were initially studied in experiments carried out to establish eligibility for a fundamental catalogue of extragalactic radio sources.

4.2 Techniques of Radio Interferometry

4.2.1 Radio Interferometers for Astrometry

Modern astrometry aims at positional coordinates accurate at the milliarcsecond level or better. To reach such a high accuracy, a necessary condition to be fulfilled by the telescope is the capability of distinguishing between point sources with angular separations at the milliarcsecond level. In other words, the resolving power of the instrument should be of the same order of magnitude as the accuracy level striven for. Expressed in radians, the resolving power is equal to the radius of the Airy disc or the angular separation of the maximum and the first zero of the diffraction pattern, namely

$$\theta = 1.22\,\frac{\lambda}{D},$$

where λ and D are the signal wavelength and diameter of the instrument's aperture, respectively. In radio astronomy, dishes of about 30 m diameter are common, and a typical receiver frequency is 5 GHz corresponding to a wavelength of 6 cm. Accordingly, the resolving power is 5 minutes of arc, much too large for astrometry. Note that the location of a point-like radio source can be determined with a remarkably better accuracy than is suggested by the resolving power of a radio telescope. This can be understood by analogy to optical observations: The power available at the antenna output as a function of the direction makes up the antenna power pattern, which is the equivalent of the Airy disc in optical astronomy. To increase the positional accuracy one performs a best fit of the theoretical intensity distribution of the antenna power pattern to the observed intensities, obtained by sweeping the antenna beam across the radio source in at least two directions. An improvement of accuracy by roughly a factor of 10 can be reached in this manner.

Because of mechanical construction difficulties, it would be unrealistic to try to increase the single dish diameter sufficiently to obtain a resolving power of the order of 1 mas. One practical way to achieve the milliarcsecond goal is to use interferometers consisting of two ordinary dishes, but spaced by 10s, 100s or even 1000s of kilometers apart. For distances not exceeding 100 km the interferometer elements can be connected by cables or via microwave communications, and one speaks of Connected Element Interferometry (CEI). A typical CEI installation and its application to astrometry is described by Ryle & Elsmore (1973). Another application of a linear array, however to brightness studies in radio sources, is given by Hogg et al. 1969. The signals from the two antennas are mixed with the signal of a common local oscillator. As the spacing between antennas is increased, unpredictable phase shifts are likely to be introduced by the communication lines, and it is indispensable to use independent local oscillators whose signals are combined at a later stage. Interferometers of this type fall in the category of Very Long Baseline Interferometry (VLBI) and can reach intercontinental distances between the antennas (Bare et al. 1967; Cohen et al. 1968). A two-dimensional extension of the interferometer configuration is realized in arrays forming intercontinental and global networks, which usually have 4 to 10 participating antennas. Examples of dedicated networks that can contain 10 or more antennas are the VLA, the Very Large Array (Thompson et al. 1980), the VLBA, the Very Long Baseline Array (Kellermann & Thompson 1985), and MERLIN, the Multi-Element Radio-Linked Interferometer Network (Thomasson 1986, MERLIN 1999).

In principle, the operation of antenna arrays (or networks) does not differ from that of interferometers. Without losing generality we deal below only with interferometers, giving emphasis to the derivation of the interferometer observables from the time-varying voltages arriving at the antenna receivers. There is a variety of observing frequencies employed in radio interferometry covering the entire radio window. Most astrometric VLBI experiments are now performed with observing frequencies in the S band (2.3 GHz, $\lambda = 13.0$ cm) and X band (8.4 GHz, $\lambda = 3.6$ cm). These frequencies are sufficiently spaced to facilitate the investigation and correction of differential effects caused by the dispersive propagation medium.

4.2.2 Signal Acquisition by Radio Interferometry

Observations by radio interferometry rest upon the analysis of interference patterns of radio waves. Two antennas located at different sites on the Earth receive radio radiation from a very distant point source, so that the incoming

1040+123 10 42 44.605212±24 +12 03 31.26407±40 Q 1.028

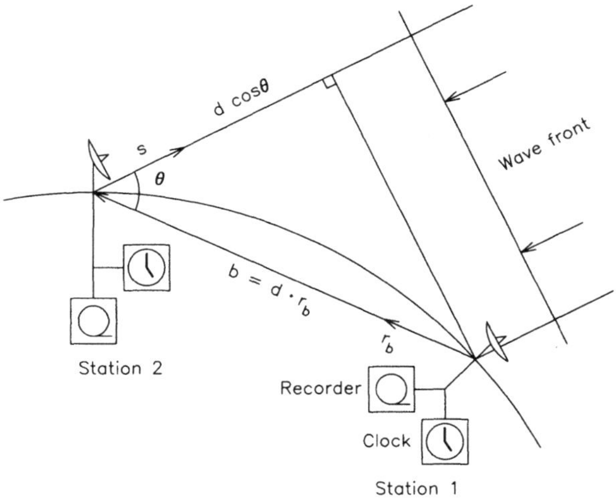

Fig. 4.3. The basic geometry of Very Long Baseline Interferometry (VLBI). Here $\boldsymbol{s}$ and $\boldsymbol{r}_{\mathrm{b}}$ are unit vectors pointing to the radio source and along the direction of the baseline, respectively; $\boldsymbol{b}$ is the baseline vector of length d

rays may be considered parallel to first approximation (Fig. 4.3). The antennas are connected by the baseline vector defined by the baseline parameters or baseline components, e.g., direction and length of the vector.

The signals arriving at the antennas are expected to originate in the same coherent zone of emission and to have the distribution of Gaussian random noise. The voltages generated in the antennas are assumed to be strictly associated with the original signals. In a connected element interferometer, the outputs of the antennas are immediately multiplied together to recover the frequency of the interference fringes. The VLBI technique, however, requires separate recording of the output of each antenna on a magnetic tape, with the outputs subsequently multiplied together for further processing at a remote facility. Multiplication and averaging of the signals takes place in a correlator, which is essentially a combination of a multiplying circuit and a lowpass filter. The correlator output provides interference fringes for the following reasons (for illustration we consider a monochromatic signal): Because of the rotation of the Earth, the two antennas generally experience different radial velocities with respect to the source, thereby causing different Doppler shifts in frequency at the antennas and, as a consequence, cause interference fringes that are detected in the correlator of a correlation interferometer. Its output is the sinusoidal *coherence function*, R, of the electromagnetic field expressed by

$$R = A_{\mathrm{f}} \cos(2\pi\nu_{\mathrm{f}}\, t + \phi_{\mathrm{f}})\,. \tag{4.2}$$

By analogy to optics, A_{f} is called the *fringe amplitude* and ϕ_{f} the *fringe phase.* Also, A_{f} measures the correlated flux, which is identical with the total flux if the angular extension of the radio source is very small compared to the resolving power of the interferometer. Due to the Earth's rotation, the fringe frequency, ν_{f}, changes slowly on the scale of minutes. At this stage of the correlator output, the original signal has undergone considerable modifications from a technical point of view; the signal's information content, however, has not yet been touched. In fact, signal processing such as amplification, filtering and recording is more conveniently performed at an intermediate frequency (IF), typically tens or hundreds of MHz, instead of directly manipulating the high-frequency (GHz) cosmic signal. To this end one converts the incoming frequency by the heterodyne technique, which mixes the signal frequencies received at the antennas with the frequency of a local oscillator (LO). Signal recording, for example, benefits from frequency conversion inasmuch as the IF signal can be completely preserved by sampling it at the lower Nyquist rate corresponding to the smaller intermediate frequency band, whereas the sampling rate of the original cosmic signal would have to be impracticably high (see, e.g., Thompson et al. 1991, p. 212). Thus, the fringe frequency appearing in the coherence function R is the result of frequency conversion, i.e. $\nu_{\mathrm{f}} = \nu - \nu_{\mathrm{LO}}$, which is the signal frequency diminished by the frequency of the local oscillator. On the other hand, the fringe amplitude and the fringe phase retain the original signal characteristics.

This line of thought on the formation of the interference pattern remains valid for natural sources which, normally, emit a band of frequencies. One should note that the *fringe amplitudes* and *fringe phases* carry the principal astronomical information from the observed source and, therefore, are regarded as the fundamental interferometer observables. How to extract astrometric information from the interferometer output will be the subject of the next section.

4.3 The Observables

4.3.1 The Phase Observable Derived from VLBI

Theoretically, no distinction exists between Connected Element Interferometry (CEI) and Very Long Baseline Interferometry (VLBI). Only from a technical point of view are distinctions required. In the case of CEI the voltages generated at the two antennas are transmitted to the correlator in real time by means of coaxial cables for baselines not exceeding 50 km, or by optical fibers or microwave communications for baselines of the order of 100 km. The present state of the art of communication systems has not yet reached that degree of progress which would allow the connection, in real time, of antenna stations separated by intercontinental or continental distances typical of VLBI. For VLBI, therefore, each data stream must be stored on magnetic tape at its site of acquisition after radio frequency conversion to the intermediate frequency (IF), digitization and sampling at the Nyquist rate. Only a cursory outline is presented here of the data acquisition process during which

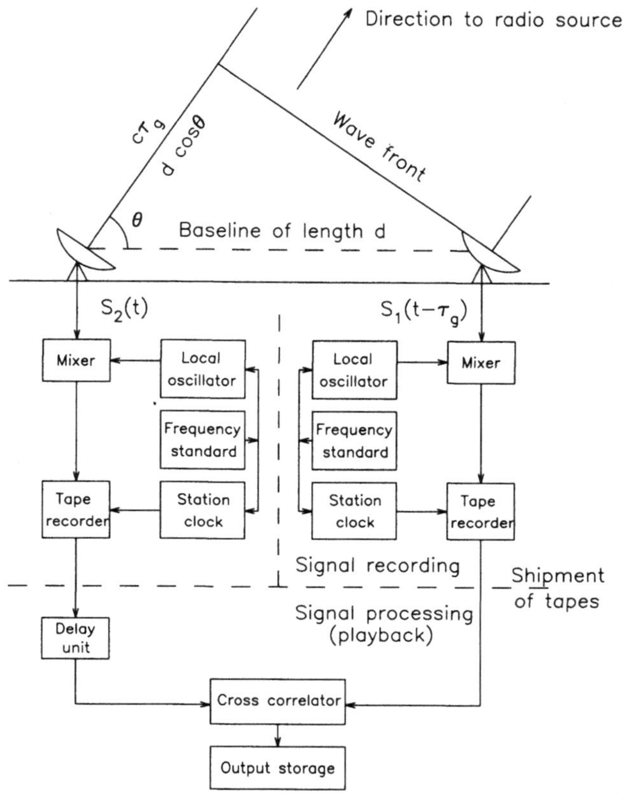

Fig. 4.4. A general block diagram of a VLBI recording system. The lower horizontal dotted line separates the terminals for signal recording from the processing terminal dedicated to the combination of the two signal streams

the many gigabytes collected during an observation of a single source are reduced to the 16 bytes representing values of the observable and its error estimate.

Special equipment is required to be installed at the stations associated with the remotely situated antennas in order to make them function as an interferometer. At the stations one needs: 1) a stable local-oscillator system for conversion of the radio signal frequency, 2) a video converter for the conversion of the signal of intermediate frequency to a video band (a few MHz), 3) a procedure for synchronization of the station clocks and 4) a device for storing the processed signals and associating them with a reference time. At the processing centre a playback system is needed to enable the correlation of the tape-recorded data streams. Schematically, Fig. 4.4 depicts the arrangement of the essential elements of a typical VLBI installation.

To ensure that the tape-recorded signals can be successfully multiplied together in the central correlator at some later stage, the antenna stations

1053+815 10 58 11.535365±118 +81 14 32.67521±27 Q 0.706

are equipped with a frequency standard or station clock of extremely high stability. Its function is twofold:

1) the frequency standard controls the local oscillator needed for frequency conversion;
2) it also controls the station clock that imprints the tape-recorded IF signal with a reference time.

Cross-correlation will be most effective when the timing pulses on both tapes are synchronized and when the local oscillator frequencies are identical at the two sites. Consequently, great attention is focused on possible timing errors caused by frequency offsets in the standards. Various methods of clock synchronization have been devised; one of them is the introduction of the timing error and its drift as additional unknowns to be estimated from VLBI observables, while another is the use of the Global Positioning System (GPS) for clock calibration (Hofmann-Wellenhof et al. 1992).

When attempting to achieve an astrometric positional accuracy of one milliarcsecond (mas) or better, one is left with no choice but to give preference to the VLBI technique. In fact, the maximum internal precision reached by CEI is estimated to be only 30 mas (Florkowski et al. 1985), whereas VLBI estimates arrive at the milliarcsec level, as we can infer by a rough guess from the geometry of Fig. 4.4. Accordingly, with c denoting the speed of light, we get for the geometric time delay, τ_g,

$$c\,\tau_g = d\cos\theta\ .$$

By definition, τ_g is positive if the wave front reaches station 2 later than station 1, i.e. for $0 < \theta < \pi/2$. It is negative for $\pi/2 < \theta < \pi$.

The variation of the time delay with source direction becomes

$$\Delta\tau_g = -\frac{d}{c}\sin\theta\,\Delta\theta \tag{4.3}$$

or

$$\Delta\theta = -\frac{c}{d\sin\theta}\,\Delta\tau_g\ .$$

A change in the time delay by 10% of a wavelength is easily detectable in the cross-correlation process at current sensitivity levels. This change is equal to $0.1\ \lambda/c$ seconds, thus causing a variation of the source direction by

$$\Delta\theta = -\frac{0.1\lambda}{d\sin\theta}\ . \tag{4.4}$$

On a 5000 km-long baseline and with an operating frequency in the X band, corresponding to $\lambda = 3.6$ cm, we obtain from (4.4) the variation of the source direction, or the fractional fringe spacing, to be approximately $0.14\ \mathrm{mas}/\sin\theta$. This means that directions should be theoretically measurable by VLBI accurate to within 0.2 mas on the average.

1057−797 10 58 43.309786±106 −80 03 54.15949±27 Q ...

It is this astrometric potential of VLBI which draws our attention from here on to the fringe amplitudes and fringe phases available at the output of VLBI correlators. As the amplitudes contain only information on source structure and brightness, we restrict the following sections to the study of the *phase*, which makes up the natural and original astrometric VLBI observable.

To gain some insight into the fringe phase of the coherence function (also called the cross-correlation function) introduced in (4.2), we return briefly to the electric fields caused by the signals at the antennas. For illustration let us consider a monochromatic signal originating in a point source, and electric fields generating the voltages

$$V_1(t) = A\cos\omega\, t$$

at antenna 1, designated as the time-reference antenna, and

$$V_2(t) = A\cos\left[\omega(t-\tau_g)\right]$$

at antenna 2, where the signal is retarded by the geometric time delay τ_g. Here A is the amplitude, $\omega = 2\pi\nu$ the angular frequency, and t the time.

Frequency conversion by mixing the antenna signals with signals from local oscillators, generating the frequencies ω_1 and ω_2 close to the signal frequency, results in signals composed of the frequencies $\omega + \omega_1$ and $\omega - \omega_1$ at antenna 1, and $\omega + \omega_2$ and $\omega - \omega_2$ at antenna 2. As soon as the high-frequency parts are filtered out, one is left with voltages suitable for recording on magnetic tape. These voltages may be expressed as

$$V_1(t) = A\cos\left[(\omega - \omega_1)\, t + \theta_1\right]$$

and

$$V_2(t) = A\cos\left[(\omega - \omega_2)\, t - \omega\,\tau_g + \theta_2\right],$$

where θ_1 and θ_2 are phase shifts introduced by the receivers and local oscillators.

Thus the phases of the two signals after mixing are

$$\phi_1 \;=\; (\omega - \omega_1)\, t + \theta_1$$

and

$$\phi_2 \;=\; (\omega - \omega_2)\, t - \omega\,\tau_g + \theta_2\,.$$

It is assumed that the frequencies of the two local oscillators are identical, i.e. $\omega_1 = \omega_2 = \omega_{LO}$. If small differences existed they would be manifested in θ_1 and θ_2, which are slowly varying phase shifts attributed to the frequency standards. Clock errors, τ_1 and τ_2, of the recorded signals cannot be excluded, and can likewise be accounted for in the phases. Furthermore, during processing the data stream at antenna 2 passes through a delay unit, which advances the time marks of the signals by τ_m, known as the provisional model time delay. The latter is calculated on the basis of the source position and the geometry of the baseline and, for these reasons, approximates the geometric time delay. Then, the realistic signal phases prior to correlation have the form

$$\begin{aligned}\phi_1^{\mathrm{r}} &= (\omega - \omega_{\mathrm{LO}})(t - \tau_1) + \theta_1\,,\\ \phi_2^{\mathrm{r}} &= (\omega - \omega_{\mathrm{LO}})(t - \tau_2 + \tau_{\mathrm{m}}) - \omega\,\tau_{\mathrm{g}} + \theta_2\,.\end{aligned}$$

The cross-correlation function R results from multiplying together the two signals V_1 and V_2. Formally R is expressed as

$$R(\tau_{\mathrm{m}}) = \frac{1}{2T}\int_{-T}^{T} V_1(t)\, V_2(t + \tau_{\mathrm{m}})\, \mathrm{d}t\,.$$

Here T is chosen so that a large number of variations of the signal amplitude occur in the time interval $2\,T$. For the above signal representation the cross-correlation produces a beat signal of the form

$$R(\tau_{\mathrm{m}}) = A\cos[(\omega - \omega_{\mathrm{LO}})\,t + \phi], \tag{4.5}$$

having the fringe phase

$$\begin{aligned}\phi &= \phi_1^r - \phi_2^r\\ &= (\omega - \omega_{\mathrm{LO}})(\tau_2 - \tau_1) - (\theta_2 - \theta_1)\\ &\quad + \omega(\tau_{\mathrm{g}} - \tau_{\mathrm{m}}) + \omega_{\mathrm{LO}}\,\tau_{\mathrm{m}}\,.\end{aligned} \tag{4.6}$$

If the station clocks are synchronized and the assumption is made that the slowly varying phase shifts attributed to the frequency standards are equal, we obtain from (4.6)

$$\phi = \omega(\tau_{\mathrm{g}} - \tau_{\mathrm{m}}) + \omega_{\mathrm{LO}}\,\tau_{\mathrm{m}},$$

which reduces to

$$\phi = \omega_{\mathrm{LO}}\,\tau_{\mathrm{g}}$$

as soon as the model time delay is chosen to coincide with the actual geometrical time delay. It is this expression which defines the interferometer fringe phase. Since τ_{g} varies as the Earth rotates, ϕ is a function of time.

4.3.2 Derivative Observables

The fringe phase, or simply phase, is the immediate astrometric observable of a two-element interferometer. In geometrical terms the phase observable is the phase difference of the two beams arriving at antennas 1 and 2 (see Fig. 4.3). It is equal to the 2π multiple of the difference of wavelengths counted along these beams. In most applications the phase observable has an ambiguity equal to a multiple of 2π, meaning that the astrometrically important difference of the path lengths is exactly known apart from this ambiguity. With this reservation, therefore, the geometric time delay is the phase delay τ_ϕ and, in anticipation of the terminology given below, the definition of the fringe phase reads

$$\phi = \omega\,\tau_\phi\,, \quad \omega = 2\pi\,\nu\,, \tag{4.7}$$

where ω is the local oscillator frequency. To interpret the phase observable, it is necessary either to resolve the inherent ambiguity or to find methods that allow the extraction of observables from the cross-correlation function without ambiguities.

For illustration of the general line of thought we consider a simplified mathematical model of the phase observable (Counselman III 1976):

$$\phi(t) = \frac{2\pi\nu}{c}\,\boldsymbol{b}(t)\cdot\boldsymbol{s} + \phi_{\mathrm{media}}(t) + \phi_{\mathrm{instr}}(t) + 2\pi k \tag{4.8}$$

with the following notation: ν is the observing frequency of the local oscillator, c is the velocity of light, $\boldsymbol{b}(t)$ is the baseline vector, $\boldsymbol{s}$ is the unit vector of the source position, which is taken to be constant in the coordinate system of the observations, and t is the time. The scalar product $\boldsymbol{b}\cdot\boldsymbol{s}$ is the geometrical path difference of the two beams. The phase differences caused by the propagation media (i.e., atmosphere and ionosphere) and the instrumental equipment at the antennas are symbolized by $\phi_{\mathrm{media}}(t)$ and $\phi_{\mathrm{instr}}(t)$, respectively. An unknown integer, k, accounts for the phase ambiguity.

Only the absence of clock errors and instrumental and environmental phase shifts ensures that the phase observable extracted from the output of the cross-correlator will be equal to the number of wavelengths along the path difference, as expressed by the first term on the right-hand side of (4.8). In practice, the use of the phase observable for astrometric applications is usually impaired due to the fact that the value of k may change during an observing session lasting longer than several minutes, since in these circumstances the individual phase contributions by the baseline, the environment and equipment are normally not predictable with accuracies better than 2π. Nevertheless, in special cases the phases are preservable over an interval of time on the scale of one hour, thus yielding very precise astrometric results concerning relative source positions (e.g., Shapiro et al. 1979; Guirado et al. 1995). For global astrometry programs, however, it became common practice to avoid the phase observable in preference of derivative observables originating from fringe phases.

Before we consider the derivative observables, it is appropriate to dwell upon the manifold nomenclature used in the literature. Our point of departure is the *fringe phase observable* or *phase observable*, which is the *fundamental interferometer observable* for astrometry. For completeness, we briefly mention that lengthy processing of the raw VLBI measurements precedes the production of the fringe phase and derivative observables. This treatment comprises a data processing chain commencing with the cross-correlation function which becomes the input for generating the cross power spectrum by Fourier transformation. From here a further Fourier transform derives the delay resolution function from the cross power spectrum (Thompson et al. 1991). Finally, by means of the frequency synthesis procedure originated by Rogers (1970) one obtains the multiband delay resolution function from which the VLBI observables are extracted. To circumvent the phase ambiguity, it is customary to resort to using observables that are derived from the phase observable. These are the phase delay and the phase delay rate on the one hand, and the group delay and group delay rate on the other. Phase delay and its time derivative are defined at a single frequency, while group delay and group delay rate involve more than one frequency.

In a dispersive propagation medium the velocity of the incoming signal depends on the signal frequency. There are two characteristic velocities associated with the radio signal: its phase velocity, which is the propagation velocity of a point of constant phase, and its group velocity, which is the propagation velocity of a light beam. Consequently, the signals received at stations 1 and 2 (see Fig. 4.3) produce two types of delay: the phase delay τ_ϕ and the group delay τ_{group}.

The phase ϕ is equal to the number n_λ of oscillations counted along the path length difference of the signals arriving at antennas 1 and 2, i.e. $\phi = 2\pi\, n_\lambda$. The phase delay is then defined as the time that elapses while the signal propagates over this path length difference at the phase velocity, which is $v_\phi = \omega/k_\lambda$ where $k_\lambda = 2\pi/\lambda$ is the wave number. Thus the phase delay becomes

$$\tau_\phi = \frac{n_\lambda\,\lambda}{v_\phi} = \frac{\phi}{2\pi}\,\frac{\lambda}{v_\phi} = \frac{\phi}{\omega}\,. \tag{4.9}$$

In contrast, group delay is based on the group velocity v_{group}. To get an idea of the group delay, we imagine that it arises from dividing the path length difference by the group velocity. Speaking of group velocity presupposes the superposition of several waves having different frequencies. For small frequency and wavelength differences, or if ω is a linear function of the wave number, the group delay is

$$v_{\mathrm{group}} = \frac{\partial\omega}{\partial k_\lambda} = \frac{\partial\omega}{\partial(\omega/v_\phi)}\,. \tag{4.10}$$

The last term follows from substitution of $k_\lambda = \omega/v_\phi$, showing that group velocity equals phase velocity if the phase velocity is independent of frequency, i.e. when dispersive effects are absent. Expressing ω/v_ϕ as $\phi/(n_\lambda\lambda)$, we obtain for the group delay from (4.9)

$$\tau_{\mathrm{group}} = \frac{n_\lambda\lambda}{v_{\mathrm{group}}} = n_\lambda\lambda\,\frac{\partial(\phi/n_\lambda\lambda)}{\partial\omega} = \frac{\partial\phi}{\partial\omega}\,. \tag{4.11}$$

Thus, group delay is the derivative of fringe phase with respect to the angular frequency, which stands for the central frequency of the observing band

and, as such, it requires bandwidth. As group delay depends on frequency, it can be modified by dispersive effects. In the absence of dispersion, group delay and phase delay are identical. This, however, is a purely theoretical discussion, since even in a perfect vacuum there may be components in the instrumentation chain whose response depends on frequency.

One of the customary observables supplied by the interferometer is the phase delay rate, $\partial\tau_\phi/\partial t$, which is also known as fringe rate or fringe frequency, ν_{f}, defined by

$$\nu_{\mathrm{f}} = \frac{\partial\phi}{\partial t} = \omega\,\frac{\partial\tau_\phi}{\partial t}\,. \tag{4.12}$$

Accordingly, the fringe frequency may be considered as the phase delay rate multiplied by the observing frequency.

The group delay rate observable, $\partial\tau_{\mathrm{group}}/\partial t$, is also provided, but it is not accurate enough to be of significant astrometric use. Problems with resolving 2π ambiguities in the signal phase over large distances usually preclude the direct use of the phase delay observable. Due to its higher precision relative to group delay rate and its more facile extraction from observations relative to phase delay, the group delay observable takes precedence for astrometric and geodetic uses. Generally, in astrometric VLBI applications the two most favoured observables free of 2π ambiguities are fringe frequency, ν_{f}, and group delay, abbreviated from here on simply by τ and generically called time delay. The next section deals with the astrometric information content of fringe frequency and time delay, in view of the fact that the current efforts in catalogue compilation using VLBI techniques rest almost entirely on these two observables.

4.3.3 Fringe Frequency and Time Delay

Expressed in physical terms the fringe frequency observable is akin to the fringe oscillations or interference pattern generated by the variation of τ_ϕ as the Earth rotates. The number of oscillations of the fringes, i.e. their frequency, is equal to the number of wavelengths contained in the time rate of change of the path length difference between the interferometer terminals. In mathematical notation this frequency is

$$\frac{1}{\lambda}\,\frac{\partial(c\tau_\phi)}{\partial t} = \nu\,\frac{\partial\tau_\phi}{\partial t}\,. \tag{4.13}$$

Apart from the factor 2π, we encounter on the right-hand side of (4.13) the definition of the fringe frequency observable given in (4.12). On these grounds, the fringe frequency observable is obtained from the variation of the phase during the observation interval. The fringe frequency changes slowly on the time scale of minutes due to the Earth's rotation.

Fringe frequency may also be interpreted as the negative Doppler shift between the two antennas. Putting $v = \mathrm{d}(d\,\cos\,\theta)/\mathrm{d}t$ for the velocity, we conclude from the geometry of Fig. 4.3 that the Doppler shift is given to first approximation by

$$\Delta\omega = -\omega\frac{v}{c} = -\omega\frac{\mathrm{d}}{\mathrm{d}t}\left(\frac{d\cos\theta}{c}\right) = -\omega\frac{\mathrm{d}\tau_\phi}{\mathrm{d}t}\,.$$

Because of effects caused by the propagation media and the site equipment, the fringe frequency is expressed realistically by

$$\nu_{\mathrm{f}}(t) = \frac{\partial\phi_{\mathrm{g}}(t)}{\partial t} + \frac{\partial\phi_{\mathrm{media}}(t)}{\partial t} + \frac{\partial\phi_{\mathrm{instr}}(t)}{\partial t}\,. \tag{4.14}$$

Source position and baseline information are inherent in the geometric phase, ϕ_{g}, of the first term of (4.8). The disturbance of the phases consists of random and short-term fluctuations. Through time differentiation of the fluctuations the disturbing effect tends to be amplified, which has the consequence that imprecision is introduced into this observable.

A more powerful observable, also avoiding phase ambiguities, is the time delay or, more precisely, the group delay. Having given above the definition of group delay, we are still left with the complex problem of extracting this observable from the raw observations by some measurement technique. For details we refer to Thompson et al. (1991), p. 256. Accordingly, the group delay can be derived from the position of the cross-correlation peak, since the cross-correlation function assumes a maximum value as soon as one of the provisionally applied (modelled) time delays, τ_i, which are precalculated for the different delay channels, approximates the group delay. Other techniques determine τ by measuring the slope of the phase versus frequency. As for fringe frequency, the definition given for the time delay is valid for the ideal case where the fringe phase is not exposed to disturbances by the propagation media and instrumental phase noise. More generally, the time delay is represented by

$$\begin{aligned}\tau(t) &= \frac{\partial\phi_{\mathrm{g}}(t)}{\partial\omega} + \frac{\partial\phi_{\mathrm{media}}(t)}{\partial\omega} + \frac{\partial\phi_{\mathrm{instr}}(t)}{\partial\omega} \\ &= \tau_{\mathrm{g}}(t) + \tau_{\mathrm{media}}(t) + \tau_{\mathrm{instr}}(t)\,.\end{aligned} \tag{4.15}$$

The astrometry of a source and the geodesy of the baseline are embedded in the geometric part of the phase given in the first term of (4.14) and (4.15). We elaborate on this crucial part in Sect. 5.4.2 and, as far as the fringe frequency observable is concerned, in Sect. 5.4.3. With regard to the disturbing parts of the fringe frequency and time delay, atmospheric models are adopted to estimate τ_{media}. Clock synchronization is performed either by direct solution for the clock offsets or by calibration using the global positioning system (GPS). To be more adaptable to realistic conditions, it is nowadays customary to introduce parametrized models representing the delays of the propagation media and instruments. These parameters are usually estimated simultaneously with the unknown source coordinates and baseline components as outlined in Sect. 5.4.7.

4.3.4 Uncertainties in the Interferometer Observables

We are already aware that a considerable amount of the observable uncertainty is contributed by fluctuations of the frequency standards, the propagation media and clock synchronization. What follows here deals exclusively with the accuracy to which the observables are measurable in the presence of Gaussian noise of the receivers, also called the 'system noise'. This accuracy is related to the instrumental signal-to-noise ratio (SNR).

The estimated error of the fringe phase, expressed in radians, is approximately equal to the inverse of the signal-to-noise ratio (Moran 1975),

$$\delta\phi \approx \frac{T_{\mathrm{R}}}{T_{\mathrm{A}}\sqrt{2\Delta\nu T}} \equiv (\mathrm{SNR})^{-1}\,.$$

Using (4.12) the error of fringe frequency, expressed in Hz, is approximately

$$\delta\nu_{\mathrm{f}} \approx \frac{\delta\phi}{T}\,,$$

and, using (4.11), the error of the time delay, expressed in seconds, becomes

$$\delta\tau \approx \frac{\delta\phi}{2\pi\Delta\nu_{\mathrm{eff}}}\,.$$

More details on the observable errors are derived in the context of interferometer techniques in Thompson et al. (1991), p. 392.

The following notation is used above: T_{A} and T_{R} are the geometric means of the two antenna temperatures and the receiver temperatures, respectively. The recorded bandwidth given in Hz is $\Delta\nu$ with the mean observing frequency at its centre, and $\Delta\nu_{\mathrm{eff}}$ the effective bandwidth, again in Hz. One speaks of 'effective bandwidth' if two or more single frequency bands of bandwidth $\Delta\nu$ are recorded, spaced over some total frequency range; this total frequency range is called the effective bandwidth. Large effective bandwidths reduce the delay uncertainty and are achieved by recording the signals at a number of frequencies within a given observing band. The time T is given in seconds and signifies the integration time of the two antenna signals in the correlator. It is much greater than the reciprocal bandwidth and is limited by the coherence time, which can be as long as several minutes for intercontinental baselines and medium sized antennas. The quantity $2\Delta\nu \cdot T$ is the number of data samples averaged in the correlator in the course of a single observation.

In performing the transformation from the errors of the observables to the corresponding errors of the angular measurements, we make use of (4.3), from which the relationship can be inferred between the variation of fringe phase and time delay as a function of θ. The variation of the fringe frequency follows by differentiation from

$$\nu_{\mathrm{f}} = \omega\,\frac{\partial\tau}{\partial t}\,,$$

1148−671 11 51 13.426591±88 −67 28 11.09423±59 ? . . .

yielding

$$\delta\nu_{\mathrm{f}} = -\omega \frac{d}{c} \dot{\theta} \cos\theta \, \delta\theta \, ,$$

where θ is the angle between the source direction and the baseline, and $\dot{\theta}$ is the rate of change of the source direction relative to the baseline. It is proportional to the angular velocity, ω_{e}, of the Earth's rotation. On substituting the aforementioned observable errors, one gets the corresponding errors or sensitivities of the angle θ of the source direction, in radians:

$$\begin{aligned}
\sin\theta \;\; \delta\theta(\phi) &\approx \frac{1}{2\pi} \frac{\lambda}{d} (\mathrm{SNR})^{-1} \, , \\
\cos\theta \;\; \delta\theta(\nu_{\mathrm{f}}) &\approx \frac{1}{2\pi} \frac{\lambda}{d} (\mathrm{SNR})^{-1} \frac{1}{\omega_{\mathrm{e}} T} \, , \\
\sin\theta \;\; \delta\theta(\tau) &\approx \frac{1}{2\pi} \frac{\lambda}{d} (\mathrm{SNR})^{-1} \frac{\omega}{2\pi \Delta\nu_{\mathrm{eff}}} \, .
\end{aligned}$$

These error estimates are due entirely to signal-to-noise limitations of angular measurements inferred from VLBI observables. They reflect the ideal case when the source is unresolved and processing losses do not occur. Geometric effects caused by the propagation media, clock synchronization errors etc. have been ignored.

Antenna diameters of typically 30 m or larger are customary in interferometer installations for astrometric and geodetic experiments. A signal-to-noise ratio of 20 is not unusual for such interferometers on the assumption of a flux density of one jansky, which is an average in astrometric observation campaigns. Moreover, our estimates of the uncertainties of the observables derived from signals with $\lambda = 3.6$ cm (X band) can be based on an integration time, T, of 100 s and an effective bandwidth of 56 MHz, roughly corresponding to the original Mark III system (Clark 1980). We then find for the observable errors on a 5000 km baseline in turn $\delta\phi = 0.05$ rad, $\delta\nu_{\mathrm{f}} = 0.5$ mHz and $\delta\tau = 0.14$ ns, corresponding to angular sensitivities of approximately 0.01, 1.6 and 1.7 milliarcseconds (mas) for phase, fringe frequency and delay, respectively. The error in the time delay, especially, has been reduced to near 10 ps during the past decade by extending the bandwidth to several hundred MHz. On the whole, the errors arising solely from the sensitivity of the antenna and receiver system do not seriously limit astrometric VLBI experiments.

Compared with the receiver noise, the observable errors introduced by the propagation media are much larger. For example, the ionospheric delay amounts to several nanoseconds and is a function of the electron density and observing frequency. Simultaneous measurements in the S band (2.3 GHz) and X band (8.4 GHz), however, can eliminate the ionosphere delay almost completely by applying the dual frequency procedure. A more serious limitation to the accuracy of fringe frequency and time delay is imposed by the unknown dry and wet parts of the troposphere. This subject has received detailed treatment by Ronnang (1989). We confine ourselves here to mentioning that the tropospheric contributions to fringe frequency and time delay are of the magnitude order of 100 mHz and 8 ns, respectively. Most of these effects of the propagation media are due to the dry component of the troposphere and are predictable from the surface pressure to within 0.01 ns in the case of time delay. Approximately 0.5 ns are ascribed to the wet component, which is a priori unmodellable because of its variability and unpredictability from Earth surface meteorology. This estimate underlines the fact that the unmodelled error sources due to the atmosphere are significantly larger than the uncertainties caused by the noise of the antenna and receiver system.

4.4 Requirements for Astrometry

4.4.1 Geometric Delay Models

Careful modelling of the observed delay is one of the indispensable tasks in preparing the parameter estimation process for high precision astrometric applications of radio interferometry. A variety of causes contribute to the observed delay. These are: baseline geometry, station positions, Earth orientation, antenna structure, instrumentation, atmosphere and source structure. The largest component of the observed delay is the geometric delay. It is defined as the difference in arrival time of a signal at two geometrically separate points. This time difference would be measured by perfect instrumentation, perfectly synchronised, and as if there were a perfect vacuum between the observed object and the Earth-based observing sites. In other words, the geometric delay measures the scalar product of the baseline and source direction vectors. Therefore, the data determine only the relative directions of the sources and baseline, which is equivalent to the determination of the orientation of the whole Earth relative to the sources. A rigid link of the baseline to geographic features of the Earth can be provided by the introduction of a reference station with known coordinates in the terrestrial reference frame, and the adoption of a conventional origin for celestial orientation, e.g., the right ascension of a selected source.

Even this geometric delay is remarkably complex, requiring extensive modelling related to, e.g., the wave front arrival time difference, time information, station location, Earth orientation, Earth orbital motion, antenna structure and source structure. Much of the burden of the delay modelling arises from the numerous coordinate transformations that are necessary to relate the celestial reference frame, used for locating the radio sources, to the terrestrial reference frame to which the station locations refer. Ultimately, the delay modelling serves the purpose of removing from the observable in the best possible way those disturbing effects which are unwanted in the parameter estimation.

To give an overview of the scope of the task, we present below the principal steps of an approach applied to VLBI delay modelling while referring to the specialist literature for details (e.g., Sovers et al. 1998). On occasion we deal in the succeeding sections with exceptional components of the geometric delay such as the retarded baseline and the gravitational delay, in order to emphasize the complexity of observable modelling. In the context of parameter estimation the problem of modelling is encountered again in Sect. 5.4.7.

The construction of the VLBI model for the observed delay may be summarized in seven steps (Sovers et al. 1998):

1) Specify the proper locations of the two stations as measured in a defined Earth-fixed frame at the time that the wave front intersects station 1. Let this time be the proper time t, as measured by a clock in the Earth-fixed frame.
2) Modify the station location for Earth-fixed effects such as solid Earth tides, tectonic motion and station and antenna motions.
3) Transform these proper station locations to a geocentric celestial coordinate frame with its origin at the centre of the Earth and moving with the Earth's centre of mass. For instance, the spherical coordinate system of right ascension and declination may be adopted for this geocentric coordinate frame.
4) To account for effects of the Special Theory of Relativity, perform a Lorentz transformation of the proper station locations from the geocentric celestial frame to a frame at rest relative to the centre of mass of the solar system, and rotationally aligned with the geocentric celestial frame.
5) Compute the proper time delay for the passage of the specified wave front from station 1 to station 2 (see also Sect. 4.4.3) in this frame referring to the solar system barycentre (SSB). Correct for antenna and source structure. Add the effective change in proper delay caused by the gravitational delay of the signal within the solar system (see Sect. 4.4.4) yielding the SSB geometric delay.
6) Perform a Lorentz transformation of the SSB geometric delay back to the celestial geocentric frame moving with the Earth. This completes the model calculations for the geometric portion of the observed delay.
7) Add to this geometric delay, obtained in an Earth-fixed frame, the contributions due to clock offsets, tropospheric delays and effects of the ionosphere on the signal, in order to get the total modelled delay corresponding to the actual delay measurement.

By carrying out steps 1 to 4, proper station locations in the Earth-fixed frame are related to corresponding proper locations in the SSB frame with due consideration of a special relativistic transformation between proper coordinates of two local frames in relative motion. Step 5 is dedicated to the calculation of the geometric delay in the SSB frame on the basis of the SSB station locations and an a priori SSB source location. At this stage a small

`1155+251      11 58 25.787505±37   +24 50 17.96369±60      G   . . .`

delay correction is applied to account for the differential gravitational retardation introduced along the paths of the two rays through the solar system, including retardation by the Earth's gravity. Finally, step 6 transforms the SSB geometric delay to the observed geometric delay in the celestial geocentric reference frame, and step 7 provides the non-geometric portions of the observed delay.

Having constructed the model for the delay, it is easy to get the model for the phase delay rate or fringe frequency (ν_{f}) by analytical or numerical differentiation of the phase delay (τ_ϕ). The model for the delay rate (fringe frequency) is approximated as a finite difference, R, by the following algorithm (Sovers et al. 1998):

$$R = \omega\left[\tau_\phi(t+\Delta t) - \tau_\phi(t-\Delta t)\right] / (2\Delta t) . \tag{4.16}$$

Expanding τ_ϕ to third order in Δt, the numerically evaluated fringe frequency becomes

$$R = \nu_{\mathrm{f}}(t) + \omega \frac{\partial^3 \tau_\phi}{\partial t^3} \frac{(\Delta t)^2}{3!} , \tag{4.17}$$

from where ν_{f} follows with an error equal to the second term of (4.17).

The next four subsections focus on some portions of the VLBI model that are also considered to be generally pertinent to other astrometric research. In particular, a somewhat lengthy discussion is presented concerning aberration and parallactic effects. These will be important in interpreting future space astrometric measurements of some of the proposed missions that are discussed in Chap. 8. A considerable part of the present VLBI model is only as accurate as current experiments demand, and will have to be revised as measurement accuracy improves.

4.4.2 Time Information

In assembling the requirements for VLBI astrometry, some definitions must be introduced concerning time tag information in the experiments, as well as the time scales used in data reduction. With reference to the definitions and notation in Sect. 2.2.3, the epoch of the radio measurements is taken from the time tags in Universal Time Coordinated (UTC) in the data stream of station 1, i.e., UTC_1. This time is converted to Terrestrial Time (TT) following, in principle, the conversion given below (Sovers et al. 1998):

$$\begin{aligned} \mathrm{TT} &= (\mathrm{TT} - \mathrm{TAI}) + (\mathrm{TAI} - \mathrm{UTC}_{\mathrm{IERS}}) \\ &\quad + (\mathrm{UTC}_{\mathrm{IERS}} - \mathrm{UTC}_1) + \mathrm{UTC}_1 . \end{aligned} \tag{4.18}$$

The meanings of the offsets are as follows:

1) TT − TAI is 32.184 s by definition (Sect. 2.2.3).

2) TAI − UTC_{IERS} is the offset between atomic and coordinated time. It is a published integer second for any epoch after 1 January 1972, accumulating the leap seconds. The International Earth Rotation Service (IERS) is responsible for maintenance of this offset.
3) UTC_{IERS} − UTC_1 is the offset between UTC kept by station 1 and the coordinated time scale maintained by the IERS.

The conventional time scale, UT1, is obtained from tabulated values of the offset UT1 − UTC maintained by the IERS, and is used to model the instantaneous orientation of the Earth.

Transition to the IAU conventions on the time scale (TDB) and unit of time (Julian century) is provided by the following definitions (USNO 1981).

- The standard epoch J2000.0 is equivalent to JD2451545.0 TDB.
- The time argument is measured in Julian centuries of 36525 days relative to the epoch J2000.0, i.e., T = (JD − 2451545.0) / 36525. If the time scale needs to be specified for a time expressed as a Julian date, it should be given right after the date, as exemplified under the item immediately above.
- For calculations of precession and nutation, and for references to solar system ephemerides, Barycentric Dynamic Time (TDB) is used. TDB is related to TDT by the following approximation, which is currently adequate for VLBI data reductions:

$$\mathrm{TDB} \;=\; \mathrm{TDT} \;+\; 0\overset{s}{.}001658 \sin g \;+\; 0\overset{s}{.}000014 \sin 2g \;,$$

where

$$g \;=\; (357\overset{\circ}{.}528 \;+\; 35999\overset{\circ}{.}050\; T) \times 2\pi \;/\; 360^\circ$$

is the mean anomaly of the Earth in its orbit. TDT is interchangeable with TT (see Sect. 2.2.3).

Modelling of the VLBI observations subsequently uses TT and TDB rather than the original UTC time tags of the observations.

4.4.3 Retarded Baseline

In (4.31) below we have expressed the geometric time delay as its zero-order approximation, which reads in vector notation:

$$\tau_{g0} = \frac{d}{c} \boldsymbol{r}_b \cdot \boldsymbol{s} \,, \tag{4.19}$$

where $d\,\boldsymbol{r}_b = \boldsymbol{r}_2 - \boldsymbol{r}_1$ is the instantaneous baseline (see Fig. 4.5). As the Earth moves during the time elapsed between the arrival of a wave crest at the one station and at the other, a small error is committed if the instantaneous baseline is used for delay calculations (Thompson et al. 1991, p. 258). This correction does not have negligible consequences, since the efficacy of the signal processor of the VLBI receiver system depends on an accurate estimate of the model time delay. Therefore, the delay is not determined from the instantaneous baseline, but from the 'retarded' baseline, which takes account of the relative motion of the two stations due to the Earth's rotation. The total geometric time delay is

$$\tau_{\mathrm{g}} = \tau_{\mathrm{g}0} + \Delta\tau = \tau_{\mathrm{g}0}(1+\Delta)\,, \tag{4.20}$$

and we have to estimate Δ. For this purpose, we consider the case where a plane wave reaches station 1 first at time t_1 and station 2 later at time t_2 (see Fig. 4.5). Then, denoting the wavelength and frequency of the radiation by λ and ν, respectively, one gets the phase difference

$$\frac{2\pi}{\lambda}\,\boldsymbol{s}\cdot[\boldsymbol{r}_2(t_2)-\boldsymbol{r}_1(t_1)] = 2\pi\nu(t_2-t_1)\,, \tag{4.21}$$

where

$$\tau_{\mathrm{g}} = t_2 - t_1\,.$$

Taylor expansion yields

$$\boldsymbol{r}_2(t_2) = \boldsymbol{r}_2(t_1+\tau_{\mathrm{g}}) = \boldsymbol{r}_2(t_1) + \dot{\boldsymbol{r}}_2(t_1)\,\tau_{\mathrm{g}}\,.$$

On substituting this expression, (4.21) becomes

$$2\pi\nu\tau_{\mathrm{g}} = \frac{2\pi}{\lambda}\,\boldsymbol{s}\cdot[\boldsymbol{r}_2(t_1)-\boldsymbol{r}_1(t_1)+\dot{\boldsymbol{r}}_2(t_1)\,\tau_{\mathrm{g}}]\,.$$

By referring to the instantaneous baseline and solving for τ_{g}, one obtains

$$\tau_{\mathrm{g}} = \frac{d}{c}\,\boldsymbol{r}_{\mathrm{b}}\cdot\boldsymbol{s}\,(1-\boldsymbol{s}\cdot\dot{\boldsymbol{r}}_2/c)^{-1}\,,$$

or, by approximation,

$$\tau_{\mathrm{g}} = \frac{d}{c}\,\boldsymbol{r}_{\mathrm{b}}\cdot\boldsymbol{s}\,(1+\boldsymbol{s}\cdot\dot{\boldsymbol{r}}_2/c)\,. \tag{4.22}$$

Since $\dot{\boldsymbol{r}} = \boldsymbol{\omega}_{\mathrm{e}}\times\boldsymbol{r}$, where $\boldsymbol{\omega}_{\mathrm{e}}$ is the angular velocity vector of the Earth, we get

$$\tau_{\mathrm{g}} = \frac{d}{c}\,\boldsymbol{r}_{\mathrm{b}}\cdot\boldsymbol{s}\,[\,1+\boldsymbol{s}\cdot(\boldsymbol{\omega}_{\mathrm{e}}\times\boldsymbol{r}_2)/c\,] = \tau_{\mathrm{g}0}\,(\,1+\Delta\,)\,. \tag{4.23}$$

The correction Δ remains to be estimated. As reference coordinate frame, we have chosen the space-fixed frame using the coordinates right ascension and declination. In this frame the angular velocity vector and the station vector are expressed by

$$\boldsymbol{\omega}_{\mathrm{e}} = \begin{pmatrix} 0 \\ 0 \\ \omega_{\mathrm{e}} \end{pmatrix} \quad \text{and} \quad \boldsymbol{r}_2 = r_2 \begin{pmatrix} \cos\delta_2\cos\alpha_2 \\ \cos\delta_2\sin\alpha_2 \\ \sin\delta_2 \end{pmatrix}\,,$$

where α_2, δ_2 are the spherical coordinates of station 2 and r_2 is the length of the station vector. Thus

$$\boldsymbol{\omega}_\mathrm{e} \times \boldsymbol{r}_2 = r_2 \begin{pmatrix} -\omega_\mathrm{e} \cos\delta_2 \sin\alpha_2 \\ \omega_\mathrm{e} \cos\delta_2 \cos\alpha_2 \\ 0 \end{pmatrix}$$

and, using (4.23),

$$\begin{aligned} \Delta &= \boldsymbol{s} \cdot (\boldsymbol{\omega}_\mathrm{e} \times \boldsymbol{r}_2)/c \\ &= \omega_\mathrm{e} \frac{r_2}{c} \cos\delta \cos\delta_2 \sin(\alpha - \alpha_2)\,. \end{aligned} \tag{4.24}$$

Accordingly, the upper limit of Δ is approximately 1.6×10^{-6}. On the Earth, simple geometry yields the maximum possible value of $\tau_{\mathrm{g}0}$, which is equal to the Earth's radius divided by the speed of light, or 0.021 s. Keeping in mind the above estimate of Δ we realize by means of (4.23) that the delay on the retarded baseline can differ from the delay of the instantaneous baseline by not more than 33 ns. This is much larger than the precision of the group delay estimated in Sect. 4.3.4. It is therefore mandatory to model the effect of the retarded baseline in order to obtain the optimum delay estimate, already at the correlator stage of the data analysis.

4.4.4 Gravitational Delay

Because an electromagnetic signal propagating in a gravitational potential does not follow a rectilinear path and is retarded relative to its travel time in field-free space, as predicted by the General Theory of Relativity, the computed value for the differential time of arrival of the signals at the two observing stations must be corrected for gravitational effects. Shapiro (1964, 1967) first pointed out the importance of the Sun's gravitational delay on interplanetary distance scales, and this was experimentally confirmed in measurements of radar signals reflected by Mercury and Venus. More recently Jupiter-grazing VLBI measurements (Treuhaft & Lowe 1991) have also confirmed planetary 'gravitational lensing'. Such gravitational potential perturbations are relatively small ($\leq 1.''75$ for Sun-grazing rays). At contemporary milliarcsecond accuracies, however, these gravitational delay effects remain important even at large impact angles. The Sun's influence must certainly be included in VLBI modelling, and any intentional or fortuitous close passages to other solar system bodies are also cause for concern. Note that more distant gravitating bodies, while undoubtedly affecting the ray paths which are intercepted on Earth, do not produce significant differential delays at the observing stations.

There is an immense concentration of mass at the galactic centre (on the order of 10^{11} solar masses), which bends signals from sources observed in that direction and contributes an additional delay. The estimated gravitational influence of the galactic centre on electromagnetic signals exceeds that of the Sun approximately 40-fold. Geometrically, it produces a bending of 4 arc seconds for signal paths within $\approx 10°$ of the galactic centre (the currently closest routinely observed radio source). The relatively slow motion (5 mas/yr) of the solar system on galactic scales, however, makes the time variation of galactic bending extremely slow. Its only practical consequence for astrometry is to produce a quasi-static distortion of the sky, which is absorbed into the estimated source coordinates.

For the geometry appropriate to detection of signals from an extremely distant source by two receivers on Earth, the differential relativistic light travel time due to a perturbing body p can be written as

$$\Delta_G = \frac{(1+\gamma)\mu_p}{c^3} \cdot \ln\left(\frac{r_1 + \mathbf{r}_1 \cdot \mathbf{s}}{r_2 + \mathbf{r}_2 \cdot \mathbf{s}}\right). \tag{4.25}$$

Here γ is the γ factor in the parametrized post-Newtonian gravitational theory (e.g., Misner et al. 1973). In the General Theory of Relativity, $\gamma = 1$. (However, allowing γ to be an estimated parameter permits experimental tests of general relativity.) Further, μ_p is the gravitational constant $\mu_p = Gm_p$, where G is the universal gravitational constant, and m_p is the mass of body p. As outlined in Sect. 4.4.1, the correction Δ_G is added to the modelled delay in the solar system barycentre in step 5.

4.4.5 Aberration and Parallactic Effects

The simplified model of interferometric delay (e.g. (4.19)) must of necessity be made more complete, according to the steps 4 to 6 outlined in Sect. 4.4.1. The reason for introducing refinements is that contemporary data accuracy demands accurate modelling of the Earth's motion relative to the solar system barycentre. Any catalogued extragalactic source positions are defined in a reference frame centred at the SSB at a stated epoch. While such a convention eliminates the complications that would arise if the catalogue positions were to be defined in an Earth-centred frame, it requires an equivalent amount of modelling of aberration and parallactic effects due to the Earth's motion about the Sun. Similar complications caused by the motion of the solar system about the galactic centre, by the motion of our galaxy relative to the cosmic microwave background, and by the presence of gravitational radiation, have not yet become important enough to demand inclusion in models of the VLBI observables. It can be expected that, as the time span of the data to be analysed extends well beyond two decades, and as experimental techniques become more sensitive, such cosmic phenomena will also need to be modelled.

Accounting for the Earth's motion in the solar system is taken care of automatically in the course of Lorentz transformations between the geocentric and solar system barycentric coordinate systems. The necessary positions and velocities are obtained from the planetary ephemeris in the J2000 frame

1221+809   12 23 40.493698±123   +80 40 04.34031±30   L ...

(Standish 1982a, Standish & Newhall 1996). Modelling usually employs either the JPL DE200 or DE403 ephemerides. The more recent DE403 is rotationally aligned with the ICRF celestial reference frame, and differs from DE200 by a few mas in rotation.

To give an example of these transformations, the source unit vector $\mathbf{s}$ in the geocentric celestial frame is related to its counterpart $\mathbf{s_0}$ in the SSB frame by the Lorentz transformation

$$\mathbf{s} = a_s \mathbf{s}_0 + a_\beta \beta \tag{4.26}$$

with the coefficients

$$a_s = \frac{1}{\gamma(1+\beta \cdot \mathbf{s_0})} \qquad \text{and} \qquad a_\beta = a_s \left[(1-\gamma)\frac{\beta \cdot \mathbf{s_0}}{\beta^{\mathbf{2}}} + \gamma\right] , \tag{4.27}$$

where $\beta = v/c$ (v = Earth velocity), and $\gamma = (1-\beta^2)^{-1/2}$.

At present, the Earth's orbital motion is the only aberration effect which is normally modelled in routine VLBI data analyses. We note parenthetically that weak ties of the baseline to geographic features of the Earth are provided by effects such as the Earth's motion in its orbit (aberration), tidal displacements, and tropospheric delay. These fix the baseline in the terrestrial frame at an uncertainty level of a few tenths of an arcsecond. Future extensions of modelling may have to account for numerous much smaller geometric and aberration effects. These have been considered in detail by Sovers and Jacobs (1996), and some of the leading candidates are mentioned below.

Working in a frame at rest with respect to the centre of mass of the solar system may cause relativistic effects due to the motion of the solar system in the quasi-inertial frame of the extragalactic radio sources to be absorbed into the mean positions of the sources and their proper motions. When observational data extend over a sufficiently lengthy time span, this motion in inertial space will eventually become separable from terrestrial and intra-solar-system dynamics. The SSB's velocity relative to the Cosmic Microwave Background (CMB) has been measured by the Cosmic Background Explorer (COBE) project (Kogut et al. 1993) to be ≈ 370 km/sec. This motion of the SSB relative to the CMB is on the order of $10^{-3}c$, indicating that relativity should play a significant role in modeling its consequences for VLBI.

The extragalactic radio sources have a median red shift $z \approx 1.2$, whereas the more distant CMB (Melchiorri & Melchiorri 1990) is characterized by a red shift $z \approx 10^3$. If one assumes that the extragalactic radio sources are at rest relative to the much more distant CMB, the above $10^{-3}c$ can be taken as an estimate of the SSB velocity in the extragalactic radio reference frame. The motion of the SSB relative to the frame of the extragalactic radio sources produces three effects that contribute to the observed delay. The first of these is the geometric effect on source angles caused by the movement of the SSB. The second, related effect, is due to changes in the gravitational time delay caused by the motion of the SSB relative to the galactic mass distribution, and has already been discussed in the previous section. Third, aberration effects produced by the SSB's velocity relative to the radio sources must be considered. Detection of this motion could contribute significantly to understanding of the large-scale structure of the universe.

Parallactic effects. The geometric effects of galactic rotation can be easily estimated from its period of approximately 240 million years. The solar system angular velocity about the galactic centre is $\approx 2\pi/2.4\times10^8 = 2.6\times10^{-8}$ radians/year. For sources within the Galaxy, at distances approximately equal to our distance from the galactic centre, the apparent positions could change by $\approx$ 5 mas/yr. Since our distance from the galactic centre is 8.5 $\pm$ 1 kpc $\approx 2.7\times10^4$ light years (Binney & Tremaine 1987), and most extragalactic radio sources are $\approx 10^9$ light years distant, the potential error is scaled by the ratio of these two distances, $\approx 3\times10^{-5}$, and becomes only $\approx$ 0.2 μas/year. Even with the present 20-year history of VLBI data, the purely geometric systematic error due to galactic rotation is thus negligible for sources more distant than 10 million light years.

Aberration effects. The SSB velocity relative to the CMB of 0.0012 c (see above) causes large ($\approx$ 4 arcmin) changes in apparent source positions due to aberration. To the extent that the SSB velocity does not change on time scales of decades, however, one is free to absorb these aberration effects into catalogued source positions. With such a convention, the problem is reduced to considering *changes* in the SSB velocity. The hierarchy of cosmic structures to which the Earth belongs includes the solar system (SSB), galactic centre (GC), local standard of rest (LSR), local group (LG), and finally the cosmic microwave background. Relative motions of these categories are known to within $\approx$ 10%, and the LG–CMB velocity is the largest contributor to the SSB–CMB motion, which is of the order $10^{-3}c$. Only the relative acceleration of the SSB and GC is presently well known; using the rotational period given in the preceding paragraph and the SSB–GC distance of 8.5 kpc produces an estimated change in velocity of $\approx 2\times10^{-11}c$/yr. Such a velocity change will cause a maximum aberration of $\approx$ 5 μas/yr. This aberration effect is at present not included in VLBI models. Its magnitude makes it probable that it will soon be possible to estimate it from the data.

Motion of the solar system barycentre (to a first approximation, galactic rotation) may soon emerge above the detection threshold. The rotational motion of the galaxy affects all observations, and induces a maximum aberration effect of 5 μas/yr. It will need to be taken into account for observations spanning more than two decades. Galactic aberration and gravitational radiation can also contribute to apparent motion. Initial searches for VLBI evidence of the passage of gravitational waves have placed loose bounds on their existence (Pyne et al. 1996; Gwinn et al. 1997). We also note that VLBI is weakly sensitive to the difference between Newtonian and Lorentzian aberration [$\propto 1/4(v/c)^2$], which is a 2-mas effect on intercontinental baselines, but is already implicitly included in the VLBI model.

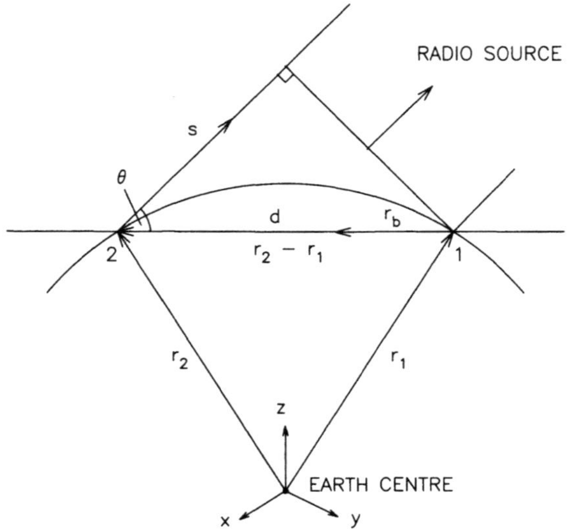

Fig. 4.5. Interferometry geometry represented in a rectangular coordinate frame with its origin at the centre of the Earth. $\boldsymbol{r}_1$ and $\boldsymbol{r}_2$ are the station vectors, while the unit vectors of the baseline and source directions are denoted by $\boldsymbol{r}_\mathrm{b}$ and $\boldsymbol{s}$, respectively

4.4.6 Sensitivity of the Observables

Up to this point we have made acquaintance with the interferometer observables known as fringe phase, fringe frequency and time delay, which are the typical outputs of an interferometer. They provide a measure of the scalar product of the baseline and source position vectors, $\boldsymbol{b} \cdot \boldsymbol{s}$. In Fig. 4.3 we already encountered this scalar product, where it was used for illustrating how time delay comes into existence. This scalar product is the core of the geometric parts of the phase, fringe frequency and time delay observables and, therefore, attention is drawn to its properties below. To establish the relationship between observables on the one hand and source positions and baseline parameters on the other, we introduce below the coordinate frame to which the source positions and baseline parameters are referred.

Let us assume a coordinate frame with origin at the centre of the Earth, the x axis pointing to the vernal equinox, the z axis to the celestial pole, and the y axis being perpendicular to the x and z axes so that the three axes form a right-handed system (see Fig. 4.5). The vectors to the antennas are designated $\boldsymbol{r}_1(t)$ and $\boldsymbol{r}_2(t)$, the unit vector pointing to the source is $\boldsymbol{s}$ and the unit vector defining the zero-order baseline is $\boldsymbol{r}_\mathrm{b}$, which is given by

$$\boldsymbol{r}_\mathrm{b} = \boldsymbol{r}_2 - \boldsymbol{r}_1/|\boldsymbol{r}_2 - \boldsymbol{r}_1|$$

and

$$\boldsymbol{b} = d\,\boldsymbol{r}_\mathrm{b}, \quad d = |\boldsymbol{r}_2 - \boldsymbol{r}_1|\,.$$

1236−684	12 39 46.651396±155	−68 45 30.89260±100	?	...

The exact baseline vector differs from the zero-order baseline by a small additive correction that is caused by the Earth's rotation while the incoming waves pass from the nearer to the more distant antenna. This correction is contained in the retarded baseline (see Sect. 4.4.3) and must be added to the zero-order baseline to yield the first-order baseline. In the coordinate frame defined above, both unit vectors, $\boldsymbol{s}$ and $\boldsymbol{r}_{\mathrm{b}}$, can be expressed in terms of right ascension, α, and declination, δ:

$$\boldsymbol{s} = \begin{pmatrix} x_{\mathrm{s}} \\ y_{\mathrm{s}} \\ z_{\mathrm{s}} \end{pmatrix} = \begin{pmatrix} \cos\delta_{\mathrm{s}}\cos\alpha_{\mathrm{s}} \\ \cos\delta_{\mathrm{s}}\sin\alpha_{\mathrm{s}} \\ \sin\delta_{\mathrm{s}} \end{pmatrix}$$

and

$$\boldsymbol{r}_{\mathrm{b}}(t) = \begin{pmatrix} x_{\mathrm{b}} \\ y_{\mathrm{b}} \\ z_{\mathrm{b}} \end{pmatrix} = \begin{pmatrix} \cos\delta_{\mathrm{b}}\cos\alpha_{\mathrm{b}} \\ \cos\delta_{\mathrm{b}}\sin\alpha_{\mathrm{b}} \\ \sin\delta_{\mathrm{b}} \end{pmatrix}.$$

Hence

$$\boldsymbol{r}_{\mathrm{b}} \cdot \boldsymbol{s} = \sin\delta_{\mathrm{s}}\sin\delta_{\mathrm{b}} + \cos\delta_{\mathrm{s}}\cos\delta_{\mathrm{b}}\cos(\alpha_{\mathrm{b}} - \alpha_{\mathrm{s}})\,. \tag{4.28}$$

On substituting (4.28) into the first term of (4.8), which contains the scalar product $\boldsymbol{r}_{\mathrm{b}} \cdot \boldsymbol{s}$, we establish, for the geometric part of the fringe phase, the relationship between the observables on the one hand, and astrometric and geodetic quantities on the other. These latter quantities are represented by the source and baseline coordinates. One obtains:

$$\begin{aligned} \phi_{\mathrm{g}} &= \frac{2\pi\nu}{c}\,\boldsymbol{b}\cdot\boldsymbol{s} + 2\pi k \\ &= 2\pi\,\frac{d}{\lambda}\left[\sin\delta_{\mathrm{s}}\sin\delta_{\mathrm{b}} + \cos\delta_{\mathrm{s}}\cos\delta_{\mathrm{b}}\cos\left(\alpha_{\mathrm{b}} - \alpha_{\mathrm{s}}\right)\right] + 2\pi k\,. \end{aligned} \tag{4.29}$$

Likewise, from (4.14) and (4.15) follow the geometric parts of fringe frequency and group delay by substitution of (4.28). They become, respectively,

$$\begin{aligned} (\nu_{\mathrm{f}})_{\mathrm{g}} &= \frac{2\pi\nu}{c}\,\frac{\partial}{\partial t}\,(\boldsymbol{b}\cdot\boldsymbol{s}) \\ &= -\omega\,\frac{d}{c}\left[\omega_{\mathrm{e}}\cos\delta_{\mathrm{s}}\cos\delta_{\mathrm{b}}\sin\left(\alpha_{\mathrm{b}} - \alpha_{\mathrm{s}}\right)\right], \end{aligned} \tag{4.30}$$

with $\omega_{\mathrm{e}} = \dfrac{d\alpha_{\mathrm{b}}}{dt}$ equal to the angular velocity of the Earth's rotation, and

$$\begin{aligned} \tau_{\mathrm{g}} &= \frac{\partial}{\partial\omega}\left(\frac{\omega}{c}\,\boldsymbol{b}\cdot\boldsymbol{s}\right) \\ &= \frac{d}{c}\left[\sin\delta_{\mathrm{s}}\sin\delta_{\mathrm{b}} + \cos\delta_{\mathrm{s}}\cos\delta_{\mathrm{b}}\cos(\alpha_{\mathrm{b}} - \alpha_{\mathrm{s}})\right]. \end{aligned} \tag{4.31}$$

The geometric parts elaborated above provide the key to estimating the sensitivity of the group delay and fringe frequency observables to small errors

1252+119 12 54 38.255601±19 +11 41 05.89507±32 Q 0.870

of the source positions and baseline parameters. We derive these estimates from the partial derivatives of the group delay and fringe frequency with respect to the source right ascension and declination on the one hand, and with respect to the baseline parameters on the other.

First we deal with the sensitivity to source position. The delay partials are

$$\frac{\partial\tau}{\partial\alpha_s} = \frac{d}{c}\cos\delta_s\cos\delta_b\sin(\alpha_b-\alpha_s) \tag{4.32}$$

$$\begin{aligned}\frac{\partial\tau}{\partial\delta_s} &= \frac{d}{c}\left[\cos\delta_s\sin\delta_b - \sin\delta_s\cos\delta_b\cos(\alpha_b-\alpha_s)\right]\\ &= \frac{p}{c}\cos\delta_s - \frac{d}{c}\left[\sin\delta_s\cos\delta_b\cos(\alpha_b-\alpha_s)\right],\end{aligned} \tag{4.33}$$

where p is the projection of the baseline onto the z axis, i.e., the polar projection as opposed to the equatorial projection.

For the fringe frequency partials one gets

$$\frac{\partial\nu_f}{\partial\alpha_s} = \omega\frac{d}{c}\left[\omega_e\cos\delta_s\cos\delta_b\cos(\alpha_b-\alpha_s)\right] \tag{4.34}$$

$$\frac{\partial\nu_f}{\partial\delta_s} = \omega\frac{d}{c}\left[\omega_e\sin\delta_s\cos\delta_b\sin(\alpha_b-\alpha_s)\right]. \tag{4.35}$$

An immediate conclusion from the partial derivatives is the strong dependence of time delay and fringe frequency observables on baseline length. But it is also immediately realized that, for source declinations near zero, the fringe frequency is insensitive to declination, which implies that this observable is poor in determining declinations of sources in the vicinity of the equator.

Let us try to assess the partial derivatives numerically and relate them to the expected errors of the observables (Sect. 4.3.4). In this way estimates are provided for the sensitivities of time delay and fringe frequency with respect to the source coordinates for a given baseline length.

For a baseline length of d=5000 km the group delay partials, (4.32) and (4.33), have the order of magnitude (d/c) s/rad which equals 0.08 ns/mas; i.e., a change in the source position of 1 mas translates into a change of the group delay of 0.08 ns. This quantity is a measure of the sensitivity of the delay, and it must be considered in relation to the error of the group delay observable. From experience, a change of the time delay equal to the equivalent of 10% of the wavelength is detectable at cross-correlation. Assuming $\lambda = 3.6$ cm (X band), the corresponding change in time delay is $\Delta\tau = 0.01$ ns. In relating this variation to the above delay sensitivity, it is concluded that the baseline is capable of measuring positions accurate to fractions of 1 mas.

By analogy, in the case of the frequency observable, (4.34) and (4.35), an order of magnitude calculation yields approximately 0.3 mHz/mas for the fringe frequency sensitivity with respect to source coordinates, again taking

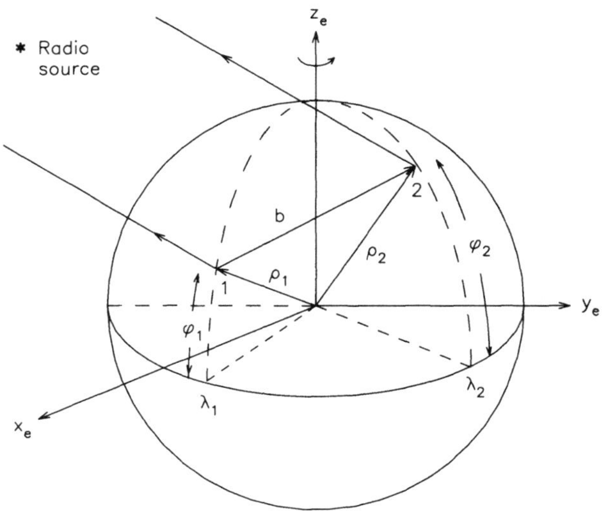

Fig. 4.6. Baseline vector ***b*** referred to the rectangular terrestrial coordinate frame $(x_\mathrm{e}, y_\mathrm{e}, z_\mathrm{e})$, and stations 1 and 2 described by the distance (ϱ) from the centre of the Earth and geographical longitude and latitude (λ, φ)

the same baseline length and frequency as above, and $\omega_\mathrm{e} = 0.73 \times 10^{-4}$ rad/s for the Earth's rotation. As estimated in Sect. 4.3.4, the precision of the fringe frequency is about 0.5 mHz. From this precision along with the above sensitivity, it follows that the baseline is capable of measuring source positions at a level of 1 mas.

Now we turn to the sensitivity of the observables to baseline components. In order to develop the partial derivatives of group delay and fringe frequency, it is necessary to represent the observables in terms of the vector components of the baseline. These vector components refer to an Earth-fixed coordinate frame of geographical longitude (λ) and latitude (β), in which the latitude may be set equal to the baseline declination δ_b bearing in mind the order of magnitude study pursued here. The Earth-fixed coordinate system is defined by the equatorial plane with the x_e axis pointing along longitude 0° and the y_e axis along 90° east, while the z_e axis is aligned with the direction to the north pole (Fig. 4.6). In this coordinate frame, the components of the baseline vector are given by

$$
\begin{aligned}
x_\mathrm{e} &= d \cos\delta_\mathrm{b} \cos\lambda_\mathrm{b}\,, \\
y_\mathrm{e} &= d \cos\delta_\mathrm{b} \sin\lambda_\mathrm{b}\,, \\
z_\mathrm{e} &= d \sin\delta_\mathrm{b}\,.
\end{aligned}
$$

As $\alpha = \alpha(G) + \lambda$, where $\alpha(G)$ is the right ascension of Greenwich, the right ascension difference $\alpha_\mathrm{b} - \alpha_\mathrm{s}$ in (4.30) and (4.31) is replaceable by $\lambda_\mathrm{b} -$

1257+145 13 00 20.918799±38 +14 17 18.53107±63 ? . . .

λ_s. Then, omitting the subscripts 'e' for simplicity, group delay and fringe frequency can be written as

$$\tau_g = \frac{1}{c}\left[z \sin\delta_s + x\cos\lambda_s\cos\delta_s + y\sin\lambda_s\cos\delta_s\right]$$

and

$$(\nu_f)_g = \frac{\omega}{c}\,\omega_e\left[x\sin\lambda_s\cos\delta_s - y\cos\lambda_s\cos\delta_s\right].$$

The dependence of the group delay on the baseline components is described by

$$\begin{aligned}\frac{\partial\tau}{\partial x} &= \cos\lambda_s\cos\delta_s/c\,,\\ \frac{\partial\tau}{\partial y} &= \sin\lambda_s\cos\delta_s/c\,,\\ \frac{\partial\tau}{\partial z} &= \sin\delta_s/c\,,\end{aligned}$$

indicating an order-of-magnitude value of $1/c$ or 3 ns/m. The 0.01 ns X-band group delay precision then implies baseline coordinate sensitivity of 3 mm.

By analogy, the dependence of the fringe frequency on the baseline components is described by the fringe frequency partials:

$$\begin{aligned}\frac{\partial\nu_f}{\partial x} &= \frac{\omega}{c}\,\omega_e\sin\lambda_s\cos\delta_s\,,\\ \frac{\partial\nu_f}{\partial y} &= -\frac{\omega}{c}\,\omega_e\cos\lambda_s\cos\delta_s\,,\\ \frac{\partial\nu_f}{\partial z} &= 0\,.\end{aligned}$$

Accordingly, the sensitivity of fringe frequency to the x and y components of the baseline amounts to approximately 12 mHz/m. The fringe frequency precision of 0.5 mHz then implies a baseline x and y component sensitivity of 4 cm. There is total lack of sensitivity to the polar component of the baseline, i.e., the fringe frequency observable does not provide any information concerning the z component of the baseline. This is another drawback of fringe frequency, in addition to its lesser accuracy and limited sensitivity to source declinations near zero.

Application of arguments similar to the above to real observing stations is helpful in designing networks that permit the maximum return from observing sessions. The general conclusion is that, in order to achieve the best determinations of terrestrial and celestial model parameters, the network baselines should be of equal extent in the north-south and east-west directions, and the celestial sphere should be covered as uniformly as possible.

5. Fundamental Catalogues of Extragalactic Radio Sources

As pointed out in Sect. 1.8 an alternative to the conventional stellar reference system of the FK5 is presented by extragalactic reference systems. The advantages of an extragalactic system rest, first, upon the observed positions of extragalactic objects (EGOs) whose rotation, when averaged over a large number of objects, would be representative of the rotation of the Universe, which, however, is assumed to be zero according to the discussion in Sect. 4.1.2. Second, these advantages rest upon the possibility of introducing explicitly the General Theory of Relativity for the definition of the celestial space-time reference frame, thereby meeting better the accuracy requirements of modern astrometry.

Considering the need for defining an up-to-date coordinate system with its spatial origin at the barycentre of the solar system, the International Astronomical Union (IAU 1992) decided that the high-precision coordinates of extragalactic radio sources should form the core of this new conventional celestial reference system. Being based on the kinematic behaviour of distant objects, the theoretical concept of the system is underlain by a kinematic definition, which is the chief feature distinguishing it from the essentially dynamical definition of the FK5 system. Over the course of the years the International Celestial Reference System (ICRS) was developed (Arias et al. 1995). The following sections present details of the construction of catalogues of extragalactic radio sources with emphasis on the catalogue associated with the International Celestial Reference Frame (ICRF). This frame is the realization of the ICRS, defined by the International Earth Rotation Service (IERS) under whose auspices the individual contributions of source positions were incorporated into yearly preliminary realizations of the ICRS. Finally, we discuss details of the origin and generation of the first officially sanctioned realization of the ICRF (IAU 1999), which became the fundamental reference frame for astronomical measurements at the beginning of 1998.

5.1 System Definition

At its 1991 General Assembly (GA), the International Astronomical Union adopted Resolution A4 (IAU 1992), which established the theoretical basis of a new conventional reference system. Its practical realization was adopted

1324+224   13 27 00.861311±20   +22 10 50.16306±31   ? 1.400

as the new ICRF six years later at the 1997 GA (IAU 1999). The theoretical basis is a kinematic definition and is subject to the following conditions:

- The system is barycentric, which means that the origin of its spatial coordinates coincides with the centre of mass of the solar system.
- The reference frame representing the system shows no global rotation with respect to a set of distant extragalactic reference points.
- Selected extragalactic radio sources are chosen as reference points that are part of the definition of the reference system.
- The principal plane of the system is as near as possible to the mean equator at J2000.0, and the origin in this plane is as near as possible to the dynamical equinox at J2000.0. Keeping in mind that the FK5 equator and equinox also refer to J2000.0, this condition thus avoids discontinuities in the positions of stars when the FK5 frame is replaced by the extragalactic reference frame.
- The positions of the extragalactic objects representing the reference frame are computed initially for the equator and equinox at J2000.0 using the best available values of the celestial pole offset with respect to the IAU expressions for precession and nutation, in order to avoid the introduction of spurious proper motions into the positions of the extragalactic objects. Through this procedure the positions of the objects are referred to the FK5 system at the standard epoch J2000.0.
- The reference system is realized by a reference frame that is accessible to astrometry in visual as well as radio wavelengths.

In defining the ICRS one resorts to selected extragalactic objects such as quasars or active nuclei of distant galaxies assuming a non-rotating Universe. Consequently, the distant objects are not exposed to any global motion that could be identified with a rotation. It is characteristic of this system definition that the axes of the coordinate frame or triad, which eventually realize the system, are fixed to matter at infinite distance, and that this matter is represented by point-like extragalactic objects. The nucleus of the system definition is formed by 212 so-called defining sources. They are chosen from approximately 600 objects according to certain criteria given, e.g., in Ma et al. (1998), and constitute a set of reference points, whose positions are used to fix the directions of the axes of the triad that is to be kept invariant from now on. The definition is purely geometrical. As it is based on the kinematics of EGOs with, however, negligible apparent motions, the definition is also known to be kinematic, sometimes also called static.

The postulated non-rotation of the reference frame rests upon the absence of measurable proper motions of the EGOs. Apart from a rotational motion common to all objects, monitoring of the arcs between EGOs provides a practical means to check the assumption that proper motions are undetectable. To this end, observations are performed using differential VLBI and, in future, interferometry in space to check the existence of relative motions. In this context potential secular motions may also be assessed, which are probably caused by source structures detected on a milliarcsecond scale (Kellermann & Pauliny-Toth 1981, Fey & Charlot 1997), and by gravitational effects on the solar system and on the source directions. Estimates of the last two effects lie below 10 microarcseconds per year (Eubanks et al. 1995).

Resolution B2 of the IAU (IAU 1999) states that, as of 1 January 1998, the IAU celestial reference system is the International Celestial Reference System (ICRS) as specified above (see also Arias et al. 1995).

In terms of the guidelines for the definition of celestial reference systems given in Sect. 1.3.2 we summarize below the items defining the ICRS:

Theoretical concept:

- Availability of a set of defining extragalactic objects.
- The axes of the orthogonal coordinate frame (triad) have fixed directions defined by the positions of extragalactic radio sources that are at rest with respect to the Universe.
- Target: establishment of an inertial (non-rotating) system.

Procedures:

- None, see Note 1 below.

Models:

- Model of the non-rotating Universe.
- Model of the motion of the extragalactic objects with respect to the Universe, see Note 2 below.
- Model of the atmosphere.
- Model of light deflection.

Parameters and constants:

- None, see Note 1 below.

Note 1: 'Procedures' and 'Parameters and constants' are needed only for the initial establishment of the frame insofar as the motion of the Earth must be taken into account. During this phase the IERS Conventions (IERS 1996) are employed. Once the coordinate axes of the frame are specified, they are kept fixed, and the connection between the definition of the system and the kinematics of the Earth is severed.

Note 2: The model consists simply of the assumption of zero motion of the EGOs or, as a more elaborate version, of the knowledge of the laws of motion enabling their modelling.

5.2 Some Specific Features of the ICRS Definition

In principle, any fixed coordinate axes forming an orthogonal triad can be chosen with respect to the distant objects. For reasons of continuity, priority is given to the triad defined by the mean equator of the FK5 and the dynamical equinox at J2000.0, with the option to eventually rotate this triad to some other preferred principal plane and direction in this plane, while retaining J2000.0 as the standard epoch.

A crucial point of the ICRS concept is the fixing of axes. It results from a lengthy iterative procedure which has been described in the IERS Annual Reports between 1989 and 1996 (e.g., IERS 1995a, IERS 1996a). For determining the fixed axes only the so-called defining sources are eligible, because of the empirically and statistically ascertained stability of their coordinates. A variety of observing and analysis centres supplied the IERS with individual position catalogues constructed from VLBI observations of extragalactic objects. The catalogued source positions were obtained from analyses that adhered to common standards of data reduction (e.g., IERS 1992). In particular, the observations were referred to J2000.0 by employing the standard IAU 1976 precession (Lieske et al. 1977) and the IAU 1980 theory of nutation (Seidelmann 1982). In performing the reductions, however, the coordinates were freed from systematic errors caused by the current imperfect precession and nutation models as has been proved by Charlot et al. (1995). For this purpose the coordinate estimates that were submitted to the IERS either took into account the celestial pole offsets for each VLBI session lasting up to 24 hours, or they solved for the luni-solar precession and the major coefficients of the nutation theory simultaneously with the estimation of source positions and supplementary parameters.

At IERS, the first step dealt with the combination of the individual catalogues emanating from the analysis centres by applying rigid rotations and determining optimum coordinates of the defining sources referred to the triad defined by the FK5 frame. When, in the course of time, the defining sources were reobserved and the quantity of sources increased, the observing and analysis centres provided updated catalogues, and IERS undertook a new compilation of the combined catalogue, constraining the axes of the updated frame realization to those of the previous year's version. Thus, each successive iteration generated a new set of source positions and, at the same time, the number of defining sources usually increased. The alignment of the axes of successive frame realizations was maintained at a level better than 0.005 mas (IERS 1996a). From Sect. 5.5.3 a deeper insight into the subject may be gained.

The procedure described above guarantees stability of the axes of the ICRF precursors, while the source positions may be subject to change due to random and systematic effects that cannot be absorbed by rigid rotations. At first glance, it seems as if the realization of the ICRS by the ICRF would circumvent the impact of procedures and astronomical and geophysical con-

1347+539 13 49 34.656623±34 +53 41 17.04028±32 Q 0.976

stants on deriving coordinates from the original observations of radio sources. Actually, the observing and analysis centres shoulder this burden of employing consistent procedures and constants in order to avoid spurious motions, which may corrupt the source positions during the establishment phase of the ICRF.

The next three sections show how the ICRS fulfills the system requirements imposed by IAU (IAU 1992).

5.2.1 Origin of Coordinates

Application of refined models and improved standards (IERS 1996b) for the reduction of the VLBI observations of extragalactic objects in accordance with the requirements of the Special and General Theories of Relativity for aberration, light deflection and time transformations, secures the coincidence of the origin of the coordinate axes of the ICRS with the barycentre of the solar system.

Possible offsets between the spatial origin defined by the ICRS and the centre of mass of the solar system may be ascribed to the frame of the solar system ephemerides (DE200) and, especially, to the Earth's ephemeris. In fact, for reducing the VLBI observations this ephemeris was used in order to account for annual aberration and light deflection. While the DE200 had been created in 1981 (Standish 1982a), the DE403 came into being in 1995 (Standish & Newhall 1996). One of its distinguishing features is the inclusion of recently processed differential VLBI observations of the Magellan spacecraft orbiting Venus and the Phobos spacecraft approaching Mars, as well as recent radar-ranging observations to Mercury, Venus and Mars. Comparison of the ephemerides DE403 and DE200 gives an indication of the uncertainty of the Earth's ephemeris provided by DE200. Accordingly, triaxial rotations by some 10 mas in each direction tie one ephemeris to the other; for the inner planets the longitudes and latitudes agree within ± 5 mas and ± 20 mas, respectively, and there is a mean motion difference of 0.5 mas/yr for the longitude difference, $\lambda_{403} - \lambda_{200}$. For the purpose of error estimation, all differences between the two ephemerides are interpreted as aberrational effects, leading to an upper limit of the lump sum covering these alignment differences that does not exceed 40 mas during an interval of a few years. Therefore, a conservative estimate of the uncertainty of the barycentric Earth velocity is less than 10^{-1} cm/s and, consequently, the frame distortion due to errors of aberration definitely remains below 10^{-2} mas.

Considerations similar to those of aberration apply to the calculation of light deflection by the Sun and other celestial bodies. Partly, small differences may also be explained by the metric adopted in (1.1), which is valid only for inertial frames.

1416+067 14 19 08.180173±83 +06 28 34.80349±129 Q 1.439

5.2.2 Principal Plane – Equator

The mean celestial pole of the ICRS is defined by the IAU 1976 and the IAU 1980 standard models of precession and nutation, respectively. Both models are known to be in error, thus causing offsets of the Earth's celestial pole when it is determined from the standard models on the one hand, and from modern observations on the other. Charlot et al. (1995), using VLBI and lunar laser ranging observations, and Souchay et al. (1995), using VLBI observations only, have shown that the ICRS celestial mean pole based on the IAU standard models is offset by approximately 20 mas from the mean pole determined with the aid of these high precision techniques. In other words, this fact demonstrates close agreement of the mean equator at J2000.0 with the equator defined by ICRS.

Furthermore, since the IAU recommendations stipulate continuity between the new conventional celestial pole and that of the FK5, it must be demonstrated that the two poles are consistent at J2000.0. Making the assumption that the obvious imperfections of the precession model are nearly absorbed by the stellar proper motions, the uncertainty of the FK5 pole at J2000.0 may be estimated from the standard deviations of the equator amounting to ± 20 mas (Fricke 1982) and the residual rotation of the FK5 proper motion system of ± 0.7 mas/yr (Schwan 1988a) accumulated during about 60 years, which is the difference between J2000.0 and the mean epoch of the FK5 system. By quadratic summation of these quantities one finds an uncertainty of the FK5 pole at J2000.0 of not more than ± 50 mas relative to the mean pole at J2000.0. Recalling from above the shift of the ICRS pole relative to the mean pole at J2000.0, we conclude that the ICRS pole is consistent with that of the FK5 within the uncertainty of the latter. Consequently the mean equator of the ICRS fulfills the condition that it should be close to the FK5 equator (IAU 1992).

5.2.3 Right Ascension Origin

In the analysis of radio interferometric observations, the origin of right ascension and the longitude of the interferometer baseline are not separable as long as the right ascension zero point is not fixed. The x axis of the initial realization of the ICRF, which is equivalent to the right ascension zero point, was implicitly defined by adopting the mean right ascensions of 23 primary radio sources (Arias et al. 1995). These coordinates were taken from a group of observation catalogues that were compiled by fixing the right ascension of quasar 3C 273B to the usual value given by Hazard et al. (1971) and transformed into the FK5 value, which is $12^{\mathrm{h}}\,29^{\mathrm{m}}\,06^{\mathrm{s}}.6997$ at J2000.0 (e.g., Kaplan et al. 1982).

Folkner et al. (1994) determined the link between the preliminary ICRF and the solar system ephemeris frame. They found an offset of 78 ± 10 mas between the x axis of the ICRF and the mean dynamical equinox at J2000.0.

`1418+546    14 19 46.597401±31   +54 23 14.78721±27    L  0.152`

This discrepancy is compatible with the IAU recommendation that the right ascension origin of the ICRS be close to the dynamical equinox at J2000.0.

Further, for the FK5, the dynamical equinox at J2000.0 has been adopted as the right ascension origin with an estimated error of about ±90 mas, which is derived from the quadratic sum of the accuracies of the FK5 motion of the equinox given by Fricke (1982) and of the residual rotation of the FK5 system (Schwan 1988b), assuming 1955 as mean epoch for the proper motions in right ascension.

We conclude that, at J2000.0, there is agreement of the ICRS and FK5 right ascension origins at an uncertainty level of about ±100 mas. This is small enough to comply with the continuity condition imposed on ICRS and FK5 (IAU 1992). For more details see Arias et al. (1995).

5.3 The Extragalactic System Versus the FK5 System

The definition of the conventional extragalactic celestial reference system is remarkably simple and undemanding with regard to models. It only presupposes the existence of objects at cosmological distances whose directions are invariant with respect to the Universe.

In contrasting the extragalactic and FK5 systems there is one principal difference: In implementing the celestial reference system on the basis of observed positions of some 200 defining extragalactic radio sources, the coordinate axes remain fixed with respect to these positions. Especially, the axes are not to be rotated into other directions if the source coordinates change as inferred from future observations. In other words, the previously adopted positions may require revision, but the coordinate axes will be maintained by applying the statistical condition that the coordinates of the defining sources exhibit no global rotation in the course of the frame revision, which takes into account recent observations. This means that the fundamental plane and the zero point chosen on that plane are kept fixed, while the individual object coordinates may change over the years.

On the other hand, the fundamental plane and origin of the FK5 system, say the mean equator and the mean equinox at some epoch, are both moving due to the motion of the Earth's axis in space. The coordinates of the catalogue stars are given constant values in this frame. Ignoring stellar proper motions, we face the situation that the positions of stars are fixed in a moving frame whose motion is essentially dictated by precession and nutation and their uncertainties.

In the ICRS, purely conventional coordinate axes have been adopted that are fixed by the positions of the defining radio sources. To maintain continuity these coordinate axes are aligned with those of the FK5 system at the standard epoch J2000.0 within the uncertainty of the latter. The zero points of right ascension and declination of the ICRS are implicitly introduced by this procedure. In principle, however, arbitrary directions could have been chosen for the axes. Therefore, the fundamental planes referred to in the FK5 system, the mean equator and ecliptic, have lost their dominant significance in the framework of the extragalactic reference system.

In these circumstances, there is no room left to speak of what is called 'the equinox motion' in the construction of the FK5, and no specific epoch date needs to be associated with the ICRS right ascension origin which, however, has been chosen close to the mean dynamical equinox of the J2000.0 coordinate frame for the convenience of catalogue application. Actually, it would be imaginable to adopt formally other designations to the right ascensions and declinations defined by the ICRS to distinguish them from the conventional usage of α, for right ascension, and δ, for declination, in the context of the FK5 system. Such a change of nomenclature, of course, has not been carried out in order to maintain continuity of customary practice.

As reported in Sect. 5.2, the construction of the International Celestial Reference Frame (ICRF) ensures a smooth transition from the FK5 frame to the ICRF, to the extent that discontinuities do not arise in the FK5 equator and equinox of J2000.0 which exceed the uncertainties of the FK5 frame.

Here is also the proper place to recapitulate the fundamental nature of the FK5 system and the ICRS: As long as we remain in the realm of the Special Theory of Relativity, there are finite regions in space where material particles move freely without acceleration and in remarkable agreement with the laws of that theory (Hohenkerk et al. 1992). A frame attached to such a region can be regarded as a quasi-inertial frame of reference. The FK5 frame and the ICRF are embedded in such regions and, therefore, both frames share the property of being quasi-inertial with, however, different definitions of the frames as stated below.

- The FK5 frame is based on the theory of motions of the bodies of the solar system. Consequently it has a dynamical definition from this point of view. Besides, the FK5 system is based on assumptions of the proper motions of stars in the neighbourhood of the Sun and as such has a kinematic definition. In sum, the definition of the FK5 frame is a hybrid one, as was already discussed in more detail in Sect. 2.2.
- The ICRF is constructed from extragalactic sources that are assumed to be free from rotational components to their motions. Again, this frame falls in the category of the kinematic definitions. Alternatively, one may regard it as a static definition since observations of sources using current high-precision techniques give evidence that the sources are effectively at rest with respect to the Universe.

While the FK5 system provides access to visible wavelengths, the extragalactic system is defined in the range of radio wavelengths and represented by some 600 radio sources. Chapter 7 will show how this 'radio system' can be made accessible to visible wavelengths through its link with the Hipparcos catalogue. This link enables optical astrometry to benefit from the unprecedented properties of the extragalactic celestial reference system.

5.4 Building Blocks for Catalogue Establishment

5.4.1 Absolute Astrometry

In Sect. 4.4 the investigations of the VLBI observable sensitivity to source coordinates and baseline components, as well as consideration of the retarded baseline effect, were confined to the geometric parts of group delays and fringe frequencies. It must be recalled, however, that both observables are also affected by the propagation media and the instrumental equipment as indicated in (4.14) and (4.15). Among the effects of the instrumental equipment, it is especially the behaviour of the clocks at the two completely separated stations, which contributes unknown quantities. Numerous other effects are absorbed by the observables, and have to be taken into account in order to isolate the undisturbed geometric part of the group delay and fringe frequency. These come from the complex motion of the Earth, known as polar motion, rotation, nutation and precession. Furthermore, crustal motions, solid Earth and ocean tides, source structure and the effects of Special and General Theories of Relativity also have some bearing on the observables by causing variations of the source and baseline vectors. Provided that these effects are modelled by suitable parametrisations, it is even possible to obtain estimates of any relevant parameters from the analysis of the observables. Successful analyses require measurements that cover a sufficiently long interval of time. The customary estimation procedure is a multi-parameter adjustment by means of least squares methods, necessitating a combination of data and unknowns in such a way that degeneracies are avoided. A comprehensive discussion of the explicit modelling of the diverse effects on the VLBI observables is given, for instance, by Sovers & Jacobs (1996).

Instead of immediately applying a multi-parameter fit to the observables covering a time interval of days, weeks, months or even years, we first pursue a simplified line of thought of fundamental astrometry by inquiring into the determinability of basic astrometric quantities from a minimal set of observables. Any external references are excluded as far as possible. This is comparable to a bootstrap method, and has its counterpart in optical astrometry in the situation when absolute right ascensions and declinations are to be determined from meridian circle observations (Sect. 2.3.2). In order to gain a clear view of the problem of determinability, a few simplifications may be sensible. First, we ignore propagation medium effects and the instrumental effects with the exception of synchronization errors of the station clocks. In fact, the recorded VLBI signals are based on readings of these clocks, operating independently, therefore risking differences in both the epoch settings and clock rates at the stations. Accordingly, the clock synchronization errors and the clock rates should be considered as unknowns, since they are unavoidably entangled in the observables. Second, to remove small time-variable effects, we assume a rigid Earth rotating uniformly with a known and constant angular velocity about an axis fixed in an inertial frame and also fixed with respect to the Earth's crust. Third, we consider point-like sources at infinite distances, which are motionless with respect to the inertial frame and are emitting radio waves that travel with the speed of light.

With this simple model in mind we study in the following sections the information content of group delay and fringe frequency observables. It will be shown that these observables have the potential to provide absolute or, at least, quasi-absolute source coordinates, though with a slight reservation.

5.4.2 The Group Delay Observable

With simplifications according to the above scenario, we find that the group delay observable of (4.15) transforms into the simple and easily interpretable expression

$$\tau_{\text{group}} = \frac{d}{c}\, \boldsymbol{r}_{\text{b}} \cdot \boldsymbol{s} + \Delta\tau_{\text{clock}}\,, \tag{5.1}$$

which contains, as the immediate basic unknowns, two source coordinates ($\boldsymbol{s}$) and three baseline components ($d, \boldsymbol{r}_{\text{b}}$). In addition, there are the clock calibrations, represented by two unknowns, which are the clock synchronization or epoch setting at $t = 0$, C_0, and the clock rate, C_1, i.e., $\Delta\tau_{\text{clock}} = C_0 + C_1\, t$. In total, (5.1) comprises seven unknowns.

As the first term on the right-hand side of (5.1) is equal to the geometric time delay explicitly written out in (4.31), τ_{group} is composed of a constant part, a part proportional to time and a sinusoidally varying part, i.e.,

$$\tau_{\text{group}} = B + C_1 t + A\cos(\omega_{\text{e}} t + \phi)\,, \tag{5.2}$$

where

$$B = \frac{d}{c} \sin\delta_{\text{s}} \sin\delta_{\text{b}} + C_0\,,$$

$$A = \frac{d}{c} \cos\delta_{\text{s}} \cos\delta_{\text{b}}\,,$$

$$\omega_{\text{e}}\, t + \phi = \alpha_{\text{b}}\,(t) - \alpha_{\text{s}}\,.$$

Here ω_{e} is the Earth's angular velocity, which is assumed to be constant. The phase ϕ is the angular difference between the projections of the baseline and the source vectors onto the equatorial plane at time $t = 0$, i.e. the right ascension difference between the two vectors (see Fig. 4.6).

In order to comprehend the potential of delay measurements for performing absolute astrometry we analyse the information content of (5.2). Obviously, this expression represents a link between the observables and a set of intermediate unknown parameters that are related to the real unknowns, i.e., source coordinates, baseline components and clock calibrations.

To begin with, let us consider the observation of a single source in the course of a VLBI session that lasts several hours and acquires sufficient observations during the time interval of simultaneous visibility of the source from both stations. From (5.2) it follows immediately that a minimum of four delay measurements reasonably spaced in time will suffice to determine these four unknowns B, C_1, A and ϕ by means of curve fitting. Concerning the determinability of the four unknowns, any further delay measurements are redundant. They would only contribute to the error assessment of these unknowns, but cannot provide any information about additional unknowns in view of the model described by (5.2). Consequently, we have obtained solutions for four unknowns, while the total number of unknowns is as large as seven. This is, at first glance, a disappointing result from the point of view of absolute astrometry. To play a 'winning game' (Shapiro 1976), we try the strategy of observing a second and third source during the same VLBI session, employing the same baseline and station clocks.

Since the slope, C_1, of the linear term in (5.2) is already known from curve fitting for the first source and since the slope is independent of the source, we realize that a minimum of only three delay measurements of the second source provide solutions of the three unknowns, B, A and ϕ, related to the second source but, of course, adds the two new unknowns of the source coordinates. Now the budget of intermediate parameters and unknowns looks more favourable, being 7 and 9, respectively. As soon as a third source is included in the observation programme, this budget is further improved to 10 and 11, respectively, again by solving for the three unknowns, B, A, and ϕ related to the third source, and the augmentation by two positional unknowns due to the additional source. Note that the choice of sources is to be made with some care to avoid degeneracies.

It would be a logical flaw to continue this game by increasing the number of sources in order to arrive at a sufficient number of equations for determining the unknowns. Only redundancies would be produced. Indeed we cannot expect to solve for all 11 unknowns since, in the theoretical expression for the delay observable, differences appear between baseline right ascensions and source right ascensions, as indicated by the phase term in (5.2). In other words, a rotation of the baseline vector and the radio source vector about the Earth's axis of rotation leaves the phase invariant and, consequently, this rotation is indeterminable. It is therefore imperative to introduce a constraint by, for example, fixing the origin of the right ascension (RA). Thus, observables of a minimum of three sources and, as the only external reference, the origin of RA are needed to determine six source coordinates, three baseline components and two clock parameters. Due to the external fixing of one right ascension, it is more exact not to speak of absolute but, instead, of quasi-absolute right ascensions. How one proceeds in adopting such a zero point is explained in Sect. 5.4.5.

1459+480 15 00 48.654199±34 +47 51 15.53826±38 ? . . .

For completeness of the data chain rather than for its intrinsic importance, we briefly comment on the determination process of the 11 basic unknowns. Once the RA of one of the three sources is fixed, say $\alpha_{s(1)}$, the remaining 10 unknowns are determinable from curve fitting: C_1 follows immediately from curve fitting, and the other 9 unknowns are determined from selected combinations of pairs of equations belonging to one of the types 'B', 'A' and 'ϕ' appearing in (5.2). The procedure is mathematically sound though lengthy, and therefore not carried out here.

5.4.3 The Fringe Frequency Observable

For fringe frequency we proceed in the same manner as for group delay. By analogy to (5.2) the theoretical expression for the fringe frequency is inferred from (4.14) and (4.30). One obtains

$$\begin{aligned} \nu_\mathrm{f} &= \omega \frac{\partial}{\partial t}\left(\frac{d}{c}\,\boldsymbol{r}_\mathrm{b}\cdot\boldsymbol{s}\right) + \frac{\partial}{\partial t}\,\Delta\tau_\mathrm{clock} \\ &= -\omega\,\frac{d}{c}\,\omega_\mathrm{e}\cos\delta_\mathrm{s}\cos\delta_\mathrm{b}\sin(\alpha_\mathrm{b}-\alpha_\mathrm{s}) + C_1\,. \end{aligned} \tag{5.3}$$

We realize that the fringe frequency is composed of a constant and a sinusoidal term:

$$\nu_\mathrm{f} = C_1 + A\sin(\omega_\mathrm{e}\,t + \phi)\,, \tag{5.4}$$

where

C_1 is the clock rate error,

$$A = -\omega\,\frac{d}{c}\,\omega_\mathrm{e}\cos\delta_\mathrm{s}\cos\delta_\mathrm{b}\ ,$$

$$\omega_\mathrm{e}\,t + \phi = \alpha_\mathrm{b}(t) - \alpha_\mathrm{s}\,.$$

As shown in (4.12), the fringe frequency observable is a multiple of the time derivative of the phase delay. Therefore, with fringe frequency alone it is not possible, in principle, to determine the epoch setting or clock offset of the station clocks. Furthermore, we know from Sect. 4.4.6 that fringe frequency is not sensitive to the polar component of the baseline. Consequently only two baseline components are determinable from fringe frequency observables.

Assuming that fringe frequency observations of a single source span a reasonable fraction of the diurnal circle, curve fitting of a minimum of three observables applied to (5.4) yields three intermediate unknowns: C_1, A and ϕ. One of them, C_1, is the clock rate offset or clock rate error, the other two are related to the set of four unknowns comprising the two source coordinates and the two equatorial baseline components. What we have constructed are three equations for the determination of five unknowns. The obvious deficit of two equations, however, cannot be remedied by adding observations of a second source. It is true that this procedure would augment by two the intermediate unknowns estimated by curve fitting, but it also increases the number of the unknowns to be determined by the two additional source coordinates, i.e., five equations for the determination of seven unknowns. Concerning right ascension we face the same situation as in the case of delay observables. Again, the theoretical expression for the fringe frequency observable in (5.4) contains only right ascension differences, necessitating the introduction of a constraint that fixes the right ascension origin. To remove the remaining deficit of one equation, one can decide to fix the declination of a single source by adopting an external value, e.g., the declination from optical astrometry or from a group delay solution. Preferably, one chooses a source near the equator since, as outlined in Sect. 4.4, fringe frequency is insensitive to the source declination zero. Consequently, the numerical value of A is hardly affected by an unintentionally introduced uncertainty of the adopted source declination.

Having fixed the right ascension and declination of one source each, s(1) and s(2), we now turn the tables to determine the unknowns from (5.4). Given the two constraints, $\alpha_{\mathrm{s}(1)}$ and $\delta_{\mathrm{s}(2)}$, one finds α_{b} from $\omega_{\mathrm{e}}\, t + \phi$, and $d \cos \delta_{\mathrm{b}}$ from A. Hereby the equatorial components of the baseline are determined. Any fringe frequency measurements of additional sources provide their right ascensions and declinations relative to $\alpha_{\mathrm{s}(1)}$ and $\delta_{\mathrm{s}(2)}$. In this context account is taken of the variation of α_{b} with the right ascension of Greenwich.

To sum up one can say that fringe frequency observables are unable to provide the full set of baseline components. Furthermore, the source coordinates derived from fringe frequency observables fall in the category of quasi-absolute RAs and Decs because of the necessity to adopt one external reference each in RA and Dec.

5.4.4 Accumulation of Source Observations

In the case of group delay observables, the observations of three sources during a normal 24-hour VLBI experiment are, in principle, sufficient to permit estimates of all the unknowns involved in the problem of determinability: 3×2 source coordinates, 3 baseline components and 2 clock offsets, one for epoch setting and one for the clock rate. This is valid provided that the origin of RA is adopted from an external reference. In contrast, the processing of fringe frequency observables results in estimated unknowns that are a genuine subset of those unknowns which are determinable from delay observables. Fringe frequency measurements, therefore, are complementary to time delay measurements; they do not, however, provide solutions for unknowns which cannot also be determined from delay observables. Through their redundancy fringe frequency measurements add to the robustness of the combined solution based on both delay and fringe frequency observables.

`1514+197      15 16 56.796194±26   +19 32 12.99187±49      L   ...`

The observables of at least three sources entered the discussion in connection with absolute astrometry. During a typical 24-hour session 30 to 50 or more sources are easily observable several times while pointing at a single source for several hundred seconds. Results for absolute astrometry can be achieved from these observables as in the case of only three sources. Successive 24-hour sessions provide the source coordinates of another batch of 30 to 50 sources, usually comprising observations of all or subset of the sources of the previous batch plus new sources. Along these lines an observation catalogue of extragalactic radio sources is produced, which is the subject of Sect. 5.4.6.

5.4.5 The Right Ascension Zero Point

Apart from the need to adopt the zero point of right ascension, the VLBI technique is capable of performing absolute astrometry by providing self-contained solutions of clock calibrations, baseline components, absolute source declinations and right ascension differences, but not absolute right ascensions. A customary method practiced in establishing many of the early radio astrometric catalogues adopted the value $12^{\mathrm{h}}\,29^{\mathrm{m}}\,06^{\mathrm{s}}.6997$ at J2000.0 for the right ascension of the reference source 3C 273B (1226 + 023). This coordinate was obtained by transforming the position derived by Hazard et al. (1971) from lunar occultation measurements to the reference frame J2000.0 defined by the FK5. The source 3C 273B is a privileged source because of its strong emission at both optical and radio wavelengths and its nearly zero declination, providing accessibility to observers in both the northern and southern hemispheres. Observations of 3C 273B, however, reveal time-variable radio structure at the level of 5 milliarcseconds, giving rise to the fear that this structure may corrupt the coordinates of the other sources in the respective catalogue. To reduce this vulnerability, the alignment of the radio source right ascensions with the FK5 frame (Fricke et al. 1988) is an alternative approach: The right ascension zero point of the radio reference frame is defined by the FK5 positions of the optical counterparts of extragalactic radio sources to such an extent that the average right ascension difference between the VLBI and FK5 positions is constrained to zero (Ma et al. 1990).

Another procedure, similar to the previous one, prefers the choice of the right ascension origin to minimize the rms difference between the radio and optical positions of a number of sources, i.e.

$$D\,(\Delta\alpha) = \frac{1}{N}\sum_i [(\alpha^i + \Delta\alpha)_{\mathrm{radio}} - \alpha^i_{\mathrm{opt}}]^2 = \min\,.$$

Both the averaging as well as the minimization procedure have the advantage of absorbing any real differences between the radio and optical emission centres.

Up to this point the definition of the radio astronomical right ascension zero point or origin resorted to the results of optical astrometry. One may inquire into the possibility of defining the right ascension origin on purely radio astronomical grounds. A few remarks on this problem seem appropriate: While the Earth's spin axis serves to define an instantaneous reference for declination measurements, there is no analogous natural point which could play the role of a preferred origin of right ascension. A possible exception lies in the weak sensitivity of VLBI delays to the Earth's position in its orbit and to the position of the Sun (via gravitational bending). Unfortunately, these higher-order effects can only determine a right ascension origin to an accuracy that is one or two orders of magnitude inferior to the desired milliarcsecond level. Because such a strong fiducial point does not exist, it is necessary to define an origin arbitrarily but, of course, as realistically as possible to facilitate comparisons of coordinates. This situation is not confined to VLBI but is also faced by other systems of measurements. For instance, the so-called absolute meridian circle measurements provide primarily right ascension differences of stars with respect to the Sun and members of the planetary system. In a separate procedure the absolute right ascensions of these objects are established allowing to absolutize the differential stellar right ascensions and, in addition, to connect them to the solar system which is known to represent an inertial frame in the sense of post-Newtonian dynamics. For more details on this problematic area we refer to Sects. 1.7 and 2.2.

The classical method of zero point determination, outlined in Sect. 2.2.2, defines the origin of right ascension as the Sun's absolute right ascension at the instant of the passage of the vernal equinox. Because of the weak and scattered radio emission of the Sun, this method does not satisfy radio astrometric requirements. Other methods of radio astronomical equinox determination, therefore, have been devised and are delineated below.

The preceding discussions on absolute astrometry stressed the fact that VLBI observables alone do not have potential of immediately determining the direction of the vernal equinox. Instead, we were obliged to adopt a catalogue equinox as the origin of right ascension by resorting to means which are outside the domain of radio astronomy. We now discuss methods that have been invented to tie the radio interferometric right ascension differences to the dynamical equinox. Some of these have reached fruition, while others are still in an experimental phase. While a catalogue equinox may refer to some arbitrary point on the celestial equator, the dynamical equinox is defined by the line of intersection of the mean plane of the equator and the ecliptic. The intersection of these two planes, where the apparent path of the Sun crosses the equator from south to north, was declared to be the zero point for measurements of right ascensions. It is for this reason that the dynamical equinox plays an important role in relating the differential right ascensions derived from interferometric observations to the zero point of right ascension.

One promising method for relating the differential right ascensions of extragalactic radio sources to the dynamical equinox has been developed by Folkner et al. (1994). This method determines the link between the extragalactic frame, established by means of VLBI, and the planetary frame, based on lunar laser ranging (LLR) measurements. Since the orbits of the inner planets are known from radar ranging observations, it is evident that the comparison of the planetary reference frame with the extragalactic radio reference frame implicitly refers to the orbits of the four inner planets, especially those of Earth and Mars. The implicit character of the link of the frames derives from the fact that both techniques, VLBI and LLR, are sensitive to the station locations in their respective celestial reference frames. Therefore, the relative orientation between the extragalactic radio frame and the planetary ephemeris frame, which is oriented towards the vernal equinox by definition, can be inferred from a comparison of the relative orientation of VLBI and LLR terrestrial frames, and the transformations needed to map Earth-fixed station locations to the VLBI and LLR celestial frames. A rotation vector is derived from the offsets of the VLBI and LLR station coordinates, thus providing the link between the extragalactic frame and the inertial planetary ephemeris reference frame. One component of this vector causes a rotation about the axis to the celestial pole. This rotation has to be applied as correction to the right ascensions of the extragalactic radio frame in order to refer them to the dynamical equinox of the planetary ephemeris frame. Based on currently existing measurements, the accuracy of this link is found to be 3 mas.

Another, rather conceptual approach to the problem of determining the direction of the vernal equinox involves radio interferometric observations of selected minor planets whose orbits are related to the planetary ephemeris frame (Johnston et al. 1982). The idea is to observe the thermal radiation of minor planets by means of the Very Large Array (VLA), aiming ultimately at high positional accuracy. Theoretically, it should be possible to locate the dynamical equinox from radio observations alone and, thereby, avoid the adoption of a non-radio astronomical zero point. Along these lines, absolute right ascensions would result from joint radio interferometric observations of extragalactic radio sources and minor planets. In principle, the differences between the ephemeris right ascensions of minor planets and those obtained from interferometric observations relative to extragalactic sources indicate the shift that should be applied to the right ascensions of the extragalactic sources in order to calibrate them relative to the dynamical equinox. So far a few drawbacks have retarded the maturation of the method. These are principally the extremely low flux densities (fractions of a millijansky) that are found at 2 and 6 cm wavelengths for Ceres and Pallas, as well as the finite angular sizes of the larger minor planets.

Likewise, VLA observations of planets and their natural satellites may be useful to provide absolute right ascensions of extragalactic radio sources. The radio flux emitted from the larger satellites of Jupiter and Saturn and from planet Uranus, which is of small size, suffices for determining accurate radio positions. Early results suggested a discrepancy of roughly −0.2 arcsec in right ascensions of the three outer planets between the ephemeris reference frame and the radio reference frame based on extragalactic sources that are aligned with the optically determined right ascension of the quasar 3C 273B (Muhleman et al. 1985).

A similar line of thought for an accurate tie between the radio and ephemeris frames uses differential VLBI applied to planet-orbiting spacecraft and angularly nearby quasars (Newhall et al. 1986). This method overcomes the two drawbacks mentioned above: The angular size of the spacecraft is relatively small, while the intensity of the radio emission may be chosen to be quite sizeable.

A third method takes advantage of pulsars (Bartel et al. 1985). On the one hand, the celestial coordinates of pulsars and extragalactic radio sources are determined by VLBI and, as such, they refer to the Earth's axis of rotation. Furthermore, these pulsar coordinates are relative to an extragalactic reference frame established from VLBI observations of extragalactic radio sources having some adopted right ascension origin. On the other hand, the timing measurements of pulsars yield positions relative to the Earth's orbit. Therefore, the celestial coordinates obtained from pulse arrival times (PAT) are originally expressed in ecliptic longitude and latitude (λ, β), while those obtained from VLBI are given by their right ascensions and declinations (α, δ). Between these two position vectors, $\boldsymbol{r}_{\mathrm{PAT}}$ and $\boldsymbol{r}_{\mathrm{VLBI}}$, the following relationship holds:

$$\boldsymbol{r}_{\mathrm{PAT}}\,(\lambda, \beta) = \mathbf{R}_x(\varepsilon + \Delta\varepsilon)\,\mathbf{R}_z(\Delta\alpha)\,\boldsymbol{r}_{\mathrm{VLBI}}(\alpha, \delta)\,. \tag{5.5}$$

This expression allows the determination of a correction $\Delta\varepsilon$ to the obliquity of the ecliptic, (ε), and a shift $\Delta\alpha$, which adjusts the right ascensions of the objects constituting the extragalactic reference frame to the intersection of the Earth's orbit with the celestial equator, i.e., to the direction of the dynamical equinox. In (5.5) we have assumed a right-handed rectangular coordinate frame x, y, z with the x axis lying in the equatorial plane pointing along the VLBI-adopted zero point of right ascension, the y axis running perpendicular to x in the equatorial plane, and the z axis pointing to the north pole. The matrices $\mathbf{R}_x$ and $\mathbf{R}_z$ stand for rotations about the x and z axes, respectively.

The pulsar positions determined from radio interferometric measurements and those determined from pulse-timing measurements have precisions of 0.″01 or better, which is especially true for millisecond pulsars (Fomalont et al. 1992). Once the positions of a few dozen suitable pulsars are inferred from both VLBI and pulse-timing measurements, milliarcsecond accuracy can be expected for the relative orientation of the extragalactic Earth-spin-oriented and the planetary Earth-orbit oriented reference frames.

1549−790 15 56 58.869899±111 −79 14 04.28134±32 S 0.149

5.4.6 Observation Catalogues of Extragalactic Radio Sources

In realistic circumstances an observation campaign (session) during one diurnal cycle can be extended to $m > 3$ extragalactic radio sources giving rise to a total of $2m+3+2$ unknowns, namely $2m$ source coordinates, 3 baseline components and 2 clock parameters. Let us first assume that the session supplies only delay observables. From the preceding discussion on absolute astrometry we conclude that $4m+1$ equations are available. They are composed of $4m$ equations each of the types B, C_1, A and ϕ (see Sect. 5.4.2), and the right ascension constraint, which is dictated by the necessity of defining the zero point of right ascension. Not all of these equations are independent. There are, in general, among them $2m+3+2<4m+1$ independent equations for the determination of the identical number of unknowns. With m increasing further, more and more redundant equations will be produced to enable refinement of the error estimation of the unknowns.

In the case that fringe frequency observables are also supplied for m sources, nominally $3m+2$ equations will be available (see Sect. 5.4.3), including the right ascension and declination constraints, provided that the latter are not replaced by declinations inferred from delay measurements. We can expect to solve for $2m+2+1$ unknowns comprising $2m$ source coordinates, 2 baseline components, and the clock rate offset.

After these preliminaries we now illustrate the construction of an observation catalogue of extragalactic radio sources, still using the simple model introduced in Sect. 5.4.1. Imagine that successive observation sessions of 24 hours duration take place, and that additional sources are observed during the following days, weeks and months. Also, the same sources may be observed on repeated occasions. In principle, the delay measurements of a group of three sources could be analysed for a 24-hour interval, and, after some time has elapsed, other groups of three sources containing all or at least a subset of the initial three sources could again be analysed independently. Source positions and baseline components at different observation epochs would be obtained. As a result, variations of these quantities as a function of time will almost certainly manifest themselves since the simplified model has neglected short term effects, of the order of days and even hours, while VLBI is sensitive to such effects. Likewise, medium and long term effects are detectable by VLBI observables provided they cover an interval of time of sufficient length. Relevant effects belonging to this category are, for instance, polar motion, the velocity of the Earth's rotation, the crustal motion, the solid-Earth tides, nutation and precession of the Earth, but also source structure and motion.

The simplified model was instrumental in demonstrating that the basic quantities such as source coordinates and baseline components are determinable from delay and fringe frequency observables. Eventually, astronomical, geodetic and geophysical effects causing variations of the basic quantities, source positions and baseline components, may be identified by fitting suitable model parameters to the data. In practice, however, this approach

1600+335	16 02 07.263468±27	+33 26 53.07267±53	?	...

is inconvenient. Instead, one uses a multi-parameter adjustment procedure, which stands on safe ground after the determinability of the basic quantities has been demonstrated. Its core is the modelling of the observables as a function of not only the source coordinates and baseline components, but also depending on the parametrisations of the astronomical, geodetic and geophysical effects, and of the propagation media and instrumental equipment, as indicated, e.g., in (4.15). Provided the observables are consistent and accurate, and cover a sufficiently long interval of time, one can expect to obtain estimates of these parameters or subsets from the adjustment process. Modelling the effects does not necessarily mean that the respective parameters are completely unknown. Solving for those parameters can be treated on an optional basis, or alternatively the parameter values can be supplied from external sources.

The number of institutions operating VLBI networks is limited, as is the number of centres which deal with the compilation of individual observation catalogues of positions of extragalactic radio sources. Unfortunately, the majority of these catalogues are not completely independent. The data sets and modelling software overlap in most cases. Such observation catalogues have been produced at the Goddard Space Flight Center (GSFC), the Jet Propulsion Laboratory (JPL), the National Oceanic and Atmospheric Administration (NOAA), the United States Naval Observatory (USNO), the National Astronomical Observatory of Mizusawa (NAOMZ) and the Geodetic Institute of the University of Bonn (GIUB), to mention the most productive contributors during the 1980s and 90s. Typical examples of individual position catalogues of extragalactic radio sources are the catalogues by Fanselow et al. (1984), Sovers et al. (1988), Ma et al. (1990), Robertson et al. (1993), Manabe & Yokoyama (1994), and Johnston et al. (1995). This list of catalogues is open-ended, and in fact, the International Earth Rotation Service (IERS) keeps track of new VLBI catalogues by publishing submissions from participating institutions in its Annual Reports, e.g., IERS (1994a). During the past decade, this organization has decided whether new catalogues are eligible for the maintenance of the extragalactic reference frame, which is one of the IERS formal responsibilities. Especially in the early days, the catalogues contained, in addition to the positional information, an instructive narrative section describing the procedures that finally led to the source positions.

5.4.7 The Physical Models Used for Parameter Adjustment

Instead of the simplified expression of (4.15) we introduce now the more sophisticated observation equations for a multi-parameter adjustment process for group delay observables as

$$\tau(t) = \tau_{\rm g} + \tau_{\rm instr} + \tau_{\rm misc} + \tau_{\rm media} + \tau_{\rm struc} \,, \tag{5.6}$$

```
1604−333     16 07 34.762344±47   −33 31 08.91313±48     Q   . . .
```

where each of the terms on the right-hand side represents a special type of physical model described below.

The *geometric delay*, τ_g, is obtained at the time t of observation. It can be written as

$$\tau_g = (\mathbf{P}\,\mathbf{N}\,\mathbf{U}\,\mathbf{X}\,\mathbf{Y})\,\boldsymbol{b}_{\text{terr}} \cdot \boldsymbol{s}/c, \tag{5.7}$$

with a symbolic indication of the models that determine at some observation time, t, the baseline orientation in the celestial geocentric reference frame at the standard epoch J2000.0: $\mathbf{P}$, $\mathbf{N}$, $\mathbf{U}$, $\mathbf{X}$ and $\mathbf{Y}$ denote the rotation matrices of precession ($\mathbf{P}$), nutation ($\mathbf{N}$), universal time or diurnal rotation of the Earth ($\mathbf{U}$), and polar motion ($\mathbf{X}, \mathbf{Y}$), respectively. For the sake of completeness the effect of the high-frequency polar motion must also be added. Assuming that $\boldsymbol{s}$ is the source unit vector at observation time relative to the celestial geocentric frame at J2000.0, the problem is that the baseline vector, $\boldsymbol{b}_{\text{terr}}$, has to be transformed to the celestial geocentric frame for reasons of homogeneity. Originally, $\boldsymbol{b}_{\text{terr}}$ refers to the terrestrial reference frame fixed with respect to the Earth's crust and the 1903.0 CIO (Conventional International Origin), also known as the 1903.0 CIO frame. This transformation involves the precession and nutation of coordinates at observation time to the corresponding J2000.0 coordinates. Therefore, to be precise, the matrices $\mathbf{P}$ and $\mathbf{N}$ in (5.7) do not represent the standard formulation typically used in astrometry but they are the transposes of the conventional matrices applied to transform from the frame at J2000.0 to coordinates of date. Subsequent to these transformations, the baseline and source vectors refer to the same frame, and the scalar product of the two vectors models the geometric part of the observed time delay.

The *instrumental delay*, τ_{instr}, is composed of the propagation time of signals within the electronic equipment at each station, and of the clock offsets. Antenna deformation dependence on time and elevation also plays a part here. The latter effects could be included either in the geometric delay ($\boldsymbol{b}_{\text{terr}}$ above) or instrumental delay.

The *miscellaneous delays*, τ_{misc}, are caused by sundry effects which perturb the observation geometry and therefore require modelling. These effects are, for instance, solid-Earth tides, ocean tides, seafloor spreading, ocean loading, antenna structure and relativistic gravitational deflection. Some of these effects, such as the solid-Earth tides, cause temporal oscillations of the baseline vector, $\boldsymbol{b}_{\text{terr}}$, and have short-term repercussions on the geometric delay.

The *propagation delay*, τ_{media}, contains two contributions: one caused by the troposphere, the other by the ionosphere.

– Tropospheric delay contributions consist of a dry and wet component. The dry component is predictable and can be estimated to a high precision from the total atmospheric surface pressure (Ronnang 1989). Under

standard conditions the excess dry delay amounts to the equivalent of approximately 6 nanoseconds.
The wet component is caused by the dipole moments of any atmospheric water molecules and depends on the water vapour content along each line of sight. Since the water vapour distribution in the atmosphere is not well known, the wet component is difficult to model. Microwave radiometer measurements of the brightness temperatures of the troposphere at 22 GHz indicate that the path length of the wet component was measurable to better than 1 cm in the 1980s (Ronnang 1989), and nearly an order of magnitude better in the 1990s (Keihm & Marsh 1996). The magnitude of the wet component ranges from approximately 5 to 20% of the dry component.
A completely different method of modelling the wet component takes advantage of the interferometer measurements by estimating it directly from the observables. Such estimates can be done either at frequent time intervals, or by employing Kalman filtering techniques (Ronnang 1989).

– The ionospheric delay contribution is associated with a plasma effect generated by charged particles in a layer at about 350 km altitude. While at X band (8.4 GHz) the ionospheric path delay is only of the order of 10% of the dry tropospheric component, and has its maximum during the local day, it increases by a factor of 10 at S band (2.3 GHz). These plasma effects can, however, be removed by the technique of observing the sources at both X and S bands, which are the frequencies usually employed for astrometric and geodetic VLBI. Provided that the two observing frequencies are significantly larger than the plasma frequency, the combination of the observables at two frequencies allows nearly complete elimination of the charged particle contribution from delay observables.

The *source structure delay*, τ_{struc}: It cannot be excluded that source position offsets exist for X- and S-band observations. If so, they will be unintentionally modelled into the ionospheric group delay in the case of dual frequency observations, and consequently the geometric time delay will be contaminated. Apart from this frequency-dependent effect, the intrinsic structure of the source itself also degrades accuracy. In fact, structure on a milliarcsecond scale has been detected in many compact extragalactic radio sources (Kellermann & Pauliny-Toth 1981; Fey & Charlot 1997, 2000). Moreover, temporal variations of structure have been confirmed in the past (Zensus & Pearson 1987).

As extragalactic radio sources are candidates eligible to serve as fiducial points in a rigid reference frame, it is important to model these structural effects aiming, ultimately, at the definition of a stable reference point for any instant. How such modelling of a non-point-like distribution can be achieved is described, for example, by Charlot (1990).

What has been said above about modelling of the group delay observable is, whenever applicable, also valid for the delay rate or fringe frequency observable. Since, however, the time differentiation produces an amplification of the random, short term fluctuations of ϕ_{media} and ϕ_{instr} in (4.14), modelling in general is less precise for fringe frequency than for group delay. In fact, modelling may even be seriously impaired in the presence of a turbulent troposphere. Also, the effects on the observation geometry caused, for instance, by solid Earth tides and ocean loading carry the risk of becoming less predictable in the case of fringe frequency.

A closing remark on the numerous physical effects contributing to the interferometer observables seems to be appropriate. The list of these effects and of the corresponding physical models is open-ended due to the discovery of hitherto unknown phenomena and the steady increase in geophysical knowledge and improvement of measurement accuracy. In the above exposition, only the most common effects have been outlined. A state-of-the-art treatment of the multitude of geometrical, instrumental, observational, environmental and structural effects and their modelling has been compiled in a comprehensive manner by Sovers & Jacobs (1996). With the advent of further experimental modernization, in the course of which delay accuracies are expected to approach a few picoseconds (ps), modelling at the mm level will be required instead of at the cm level. In these circumstances, revisions of the Earth tidal models, the Earth orientation model and the model of general relativity will become imperative. Likewise, the effects caused by source structure, troposphere and antenna deformation will have to be examined thoroughly.

5.5 Methods of Fundamental Catalogue Construction

We have seen that radio interferometry can be instrumental in generating catalogues of absolute coordinates provided that a zero point of right ascension is adopted. On the assumption that the catalogue objects are extragalactic radio sources at large distances, the condition of a kinematic definition of a fundamental reference system is fulfilled (see Chap. 1). Any such observation catalogue, per se, may be considered as a fundamental catalogue, which represents a fundamental reference frame. We recall that the construction of a conventional fundamental catalogue relies on conventional astronomical constants whose values are needed for reducing the raw observations to a prescribed epoch. Therefore, it would be ideal to determine certain astronomical constants such as precession, nutation and aberration in conjunction with the establishment of the catalogues. To a certain degree, this is not necessary because there exist high standards for these astronomical constants and related conventions. These are laid down, e.g., in the International Earth Rotation Service (IERS) Standards (IERS 1992) and the IERS Conventions (IERS 1996b). One current exception is the 1980 IAU nutation model, which is known to have defects at the level of many mas. In order to produce accurate inter-source arc positions, most customary modelling procedures have

1619−680 16 24 18.437150±71 −68 09 12.49811±57 Q 1.354

corrected these defects by estimating a pair of nutation angle corrections for each VLBI observing session.

In the following sections we present three methods for the compilation of fundamental catalogues from either observation catalogues of source positions or batches of VLBI observing sessions. First, a rather classical method is treated which, in the times of meridian circle astrometry, was applied to the construction of fundamental catalogues, but is equally applicable to radio astronomical observation techniques. The point of departure is the collection of individual VLBI position catalogues that have accumulated during the last two decades. The second method starts directly from the VLBI observables of different networks, and the third method again deals with preprocessed individual position catalogues that are combined to a fundamental catalogue through the optimization of triaxial rotations.

5.5.1 The Classical Method

The construction of a fundamental catalogue in accordance with the classical method is based on a series of independent observation catalogues of extragalactic radio sources produced by different VLBI networks. Without loss of generality we assume that the source positions, listed in the observation catalogues as right ascension (RA, α) and declination (Dec, δ), refer to the coordinate frame defined by the equator and equinox of J2000.0. Furthermore, the right ascension origin of each catalogue is assumed to be fixed to the right ascension of some common source. The accuracy of the observation catalogues is degraded by both random and systematic errors, the latter being caused by properties of the network configuration, the receivers and the data reduction procedures. Any observed position is composed of the true source position and a systematic part, which for each source takes the form

$$\alpha_{\text{true}} + \Delta c^{\alpha} = \alpha_{\text{obs}}, \qquad \delta_{\text{true}} + \Delta c^{\delta} = \delta_{\text{obs}}\,. \tag{5.8}$$

On these grounds it is possible to set up a fundamental catalogue in its simplest form and with a minimum of presuppositions. Assuming that the position of a radio source appears in n observation catalogues, there will be $2n$ observational equations, n each in RA and Dec:

$$\begin{aligned} \Delta\alpha + \Delta c_i^{\alpha} &= (\alpha_{\text{obs}})_i - \alpha_0, \\ \Delta\delta + \Delta c_i^{\delta} &= (\delta_{\text{obs}})_i - \delta_0, \\ & \quad i = 1, ..., n, \end{aligned} \tag{5.9}$$

where $\Delta\alpha$, Δc_i^{α} and $\Delta\delta$, Δc_i^{δ} are the unknowns and α_0, δ_0 some approximation of the true position. The systems of observational equations (5.9), established for each source, consist of $2n$ equations for $2n+2$ unknowns: two unknowns signifying the corrections of the position and $2n$ unknowns standing for the systematic corrections in RA and Dec of each of the catalogues.

It is common practice to define a fundamental catalogue as the expectation value of the weighted systematic corrections of the observation catalogues (see, e.g., Zverev 1963), with their relative weights w_i being inferred from the observational accuracy of the catalogues. Note that this recipe concerns the implementation of the system and not its kinematic definition (see Chap. 1). The observation catalogues themselves have been set up in consistency with models and parameters given in the standards of the IERS, in striving to satisfy the system definition of the fundamental catalogue. If the number of catalogues is sufficiently large, the systematic corrections follow a normal distribution about zero. Consequently, it is meaningful to constrain to zero the weighted means in RA and Dec, i.e.,

$$\sum_{i=1}^{n} w_i^{\alpha} \Delta c_i^{\alpha} = 0, \qquad \sum_{i=1}^{n} w_i^{\delta} \Delta c_i^{\delta} = 0. \tag{5.10}$$

Thus there are $2n{+}2$ equations for the determination of $2n{+}2$ unknowns: $2n$ observational equations of the form (5.9) and two constraints according to (5.10).

For each source the coordinates $\alpha_0 + \Delta\alpha$, $\delta_0 + \Delta\delta$ are obtained relative to the fundamental system. This procedure also yields, as a by-product, the systematic catalogue corrections $\Delta c_i^{\alpha}, \Delta c_i^{\delta}$ of the i-th observation catalogue in the vicinity of the source location. The ensemble of these coordinates of extragalactic objects constitutes a fundamental catalogue that materializes an extragalactic reference system. Details concerning this construction method, error estimation included, are found in a pilot study (Walter 1989), which may be considered as a precursor of a fundamental catalogue.

5.5.2 The Observable Method

In contrast to the classical method, the observable method deals with the original VLBI observations obtained by using the Mark II recording system (Rogers et al. 1983) and its updated version Mark III (Clark et al. 1985) between late 1979 and the end of 1993 (Johnston et al. 1995). All of these observations are made at the standard astrometric and geodetic frequencies of 2.3 GHz (S band) and 8.4 GHz (X band). Group delay and fringe frequency observables result from these observations after correlation at the Mark III processors. The observables originating from different observing agencies are amalgamated into a single data base in a first step of data analysis.

Once the observation equations are set up, a weighted least squares solution is performed to estimate the source positions and a multitude of additional parameters such as baseline parameters, Earth orientation parameters, station clock settings and atmosphere parameters. This analysis is subdivided into two stages. First, the least squares solution is performed on individual data sets associated with the experiments of the respective observing agencies, in order to determine their parametrisation and proper weights. This includes estimates of the local parameters describing the station clocks, the atmosphere at each site and, as will be explained below, nutation offsets. In the second stage, the individual data sets are combined to perform a least squares solution for the source positions from the observation equations of all data sets by elimination of the local parameters.

These source positions are obtained from first principles, i.e., as few conditions as possible are imposed on the source positions for establishing an inertial frame. Whenever models and parameters enter the solution, they are chosen to be consistent with the International Earth Rotation Service (IERS) Standards. Only minimal a priori information concerning station locations is included, in order not to corrupt the determination of the source coordinates by a presupposed terrestrial frame. In fact, only the position of one station in each experiment is normally fixed to its a priori value, serving as a local zero point of the terrestrial frame.

As mentioned previously, inadequate knowledge of nutation necessitates special measures in combining data sets referring to different epochs. Otherwise the accuracy of the source positions would be impaired. In order to relate the global solution to a defined celestial pole, a reference day is selected by adopting the IAU standards for precession and nutation in longitude and obliquity on that day without modification. Offset parameters of nutation in longitude and obliquity with respect to the pole of the reference day are estimated as local parameters in each experiment. Since, for each experiment, a pair of nutation offsets is estimated with respect to the corresponding parameters provided by the nutation model on the reference day, the pole of the combined catalogue of source positions is determined by the celestial ephemeris pole of the reference day. Therefore, it should be noted that, through this procedure, the conventional mean observation epoch of the combined experiments has been substituted by the reference day, a fact that needs to be considered when catalogues are analysed.

Originally, the observable method was applied to the VLBI observables by the independent analysis centres for establishing the individual observation catalogues referred to in Sect. 5.4.6. Also by the observable method, the radio positions of some 600 sources were estimated that formed the basis of the radio/optical reference frame (RORF) constructed by Johnston et al. (1995) from combining VLBI observables of a variety of observing networks. This is the first large-scale application of the observable method, which will be revisited in Sect. 6.1. Only those objects were eligible for the catalogue which had weighted root-mean-square (wrms) position errors of better than 3 mas in both coordinates; 436 objects fulfilled this condition. The wrms errors are derived from the positions obtained in the course of the first stage of processing dealing with the individual data sets.

Hence, the final RORF catalogue consists of 436 radio sources, the positions of which define the radio reference frame. Details of the catalogue establishment including the list of source positions are given in Johnston et al.

`1642+690    16 42 07.848514±50   +68 56 39.75640±27    G  0.751`

(1995). The positional uncertainties quoted therein are formal errors of the least squares estimates; they are at the submilliarcsecond level. The catalogue positions have been derived in consistency with the IERS Standards, which is an important precondition for comparison with the reference frame established by IERS as treated in the next section.

According to its basic design, the RORF does not only constitute an extragalactic radio reference frame but has the additional potential for developing into a radio/optical reference frame since, in selecting the frame objects, the requirement was met that all the radio sources are identified with optical counterparts. The long-range goal is to establish a supplementary extragalactic optical reference frame at the accuracy level of 10 mas, compared with 30-40 mas reached at present for the positions of the optical counterparts (Johnston et al. 1995), and to attempt to link the radio and optical frames. A partial result of this goal is reported by Zacharias et al. (1999). Even in the presence of a radio reference frame, it is no luxury to strive for an extragalactic optical reference frame. In fact, precise optical astrometry of radio sources is a prerequisite for the unique identification of radio source and its optical counterpart. Another field in which a unified radio/optical reference frame is of crucial importance is the study of radio and optical structures, which require that both spatial structures be displayed in the same coordinate frame. Furthermore, if in the long run the positions of the optical counterparts have been determined relative to the Hipparcos Catalogue (see Chap. 7), then comparison with the corresponding radio positions of the frame objects will presumably open new avenues for interpreting the astrometry and astrophysics of extragalactic objects, and, perhaps, touch cosmology.

5.5.3 The IERS Catalogue Combination Method

In 1987 the International Astronomical Union (IAU) and the International Union of Geodesy and Geophysics (IUGG) established the International Earth Rotation Service (IERS) and entrusted to it the definition and maintenance of a conventional celestial reference system based on extragalactic radio sources (IAG 1988). During the ensuing decade, the IERS carried out this task and produced annually updated celestial radio reference frames. The method of accomplishing this did not follow either the classical or the observable method described above.

In contrast to the observable method described in Sect. 5.5.2, the IERS did not use the raw VLBI observables, but instead derived a combination catalogue by averaging individual position catalogues that had been set up by a variety of essentially independent analysis centres. Each such catalogue was constructed by the observable method, and used common models and parameters for the reduction of the original VLBI observables (IERS 1994a). The numerical values of astronomical constants and other parameters required for reduction were the results of recent analyses, and are laid down in the IERS Standards (e.g., IERS 1992). As proposed by Guinot (1979), the IERS reference frame is defined by the directions of selected extragalactic radio sources, the positions of which are assumed invariant. This frame has its origin in the barycentre of the solar system. The coordinate axes were fixed at the epoch J2000.0 as follows: The polar axis or z axis lies along the direction defined by the IAU recommended value of precession (IAU 1977) and the 1980 IAU Theory of Nutation (Seidelmann 1982), and the x and y axes are given by $\alpha = 0\,\mathrm{h}$, $\delta = 0°$ and $\alpha = 6\,\mathrm{h}$, $\delta = 0°$, respectively. In the early years of the IERS catalogue compilations by the combination method, the zero point of right ascension was adjusted to the right ascension of the source 3C 273B = 1226 + 023, for which the value $\alpha = 12^{\mathrm{h}}\,29^{\mathrm{m}}\,6.^{\mathrm{s}}6997$ was adopted in J2000.0 coordinates, consistent with the value for B1950.0 (Hazard et al. 1971). After an initial phase, characterized by progress in maintenance and stabilization of the combined catalogue, the process evolved in subsequent years to keeping the right ascension origin fixed at the zero point of the preceding IERS catalogue version (IERS 1994a).

A special feature of the frame represented by the IERS combination catalogue is the invariant orientation of the axes. No attempt was made to readjust the axis directions, because the sources are considered to be at rest with respect to the Universe within the present measurement accuracy at the milliarcsecond level. We briefly outline how these axes are established in the course of the averaging process referred to above. The source positions are derived from individual position catalogues by determining the small rotation angles A_1, A_2 and A_3 about the x, y and z axes that transform the coordinates from the combined (c) catalogue to the individual (i) catalogues (e.g., Arias et al. 1988). For any object this rotation is expressed by

$$\boldsymbol{s}_i = \mathbf{R}\,\boldsymbol{s}_c\,, \tag{5.11}$$

where

$$\boldsymbol{s} = \begin{pmatrix} \cos\delta\,\cos\alpha \\ \cos\delta\,\sin\alpha \\ \sin\delta \end{pmatrix}, \quad \mathbf{R} = \begin{pmatrix} 1 & A_3 & -A_2 \\ -A_3 & 1 & A_1 \\ A_2 & -A_1 & 1 \end{pmatrix}. \tag{5.12}$$

Introducing $\Delta\boldsymbol{s} = \boldsymbol{s}_i - \boldsymbol{s}_c$ in terms of spherical coordinates and considering that $\Delta\alpha, \Delta\delta$ are the differences between the individual catalogue position and that of the combined catalogue, one finds for the object j in catalogue i the conditional equations (Arias & Feissel 1990)

$$\begin{aligned} &A_1^{(i)}\sin\delta_{ij}\cos\alpha_{ij} \\ &+ A_2^{(i)}\sin\delta_{ij}\sin\alpha_{ij} - A_3^{(i)}\cos\delta_{ij} = (\alpha_{ij} - \alpha_{cj})\cos\delta_{ij}\,, \end{aligned} \tag{5.13}$$

$$-A_1^{(i)}\sin\alpha_{ij} + A_2^{(i)}\cos\alpha_{ij} = \delta_{ij} - \delta_{cj}\,. \tag{5.14}$$

If, for instance, an individual catalogue comprises n objects, it provides $2n$ conditional equations for the $2n$ positional unknowns, α_{cj}, δ_{cj}, as well as the three rotational unknowns A_1, A_2 and A_3. Any additional individual catalogue, comprising the same objects or a subset of them, increases the number of conditional equations by $2n$ or correspondingly less, but adds only the three unknown rotation angles. In general, there will be a redundant number of equations allowing a least squares fit to estimate the unknowns. For the solution only the defining sources are used, which have the property of belonging to at least two individual catalogues.

A word of caution is in order here: The individual catalogues are treated as if they were independent. Some of them, however, are derived from partly overlapping sets of observables and, hence, non-negligible correlations may exist between the different estimated spherical coordinates. Because the catalogues are generated in separate analysis centres, these correlations remain undetected and are assumed to be zero in this catalogue combination method. These neglected correlations may have minor repercussions on the positions and their uncertainties in the final combination catalogue.

The rotations with respect to the combined catalogue quantify systematic differences of the individual catalogues. From the point of view that a fundamental catalogue is defined as the weighted mean of the systematic corrections of k individual catalogues as described in Sect. 5.5.1, the three constraints

$$\sum_{i=1}^{k} w_i A_s(i) = 0, \qquad s = 1, 2, 3$$

complete the above system of conditional equations enhancing its robustness. In practice, IERS applies an alternative method for fixing the axes of the system. In the course of system maintenance the directions of the axes are constrained to those of the realization of the previous IERS catalogue.

Only the principles of establishing the IERS reference frame were treated above. In reality, additional refinements are included in the conditional equations that cope with regional distortions in right ascension and declination as functions of declination. As an example of this kind of catalogue construction, we mention the IERS celestial reference frame for 1994. It involves 531 extragalactic radio sources; 209 among these have been identified with high positional standards to such an extent that they are eligible for defining the orientation of the axes of the frame (IERS 1994a).

5.5.4 Observable Method Versus Combination Method

In contrast to optical astrometry, the classical method of radio catalogue construction has been applied only in pilot studies, probably due to the relatively limited number of individual observation catalogues and observed objects. Among recently published radio source catalogues the construction of

1706−174   17 09 34.345380±39   −17 28 53.36480±56   ?   ...

the RORF and of the ICRF (Chap. 6) employed the observable method, while the compilation catalogue by Yatskiv & Kuryanova (1990) and the successive versions of the IERS catalogues rest upon the catalogue combination method. In the past, both methods proved to be worthwhile in establishing position catalogues of extragalactic radio sources, and each of these catalogues may be considered as a realization of a radio reference frame. To illustrate the process of comparing the two types of catalogues, we consider the particular case of the RORF and IERS combination catalogues.

The RORF frame realization of Johnston et al. (1995) is based on the observable method and consists of 436 sources. Among these, 225 sources have formal standard deviations between 1 and 3 mas, while 211 sources have standard deviations of better than 1 mas. It is this latter group that constitutes the set of defining sources, which represent the frame. By its design, the observable method is as independent as possible of the terrestrial frame or Earth orientation parameters, and is capable of providing a rigid non-rotating frame. Typical of this frame, also known as an Independent Celestial Frame (ICF), is the arbitrary choice of the pole and right ascension zero point. Consequently, three degrees of freedom for three rotation angles are left for the determination of the orientation of this frame relative to any other rigid non-rotating frame.

On the other hand, the catalogue combination method of IERS materializes the extragalactic frame by a catalogue of 531 sources (IERS 1994a). As opposed to the ICF, the IERS catalogue reflects strictly the IERS system. In particular, the station coordinates and Earth orientation parameters (terrestrial pole coordinates, celestial pole offsets, and universal time or length of the day) were treated in the same manner in generating the individual catalogues that entered the IERS combination. A subsidiary combination method yielded the IERS terrestrial system. Therefore, a direct comparison of the ICF and IERS catalogues would also reflect discrepancies of the two terrestrial systems. In order to remove this potentially obscuring contribution of the terrestrial discrepancies to differences of the celestial frames, a modification of the ICF solution was generated by Johnston et al., called CTF (Celestial Terrestrial Frame). This solution takes full advantage of the IERS-defined terrestrial reference frame, having the consequence that the CTF is expected to be consistent with the IERS celestial reference frame. Using the sources common to both catalogues, the rotation angles between the two frames, A_1, A_2, A_3, are determined by means of least squares adjustment from the rearranged (5.13) and (5.14) after they are tailored to the present application, i.e.,

$$\begin{pmatrix} \alpha_{\mathrm{IERS}} - \alpha_{\mathrm{CTF}} \\ \delta_{\mathrm{IERS}} - \delta_{\mathrm{CTF}} \end{pmatrix} = \begin{pmatrix} \tan\delta\cos\alpha & \tan\delta\sin\alpha & -1 \\ -\sin\alpha & \cos\alpha & 0 \end{pmatrix} \begin{pmatrix} A_1 \\ A_2 \\ A_3 \end{pmatrix} . \quad (5.15)$$

The rotation angles, A_i, are found to be at the submilliarcsecond level, lying well within the year-to-year variations of the early IERS frames. This

1718−649 17 23 41.029765±92 −65 00 36.61518±106 S 0.014

is a gratifying result, which demonstrates the extremely good agreement of two independently constructed extragalactic reference frames. An explanation of the non-zero rotation angles presumably lies in the different methods of catalogue construction: The CTF catalogue is derived from a global solution using the original VLBI observables, while the IERS catalogue is a combination of preprocessed individual position catalogues and, therefore, loses correlation information that was available for the CTF construction. Other sources of the rotational offset may be ascribed to diversities of the data acquisition equipment, the techniques and facilities of processing, and the modelling of physical effects. Especially at the milliarcsecond level, the results may be sensitive to different models of the atmosphere, as well as to the unmodelled source structure.

In spite of the small rotational offset, the two extragalactic reference frames provided by the CTF and IERS catalogues deserve to be regarded as equivalent. Either catalogue may be considered to be the precursor of the new conventional reference frame of the International Astronomical Union (IAU 1992). More details concerning this topic are given in Chap. 6.

1726+455 17 27 27.650808±24 +45 30 39.73139±26 Q 0.714

6. The International Celestial Reference Frame: ICRF

6.1 The Principles of ICRF Construction

The radio source catalogue which was adopted as the official International Celestial Reference Frame (ICRF) by the IAU at its General Assembly in 1997 belongs to the category of conventional fundamental catalogues. It does not differ fundamentally from the numerous radio catalogues produced during the preceding two decades. This catalogue is merely another member of the category of reference frames produced by the 'observable method' discussed in Sect. 5.5.2. It is revolutionary in the sense that for the first time in history the official coordinate system of astronomy is no longer directly connected to the equinox and the ecliptic plane. In accordance with resolutions adopted by the 1991 IAU General Assembly, materialization of the conventional celestial reference frame is achieved via the coordinates of 'primary' or 'defining' extragalactic radio sources. What distinguishes the ICRF from its predecessors is the breadth of the data base, the care taken to ensure that only sources of the highest quality were selected as the primary defining objects, and considerable agonization to ensure that the best models were used in the data analysis during a period when substantial improvements in tropospheric and Earth-tidal modelling were rapidly starting to emerge and find acceptance.

As an internationally sanctioned catalogue of unique status, the ICRF deserves detailed discussion of its method of construction, accuracy assessment, and future maintenance. This section recounts some of the considerations that entered the construction of a definitive extragalactic radio frame in 1995. The production of this frame was timed to coincide with the coming to fruition of Hipparcos data analysis in late 1995, in order to provide a radio-wavelength counterpart to the optical-wavelength Hipparcos Catalogue. Since a handful of radio stars are observed by both VLBI and Hipparcos, the Hipparcos catalogue can be directly related to the extragalactic reference frame. Several years later, the 1995 Hipparcos radio frame was also proposed and adopted as the ICRF: the first radio-based fundamental astrometric reference frame (Ma et al. 1998). Some of the relevant aspects of its construction include:

- The observational VLBI data base
- Selection of a set of frame-defining sources
- Modelling and minimization of systematic errors

1727+502 17 28 18.623853±140 +50 13 10.47001±98 L 0.055

– Realistic error estimates (see also Sect. 6.3)
– Imposition of the ICRS as the underlying reference system

The Working Group on Reference Frames (WGRF) was commissioned by the IAU with the responsibility of constructing the ICRF. This task was delegated to a subgroup composed of representatives from most of the major VLBI analysis centres of the 1990s. In the course of annual or semiannual meetings as well as electronic exchanges of information and experiences, the subgroup reached a consensus concerning the optimum methods of constructing the extragalactic reference frame. The main basis for the work was the collection of dual-frequency bandwidth synthesis VLBI data accumulated over more than 15 years by various networks for geodetic and astrometric purposes. The sizes of the dish antennas that were used in these experiments ranged from 3 m to 100 m, and the vast majority of observing sessions included intercontinental baselines. There were approximately 1.6 million pairs of delay and delay rate observations of 608 sources, collected over a time period extending from late 1978 to mid-1995.

During the development of VLBI techniques starting in the 1970s, a list of several hundred extragalactic radio sources evolved, which forms the basis of radio reference frames. As instrumental techniques were improved over the course of time, this list was successively extended to include objects with weaker flux densities. The flux densities of the 608 sources in the ICRF data base range down to a few tenths of a jansky. They provide reasonably dense sky coverage in the northern hemisphere, but the well-observed sources are considerably more sparse in the south due to the relative paucity of observatories (and land area) in the southern hemisphere. Since the observing sessions were carried out for diverse and sometimes disparate purposes, the quantity of data available for a given source vary widely, from only a few observations of weak and newly investigated sources to nearly 100 000 observations of some strong sources which have been regularly monitored since the early days of VLBI. The frequency of observation can thus be one criterion for eliminating sources that have not been observed often enough to permit adequate judgment of their potential for serving as stable benchmarks in the reference frame. It was decided to require a minimum of 20 observations spread over a time span of at least two years to make a source eligible for inclusion in the frame-defining category.

Further important criteria for acceptable primary sources are based on the stability of each measured source position with time. Stability can be evaluated in two ways:

1) empirically, by inspecting the time evolution of source coordinates estimated during relatively short time spans or, alternately, by estimating the time rates of change of the coordinates over the entire observation history,
2) by scrutinizing maps of the source structure when such information is available from imaging experiments.

```
1725+044     17 28 24.952716±20  +04 27 04.91401±41     S  0.293
```

Thresholds for identifying problematic sources were set at 50 μas/yr or 3 times the formal uncertainty of the time rates of change of source coordinates. Such apparent motion is most probably related to source structure changes, and was taken as an indication that the source position is not a suitable invariant point on the sky. Of the 608 sources in the data base, the coordinates of 102 were found to exhibit unacceptable stability by these criteria. Structural maps were available for only a small fraction of these sources, making it impossible to provide detailed explanations for the majority of the apparent motions. At the time of construction of the ICRF, dual-frequency maps were only available for 42 sources, which however accounted for 55% of the total observations in the data base. Even this modest beginning of a more comprehensive mapping effort stimulated the development of methods of using structure information as a selection criterion for stable point-like sources. Fey & Charlot (1997) define a 'structure index' which groups sources into four categories, of increasing likelihood to be unsuitable as fiducial points in a reference frame. This index is based on median calculated structure corrections to VLBI delays (relative to a point source) observed on all hypothetical Earth-bound baselines. The S-band and X-band delay corrections of 193 sources are shown in Sect. III.3 of IERS Tech. Note 23 (IERS 1997), and their structure indices are given in Tables 5 to 7 of that report. The majority of these sources were mapped after the ICRF was constructed, and thus their structure indices only serve as a posteriori indicators of source quality. By the end of 1999, additional experiments had extended the total number of sources with single-epoch maps to 389 (Fey & Charlot 2000).

Modelling inadequacies are known to dominate over the random recording system noise in the overall VLBI error budget (e.g., Sect. 4.3.4). Much attention was therefore focused by the Working Group on ensuring that the best contemporary modelling was used in the VLBI data analysis. The ICRF was based on a monolithic least squares fit to the 1.6 million observation pairs. Initially, its right ascension zero point was fixed by adopting the right ascension (RA) of the source 0235+164 = J023838.9+163659 as its value in the latest available IERS combination catalogue. The observable modelling used the best models available in 1995, including estimation of parameters for those aspects that were judged to be inadequately known a priori. In addition to the structure effects that manifest themselves for some sources at the milliarcsecond level, some other significant sources of modelling errors are the treatment of tropospheric delay, nutation and precession, and variations in Earth orientation caused by tidal motions of both the solid Earth and the global ocean. Some of these are discussed in more detail in the next two paragraphs.

Source structure effects cannot presently be treated adequately for all members of the diverse collection of objects. Their impact on the ICRF was presumably minimized by eliminating problem sources via the winnowing processes described in the preceding discussion. To a large extent the stochastic tropospheric delay variations are also not amenable to calibration except via independent experiments, such as water vapour radiometer (WVR) measurements (see also Sect. 6.3.3) that are carried out at the same place and time as the VLBI measurements. High-quality WVR determinations of the tropospheric delay are available for only a tiny fraction of the observations in the ICRF raw data base. Fortunately, just at the time of the ICRF construction, a troposphere gradient model had been developed which appeared to correct a considerable portion of the systematic error that is inherent in assuming a simple azimuthally symmetric troposphere. With suitable adjustment of parameters, it was shown to eliminate systematic errors as large as 0.5 mas in the mid-range of declinations for the ICRF.

The two remaining categories of error (nutation/precession and tidal variations) had already been identified as major contributors to systematic errors in VLBI analyses in the mid-1980s. By the time of ICRF construction in 1995, these models had improved to the point of nearly eliminating these Earth orientation variations as error sources at the sub-milliarcsecond level. In the analysis yielding the ICRF, estimates were made of two nutation angles per observing session, as well as Earth orientation amplitudes at four diurnal and four semidiurnal frequencies. The resulting time series of the nutations in longitude and obliquity were separately analysed, and yielded corrections to the 1980 IAU nutation model that were as large as 6 mas for the amplitudes at the dominant 18.6-yr period, as well as a number of non-zero 'out of phase' amplitudes that are caused by ocean tidal effects. Time-linear departures from the 1980 IAU model were also clearly detected: -2.8 mas/yr in longitude (precession), and -0.3 mas/yr for the rate in obliquity. The diurnal and semidiurnal amplitudes of variations in the orientation of the Earth were generally small, but quite significant at the level of VLBI data accuracy. In summary, the treatment of nutation/precession and Earth orientation in the ICRF analysis should eliminate modelling errors at a level well below the accuracy of the ICRF coordinates.

After total or partial removal of known systematic problems, the Working Group also sought ways of assessing the magnitude of any remaining (unknown) systematic errors in order to be able to provide best estimates of the accuracy of the ICRF source coordinates. This goal was achieved by an empirical approach, in the course of which many subsidiary catalogues were generated and intercompared. The subsidiary catalogues were generated by modifying either the data base or the modelling in the data analysis. In either case, catalogue discrepancies in pairwise comparisons of the subsidiary catalogues were used to place bounds on unknown error contributions. These comparisons indicated that the remaining errors are in the range of 0.1–0.3 mas, and led the WGRF to conclude that 0.25 mas should be adopted as an additive error contribution to the formal source coordinate uncertainties. An earlier study by Ryan et al. (1993) had concluded that VLBI parameter formal uncertainties should be inflated by approximately 50%. In combination, these considerations led to the following simple algorithm for estimating the realistic error of a source coordinate:

$$\sigma_{\mathrm{real}}^2 = (1.5\sigma_{\mathrm{formal}})^2 + (0.25)^2 \text{ mas} \tag{6.1}$$

where σ_{formal} is the formal statistical uncertainty in the ICRF least squares fit. While more detailed investigation might have led to somewhat more realistic error estimates, the virtues of the adopted form are its simplicity and relative conservatism. True errors are unlikely to exceed these values, which can be as much as one order of magnitude larger than the extremely small formal errors given by the parameter estimation procedure for many sources.

The adopted orientation of the ICRF is essentially a continuation of that of the historical series of IERS yearly reference frames, which were originally aligned with the ICRS and were forced to maintain that alignment to within a small fraction of a milliarcsecond over the years. This alignment was accomplished by transforming the ICRF coordinates yielded by the VLBI fit with a rigid three-dimensional rotation. Because the ICRF was already quite well aligned with the IERS frame (and thus with the ICRS) through the adopted RA of the reference source 0235+164 = J023838.9+163659, this rotation was quite small. Additional distortion terms were introduced in this transformation when quantitative comparisons were made between the ICRF and the last IERS reference frame. Only the 117 common 'defining' sources in both the ICRF and the 1995 IERS catalogues were utilized to calculate the rotation parameters, augmented by 16 IERS defining sources to compensate for the relatively sparse distribution at southern declinations. Additional tests indicated that the axes are stable to within 20 μas.

In summary, the ICRF is the result of a single analysis of all relevant VLBI measurements in late 1995. Depending on indications of time-varying source structure and strength of the observational base, each source was evaluated for suitability for inclusion in the frame-defining category. The resulting decimated catalogue containing 212 sources then underwent a small three-dimensional rotation to place it in the reference frame defined as the ICRS. As mentioned in the Preface, the coordinates, object types, and red shifts of the ICRF defining sources are given in the bottom margins of this book. On a decreasing scale of accuracy, 294 'candidate' and 102 'other' sources serve to densify coverage of the celestial sphere. The three categories include a total of 58 sources that serve as links to the Hipparcos optical frame.

6.2 Appraisal of the Origins, Context, and Role of the ICRF

Establishment of a radio reference frame is probably the one accomplishment of the VLBI technique that is of greatest fundamental significance. It makes possible quantitative treatment of the dynamics of the Earth and solar system

```
1749+701      17 48 32.840231±77   +70 05 50.76882±37      L  0.770
```

at unprecedented levels of accuracy. By the end of the 20th century astrometric radio interferometry has fulfilled the promise foreseen for the technique at its inception in the late 1960s. Within these few decades, the VLBI technique has produced a nearly inertial celestial reference frame that is accurate at the level of fractional milliarcseconds, and has shown the capability of point positioning on the Earth and determining its rotational variations with similar accuracies. Its evolution has involved many fields of physics, and it is still developing vigorously in both experimental and theoretical aspects. Provided that the measurements can be continued at the same level as during the past two decades, the future promises unexpected and exciting results to help characterize the behaviour of the Earth, the structure and emission mechanisms of extragalactic radio sources, and the motion the Earth in the Universe. Such future advances depend on continuity of the reference frame, i.e. *maintenance* via periodic monitoring of the behaviour of its constituent radio sources, as well as continuing updated analyses to improve the theoretical model.

During the last quarter of the 20th century, several research groups have used the VLBI technique to catalogue the positions of extragalactic radio sources (Robertson et al. 1986; Sovers et al. 1988; Ma et al. 1990; Johnston et al. 1995). The coordinates of over 400 objects are now known at the milliarcsecond level. Regularly scheduled experiments are continuing periodic monitoring of a substantial fraction of these sources. Survey campaigns (e.g., Patnaik et al. 1992 with the MERLIN and VLA arrays), meanwhile, have accumulated somewhat less precise coordinates of several thousand additional radio sources, which form a valuable pool of candidates for future inclusion in a higher-precision reference frame. Some applications of radio reference frames have been to Earth orientation measurements (e.g., IERS 1994b), astrometry (e.g., Bartel et al. 1985; Treuhaft & Lowe 1991; Lebach et al. 1995), geodesy (e.g., Fallon & Dillinger 1992), as well as to deep space navigation (e.g., Kahn et al. 1994). All of these diverse applications rely on accurate and stable positions of the objects composing the reference frame. In order to provide a more stable and accurate reference frame for astronomical research, as well as to standardize the VLBI results and to make the extragalactic radio source catalogue more widely known and available for general astronomical research, the International Astronomical Union has adopted a new fundamental celestial reference frame (the International Celestial Reference Frame, ICRF) that is based on the angular coordinates of 212 extragalactic radio sources (IAU 1996; Ma et al. 1998). Figure 6.1 illustrates the distribution of the ICRF defining sources over the sky. As will be discussed in the next chapter, the Hipparcos optical catalogue has been linked to the radio frame via measurements of approximately a dozen radio stars (Lestrade et al. 1995). This is the first time in the history of astronomy that the fundamental celestial coordinate system is no longer based on observations at visible wavelengths. At J2000.0 the ICRF is approximately

1751+441 17 53 22.647901±32 +44 09 45.68608±33 Q 0.871

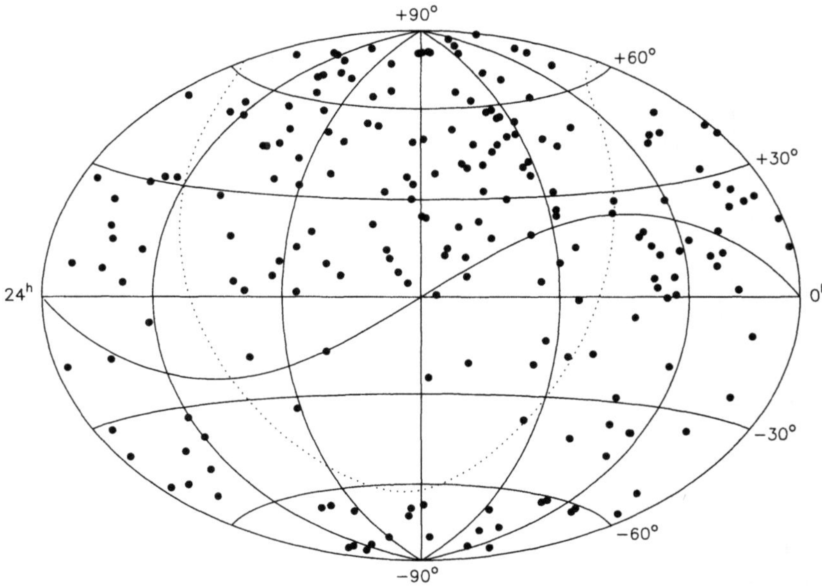

Fig. 6.1. Distribution of the 212 best-observed extragalactic sources comprising the new IAU celestial reference frame (ICRF). An Aitoff equal-area projection is used. Note the relatively sparse population at negative declinations (After Ma et al. 1998)

100 times more accurate than the FK5 catalogue, the traditional realization of the fundamental optical celestial frame based on Earth-bound measurements. At the time of generation of the Hipparcos optical frame, the radio and optical reference frames had approximately comparable (milliarcsecond) accuracy. While the accuracy of the ICRF is not expected to degrade nearly as rapidly as that of the Hipparcos catalogue, whose objects show sizeable proper motions, it will require future monitoring for a number of reasons.

Limitations of reference frames that are based on extragalactic radio sources have been recognized for some time. While estimates of the proper motions of quasars presently give null results at the approximate level of tens of μas/yr (Eubanks et al. 1995), extended structure of the emitting objects at the milliarcsecond level is ubiquitous. Structure that is constant in time can be accounted for by carefully defining a fiducial point for each source. Unfortunately, many radio sources also show considerable time variability, which is manifested as apparent proper motion in VLBI analyses. Constant monitoring is therefore required to ensure stability of the reference frame. Such variability can be considered to belong in the category of systematic errors. Specialized imaging experiments are being carried out in order to correct for source structure and its variation (Fey et al. 1996). Imaging is also feasible via reanalysis of older data collected primarily for geodetic purposes (e.g., Charlot 1994). Figure 6.2 shows an example of such results for the

1800+440 18 01 32.314854±36 +44 04 21.90031±46 Q 0.663

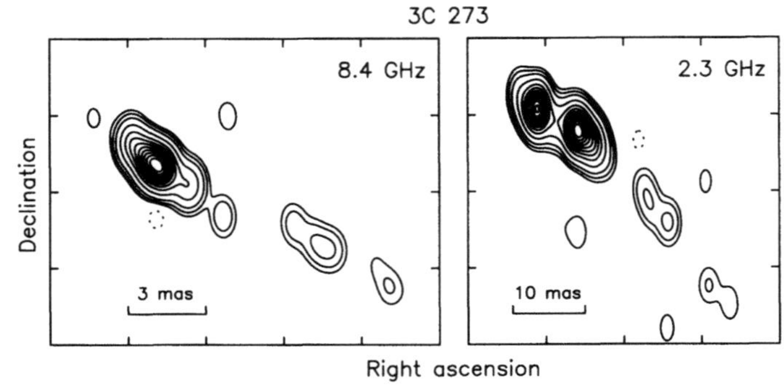

Fig. 6.2. Typical maps of the X- and S-band intensity distribution of the source 3C 273B, generated from geodetic VLBI data for the epoch 1986.27 (After Charlot 1994)

source 3C 273B in 1986. It can be seen that the central core and neighbouring components ('jet') extend over several mas, making it impossible to establish a fiducial mark at the sub-milliarcsecond level without detailed study. Similar images at other epochs show that the components of the jet move rapidly, and new components are ejected sporadically. After the structure and its time variation were characterized in the 1980s, this particular source was dropped from most astrometric observing schedules. While many of the defining sources in the ICRF show measurable internal structure, fortunately the vast majority are much more point-like than 3C 273B.

Another cause of systematic instability of the extragalactic reference frame originates in the motion of the solar system caused by the rotation of our Galaxy relative to the extragalactic radio sources. Detection of this acceleration of the solar system barycentre (SSB) is now on the borderline of possibility (see also Sect. 2.2). This motion of the solar system in inertial space manifests itself in observational data that are acquired over a sufficiently long time span. To the extent that the Earth moves along with the uniform rotation of our Galaxy and the distance to the galactic centre is known, detection of this motion amounts to an indirect measurement of the period of galactic rotation. Such results could also make a contribution to our understanding of cosmology from comparisons to motion of the SSB with respect to the cosmic background radiation. A related topic is the proposed use of direct VLBI measurements to determine the distance to the galactic centre (Reid 1993), which would be of importance in establishing a more reliable cosmic distance scale.

A further influence of the local galaxy is rooted in its gravitational deflection of electromagnetic waves. The immense concentration of mass at the galactic centre can be estimated to produce additional VLBI delays that exceed those of the Sun by a factor of 40 at comparable impact parameters. The displacement of the position of an extragalactic radio source is approxi-

1758−651 18 03 23.496605±85 −65 07 36.76177±54 G ...

mately 4 arc seconds at 10° from the galactic centre (Sovers et al. 1998), and only decreases to tens of milliarcseconds at 180°, in the direction directly away from the centre. Of course the galactic centre has similarly affected all optical astrometric measurements throughout the history of astronomy. The time variation of this distortion is infinitesimally slow, however, and it can be safely ignored and implicitly absorbed into our distorted view of the sky with no practical consequences.

It should be noted that all current celestial reference frames exhibit a pronounced northern bias. Due to the predominance of observing stations in the northern hemisphere, there has been nonuniform observing coverage of both the Earth's surface and the celestial sphere. For example, fewer than one third of the 212 defining sources of the new ICRF are at negative declinations. It can be hoped that future development of observatories in the southern hemisphere will remedy this situation, to the extent possible with the limited land area available south of the Earth's equator.

The two following sections consider two important aspects of the radio reference frame, namely assessment of its present accuracy, and maintenance and improvement of this accuracy level during future years. Accuracy assessment is performed by means of the conventional methods of searching for systematic errors in physical measurements. Most simply, the consistency of results is examined by comparing the results of analyses of different subsets of the data. More stringent tests, which fortunately have been possible in astrometric VLBI, rely on such comparisons among data that have been independently collected and analysed by different research groups. These accuracy assessments point to possible improvements in the theoretical model to take advantage of new developments in related areas of science, to minimize any remaining model deficiencies and reduce the 'error budget'. Such continuing model improvements, along with continuous monitoring of the behaviour of the reference frame objects in VLBI measurements, are part of the maintenance of the ICRF.

6.3 Accuracy Assessment of the ICRF

The extragalactic radio sources in the ICRF have been intensively observed during the past two decades, with tens of thousands of individual delay measurements now accumulated for many of these objects. This multitude of measurements makes the error contributions from the individual observation noise very small, and is suspected to produce formal errors that are not meaningful measures of the uncertainties of source coordinates. In order to obtain more realistic estimates of the true accuracy of source positions, it is therefore necessary to consider a number of other factors. One of these is a thorough investigation of the statistical validity of the formal errors, which can be as small as a few tens of microarcseconds for frequently observed sources. Another is the cumulative influence of all modelling errors and data editing decisions that were made while analyzing the raw data. Yet another is the magnitude of specific, identifiable systematic errors that may distort the results.

As in any large-scale parameter estimation procedure, many tests of the internal consistency are possible for the analysis which produced the ICRF. Such tests include examination of the fit results for various aspects of the theoretical model related to station coordinates, instrumental, troposphere, tidal, and relativistic effects. In addition to internal consistency tests, external tests can also be made to assess the accuracies of radio reference frames. The existence of several independently developed software packages permits comparisons of different computer implementations of theoretical models. Likewise the results of independent astrometric observation and analysis programmes can be intercompared to infer error contributions from differences in data sets and analysis methods.

The cumulative effects of modelling errors and data editing can be examined in detail by comparing radio source catalogues derived from independent analyses using different data and/or different analysis software. Intercomparisons of such variant radio source catalogues derived from the same data addresses the problem of mismodelling and the resulting systematic errors. Catalogue comparisons probe aspects such as:

1) agreement between independent data sets,
2) processing differences in different analyses,
3) agreement between subsets of the same data, and
4) effects of modifying the theoretical modelling.

Some of these are considered in detail in the remainder of this section, using examples taken from the tests applied during the generation of the ICRF (Ma et al. 1998) and a recent Jet Propulsion Laboratory (JPL) catalogue (Jacobs et al. 1998b).

6.3.1 Internal Consistency Tests

Internal consistency tests can point out the need for augmenting the formal statistical uncertainties with additional components, and provide evidence for existence of systematic mismodelling. Under optimum circumstances, they can be used to infer scale factors that should be applied to the formal uncertainties to obtain true accuracies. The VLBI data that are used to derive radio frames are also normally analysed for geodetic purposes. Tests of such geodetic VLBI analysis results in the past (Ryan et al. 1993) have indicated that application of a multiplicative factor of 1.5 to the formal errors gives a proper representation of the actual parameter variation over subsets of data. Similar analyses of astrometric results are much more demanding of computing resources and have not yet been systematically undertaken. By analogy with the geodetic analyses, however, it can be reasonably conjectured that a

```
1830+285     18 32 50.185631±35  +28 33 35.95530±65     Q  0.594
```

similar scaling factor probably needs to be applied to the formal errors of the source positions. Tests on a limited data set by Jacobs et al. (1998b) indicate that source position formal uncertainties are too small by approximately a factor of 2.

At the time of construction of the ICRF in 1995, some repercussions of alternate modelling were tested by creating three additional catalogues. In that work, they were named WGRFa, WGRFel, and WGRFng (Ma et al. 1998). In the solution used to produce the WGRFa catalogue, some source coordinates were treated as 'arc' parameters (i.e. positions of sources were re-estimated for every observing session). For the WGRFel catalogue, the threshold for eliminating low-elevation observations was raised from 6° to 7°. Finally, for the WGRFng catalogue, no troposphere gradient parameters were estimated as in the ICRF solution. In each of these three modified analyses, all other parameterization was identical to that of the ICRF solution. Catalogue comparisons with the ICRF indicated that such modelling perturbations affect the global source coordinates at a level much below the formal uncertainties. Estimation of troposphere gradients, however, compensates for a large-scale deformation in the reference frame, broadly centred around zero declination. Figure 6.3 shows the differences between source declinations from analyses with and without gradient estimates. The gradient effect is much larger than the formal uncertainties and is caused by the greater troposphere thickness nearer the equator (MacMillan & Ma 1997). While it is not large in absolute terms, the effect is systematic and would have distorted the celestial reference frame if ignored.

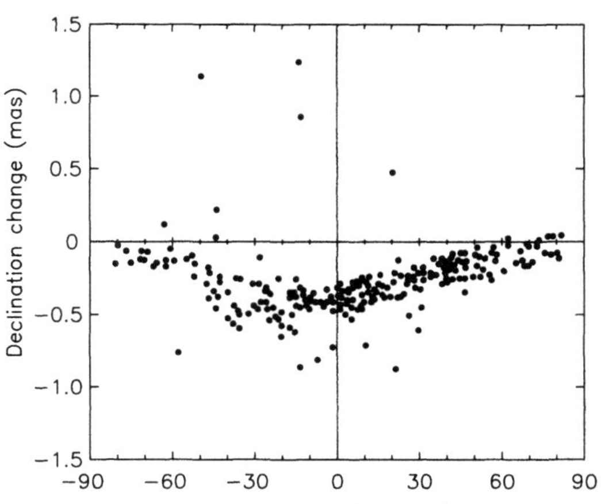

Fig. 6.3. The effect of tropospheric gradients on declinations as a function of declination. The sense is declination with gradients estimated minus declination without gradients estimated (After MacMillan & Ma 1997)

Another test of the internal consistency of the analysis estimates new vector baselines for each observing session. The repeatability of such estimates throughout the time span of available data serves as a measure of the true level of error in the analysis. A number of internal consistency tests are described below, which were performed on the data set of Deep Space Network (DSN) VLBI observations carried out by JPL during 1978-96. The reference frame which can be derived from this much smaller data set is of comparable quality to the ICRF itself. For the JPL data set (Jacobs et al. 1998b), after removing a best-fit linear drift to account for tectonic motion, the California-Spain baseline length (8 400 km) estimates had a weighted root mean square (wrms) repeatability of 13.0 mm, and chi square per degree of freedom $\chi^2_\nu = 1.8$ for 79 observing sessions during 1978-1996. For another 75 sessions during the same time period, the baseline length estimates for the California-Australia baseline (10 600 km) had a wrms repeatability of 23.8 mm and $\chi^2_\nu = 1.6$. These tests indicate that unmodelled systematic errors are present at the level of ≈ 9 and 15 mm on the two baselines, respectively. Such baseline errors of 1 to 1.5 parts per billion correspond to errors of approximately 0.2 to 0.3 mas in source positions.

Similarly, the repeatability of the daily estimates of the celestial pole position $(\Delta\psi, \Delta\varepsilon)$ provide another measure of the true error. For the above-mentioned 154 DSN VLBI observing sessions, after removing a simple model (linear drifts and harmonic terms with 18.6-yr, annual, and semi-annual periods for each pole coordinate) which compensates for deficiencies in the a priori nutation model, the pole position estimates had wrms repeatabilities of 0.28 and 0.25 mas in ecliptic longitude and obliquity, respectively. The associated χ^2_ν was 5.5. Analogous calculations of celestial pole offsets for the ICRF data set gave wrms repeatabilities of 0.30 and 0.37 mas, and $\chi^2_\nu = 3.2$. These tests again indicate the presence of unmodelled systematic errors at the level of 0.3 mas.

In another subcategory of internal checks, some tests of model modifications with the smaller JPL data set included estimates of the horizontal and vertical Earth tide Love numbers h and l, amplitudes of Earth orientation variations at subdiurnal frequencies, and the parametrised post-Newtonian γ factor of general relativity, which characterizes the curvature of space-time produced by the Sun. None of these perturbations yielded parameters that differed significantly from the a priori values of the corresponding portions of the model, and affected the radio source coordinates only to the extent of < 0.02 mas.

For investigations of reference frame stability, searches can be made for apparent proper motions of individual sources relative to the frame as a whole. Such motions are of particular concern in applications which use a small number of objects from a limited region of the reference frame. Examples of applications of this type are spacecraft navigation, occultations of radio sources, and measurements of pulsar positions. Searches for proper motion

`1842+681    18 42 33.641636±61   +68 09 25.22788±34    Q  0.475`

have been part of the evaluation of numerous catalogues since the early 1990s for the purposes of exploring the limits of the VLBI technique, as well as for investigating whether the extragalactic radio sources are truly stationary. They usually estimate linear time rates of change in right ascension, $\dot{\alpha}$, and declination, $\dot{\delta}$. The overall rotation of the frame is normally constrained by fixing to zero the rates of three coordinates of geometrically well separated and frequently observed sources (e.g., $\dot{\alpha}$, and $\dot{\delta}$ of OJ 287 = 0851 + 202 = J085448.8+200630, and $\dot{\delta}$ of CTD 20 = 0234 + 285 = J023752.4+284808). These constraints supplement the single constraint on the right ascension of a reference source (e.g., 0235+164 = J023838.9+163659) that is imposed on the standard solution.

Coordinate rate estimates from the JPL data set yield median formal uncertainties of 55 and 70 μas/yr in the rates $\dot{\alpha}\cos\delta$ and $\dot{\delta}$, respectively (consistent with the previously quoted results of Eubanks et al. (1995) from a much larger data set). It has been verified that there are no biases or net rotation rates in the set of estimated source rates at the 0.01 mas level. This confirms that the imposed rotational rate constraints enforce the stability of the solution as expected. The source rate formal uncertainties indicate the limit of sensitivity to individual proper motions. A handful of sources were found to have significant apparent motion. In particular, a highly significant apparent proper motion of 60 μas/yr was observed for the right ascension of one of the ICRF sources. At the distances of the extragalactic objects that are estimated from their red shifts, such motions are superluminal, and are therefore thought to be artifacts caused by time variation of the source structure. They are manifestations of changes in source structure averaged over time spans of many years. For the well-mapped source 4C 39.25 = 0923 + 392 = J092703.0+390220, for example, the significant component of apparent motion corresponds to the direction of large time-dependent changes in the source structure. Some preliminary results of Charlot (1994) indicate that such structure changes can be successfully incorporated into VLBI models as corrections on the basis of interpolated maps, and that such corrections may help to establish an invariant fiducial point within each source.

In addition to the stability of individual sources, the stability of the celestial frame as a whole must also be considered. In order to make use of the inherent high angular stability of the radio frame for Earth-based observing stations, the positions of the latter (which move slowly in a frame rotating with the Earth) must be related to the inertial radio frame. For such applications, the usable stability of the extragalactic radio reference frame depends on the accuracy with which the motion of the Earth's celestial ephemeris pole (CEP) can be theoretically or empirically modelled. Presently this accuracy is somewhat limited by the imperfect knowledge of the precession constant and the amplitude of the long-term (18.6-year period) nutation, but these limitations were minimized by estimating nutation corrections in the process of generating the ICRF.

`1849+670      18 49 16.072300±48   +67 05 41.67993±28      Q  0.657`

During the past decade, ever since the initial observation of Herring et al. (1986), who found that VLBI results were inconsistent with the 1980 IAU models of precession and nutation, there have been numerous ever-improving determinations of the precession value and nutation amplitudes. Only recently, however, has the time span of available VLBI data reached one full cycle of the 18.6-yr nutation, which is difficult to separate from precession. Current results (e.g., Charlot et al. 1995) indicate an error of −3 mas/yr in the standard value of precession, and several mas in a number of nutation amplitudes. These corrections have uncertainties of approximately 0.1 mas/yr and 0.1 mas, respectively. Thus the motion of the CEP is known to within a few tenths of mas, with a long-term stability of ≈0.1 mas/yr.

Two parenthetical remarks concerning the validity of CEP modelling relate to the choice of components of the a priori nutation series, and to the method of deriving corrections. In connection with the first point, it appears to be important to include many small-amplitude nutation terms that have been derived theoretically by, e.g., Souchay & Kinoshita (1996). Some of these arise from interactions of the Earth with solar system bodies other than the Sun and Moon, predominantly Venus. It has been observed that results obtained on the basis of such more complete a priori series can differ by ≈ 0.1 mas from those based on the 1980 IAU series. The second point involves comparison of results of two different methods of inferring the motion of the CEP: first by directly estimating the precession along with the amplitudes of a set of nutation terms, and second by instead estimating a time series of daily bulk corrections $\Delta\psi$ and $\Delta\varepsilon$. These two methods agree only to within 0.1−0.2 mas, both for the nutation amplitudes and source coordinates. This indicates that present-day compensation for defects in CEP modelling is also not quite adequate, at a level that is similar to the accuracy level of the radio source positions.

The general conclusion from internal tests of the VLBI data set is that the formal uncertainties of the source positions in the ICRF can be nearly an order of magnitude smaller than their true accuracies. This was taken into account in reporting the ICRF source coordinate uncertainties, which essentially have a lower limit of 0.25 mas. In addition, the accuracy of applications of the ICRF to Earth-based measurements is limited by inadequate knowledge of the orientation of the Earth in inertial space, to the extent of ≈ 0.1 mas and ≈ 0.1 mas/yr, respectively.

6.3.2 External Comparisons

In contrast to the single fit to all available VLBI data that was used to generate the ICRF, the method which was used by the IERS until 1995 for its yearly realizations of a standard extragalactic reference frame entailed combining individual VLBI frames by applying an algorithm based on pairwise comparisons (see Sect. 5.5.3). The position uncertainties reported for the combined catalogues reflected the disagreement between individual analyses. To answer the question of whether adopting a unique 'error calibration law' for all sources can eliminate or at least minimize systematic effects in the ICRF, members of the IAU working subgroup also produced a combined catalogue based on IERS procedures. This catalogue was constructed by applying a 6-parameter transformation model (three angles, drifts in right ascension and declination as functions of declination, and a bias in declination) to four independently generated source coordinate lists. The four individual VLBI frames included in this combination were those submitted by GSFC, JPL, NOAA and USNO to the IERS in 1995 (IERS 1995b). The comparison of the 'inflated' ICRF uncertainties with those obtained from catalogue combination showed that there still existed a non-negligible number of sources whose inflated ICRF uncertainties were smaller than those resulting from the comparison of parallel analyses with a deformation correction model. In order to report more realistic errors for the purposes of the ICRF, for these sources the uncertainty for each coordinate was set to be the larger of the inflated or the comparison value.

A number of catalogue comparisons were also made between the ICRF catalogue (which is derived from all available VLBI data) and associated catalogues derived from subsets of the same data base that were created for test purposes, as well as previously published radio source catalogues. The latter included the 1994 and 1995 IERS realizations of the celestial reference frame (IERS 1995a and IERS 1996a) and the radio-optical reference frame of Johnston et al. (1995) (RORF, see also Sect. 5.5.2). In some of these matches, the dividing line between 'external' and 'internal' comparisons is indistinct because a large portion of the underlying data base is common to both members of the pair. Comparing ICRF with the RORF catalogue indicates the magnitude of coordinate discrepancies to be expected between global catalogues. Evaluation of the effects of totally independent data and software was made by comparisons with two catalogues based on GSFC and JPL analyses of data collected using independent VLBI networks. The two data sets were analysed, respectively, at GSFC using CALC/SOLVE, and at JPL using the JPL Modest software package.

As in the tests discussed in the previous section, assessment of catalogue comparisons relies on several measures of the overall alignment and agreement of the coordinates. Tables 6.1 and 6.2 show such results for the six pairs of catalogues that were compared. For legibility, two-character abbreviations are used for the catalogues: ICRF = IF, IERS 1994 and 1995 = 94 and 95, RORF = RO, GSFC = GS, and JPL = JP. Rotational offsets (A_1, A_2, A_3) are the rotation angles about Cartesian axes to bring each pair of catalogues into best coincidence. This rotational transformation for catalogues i and j takes the form of (5.11) of the previous chapter:

$$\boldsymbol{s}_j = \mathbf{R}\,\boldsymbol{s}_i\,, \tag{6.2}$$

1903−802 19 12 40.019176±169 −80 10 05.94627±41 Q 1.758

Table 6.1. Summary of catalogue rotational offsets. See text for explanation of catalogue abbreviations

Catalogue pair			Rotation angles A_1	A_2	A_3
IF	vs.	95	0.1	−0.4	0.0
IF	vs.	RO	−0.2	−0.5	0.0
95	vs.	94	0.0	0.0	0.0
IF	vs.	GS	−0.1	−0.1	−0.0
IF	vs.	JP	0.1	−0.3	−0.2
GS	vs.	JP	0.2	−0.3	0.2

with

$$\boldsymbol{s}_i = \begin{pmatrix} \cos\delta_i \cos\alpha_i \\ \cos\delta_i \sin\alpha_i \\ \sin\delta_i \end{pmatrix}, \quad \mathbf{R} = \begin{pmatrix} 1 & A_3 & -A_2 \\ -A_3 & 1 & A_1 \\ A_2 & -A_1 & 1 \end{pmatrix}. \tag{6.3}$$

Since the rotations are infinitesimal, the choice of i or j as the starting catalogue is immaterial. The reduced χ^2_ν values were calculated from source position differences after the rotation was applied to one catalogue of the pair (off-diagonal covariances are neglected). Agreement between $\alpha \cos \delta$ and δ for each pair is indicated by rms differences about the respective means; another measure is an analogous quantity for arc lengths between all pairs of sources. Potentially significant internal trends in the variation of coordinate differences with α and δ were assessed by fitting linear models to all four combinations $\Delta\alpha$ vs. α, δ and $\Delta\delta$ vs. α, δ. The largest variations of these fits over the celestial sphere, $D_{\max}$, as well as their significance in units of the formal uncertainty of the slope, $D_{\max}/\sigma$, are reported in the last two columns of Table 6.2. The highly significant trends are all in $\Delta\delta$ vs. δ, with

Table 6.2. Summary of catalogue differences. See text for explanation of catalogue abbreviations

Catalogue pair			χ^2_ν	rms residuals $\alpha \cos \delta$ (mas)	δ	arc length (mas/100°)	Internal trends $D_{\max}$	$D_{\max}/\sigma$
IF	vs.	95	2.92	0.23	0.39	0.55	0.32	14
IF	vs.	RO	2.77	0.10	0.38	0.42	0.32	15
95	vs.	94	2.85	0.30	0.31	0.52	0.29	12
IF	vs.	GS	1.68	0.09	0.29	0.39	0.15	7
IF	vs.	JP	2.84	0.26	0.44	0.51	0.66	15
GS	vs.	JP	3.42	0.30	0.36	0.58	0.38	14

`1954+513    19 55 42.738273±28   +51 31 48.54623±27    Q  1.230`

the exception of $\Delta\alpha$ vs. α for the 1995 IERS vs. the 1994 IERS realizations (IERS 1996a and IERS 1995a).

Table 6.1 shows that all the tested catalogues are quite well aligned. Rotational offsets around any of the three axes do not exceed 0.5 mas. Systematic errors are seen to be present, however, as indicated by the χ^2_ν values ranging between 2 and 3 for many comparisons in Table 6.2 after the removal of the rotational offsets. Differences are as large as 0.4 mas for coordinates and 0.6 mas for arc lengths, with trends reaching 0.7 mas/100° with 15σ apparent significance. These differences are maximal for the GSFC vs. JPL comparison. Individual source coordinate differences between the GSFC and JPL catalogues are shown in Fig. 6.4. They clearly show increasing problems toward lower declinations, which are thought to arise from the presence of only a single southern-hemisphere observing station in the JPL VLBI network.

It should be noted that the significance of the systematic trends in coordinate differences is exaggerated in the results of Table 6.2. As mentioned above, the comparisons used diagonal covariance matrices. When correlations among all source coordinates are taken into account, the significance of such trends is known to decrease substantially (Sovers et al. 1998). This is an indication that the quality of the source coordinates over limited regions of the sky is considerably better than their coherence over the entire celestial

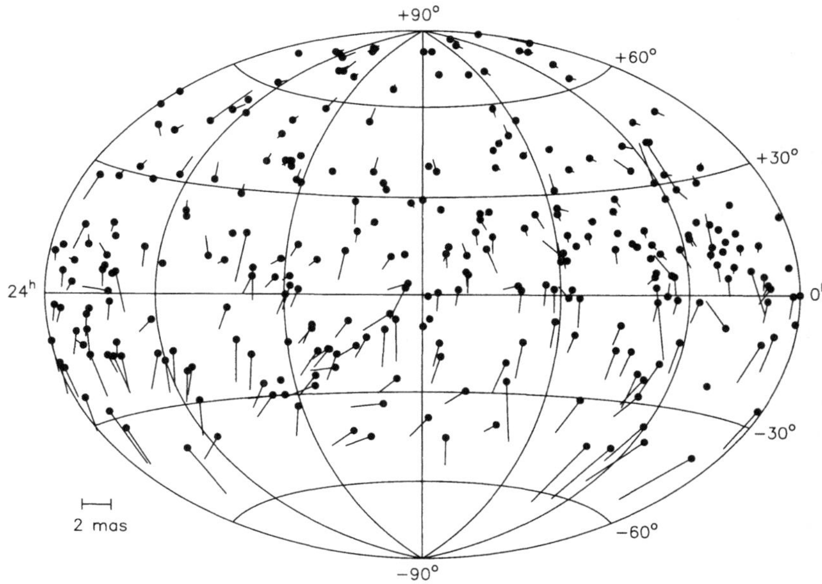

Fig. 6.4. Vector differences between JPL and GSFC catalogues. The lengths of the vectors represent the magnitude of the difference of the positions (as indicated by the key) while the orientations of the vectors represent the direction in which the positions differ on the sky

sphere. The most likely source of such behaviour lies in the correlations among observations introduced by limitations of observing networks and schedules.

Nearly two years after the ICRF catalogue was generated, an updated GSFC vs. JPL comparison was made by Jacobs et al. (1998b). These modified catalogues are denoted by primes. The GSFC′ catalogue (labeled G-1069) is also based on independent data processed with independent software. Since both catalogues were intentionally aligned to the ICRF, the rotational offsets are expected to be zero within the estimated errors, and in fact they are. The estimated rotations about the x, y, and z axes (x, $y = 0$ and 6 h RA in the equatorial plane, $z =$ spin axis) are -0.06 ± 0.05, -0.04 ± 0.06 and -0.04 ± 0.04 mas, respectively. The catalogue differences give $\chi^2_\nu = 6.0 \pm 0.1$ indicating that the combined formal uncertainties underestimate the true errors by a factor of ≈ 2.4. Full covariance matrices were used for both catalogues, and it was assumed that JPL′ and GSFC′ error covariances are independent. For the JPL′ catalogue, which is based on the limited geometry provided by two DSN baselines, the off-diagonal elements of the error covariance are important in determining the significance of zonal errors (e.g., $\Delta\delta$ vs. δ).

A least squares estimate of the $\Delta\delta$ vs. δ trend shows a large effect (nearly 1 mas over the full range of declinations), but its formal significance is only $2.9\,\sigma$. Its true significance is probably half this size and therefore insignificant. This systematic trend in the differences is another likely indication of the geometric weakness of the JPL′ frame in the southern hemisphere, rather than evidence for potential zonal errors in the ICRF. The importance of using the full source position covariance for the JPL′ reference frame is underscored by the results of a test which estimated the $\Delta\delta$ vs. δ trend using only the diagonal elements of the covariance. In this case, the estimated declination trend was nearly three times larger and had an apparent formal significance of $23\,\sigma$. The full covariance information is therefore essential for drawing meaningful conclusions concerning the size and significance of zonal errors. The GSFC′ covariance off-diagonal elements are smaller than those of JPL′, presumably due to the more varied geometry of the multiple baseline data that were used to construct the GSFC′ catalogue.

Because numerous physical effects come into play in a VLBI experiment, the software used to analyse VLBI data is of necessity very complex. In particular, the code that calculates the theoretical group delay and phase delay rates includes a variety of models, many of which are themselves quite complicated. To test for possible errors present in the implementation of the theoretical models in computer code, the JPL VLBI software was compared to two other VLBI software packages (Jacobs et al. 1998a). It needs to be emphasized that such tests can only examine the accuracy of implementing a given set of models, and cannot probe the intrinsic accuracy of the models themselves. Assessments of inherent model accuracy are usually included in the reports of research leading to the particular model extensions. Three software packages (GSFC's CALC, which was used to generate the ICRF catalogue, JPL's Modest, and Paris Observatory's GLORIA) were compared in detail for all modelled observables during one 24-hour VLBI observing session. After considerable effort to make sure that the modelling options were identical, the delay and rate observables agreed to within $\approx$1 ps and $\approx$1 fs s^{-1} wrms, respectively. Effects of software discrepancies on source positions should therefore be limited to errors on the order of $\approx$1 ps, equivalent to 0.3 mm, which on a 10 000 km baseline is only $\approx$ 0.005 mas. This is approximately a factor 60 lower than some of the systematic problems enumerated above, which shows that VLBI modelling is correctly implemented in current computer codes, and any software shortcomings do not contribute to errors in the ICRF.

Other considerations concerning catalogue comparisons are the level of agreement that would be expected from using independent analysis software, and any bias introduced by different analysts' choices during editing the raw data. Once the modelling differences were isolated, catalogues were constructed using an identical subset of the ICRF data base, but different software (CALC, Modest) and analyst choices. The rotation angles between the resulting catalogues were found to be $A_1 = 0.14 \pm 0.03$, $A_2 = -0.01 \pm 0.02$, $A_3 = 0.00 \pm 0.02$ mas. The biases in $\alpha \cos\delta$ and δ were 0.007 mas and 0.020 mas, respectively, and the corresponding wrms coordinate differences were 0.15 mas and 0.21 mas. Analyst choices may thus have introduced scatter of just under one formal error (which is 0.18 and 0.29 mas in the median for $\alpha \cos\delta$ and δ respectively) but did not significantly bias the coordinate means. The closeness of the model comparisons indicates that the level of agreement seen for the source positions is determined by data editing and model parametrisation options. The model comparisons suggest that one can place very high confidence in the correctness of the model implementations.

From a consideration of error sources such as those described in this and the previous section, the subgroup generating the ICRF concluded that a realistic error estimate for the invariant source positions could be made by inflating the formal errors by a factor of 1.5 followed by a root-sum-square increase of 0.25 mas. For the most frequently observed sources the 0.25 mas is the dominant error. This error scaling appears to be generally applicable to results of VLBI astrometry in the late 1990s.

6.3.3 Remaining Model Deficiencies and an Error Budget

Throughout the history of astrometric VLBI, data analysis and accuracy assessments such as those discussed in the two previous sections have provided continuous feedback and cross-checks by characterizing previously unknown or poorly quantified aspects of the theoretical model (e.g., precession, nutation, tidal variations, troposphere). Such interplay is expected to continue in the future, as both experimental and theoretical techniques are refined to eliminate remaining systematic errors. Here we summarize attempts to identify portions of the VLBI model that are presently the leading contributors to uncertainties of the ICRF, and to suggest means of improving modelling or minimizing these effects. Much of this discussion also applies to other Earth-based astronomical measurement techniques.

The components of the theoretical model of VLBI delays can most simply be divided into two categories: deterministic and stochastic. The 'deterministic' category includes all displacements that are governed by motions of the Earth and celestial bodies and that occur at fixed, accurately known frequencies. It includes all aspects of the model depending on either the Earth's orbital motion or solar, lunar and planetary tidal effects. The 'stochastic' category contains motions for which no underlying periodicity can be associated with the driving forces at the present state of our knowledge, and which are random or chaotic. Most of these are related to atmospheric and oceanic 'weather', but they also include the unpredictable variations of the structures of the radio sources. Model improvements in the deterministic category are simpler to achieve, since they only require more accurate determinations of amplitudes of motions with known periods. The second category is essentially unpredictable, and modelling will probably always have to rely on time series of auxiliary measurements.

Enumeration of VLBI error sources along the path of the incoming signal produces four categories: radio source structure, atmosphere, antenna structure, and Earth orientation. Estimates of contemporary model uncertainties are given by Sovers et al. (1998). Their conclusion is that the total (conservative) model uncertainty is probably just in excess of 2 cm in delay, which is equivalent to ≈ 0.5 mas on intercontinental baselines. The dominant error, which accounts for the lion's share of these 2 cm, is due to the troposphere. Antenna and radio source structure may contribute approximately 1 cm each, while tectonic, tidal, and nutation-precession uncertainties for the Earth probably add up to less than 1 cm.

Most extragalactic sources display structure on milliarcsecond scales for the strong radio emission associated with their compact cores. Temporal variations of the intrinsic structures of these objects may result in apparent motion when observations are made at several epochs (Sect. 4.1.2). Until quite recently, the intrinsic structure of the majority of the ICRF sources has been mostly unknown. The surveys of Fey et al. (1996) and Fey & Charlot (1997, 2000) show that most sources, when examined in detail, exhibit spatial structure. Their results indicate that the variation of this intrinsic structure can be quite extreme, ranging the gamut from relatively compact naked-core objects to compact double sources to complex core-jet objects. For astrometric work, the situation is exacerbated by the fact that compact extragalactic radio sources are known to have variable emission intensity as well as frequency- and time-dependent intrinsic structure. Consequently, unknown and unmodelled source structure effects may be introduced into the astrometric solutions. Charlot (1990a, 1990b) has modelled the effects of radio source structure on measured VLBI group delays and delay rates. Results of this modelling suggest that these effects can be significant for extended sources, typically at a level of 100 picoseconds in the group delay (≈ 3 cm at the surface of the Earth or ≈ 1 mas). Fey & Charlot (1997, 2000) calculate structure corrections based on the Charlot analysis using source models derived from Very Long Baseline Array (VLBA) observations of 388 extragalactic sources. Results of these calculations show that intrinsic structure contributions to the measured VLBI delay are significant, with the maximum corrections possible on any Earth-bound baseline ranging from only a few picoseconds for the most compact sources to several nanoseconds for the most extended sources. Fey and Charlot also note a correlation between the compactness of the sources and their position formal uncertainties in analyses that do not correct for structure effects, indicating that the more extended sources have larger position formal errors. A source 'structure index' can be defined, based on the median of the calculated structure corrections at S- and X-band frequencies. This index ranges over the numerical values 1 to 4 with increasing impact of source structure, and can be used as an estimate of the astrometric quality of the sources. It is subject to changes with time, however, due to occasional rapid changes of the behaviour of a source.

New techniques for characterizing the atmosphere are expected to allow more realistic modelling of the tropospheric delay than the simple spherical-shell model which has traditionally been used in VLBI analyses. For this simple model troposphere, a mapping function is now available that can map the zenith delay (which is the most important troposphere parameter estimated in data analyses) to any elevation angle at any site (Niell 1996). This mapping accurately accounts for average global weather variations, and only becomes inadequate for extreme departures from average conditions. When comprehensive atmospheric data from a region surrounding each observing site are available, present computer speeds should permit estimating the tropospheric delay by means of a complete ray-tracing solution for every observation, rather than using global average conditions. Meanwhile, improvements in tropospheric mapping can be sought by modelling the variations of the temperature vs. altitude profile as a function of season, latitude, altitude, and diurnal cycle. MacMillan (1995), MacMillan & Ma (1997), and Chen & Herring (1997) have successfully modelled azimuthal gradients in the troposphere. Persistent equator-to-pole gradients in pressure, temperature, humidity, and tropopause height suggest that a priori modelling of north-south gradients may be beneficial. East-west gradients, which are probably dominated by weather systems passing over a site, are likely to be more difficult to model without extensive weather data.

Independent quantitative estimates of the amount of water vapour along a path through the atmosphere can be made via auxiliary measurements employing *water vapour radiometers* (WVR). These instruments measure the intensity of thermal emission due to transitions between rotational energy levels of the water molecule at microwave frequencies. They are steerable

2021+317	20 23 19.017351±22	+31 53 02.30595±31	?	...

in both elevation and azimuth, and measure sky brightness temperatures at several frequencies near 22 and 31 GHz. While there is not a unique correspondence between the sky brightness temperature and water vapour content, current data retrieval procedures appear to be capable of accuracies as good as several mm of path delay (Keihm & Marsh 1996). Such wet troposphere delays agree with VLBI parameter estimates at the level of a few mm. Unfortunately, such calibrations have not been routinely available for the bulk of VLBI data collected during the past two decades and are unlikely in the future.

In order to properly account for unmodelled wet troposphere errors, a model of the spatial and temporal spectrum of wet troposphere refractivity fluctuations was developed by Treuhaft & Lanyi (1987). This model assumes that tropospheric delay errors are dominated by fluctuations in the distribution of water vapour, that these fluctuations occur in the lower 1–2 km of the troposphere, and that they are carried over a site by a constant wind. The model can be used to generate an a priori observable covariance matrix which is then included in the least squares parameter estimation procedure. While this is not a model improvement per se, but rather a modification of observable weighting, the variances of the estimates of some important parameters (e.g., baselines, source positions) are found to be substantially improved relative to results of conventional estimation schemes. Unfortunately this model has not been widely applied in VLBI analyses due to its relative complexity for multibaseline networks.

Antenna modelling uncertainties are dominated by imperfectly characterized geometric structures of the large dishes and their mounts. In most cases, the antenna structural parameters are known at the level of a few mm, but there are exceptions for which the uncertainties may approach 1 cm. Another considerable fraction of the antenna portion of the error budget is related to the unpredictable effects of temperature and pressure changes, and thus may be categorized with tropospheric effects. Thermal expansion of the antenna structure and the (predominantly vertical) motion induced by varying atmospheric pressure, are the two dominant effects.

Modelling of the Earth as a whole is under quite rigorous control. The present IAU models of nutation and precession are seriously in error, but corrections are known which reduce the errors by an order of magnitude. Uncertainties of a few mm may remain in some tidal and nutation effects, but they are expected to be reduced in the near future as development of more accurate geophysical models is completed. Present-day tectonic motions on the Earth's surface are in surprisingly good agreement with those inferred from paleomagnetic data extending millions of years into the past. Since station locations are adjusted for each observing session, this potential source of error is largely eliminated, and is not expected to contribute more than a few mm/yr to the VLBI model uncertainty. The rotational motion of the Galaxy produces aberrational effects which change by ≈ 5 μas/yr (see Sect. 4.4.5).

2030+547 20 31 47.958562±42 +54 55 03.14060±51 ? ...

This will need to be taken into account for observations spanning more than two decades.

6.4 Future Maintenance of the ICRF

The ICRF produced by VLBI astrometry is a great step forward in comparison with frames of stellar realizations. It is intrinsically simpler, much more accurate, more stable, and less susceptible to systematic deformations. The current realization of the ICRF, produced in 1995, condenses the information from a particular VLBI data set spanning a defined interval and reflects a certain state of VLBI analysis at that time. Although the IAU resolutions leading to the adoption of the ICRF did not provide for the possibility of future improvements or revisions, progress in experimental and theoretical astrometry is sure to demand amendments and extensions in the not-too-distant future. The initial step in extending the ICRF was taken in mid-1999, when the WGRF added 0.6 million new observations to the 1995 data base (IERS 1999). Except for some minor modifications, the least squares estimation procedure was identical to the original fit. Following a conservative approach, the coordinates of the 212 defining sources were kept fixed (see Sect. 5.3, while the remaining source positions, plus those of 59 newly observed objects, were presumably improved by the new data. As time progresses the realization of the ICRF is expected to evolve, although changes in the ICRF catalogue will be infrequent compared to past practice in VLBI astrometry.

Several features distinguish the ICRF from the conventional stellar catalogues that formerly defined the celestial reference frame. While the positional history of the sources is known, it cannot be predicted with certainty what future observations will reveal. Their current positions and velocities are analogous to a snapshot, and continued observations will be essential to maintain the viability and integrity of the ICRF. Many radio sources are known to change their emission intensities and structures on relatively short time scales. To compensate for potential future losses from the frame-defining list due to these shortcomings, and to allow for potential additions, new sources must be observed to replenish and expand the list of candidates, and their positions in the frame must be determined.

Of particular importance is identification of new potential radio-optical link objects to connect the ICRF and Hipparcos frames (see Sect. 7.1). Current sources need to be observed periodically to track their behaviour. As observations accumulate, it should be possible to move the secondary 'candidate' sources up or down the scale of usefulness. It is conceivable and perhaps even probable, however, that an identical categorization of sources from an analysis using twice as long an interval would show sources changing categories in unpredictable ways. For example, there is no physical reason to expect that linear position changes can continue indefinitely. Such motion would call into question the fundamental basis of the extragalactic frame, i.e.

2029+121 20 31 54.994279±19 +12 19 41.34043±34 L 1.215

the great distances of the objects. Directed position changes should cease at some time. Conversely, a source now stationary could start apparent motion. Only future data collection and analysis will show. The problem of position variation may be solved in the future if the application of source structure information will permit the identification and use of truly kinematically stable points in the sky. In contrast to the situation for stellar catalogues, however, the original VLBI observations will always be accessible for improved reanalysis.

Two areas that need to be monitored especially closely for ICRF maintenance are source selection and source time variability. Not all the ICRF sources are fully characterized: Some of their red shifts are not known, and in some cases it is not even known what type of object (quasar, galaxy, ...) gives rise to the radio frequency emission. When new sources are added, efforts should be made to add such auxiliary information as well. The other area has already been discussed in connection with source position time variability and apparent proper motion. It might also be mentioned that many radio sources (e.g., BL Lac) undergo relatively rapid changes (on the time scale of months). These are known as extreme scattering events (ESE), and may be related to ejection of new components or other changes in internal structure.

2037+511 20 38 37.034755±28 +51 19 12.66269±27 Q 1.687

7. Hipparcos Catalogue Tie with Conventional Celestial Reference Frames

The Hipparcos catalogue contains a large number of stars whose positions are known at an unprecedented accuracy level. It is therefore important to relate it both to the past (FK5) and to the future (ICRF). Useful information can be gained in both of these procedures. By looking back and relating Hipparcos to FK5, advantage can be taken of the long time spans of the FK5 proper motion measurements. By looking forward and placing the Hipparcos catalogue in the ICRS (see Sect. 5.1), its optical star positions are transplanted to a coordinate frame that is the closest contemporary approximation to an inertial system. This chapter discusses some of the details of such catalogue links.

The merging process of the provisional FAST and NDAC catalogues covering 37 months of data resulted in the combined catalogue, H37C, representing the provisional Hipparcos reference frame and denoted H in the following. This frame materializes the provisional Hipparcos reference system. In the course of the data reduction a loose connection with the FK5 system crept into the Hipparcos system since, in the framework of the data reduction procedures, some limited information was inevitably borrowed from an already existing reference system, which then was the FK5 system. For the RGC poles, for instance, the coordinates were postulated with reference to the FK5 system. As they were kept constant throughout the mission, information both on orientation and spin of the FK5 frame has been transferred to the Hipparcos astrometric parameters. Also, for calculating annual aberration and for modelling stellar parallaxes, the Earth and spacecraft ephemerides are needed. Their current versions refer to the FK5 and, hence, carry over some orientation information into the Hipparcos data reduction. In the sphere solution, occasionally, the influence of the FK5 system has been enhanced by fixing three position and proper motion components of stars in order to guarantee full rank of the normal matrix (Sect. 3.8.1).

In view of the above facts the provisional Hipparcos catalogue, which resulted from the merging process, comprises a consistent set of star parameters. Yet, it does not meet the requirements of fundamental astronomy unless an IAU-recommended conventional celestial reference system is adopted and imposed on the catalogue. The FK5 system and the extragalactic reference system, as introduced in Chap. 1, are both eligible for this purpose. One can take advantage of these conventional systems by tying the provisional Hipparcos frame, representing the Hipparcos provisional system, into either the FK5 or the extragalactic frame. The assumption is made that conditions are fulfilled which permit linking of frames by means of rigid rotations. Then, the basic principles for establishing the relative orientation and spin between two frames are common standards in mechanics. For the Hipparcos link to the extragalactic reference frame these standards have been employed in an accuracy assessment study by Froeschlé & Kovalevsky (1982). A more rigorous and complete treatment is given by Lindegren & Kovalevsky (1995). Therefore, we restrict the presentation here to those facets of the tie that are essential for understanding the extension of the extragalactic radio reference frame to visual wavelengths. Also, the link to the FK5 will be briefly treated.

Linking of frames deserves the subtle remark that the tie leaves the character of the linked system unaltered. If, for instance, the provisional Hipparcos catalogue is tied to the extragalactic reference frame, which has a kinematic system's definition, the Hipparcos system does not thereby become automatically a kinematic one. What one can say is that the positions and proper motions of the Hipparcos Catalogue have been *related* to a kinematic system. Only if a sufficient number of optical counterparts of extragalactic radio sources had been observed by the Hipparcos telescope in addition to the stars, would it be sensible to speak of a kinematic Hipparcos system.

7.1 Link with the Extragalactic Reference Frame

In linking the provisional Hipparcos frame to the extragalactic reference frame (ICRF), we are in the favourable position that the frames to be linked are already nearly coincident in orientation and spin, thus allowing small-angle approximations. Let $\boldsymbol{r}_{\mathrm{E}}(t_0)$ and $\boldsymbol{r}_{\mathrm{H}}(t_0)$ be the position vectors of objects referring to the extragalactic (E) and the provisional Hipparcos (H) frames at epoch t_0, which typically will be the epoch of the Hipparcos catalogue. The conventional extragalactic reference frame is represented by a three-dimensional rectangular coordinate system with x_{E} pointing towards $\alpha_{\mathrm{E}} = \delta_{\mathrm{E}} = 0°$, y_{E} towards $\alpha_{\mathrm{E}} = 90°, \delta_{\mathrm{E}} = 0°$ and z_{E} pointing to $\delta_{\mathrm{E}} = +90°$. On the other hand, the rectangular frame H has coordinate axes that are slightly differently oriented. Furthermore, let $\dot{\boldsymbol{r}}_{\mathrm{E}}$ and $\dot{\boldsymbol{r}}_{\mathrm{H}}$ be the rates of change of the corresponding position vectors. At time t the two vectors are related by

$$\boldsymbol{r}_{\mathrm{E}}(t) = \mathbf{M}(t)\, \boldsymbol{r}_{\mathrm{H}}(t) \,. \tag{7.1}$$

Taylor series expansion to the first order in $t - t_0$ yields

$$\begin{aligned} \boldsymbol{r}_{\mathrm{E}}(t_0) \quad &+ \quad \dot{\boldsymbol{r}}_{\mathrm{E}}(t_0)(t-t_0) \\ &= \quad \left[\mathbf{M} + \dot{\mathbf{M}}(t-t_0)\right] \left[\boldsymbol{r}_{\mathrm{H}}(t_0) + \dot{\boldsymbol{r}}_{\mathrm{H}}(t_0)(t-t_0)\right] , \end{aligned} \tag{7.2}$$

where

2051+745 20 51 33.734576±110 +74 41 40.49823±38 L ...

$$\mathbf{M} = \begin{pmatrix} 1 & A_3 & -A_2 \\ -A_3 & 1 & A_1 \\ A_2 & -A_1 & 1 \end{pmatrix}, \ \dot{\mathbf{M}} = \begin{pmatrix} 0 & \dot{A}_3 & -\dot{A}_2 \\ -\dot{A}_3 & 0 & \dot{A}_1 \\ \dot{A}_2 & -\dot{A}_1 & 0 \end{pmatrix} \tag{7.3}$$

are the unknown rotation matrices of orientation and spin of frame H with respect to frame E. Occasionally the equally common notation $\varepsilon_x, \varepsilon_y, \varepsilon_z$ and $\omega_x, \omega_y, \omega_z$ is used to replace the parameters A_1, A_2, A_3 and $\dot{A}_1, \dot{A}_2, \dot{A}_3$, respectively.

Neglecting higher order terms one gets from (7.2)

$$\boldsymbol{r}_{\mathrm{E}}(t_0) = \mathbf{M}\,\boldsymbol{r}_{\mathrm{H}}(t_0) \tag{7.4}$$

and

$$\dot{\boldsymbol{r}}_{\mathrm{E}}(t_0) = \dot{\mathbf{M}}\,\boldsymbol{r}_{\mathrm{H}}(t_0) + \mathbf{M}\dot{\boldsymbol{r}}_{\mathrm{H}}(t_0)\,. \tag{7.5}$$

Combining the last two equations and forming the vector differences gives the observational equations for determining the components of the rotation matrices at time t_0 by weighted least squares. Denoting the unit matrix by $\mathbf{I}$ one obtains:

$$\begin{pmatrix} \boldsymbol{r}_{\mathrm{E}} - \boldsymbol{r}_{\mathrm{H}} \\ \dot{\boldsymbol{r}}_{\mathrm{E}} - \dot{\boldsymbol{r}}_{\mathrm{H}} \end{pmatrix} = \begin{pmatrix} \mathbf{M}-\mathbf{I} & \mathbf{0} \\ \dot{\mathbf{M}} & \mathbf{M}-\mathbf{I} \end{pmatrix} \begin{pmatrix} \boldsymbol{r}_{\mathrm{H}} \\ \dot{\boldsymbol{r}}_{\mathrm{H}} \end{pmatrix}. \tag{7.6}$$

The inverse squares of the standard deviations of the left-hand side differences are taken as weights. In general, correlations exist between the positions and proper motions, and are usually recorded in the position and proper motion catalogues in which the link objects are listed. When neglecting the correlations, it cannot be excluded that the least squares methods will result in deterioration of both the estimates and errors. Therefore, the use of the full covariance matrix of positions and proper motions is recommended for the estimation process.

For the treatment of link observations (7.6) may be considered as a generalized expression from which the observational equations for different kinds of link observations can be derived. Several cases are distinguished for linking the provisional Hipparcos frame to the conventional extragalactic frame (Lindegren & Kovalevsky 1995):

– Comparison of positions only, which are assumed to be known for a number of objects common to the E and H frames at some epoch.

  This case is typical of those Hipparcos stars which are radio stars with only single-epoch radio observations. Catalogued at present are some 60 radio stars with single-epoch VLA positions and 10 stars with single-epoch MERLIN positions having precisions of 20-30 mas and 3 mas, respectively (Walter et al. 1997). From extrapolation of the estimates of a pilot study on 10 selected VLA stars a precision of the rotation angles of 3-4 mas is expected as soon as the entire set of VLA stars is ready for processing.

2052−474 20 56 16.359851±33 −47 14 47.62768±43 Q 1.489

One should act with caution, however, as the precision of a radio position depends critically upon the resolution of the interferometer system and on the particular structure of the star. Indeed, a large fraction of the radio stars are visual or spectroscopic binaries. Especially for stars of the latter class the radio emission has its origin in mass transfer between components. Therefore, the coincidence of optical and radio emission centres cannot be taken for granted. Since distances, diameters and other geometrical properties of radio stars can mostly be well modelled, it seems to be possible to estimate these structural properties prior to the transformation of the H to the E frame. Further, the transformation will be based on some 50 stars in the long run and, because a random distribution of the radio-optical offsets of the individual objects is likely, it can be expected that these offsets will do no damage to the link at a level of a few tenths of a mas taking into account an average 2 mas separation of the components.
Also photographic positions of quasars with respect to the Hipparcos frame and VLBI positions of the same objects determined with respect to the E frame fall in this category of link observations. From estimates based on the currently available 70 pairs of H and E quasar positions one concludes a precision of 2 mas for the orientation angles as soon as some 400 quasars are involved in the transformation. Intermediate results with formal errors of 4 mas for the orientation angles have been obtained by Zacharias et al. (1999) from the radio/optical positions of 327 extragalactic objects which are part of the ICRF.

– Comparison of proper motions only, which are known with respect to the E and H frames.

  Link observations of this type are provided by proper motion surveys with respect to extragalactic objects on the one hand, and the proper motions with respect to the provisional Hipparcos frame on the other. Moreover, the determination of apparent quasar proper motions belongs to this category of link observations. In this method use is made of photographic plates having epoch differences of up to 90 years, and of reference stars whose proper motions are given in the Hipparcos frame.

– Comparison of positions and proper motions is possible if these astrometric parameters are known for a number of stars in both the E and H frames.

  Currently a dozen radio stars are available having positions and proper motions measured by VLBI with respect to the ICRF extragalactic reference frame on the one hand (Lestrade et al. 1999), and the corresponding positions and proper motions in the Hipparcos frame on the other. Global rotations according to (7.6) furnish the angles and angular rates of orientation and spin of the H frame relative to the E frame. A preliminary

```
2059+034      21 01 38.834187±26   +03 41 31.32159±58      Q   1.015
```

study (Lestrade et al. 1995) using seven radio stars yielded the remarkable precisions of 0.5 mas and 0.5 mas/yr for the orientation and the spin, respectively. Several of the VLBI observed radio stars show structure at the milliarcsecond level, a fact which suggests modelling the geometrical properties of the structures, and basing the frame connection on as many objects as possible in order to strengthen the frame tie.

– Measurement of the angular separation between two objects for which the topocentric unit vector of the one object, $\boldsymbol{r}_{\mathrm{E}}$, is given in the E frame and that of the other object, $\boldsymbol{r}_{\mathrm{H}}$, in the H frame.

The fine guidance sensors of the Hubble Space Telescope (HST) offer the possibility of these kinds of link observations, in the course of which the angle ϕ is measured subtending the chord length between the two vector directions. In Hipparcos applications, the object in the E frame is a quasar, Q, and that in the H frame a star, S, (Fig. 7.1). Accordingly, the observed chord length at some epoch t is equal to

$$2\,\sin\phi/2 = |\boldsymbol{r}(\mathrm{S})_{\mathrm{E}} - \boldsymbol{r}(\mathrm{Q})_{\mathrm{E}}|\,,$$

and its nominal value can be approximated by $|\boldsymbol{r}(\mathrm{S})_{\mathrm{H}} - \boldsymbol{r}(\mathrm{Q})_{\mathrm{E}}|$. This quantity, however, requires a correction, $\boldsymbol{\Delta}$, if a rotational offset between the E and H frames is assumed. Thus the observational equations for a set of quasar/star pairs may be written after substitution of $\boldsymbol{r}(\mathrm{S})_{\mathrm{E}}$ by (7.1)

$$2\sin\phi/2 = |\boldsymbol{r}(\mathrm{S})_{\mathrm{H}} - \boldsymbol{r}(\mathrm{Q})_{\mathrm{E}} + \boldsymbol{\Delta}|\,, \tag{7.7}$$

where

$$\boldsymbol{\Delta} = \Big(\mathbf{M}(A_1, A_2, A_3) - \mathbf{I}\Big)\,\boldsymbol{r}(\mathrm{S})_{\mathrm{H}}\,, \tag{7.8}$$

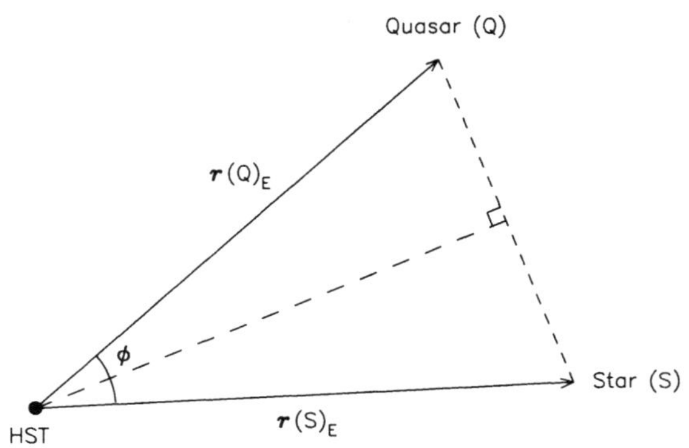

Fig. 7.1. Link observations by the Hubble Space Telescope measuring the angular separation ϕ of the topocentric directions $\boldsymbol{r}(\mathrm{Q})_{\mathrm{E}}$ and $\boldsymbol{r}(\mathrm{S})_{\mathrm{E}}$ between two objects, usually a quasar(Q)/star(S) pair. For studying potential frame offsets, $\boldsymbol{r}(\mathrm{S})_{\mathrm{E}}$ is approximated by $\boldsymbol{r}(\mathrm{S})_{\mathrm{H}}$

2059−786 21 05 44.961453±205 −78 25 34.54664±58 ? . . .

and $\boldsymbol{\Delta} \neq 0$ is indicative of different orientations of the E and H frames. Equations (7.7) and (7.8) contain the information for determining the angles of rotation from the H frame into the E frame from a minimum of three separation measurements of quasar/star pairs. With regard to the treatment of the implicit observational equations (7.7) reference is made to Lindegren & Kovalevsky (1995).

- Measurement of the rate of change of the angular separation is a means of determining the spin difference between the E and H frames.

  This procedure may be implemented through separation measurements at two or more epochs, at which the proper motions of the two objects are known in both frames, but the accurate position of the object is only known in H. Again, this kind of link observation can be provided by HST measurements for quasar/star pairs when the quasar position is not available with respect to the E frame, and its proper motion is assumed to be zero. In these circumstances, such quasars are suitable to provide information on the spin difference and, hence, are able to stop the rotation of the H frame with respect to the E frame.

- Analysis of Earth orientation parameters (EOP), i.e. the terrestrial pole coordinates, the celestial pole offsets, and the universal time (length of day).

  In contrast to the foregoing direct methods of linking the H frame to the E frame, the EOP method is an indirect procedure inasmuch it uses the terrestrial reference system as an intermediary. On the one hand, one determines from optical astrometry the rapidly changing orientation of the Earth with respect to star positions of the provisional Hipparcos Catalogue, H37C, which is the result of the merging process treated in Sect. 3.8.3. On the other hand, the EOPs are inferred from VLBI observations of extragalactic objects, i.e. relative to the E frame (Vondrák & Ron 1993). In deriving the orientation differences of the H and E frames, only those optical and radio data were exploited that have accumulated between 1980 and 1992. This limitation of the time interval is imposed by significant improvements of the VLBI observation technique around 1980, which provides extremely precise and consistent measurements since then. Ultimately, the spin differences of the H and E frames ensue from the time derivatives of the orientation differences.
  This method is not free from drawbacks. In practice, among the EOPs only the celestial pole offsets contribute to the determination of the orientation differences and, even more, the z-component of these differences is adulterated by non-alignment in longitude of the terrestrial reference frames to which the optical and radio observations are referred.

`2106−413     21 09 33.188582±32  −41 10 20.60530±42     Q  1.055`

Also, the z-component of the spin differences turned out to be unrealistically large probably due to a drift in longitude of the two terrestrial frames. At the mean epoch of the Hipparcos Catalogue, J1991.25, the x- and y-components of the orientation and spin difference vectors have been determined with precisions of 1.9 mas and 0.3 mas/yr, respectively (Vondrák et al. 1997).

For a detailed treatment of the link of the provisional Hipparcos frame to the conventional extragalactic reference frame we refer to the papers of Lindegren & Kovalevsky (1995) and Kovalevsky et al. (1997), where rigorous expressions for the relation between the H and E frames are derived, including the conditional equations for various types of link observations. It is also shown there that the small-angle approximation expressed in (7.6) has an accuracy of 0.005 mas provided that the orientation difference between H and E and the spin correction of H multiplied by the time interval of the link observations are each smaller than 1 arcsec. This limit is not exceeded in the case of the provisional Hipparcos frame and the ICRF.

In a joint effort of a variety of groups, associated with the link determination methods described above, the global orientation and spin of the provisional Hipparcos frame, H37C, have been determined with respect to extragalactic objects that are related to the ICRF (Kovalevsky et al. 1997). As a result, the coordinate frame of the Hipparcos catalogue is aligned with the extragalactic radio reference frame, ICRF, within ±0.6 mas at the epoch J1991.25 and its rotation is fixed within ±0.25 mas/yr (ESA 1997, Vol. 3, p. 408). This alignment effort made the Hipparcos Catalogue the optical realization of the ICRF as sanctioned by the Resolution B2 of the IAU (IAU 1999).

7.2 Link with the FK5 Reference Frame

Although the conventional celestial reference system is now an extragalactic one, it is nonetheless of academic interest to rotate the provisional Hipparcos frame onto the conventional reference frame of the FK5. In any case, this link is desirable for the more practical reason of comparing Hipparcos positions and proper motions with those of FK5. Above all, the comparison of the proper motions is instructive because of the nearly equal precisions of proper motions in both frames. In contrast, the precision of the FK5 positions is inferior to those of the Hipparcos catalogue by approximately a factor of 30 at epoch 1992, a fact which diminishes the precision of the rotation angles of orientation. On the other hand, this effect is compensated by the large number of link stars, namely 1535 or even more if the stars of the FK5 Extension are employed as well.

Surely, these link stars produce a firm link of high precision; its physical interpretation, however, could become subject to criticism. While the rigidity

2113+293 21 15 29.413455±20 +29 33 38.36694±28 Q 1.514

of the Hipparcos sphere is not affected by the linking process, it is clear that systematic deviations in certain parts of the FK5 frame are likely to impair the quality of the link by causing distortions of rotation angles and angular rates for the orientation and spin, respectively. Furthermore, due to imperfections of the values of precession and galactic rotation, which entered the FK5 but not the Hipparcos catalogue, a residual rotation of the FK5 frame cannot be excluded. The mean error inherent in the FK5 proper motion system is estimated to ± 0.7 mas/yr (Schwan 1988a). This basic error, plus the error of the link of the provisional Hipparcos frame to the FK5, would make up the total spin error of the final Hipparcos frame. In contrast, the extragalactic reference frame is expected to be free of any residual rotation due to the absence of measurable motions of the remote radio sources of the extragalactic frame. The spin error of the final Hipparcos frame, therefore, will be as good as the link to the ICRF.

7.3 Testing the Rigidity of the FK5 Frame

The coordinates in the FK5 catalogue refer to the mean equator and equinox at J2000.0 which are determined from the right ascensions and declinations of the FK5. Therefore, it is logical to designate the conventional reference frame represented by the FK5 catalogue by (J2000.0, FK5) to indicate that these coordinates are only meaningful in the context of the FK5 system. On the other hand, the Hipparcos catalogue is the realization of the conventional celestial reference system, ICRS, at optical wavelengths. By analogy with the FK5 but now omitting the no longer required standard epoch, the frame defined by the Hipparcos Catalogue is designated (ICRS/Hipparcos). The 1535 basic FK5 stars are available in both frames, (J2000.0, FK5) and (ICRS/Hipparcos), providing the basis for a direct comparison of the two catalogues. Considering the relatively small number of stars defining the FK5 frame, it is difficult to assess the relationship between the two frames with exactitude due to the colour- and magnitude-dependent pattern of systematic differences. We report on methods applicable to, and on results obtained from, the common data sets.

In determining global or rigid rotations of the Hipparcos frame into the FK5 frame by using identical sets consisting of $N \leq 1535$ Hipparcos and FK5 stars each, the obviously rigid sphere of the Hipparcos frame is preserved, while its spatial orientation and angular velocity are adapted to the corresponding properties of the FK5 frame. The global rotations are described by three angles of orientation at a given epoch and three angular rates concerning the stellar proper motions. These two triplets of angles are introduced in Sect. 7.1, (7.3); they are typical of the global systematic differences between the FK5 and Hipparcos frames. For the transformation from FK5 positions and proper motions to the corresponding quantities of the Hipparcos Catalogue, (7.4) and (7.5) are useful. They are equivalent to

2109−811 21 16 30.845958±180 −80 53 55.22339±39 ? ...

$$
\begin{aligned}
(\alpha_{\mathrm{FK5}} - \alpha_{\mathrm{H}}) \cos\delta &= -A_1 \sin\delta\cos\alpha - A_2 \sin\delta\sin\alpha \\
&\quad + A_3 \cos\delta \qquad (7.9) \\
\delta_{\mathrm{FK5}} - \delta_{\mathrm{H}} &= A_1 \sin\alpha - A_2 \cos\alpha \qquad (7.10)
\end{aligned}
$$

for the orientation angles, and

$$
\begin{aligned}
(\mu_\alpha \cos\delta)_{\mathrm{FK5}} - (\mu_\alpha \cos\delta)_{\mathrm{H}} &= -\dot{A}_1 \sin\delta\cos\alpha - \dot{A}_2 \sin\delta\sin\alpha \\
&\quad + \dot{A}_3 \cos\delta \qquad (7.11) \\
(\mu_\delta)_{\mathrm{FK5}} - (\mu_\delta)_{\mathrm{H}} &= \dot{A}_1 \sin\alpha - \dot{A}_2 \cos\alpha \qquad (7.12)
\end{aligned}
$$

for the spin angles. Since we deal here with small-angle approximations, it is insignificant whether the FK5 or Hipparcos values are used as arguments of the trigonometric functions. On the assumption that the FK5 and Hipparcos frames differ only by a pure rigid rotation, the conditional equations (7.9) to (7.12) yield undistorted rotation angles in a least squares fit. Since, in general, zonal and tesseral deformations are also hidden in the coordinate differences, the application of more refined methods of catalogue comparison are suggested as outlined below.

7.3.1 Vectorial Harmonics Used for Catalogue Comparison

To assess the FK5 frame relative to the final Hipparcos frame, which coincides nominally with the ICRF, Mignard & Froeschlé (1997) studied the position and proper motion differences in right ascension and declination between the FK5 and Hipparcos catalogues:

$$
\begin{aligned}
X &\equiv \Delta\alpha\cos\delta &&= (\alpha_{\mathrm{FK5}} - \alpha_{\mathrm{H}})\ \cos\delta_{\mathrm{H}} \\
Y &\equiv \Delta\delta &&= \delta_{\mathrm{FK5}} - \delta_{\mathrm{H}} \\
U &\equiv \Delta\mu_\alpha\cos\delta &&= ((\mu_\alpha)_{\mathrm{FK5}} - (\mu_\alpha)_{\mathrm{H}})\ \cos\delta_{\mathrm{H}} \\
V &\equiv \Delta\mu_\delta &&= (\mu_\delta)_{\mathrm{FK5}} - (\mu_\delta)_{\mathrm{H}}\,.
\end{aligned}
$$

Not all of the 1535 Basic FK5 stars are eligible for this comparison. Most of the omitted stars are either known double stars or, through symptoms of non-uniform motion, show evidence of being astrometric binaries. For some 80 orbiting binaries the Hipparcos position is defined relative to the centre of gravity of the double star system instead of relative to the photo-centre as in the FK5. Hence, these stars were judged to be unsuitable for comparison. In the end, 1233 apparently single FK5 stars qualified for the comparison with the respective Hipparcos stars.

The vector fields (X, Y) and (U, V) are each represented by the expansion in a series of orthogonal vectorial harmonics, where the first degree harmonics are associated with the global rotation of the FK5 frame, and the harmonics of higher degree capture the zonal distortions at wavelengths which decrease with increasing degree of the harmonic. The vectorial representation has the

Table 7.1. Angles of global orientation and spin differences between the FK5 and Hipparcos catalogues at epoch J1991.25 (ESA 1997, Vol. 3, p. 418)

Orientation [mas]	Spin [mas/yr]
$\varepsilon_x = -18.8 \pm 2.3$	$\omega_x = -0.10 \pm 0.10$
$\varepsilon_y = -12.3 \pm 2.3$	$\omega_y = +0.43 \pm 0.10$
$\varepsilon_z = +16.8 \pm 2.3$	$\omega_z = +0.88 \pm 0.10$

further advantage that the influence on the catalogue differences of right ascension and declination is accounted for simultaneously.

Let us first discuss the two global rotations: One concerns the orientation and the other the spin of the FK5 frame relative to the ICRF. Table 7.1 displays the numerical values of the respective triplets of rotation angles at the epoch of the Hipparcos càtalogue, J1991.25. For a consistent assessment of the catalogue FK5, its positions, valid for the epoch J2000.0, have been transformed to the epoch of the Hipparcos catalogue via the FK5 proper motions. The values of Table 7.1 rotate the positions and proper motions from the FK5 frame to the Hipparcos (ICRF) frame. Concluding from Table 7.1, the FK5 pole offset from the ICRF pole is expressed by the rotation angles ε_x and ε_y about the x and y axes. The offset of the right ascension origin is given by ε_z. Both offsets are within the tolerances required by the IAU for preserving continuity for the transition from the FK5 to the ICRF frame (Sects. 5.2.2 and 5.2.3). The order of magnitude of the spin components is compatible with what was to be expected from the uncertainties of the equinox motion, 1.5 mas/yr (Sect. 2.4), and luni-solar precession, −3.0 mas/yr (Sect. 6.3.1), the latter being absorbed by the proper motions, which are systematically too small because of the slightly excessive value of the precession adopted for the FK5 compilation. Both effects show up in the components of the spin vector, $\omega_x, \omega_y, \omega_z$.

Recalling the construction of the Hipparcos catalogue as a realization of the International Celestial Reference System (ICRS), there is evidence that this catalogue may differ from the FK5 not only by rigid rotations but also by regional distortions. On rotating the positions and proper motions of the FK5 into the ICRF by means of the rotation angles listed in Table 7.1, the global differences between the astrometric parameters, positions and proper motions, of the 1233 FK5 and Hipparcos stars disappear. Through this operation the basis is provided for studying regional distortions of the two sets of stars. The differences caused by the distortions exhibit a few features worth noting:

- The offset between the FK5 and the ICRF poles is confirmed by the declination differences, FK5 – ICRF, versus the right ascensions, amounting to approximately −60 mas.

- Regional differences are found from the comparisons of the position components versus right ascension and declination, reaching ±100 mas, and confirming earlier conclusions from extensive measurements by modern meridian circles (Morrison et al. 1990). The standard deviations of proper motions derived from the comparisons are as large as 2 mas/yr.
- The external errors of the FK5 positions and proper motions at the epoch J1991.25 seem to be larger by a factor of 2 than expected from the error budget of the FK5 (Fricke et al. 1988). Evidently the discrepancies are associated with zonal errors of the proper motion system of the FK5.

Bearing in mind the enormous rigidity inherent in the Hipparcos sphere solution (ESA, 1997, Vol. 1, p. 23), probably accurate to better than 0.1 mas at J1991.25 and 0.1 mas/yr on a global scale, and the alignment with the ICRF to within ±0.6 mas for the orientation at J1991.25 and ±0.25 mas/yr for the spin, it is compelling to ascribe the differences between the FK5 and Hipparcos catalogues to the FK5 positions and proper motions. Clearly, the Hipparcos observation techniques are greatly superior to those used for constructing the FK5. The latter had to rely on several hundred individual observation catalogues derived in both the northern and southern hemispheres at a variety of sites over the course of approximately one century (Sect. 2.4), while the Hipparcos project operated one single instrument over a period of only three years and, in addition, profitted from recent innovations in data reduction techniques.

7.3.2 Catalogue Comparison Using Classical Methods

Section 2.4.1 introduced selected classical methods of catalogue comparison (e.g., Bien et al. 1978, Podobed 1965, p. 193). Assuming a Hipparcos sphere of ideal rigidity with regard to positions and proper motions, we investigate the existence of regional distortions of the FK5 frame of positions and proper motions. Both a numerical and an analytical method are offered for the determination of systematic differences. In broad terms, the analytical method is more impersonal by applying statistical criteria to discriminate between the systematic and random parts of the position differences in the two frames. In addition, it takes account of the simultaneous dependence of the differences on RA and Dec.

On the basis of the analytical method of catalogue comparison (Schwan 1983) the deviations between the FK5 and Hipparcos catalogues are studied by using the method treated in Sect. 2.4.1, e.g., (2.20). For the stars of a common set, the position differences Δ_i are formed, and the unknowns A_s are solved for by least squares adjustment, yielding the systematic part of the catalogue differences. A significance test aids in selecting those terms of the series which diminish the random parts of the position differences.

In discussing this mode of catalogue comparison in some detail, we note that the Δ_i result from the position differences at the mean epoch of the

FK5 system, J1949.4. This epoch has been chosen to better disentangle the FK5 position and proper motion errors. Consequently, the star positions of the Hipparcos Catalogue had to be transformed to this mean epoch of the FK5 system using the Hipparcos proper motions, providing the residuals

$$\Delta\alpha\cos\delta = (\alpha_{\mathrm{FK5}} - \alpha_{\mathrm{H}})\ \cos\delta_{\mathrm{FK5}} \tag{7.13}$$

$$\Delta\delta = \delta_{\mathrm{FK5}} - \delta_{\mathrm{H}}\,. \tag{7.14}$$

By analogy the corresponding residuals are formed for the FK5 and Hipparcos proper motions.

Global rotations of the FK5 frames of position and proper motion relative to Hipparcos are derived from the above residuals with the aid of (7.9) to (7.12). To protect this process from any potential biases caused by actual and suspected binaries, the sample of the Basic FK5 stars was carefully examined leaving, finally, 1123 stars eligible for the determination of the angles of the global orientation, $\varepsilon_x, \varepsilon_y, \varepsilon_z$, and global spin, $\omega_x, \omega_y, \omega_z$. The numerical results are nearly identical with those of Table 7.1; the small differences are very likely due to the star selection and, above all, to the fact that possible zonal distortions are projected into the global rotation parameters. This preparatory step precedes the catalogue comparison, since the expansion in a series of products of Fourier terms, Legendre polynomials and Hermite polynomials (see (2.20)) does not provide all isolated terms of rotation.

In the next step the contributions of the global rotation are subtracted from (7.13) and (7.14), and the remaining residuals, $\Delta\alpha^R$ and $\Delta\delta^R$, are examined for regional differences along the lines that were described in Sect. 2.4.1. First the dependence on declination zones is inferred, showing features almost identical with those found by means of vectorial harmonics (see Sect. 7.3.1). In studying the dependence on right ascension, the declination-dependent differences are subtracted from the residuals step by step, so that the right ascension dependence is derived from the residuals

$$\Delta\alpha^*\cos\delta = \Delta\alpha^R\ \cos\delta - (\Delta\alpha\ \cos\delta)_\delta\,,$$

$$\Delta\delta^* = \Delta\delta^R - (\Delta\delta)_\delta\,.$$

Again, to first approximation, the regional distortions in right ascension resemble surprisingly closely those obtained by the vectorial harmonic method.

A more rigorous comparison of the FK5 with the Hipparcos Catalogue is pending (Schwan 1999). This investigation will aim to expose details of the regional distortions in positions and proper motions and, as a by-product, perform a comparison of the scalar harmonic method, applied here, and the vectorial harmonic method, presented in Sect. 7.3.1.

2146−783   21 52 03.154504±221   −78 07 06.63962±63   ?   . . .

7.4 Refinement of the Hipparcos Link with the Extragalactic Reference Frame

As discussed in Sect. 7.1, the frame of the Hipparcos catalogue has been fixed to that of the ICRF at the epoch J1991.25 with a precision of 0.6 mas. The precision of the residual rotation with time of the Hipparcos frame with respect to the ICRF is estimated to be 0.25 mas/yr. This uncertainty raises the question to what extent the displacement of the Hipparcos frame due to this residual rotation will be measurable and amenable to correction in the future.

The link of the Hipparcos frame to the ICRF is characterized by the two vectors $\boldsymbol{\mathcal{E}} = (\varepsilon_x, \varepsilon_y, \varepsilon_z)^{\mathrm{T}}$ and $\boldsymbol{\Omega} = (\omega_x, \omega_y, \omega_z)^{\mathrm{T}}$. The vector $\boldsymbol{\mathcal{E}}$ defines the position of the coordinate axes at epoch J1991.25, while $\boldsymbol{\Omega}$ stands for the annual rotation of these axes with respect to the fixed axes of the ICRF. The components of $\boldsymbol{\mathcal{E}}$ and $\boldsymbol{\Omega}$ give the angles and angular rates, respectively, for the rotations of a Cartesian coordinate frame on condition that the small-angle approximation is applicable (Sect. 7.1).

What procedures are conceivable to improve the present standard deviation of $\boldsymbol{\Omega}$, i.e. 0.25 mas/yr, and to slow down the drifting away of the optical extension of the ICRF represented by the Hipparcos catalogue? In principle the methods listed in Sect. 7.1 are applicable for the redetermination of $\boldsymbol{\mathcal{E}}$ and $\boldsymbol{\Omega}$. At short and medium term little improvement is expected from the stellar proper motion surveys contributing directly and exclusively to $\boldsymbol{\Omega}$ (Kovalevsky et al. 1997). Another direct contribution to $\boldsymbol{\Omega}$ is provided by the VLBI method applied so far to a dozen of radio stars for the simultaneous determination of positions and proper motions from observations during a ten-year interval (Lestrade et al. 1995). This method is exacting and costly. Ultimately it was chosen as the backbone of the initial link of the provisional Hipparcos catalogue to the ICRF.

For the above reasons the direct redetermination of $\boldsymbol{\Omega}$ is not advisable. More promising than the direct approach seems to be the redetermination of $\boldsymbol{\mathcal{E}}$ at some later epoch, and inference of $\boldsymbol{\Omega}$ from successive determinations of $\boldsymbol{\mathcal{E}}$. The line of thought is as follows: starting out from

$$\boldsymbol{\Omega} = \frac{\mathrm{d}\boldsymbol{\mathcal{E}}}{\mathrm{d}t} \tag{7.15}$$

and approximating the differential quotient by

$$\frac{\Delta\boldsymbol{\mathcal{E}}}{\Delta t} = \frac{\boldsymbol{\mathcal{E}}(t_2) - \boldsymbol{\mathcal{E}}(t_1)}{t_2 - t_1}, \tag{7.16}$$

the problem reduces to the determination of the orientation vectors $\boldsymbol{\mathcal{E}}_i$ at two epochs t_i, lying several years apart. Here $\boldsymbol{\mathcal{E}}_1$ may be substituted by the value obtained for the initial link, while $\boldsymbol{\mathcal{E}}_2$ is most conveniently derived from position determinations of radio stars by means of VLBI, MERLIN and VLA (see Sect. 4.2.1). Positions are derived from these radio interferometric methods with standard errors of 0.3 mas (Lestrade et al. 1995),

`2150+173      21 52 24.819405±20   +17 34 37.79482±39      L   ...`

1.7 mas (Morrison et al. 1997) and 20 mas (Florkowski et al. 1985), respectively. Since the optical positions influence the determination of the orientation vectors as well, supporting measures are required for improving the Hipparcos positions of those radio stars serving the link. Indeed, these positions may have suffered at time t_2 due to imperfections of the Hipparcos proper motions. Optical interferometry offers an opportunity for this kind of position measurement, anticipating wide-angle astrometric precision of about 2 mas (Armstrong et al. 1998), thus matching the Hipparcos precision at the catalogue epoch.

To first approximation the standard deviation of $\boldsymbol{\Omega}$, attainable along the lines of redetermining the orientation vector, is estimated from (7.16):

$$\sigma(\boldsymbol{\Omega}) = \frac{\sqrt{\sigma(\boldsymbol{\mathcal{E}}_2)^2 + \sigma(\boldsymbol{\mathcal{E}}_1)^2}}{t_2 - t_1}\,. \tag{7.17}$$

Let $\sigma(\boldsymbol{\mathcal{E}}_1) = 0.6$ mas as found for the link at epoch $t_1 = 1991.25$, and $\sigma(\boldsymbol{\mathcal{E}}_2) = 1.7$ mas based on MERLIN observations of 21 stars at the mean epoch $t_2 = 1995.7$ (Morrison et al. 1997); one calculates $\sigma(\boldsymbol{\Omega}) = 0.41$ mas/yr. On applying this estimate to $t_2 = 2000.0$ under otherwise equal assumptions one obtains 0.20 mas/yr for the precision of the updated spin vector, which is a value slightly superior to that of $\boldsymbol{\Omega}_1$. For comparison with the MERLIN-determined $\sigma(\boldsymbol{\mathcal{E}}_2) = 1.7$ mas, we give the projected error, $\sigma^{\mathrm{p}}(\boldsymbol{\mathcal{E}}_2)$, of the Hipparcos link at the epoch 1995.7 which accumulates to

$$\sigma^{\mathrm{p}}(\boldsymbol{\mathcal{E}}_2) = \sqrt{[\sigma(\boldsymbol{\mathcal{E}}_1)]^2 + [\Delta t \cdot \sigma(\boldsymbol{\Omega}_1)]^2} = 1.3 \text{ mas}$$

and, therefore, falls well within the 1σ limit of MERLIN.

In conclusion, if the number of observed radio stars is augmented while preserving or even improving the MERLIN positional precision, the spin vector would improve statistically so significantly that soon after the year 2000 a revision of the link of the Hipparcos catalogue may become desirable. In addition, a more uniform distribution of the link objects should have been achieved in the northern and southern hemispheres by then.

With some reservations due to the long lead time, the methods of plate measurements of Hipparcos stars in the vicinity of extragalactic objects and of the measurement of separations between pairs of Hipparcos stars and extragalactic objects by means of the Hubble Space Telescope (HST) will also be instrumental in strengthening the estimate of the spin vector through redeterminations of the orientation vector at some future epoch.

2204−540 22 07 43.733296±45 −53 46 33.82004±56 Q 1.206

8. Future Prospects

8.1 Interdependence of Astrometry and Fundamental Catalogues

A fundamental celestial reference system is a human artifact laid down as a convention. It is merely a snapshot of the current astrometric capabilities employed for connecting observables and their mathematical representation. Accordingly, the associated reference frame and catalogue of celestial objects, which represents the system, are transient products adopted for some interval of time. Typical of this development of a system is the FK5 reference frame that materializes, in principle, a reference system of dynamical definition, and is based essentially on meridian circle astrometry. In 1998 this dynamical system was replaced by the International Celestial Reference System (ICRS), which is a kinematic system represented by the ICRF, the International Celestial Reference Frame, and the Hipparcos Catalogue is its optical realization (IAU 1999). Astrometrically, the ICRF is based on distant extragalactic radio sources that are observed from the Earth by means of VLBI.

It is plausible that the establishment of fundamental reference frames appears in a different light with the advent of refined observational techniques. Indeed, the scientific benefits from modern astrometry foster the improvement of reference frames through, e.g., the following applications of astrometry:

- Navigation and guidance by means of positions of celestial bodies, such as planetary objects, galactic objects (stars, pulsars) and extragalactic objects.
- Providing the relationship between reference frames in different wavelengths.
- Determination of the absolute motion of objects.
- Calibration of the distance scale with the aid of accurate parallax measurements.
- Monitoring of the Earth orientation parameters for astronomical and geophysical investigations.
- Maintenance of reference frames.

2209+236 22 12 05.966318±23 +23 55 40.54388±39 ? . . .

8.1.1 New Topics Inspired by Improved Astrometric Accuracy

With improving measurement accuracies increasing numbers of stars are resolved and found to form double or multiple systems. There is, therefore, a greater need for the determination of accurate orbital data that are a prerequisite for using these stars as absolute reference points as well. Due to insufficient orbital information some stars in multiple systems have obviously dubious or incorrect astrometry in the Hipparcos Catalogue. Indeed, effects of orbital motion inherent in double and multiple systems are reflected by the proper motions of a class of Hipparcos stars which are either known binaries or are suspected to have unseen companions. While Hipparcos proper motions are only determined over the three years' period of the mission, and therefore provide proper motions of a short-term character, the FK5 proper motions are inferred from observations made at widely separated epochs up to 100 years apart and are, so to speak, of long-term character. The two types of proper motions can differ significantly. For a few hundred of the Basic FK5 stars the Hipparcos precision is almost three times worse than the average precision of Hipparcos proper motions for bright stars, which amounts to 0.7 mas/yr (Wielen et al. 1997). In compiling the FK6 as a combination of the ground-based stellar positions and proper motions of the Basic FK5 with the corresponding ones of Hipparcos Catalogue, account has been taken of the short and long term determinations of proper motions (Wielen et al. 1998). The FK6 concept is briefly introduced in Sect. 8.1.2.

Increasing accuracy of astrometric measurements also manifests itself in the demand for a wide range of photometric data required for the incorporation of corrections for refraction and detector sensitivities.

Another concomitant of improved accuracies may be seen in the possibility of establishing firm relationships between different sorts of reference frames, and in assessing their possible relative motions. In this connection a distinction of frames can be made by the spectral region (optical, radio, infrared) or by the definition of the reference system (dynamical, kinematic, hybrid).

8.1.2 A Sketch of the FK6

The driving force of establishing the Sixth Catalogue of Fundamental Stars (FK6) originates in the intention to provide proper motions and positions of optimum accuracy for a sample of stars from astrometric data available to date. Evidently, the FK5 and the Hipparcos Catalogue offer a promising starting point for this objective, and the FK6 should be understood as a combination of the results of the space astrometry mission Hipparcos and the ground-based data of the FK5, the latter one comprising the measurements of more than two centuries. Because of the underlying concept of catalogue combination, it must be accepted that the FK6 cannot represent a fundamental catalogue in the strict sense of Chap. 1.

2229+695	22 30 36.469725±71	+69 46 28.07698±34	?	...

Part I of FK6 (Wielen et al. 1999) extends over 878 stars of the Basic FK5 (Sect. 2.6) and the respective Hipparcos stars. This limit is set by the method of approach to the catalogue construction. Indeed, among the Basic FK5 only 878 stars allowed a direct solution which implies that the Hipparcos and FK5 data could be combined by immediate processing, i.e. without necessitating any preceding data treatment imposed by the properties of possible binary stars. In other words, the sample consists essentially of single stars augmented by double and multiple systems, the observations of which do not reveal signs of multiplicity. Of course, the systematic differences between the FK5 and Hipparcos frames (see Sect. 7.3) have been taken into consideration prior to the direct solutions. Specific solutions for Basic FK5 stars different from those mentioned above are intended to enter Part II of FK6.

The FK6 proper motions are determined from the Hipparcos and FK5 data according to the simplified averaging method, which is outlined below to illustrate the approach. This method is applicable on the assumption that the Hipparcos data are uncorrelated at the epoch of the Hipparcos Catalogue. Note that by definition the FK5 data are uncorrelated at the mean epoch of each star position. Let F and H be the abbreviations of FK5 and Hipparcos, respectively; let x designate the right ascension (RA) or declination (Dec) of a star, and let μ and T stand for the respective proper motion components and catalogue mean epochs. An updated proper motion, μ_0, can be derived from (Wielen 1988)

$$\mu_0 = \frac{x_{\rm H}(T_{\rm H}) - x_{\rm F}(T_{\rm F})}{T_{\rm H} - T_{\rm F}} ,$$

and the mean error of μ_0 is given by the quadratic sum of the individual positional mean errors divided by the epoch difference $T_{\rm H} - T_{\rm F}$. Finally, the FK6 proper motion, $\mu_{\rm FK6}$, results from the weighted average of the three proper motions, μ_0, $\mu_{\rm H}$ and $\mu_{\rm F}$, where the inverse squares of the respective mean errors play the role of the weights.

The rigorous determination of the FK6 positions and proper motions proceeds along the lines of a weighted least squares fit of the four FK6 unknowns, RA, Dec, $\mu_{\rm RA}$ and $\mu_{\rm Dec}$, to correlated data. These data are given in the FK5 and Hipparcos Catalogue by each star's position and proper motion at some mean epoch, and their respective errors and correlations.

Such estimates of positions and proper motions are valid only for true single stars in rectilinear motion. However, the broader category of apparent single stars is comprised of close spectroscopic binaries, double stars with known orbits, stars with hidden companions, etc. In fact, this category may be exposed to 'cosmic errors'. As shown by Wielen et al. (1997), the proper motions of the apparent single stars in the Hipparcos Catalogue are affected by a cosmic error. This cosmic error inherent in the Hipparcos proper motions (Wielen et al. 1997) was derived from a sample or 1202 apparently single FK5 stars by comparing the Hipparcos proper motions with the proper motions of the FK5. In the long-term 'prediction' mode for proper motions, therefore, the errors of $\mu_{\rm H}$ and μ_0 as well as the Hipparcos position errors have been corrected by the effects of the cosmic error prior to the estimation of the FK6 positions and proper motions by means of the method referred to above.

By rule of thumb, whenever the epoch of the predicted star position differs by 10 years or more from the epoch of the Hipparcos Catalogue, $T_{\rm H} = 1991.25$, the long-term prediction mode of the FK6 is expected to yield more accurate results for positions and error estimates than the immediate use of the Hipparcos Catalogue.

8.2 Prospective Observational Techniques

As outlined in Sect. 8.1 the maintenance of reference frames is a typical application of astrometry. For example, due to the known time-dependent structural changes of the extragalactic radio sources at the milliarcsecond level there is some need for maintaining the extragalactic radio reference frame, ICRF. For this purpose both positional observations and observations to detect changes in source structure must continue. This means, in practice, that VLBI and VLBA observation campaigns are in demand not only for the sources that compose the ICRF, but also for suitable additional sources in order to attain densification of the net.

The optical reference frame, defined as the extension of the ICRF into the visible spectral region by means of the Hipparcos stars, is represented by the Hipparcos Catalogue, and as such inevitably requires maintenance because of imperfections of stellar proper motions and potential systematic errors introduced by linking the Hipparcos frame to the ICRF. To realize this maintenance, observations are required at the level of Hipparcos' accuracy or better. At the present time, the suitable means of achieving frame maintenance include ground-based optical interferometry, CCD astrometry and, as part of natural evolution, further space missions after the avenue of space astrometry has been opened up so successfully by the Hubble Space Telescope and the Hipparcos astrometry satellite. One may add photographic astrometry especially for surveys and the brighter objects.

Among the space projects of optical astrometry which have reached the advanced study phase are: 1) SIM (standing for Space Interferometry Mission (Peterson & Shao 1997)), 2) FAME (Full-sky Astrometric Mapping Explorer (Seidelmann et al. 1995; Horner et al. 1999), and 3) GAIA (originally standing for Global Astrometric Interferometer for Astrophysics (Lindegren 1998)). These all presently seem to have high probability of being materialized in the early part of the 21st century. Other proposals for space astrometry are the collaborations known as DIVA (Bastian et al. 1996), LIGHT (Yoshizawa et al. 1997) and STRUVE (Ilin et al. 1997).

Extension of astrometry at radio wavelengths cannot become as fruitful as the projects of optical astrometry, dealing by and large with millions of ob-

2254+074 22 57 17.303120±23 +07 43 12.30284±52 L 0.190

jects, because the population of radio objects with suitably intense emission is more sparse by several orders of magnitude.

Most of the above-mentioned prospective space missions predict the target astrometric accuracy of 10 microarcsec or better for the positions, annual proper motions and parallaxes of stars as faint as the 20th magnitude. The scanning programmes comprise stellar objects that are of the order of 500 million in number. Compared with Hipparcos, improvements by approximately a factor 1000 will be achieved by means of the proposed space missions both in astrometric accuracy and number of stars. Below is included a summary of the objectives of each of the projects that rank high among the numerous proposals.

8.2.1 SIM – The Scientific Basis of the Mission

After the Hipparcos mission demonstrated the successful application of the technique of global astrometry in space (see Sect. 3.2), and broke the barrier to the fundamental problem of measuring accurate parallaxes, it was only logical to develop further along these lines. Accordingly, plans are being pursued with SIM to extend the distance measurements to astronomical objects that are substantially more distant and have much fainter magnitudes, using optical interferometry with a 10 m baseline. This mission will be operated from a heliocentric orbit which is chosen so that the spacecraft moves in an Earth-trailing orbit, but drifts slowly away from the Earth, reaching a maximum communication distance of about 95 million kilometers after 5.5 years. In this orbit the spacecraft will receive continuous solar illumination, avoiding the occultations that would have occurred in the originally considered nearly circular Earth orbit (SIM 1999). SIM is not a sky-scanning but rather a pointing instrument which is set on selected targets brighter than 20 mag. It will perform both differential astrometry within 1° fields as well as global astrometry for objects separated by angles larger than the 15° siderostat field of view. In the course of a nominal 5-year mission a throughput is expected of 10^5 targets at 4 microarcsec (μas) measurement accuracy, depending on the mix of magnitudes of the observed objects.

Feasibility studies indicate that SIM should have the capability to measure absolute parallaxes accurate to 4 μas and annual proper motions to 1–2 μas for celestial objects as faint as 20 mag. Such an enormous step of measurement accuracy will have a major impact in almost every branch of astronomy. For instance, determination of parallax to this accuracy provides distances accurate to 10% out to 25 kpc. Likewise, let us recall that a transverse velocity of 1 km/s at 10 kpc results in a proper motion of 20 μas/yr. With these estimates in mind, it is foreseeable that SIM will have extraordinary implications for studies of galactic populations, structure of the Galaxy, galaxies in and near the Local Group, and tests of the General Theory of Relativity by measuring the deflection of light by the Sun, Jupiter and the Earth.

2312−319 23 14 48.500631±50 −31 38 39.52651±103 G 0.284

8.2.2 FAME – Mission Profile and Science Summary

FAME is designed to be a small astrometric survey instrument on an artificial satellite operating from a geosynchronous orbit, thus allowing for 24-hour communication capability with the spacecraft (Horner et al. 1999). The instrument and spacecraft are being planned to fly during a 5-year mission on a slowly spinning satellite, which precesses such that it scans the complete sky several times over a period of a year, and repeats in a manner somewhat similar to the Hipparcos mission (Sect. 3.2), however at a higher level of accuracy and data yield. With regard to the instrument, FAME operates as a direct imaging telescope viewing two fields separated by approximately 80°. It measures a fixed angle between stars, and detects the position, magnitude and colour of all the stars coming through the field of view to a visual magnitude of nearly 15 mag, i.e. of approximately 40 million stars.

The primary purpose of the instrument is to obtain a catalogue of positions, proper motions and parallaxes of all stars down to about 15 mag, with an expected magnitude-dependent accuracy of positions, annual proper motions and parallaxes of 20–800 μas. Measurements are intended to be made in five different wavelength bands, supplying comprehensive information on positional and stellar properties for about 10 million stars brighter than 15 mag. Another objective of FAME concentrates on improvements in knowledge of cosmology and physics of distant objects by providing a homogeneous and complementary distance indicator. Significant improvement is expected for the distances to the Cepheid variables, the RR Lyrae stars, Hyades, Pleiades, and luminous blue and red stars. Positions, annual proper motions and parallaxes for stars to 9 mag at a 50 μas accuracy level will provide an exciting pool of scientific data for an astrometric calibration of the cosmic distance scale.

8.2.3 GAIA – Goals of the Mission

In analyzing the experience with the Hipparcos telescope which had an entrance pupil of only 29 cm, it was concluded that a bigger telescope would offer significant advantages over the Hipparcos results in terms of optical resolution and photon statistics. Now under consideration are two telescopes with an aperture of $1.7 \times 0.7\,\mathrm{m}^2$ each, by means of which virtually all stars and point-like galaxies down to 20 mag will be observable with an accuracy of 10 μas, or better for the brighter objects. The lines of sight of the two telescopes subtend the basic angle that is made as large as possible, at present 106°, to enable accurate parallax measurements. According to present plans, the observations will be performed from an artificial satellite located at the Earth-Sun libration point, L_2, i.e. at approximately 1.5×10^6 km from the Earth, arranged in the order Sun-Earth-spacecraft. This site offers a stable thermal environment, no eclipses and a low level of gravitational perturbations.

2319+272 23 21 59.862235±21 +27 32 46.44343±33 Q 1.253

GAIA is a survey-type astrometric mission which shares the characteristics of the Hipparcos concept for global astrometry (Sect. 3.2). As such, it performs continuous sky scanning according to a predefined scanning law. Consequently, GAIA is ideal for survey-type programmes but, in contrast to SIM, is inflexible with regard to the redistribution of observing time to high-priority targets. The data collected in this scanning mode are the raw observations for the determination of positions, proper motions and parallaxes. For comprehensive studies of kinematic motions GAIA aims at measuring the radial velocities of stars brighter than 17 mag by means of a slitless scanning spectrometer. Through this procedure the five astrometric parameters (i.e., two spherical coordinates, their time derivatives and the parallax) are augmented by the astrophysically determined radial velocity component, thus providing the full state vector for the majority of celestial objects.

A novel feature of GAIA is the multi-colour, multi-epoch photometry of stellar objects down to 17 mag. This detailed photometry complements the astrometric data with essential astrophysical information that is invaluable for careful calibration of the instrument and detector sensitivity, since the aberrations of reflective telescopes are wavelength dependent at the sub-resolution level where diffraction effects come into play.

The GAIA mission is optimized for the observation of large samples, perhaps as many as 10^9 stars. It is therefore well tailored to statistical studies, to the discovery of new classes of objects and to research into the kinematics of the Galaxy. Nevertheless, the capabilities of GAIA impact almost every branch of astronomy and astrophysics. These are for instance: evolution of stars, dynamics of stellar systems, structure of the Galaxy, detection of planetary systems, extragalactic astrophysics, reference frames, and general relativity. Reference is made to Perryman et al. (1997) for a broader overview with many more details.

8.3 Prospects for the Celestial Reference Frame

In the distant future, perhaps after the launch of SIM, a whole new class of optical/radio sources should become available for vast improvement of the radio-optical frame tie. The latter should be 1–2 orders of magnitude more accurate than what was possible with the handful of radio stars observed by Hipparcos. Better accuracy of proper motion determinations should also prevent the frame tie from degenerating as rapidly with time.

Preservation of historic VLBI data, as well as archiving of current results, will be facilitated by the recent formation of the International VLBI Service for Geodesy and Astrometry (IVS), whose Coordinating Centre is located at the Goddard Space Flight Center (IVS, 1999). It will ensure that the entire span of astrometric radio measurements will remain available for reanalysis in the future. This may be of great importance for improvement of the accuracy of the radio reference frame when models are improved. It is expected that

2320+506 23 22 25.982159±41 +50 57 51.96371±44 ? ...

considerable new knowledge will be generated during the next decade, which will allow the removal of much of the systematic error that is presently due to inadequate modelling of the Earth's atmosphere and the internal structures of radio sources.

A number of groups of VLBI practitioners have plans to densify the radio reference frame in the near future by observing many additional sources that have been too weak to be successfully studied in the past. Judicious selection of sources from the Veron-Cetty & Veron (1983) and MERLIN (1999) survey catalogues should provide a base of many hundreds of additional sources that will contribute to both an improved optical link and to filling in regions of the sky where present ICRF reference points are sparse. Another recently established VLBI project, CORE, is aimed at measuring Earth orientation essentially continuously, by performing uninterrupted monitoring of selected radio sources (CORE, 2000).

In summarizing ongoing activities, the prognosis may be ventured that significantly improved models and estimation techniques in conjunction with sufficient data accumulation will lead quite naturally to the construction of a new and self-contained celestial reference frame. As before, this reference frame will be a human artifact reflecting the latest level of knowledge at the time of its coming into being.

2326−477	23 29 17.704369±39	−47 30 19.11519±53	Q	1.306

Epilogue

During the last decade of the 20th century, astrometry by means of VLBI and the Hipparcos Space Project have radically revolutionized the concept of celestial reference frames. The practical consequence is the commencement of a new era of fundamental catalogues with the adoption of the ICRF. This revolution would not have been possible without these modern measurement techniques, and it has rung in the end of the venerable FK series. Nothing will remain the same as in the past:

- Seen from the perspective of the Earth the representation of the reference frame has been entrusted to fiducial points which are extragalactic radio sources that are among the most distant objects in the known Universe.
- While absolute observations of stars prevailed in the FK series of fundamental catalogues, the new reference frame is characterized first of all by a rigid sphere made up of the spherical coordinates of objects that are obtained from differential astrometry at some epoch. Second, this sphere is tied to the radio reference frame whose equator is fixed by the declinations of 212 defining extragalactic radio sources and on which a zero point of right ascension has been adopted.
- For stars, the observation history is normally known and may be extrapolated. This does not necessarily hold true for radio sources, whose positional histories are indeed known, but the results of future observations cannot be predicted. Consequently, new sources must be continually selected and observed in order to expand the list of candidates and to compensate for losses of objects due to some unexpected behaviour of the radiation mechanism of the sources.
- Progress in bringing under control the position changes related to source structure variation, along with sufficient accumulation of observations of current and new sources, holds promise for establishing an improved ICRF. In executing this step the defining sources will be constrained by the statistical condition that their coordinates do not reflect any global rotation. In these circumstances the fundamental directions of the ICRF will remain fixed in space, while the source positions may be revised. Lengthy comparisons of individual observation catalogues typical of the FK series are avoided in such a procedure. Instead, it is practicable to construct the improved ICRF from scratch by going back to the original VLBI observations,

i.e. delays and delay rates, which can be retrieved from a central data bank and combined with the newly accumulated observables by constraining the redetermined coordinates of the defining sources to the values of the initial ICRF.
- As long as the observational instruments remain under the blanket of the atmosphere on the surface of the Earth, improvements of the celestial reference frame will demand advances in understanding geophysics and the behaviour of the atmosphere. This can be avoided for instruments in Earth or solar orbit, but the price will be the necessity of unprecedented accuracy in modelling their mechanical behaviour and orbital paths.
- Extension of the ICRF to frequencies other than the optical and radio regions of the electromagnetic spectrum will be possible when such frequencies become accessible to frequent and routine astrometric measurements. The required link to the existing ICRF can then be performed by a procedure analogous to that which unified the Hipparcos and extragalactic radio reference frames.

The science of astronomy in the 21st century will continue to benefit from the revolution in astrometry at the end of the 20th century.

2329−384 23 31 59.476115±42 −38 11 47.65053±66 Q 1.195

References

Aoki, S., Guinot, B., Kaplan, G.H. et al. (1982): The New Definition of Universal Time. Astron. Astrophys. **105**, 359–361

Aoki, S., Sôma, M., Kinoshita, H., Inoue, K. (1983): Conversion Matrix of Epoch B1950.0 FK4-based Positions of Stars to Epoch J2000.0 Positions in Accordance with the New IAU Resolutions. Astron. Astrophys. **128**, 263–267

Arenou, F. (1996): Deux Sphères en Fusion. In: *Deuxième Atelier du Groupe de Recherche en Astronomie Spatiale (CNRS)*, Grasse, 26 to 27 September 1995, M. Froeschlé, F. Mignard (eds.). OCA/CERGA, 31–38

ARI (1963): Preliminary Supplement to the FK4 (FK4SUP). Veröffentlichungen Astronomisches Rechen-Institut Heidelberg, No. **11**, G. Braun, Karlsruhe, 47 pp

Arias, E.F., Feissel, M. (1990): The Celestial System of the International Earth Rotation Service. In: *Inertial Coordinate System on the Sky, IAU Symp. No. 141*, J.H. Lieske, V.K. Abalakin (eds.). Kluwer, Dordrecht Boston London, 119–128

Arias, E.F., Feissel, M., Lestrade, J.-F. (1988): Comparison of VLBI Celestial Reference Frames. Astron. Astrophys. **199**, 357–363

Arias, E.F., Charlot, P., Feissel, M., Lestrade, J.-F. (1995): The Extragalactic Reference System of the International Earth Rotation Service, ICRS. Astron. Astrophys. **303**, 604–608

Armstrong, J.T., Mozurkewich, D., Richard, L.J. et al. (1998): The Navy Prototype Optical Interferometer. Astrophys. J. **496**, 550–571

Auwers, A. (1879): Fundamental-Catalog für die Zonen-Beobachtungen am Nördlichen Himmel. Publ. d. Astron. Gesellschaft, No. **14**

Auwers, A. (1883): Mittlere Örter von 83 südlichen Sternen für 1875.0. Publ. d. Astron. Gesellschaft, No. **17**

Baade, W., Minkowski, R. (1954): Identification of the Radio Sources Cassiopeia, Cygnus A, and Puppis A. Astrophys. J. **119**, 206–214

Backer, D.C., Fomalont, E.B., Goss, W.M. et al. (1985): Accurate Timing and Interferometer Positions for the Millisecond Pulsar 1937+21 and the Binary Pulsar 1913+16. Astron. J. **90**, 2275–2280

Bare, C., Clark, B.G., Kellermann, K.I., Cohen, M.H., Jauncey, D.L. (1967): Interferometer Experiment with Independent Local Oscillators. Science **157**, 189–191

Bartel, N., Ratner, M.I., Shapiro, I.I. et al. (1985): Pulsar Astrometry via VLBI. Astron. J. **90**, 318–325

Bartel, N., Chandler, J.F., Ratner, M.I. et al. (1996): Toward a Frame Tie via Millisecond Pulsar VLBI. Astron. J. **112**, 1690–1696

Bastian, U., Röser, S., Høg, E. et al. (1996): DIVA - an Interferometric Minisatellite for Astrometry and Photometry. Astron. Nachr. **317**, 281–288

Bauschinger, J. (1922): Die Astronomische Festlegung des Trägheitssystems. Naturwissenschaften **10**, 1005–1010

Bien, R. (1987): Weights of Star Positions in Meridian Circle Catalogues. Astron. Astrophys. **188**, 225–232

Bien, R., Fricke, W., Lederle, T., Schwan, H. (1978): Methods for the Comparison of Systems of Star Positions to be Applied in the Construction of the FK5. Veröffentlichungen Astronomisches Rechen-Institut Heidelberg, No. **29**, G. Braun, Karlsruhe, 21 pp

Billaud, G. (1986): A New Astrolabe. In: *Astrometric Techniques, IAU Symp. No. 109*, H.K. Eichhorn, R.J. Leacock (eds.). Kluwer, Dordrecht Boston London, 389–395

Billaud, G., Guallino, G., Vigouroux, G. (1978): General Catalogue of FK4 Stars Observed with Astrolabes (1958-1975). Astron. Astrophys. **63**, 87–95

Binney, J., Tremaine, S. (1987): *Galactic Dynamics.* Princeton Princeton University Press, Princeton

Blanco, V.M., McCuskey, S.W. (1961): *Basic Physics of the Solar System.* Addison-Wesley, Reading

Bolton, J.G., Skimmins, A.J., Wall, J.V. (1975): The Parkes 2700 MHz Survey (7th part) Supplementary Catalogue for the Declination Zone -4 deg to -90 deg. Austral. J. of Physics, Astrophys. Suppl. **34**, 1–32

Bondi, H. (1960): *Cosmology.* Cambridge University Press, Cambridge

Boss, B. (1937): General Catalogue of 33342 Stars for the Epoch 1950, Vol. I–V. Carnegie Institution of Washington, Public. No. 486

Brosche, P. (1966): Representation of Systematic Differences in Positions and Proper Motions of Stars by Spherical Harmonics. Veröffentlichungen Astronomisches Rechen-Institut Heidelberg, No. **17**, G. Braun, Karlsruhe, 27 pp

Charlot, P. (1990a): Radio-Source Structure in Astrometric and Geodetic Very Long Baseline Interferometry. Astron. J. **99**, 1309–1326

Charlot, P. (1990b): Fourteen Extragalactic Radio Sources Mapped at 2.3 and 8.4 GHz with a 24-hour Crustal Dynamics Program VLBI Experiment. Astron. Astrophys. **229**, 51–63

Charlot, P. (1994): Evidence for Source Structure Effects Caused by the Quasar 3C 273 in Geodetic VLBI Data. *URSI/IAU Symposium on VLBI Technology – Progress and Future Observational Possibilities*, T. Sasao, S. Manabe, O. Kawaya, M. Inoue (eds.). Terra Scientific, Tokyo, 287–294

Charlot, P., Sovers, O.J., Williams, J.G., Newhall, X X (1995): Precession and Nutation from Joint Analysis of Radio Interferometric and Lunar Laser Ranging Observations. Astron. J. **109**, 418–427

Chen, G., Herring, T.A. (1997): Effects of Atmospheric Azimuthal Asymmetry on the Analysis of Space Geodetic Data. J. Geophys. Res. **102**, 20489–20502

Christiansen, W.N., Högbom, J.A. (1985): *Radio Telescopes.* Cambridge University Press, Cambridge

Clark, T.A. (1980): Mark III System Overview. In: *Radio Interferometry Techniques for Geodesy*, NASA Conference Publication 2115, NASA Scientific and Technical Information Office, 285–290

Clark, T.A., Corey, B.E., Davis, J.L. et al. (1985): Precision Geodesy Using the Mark-III Very-Long-Baseline Interferometer System. IEEE Trans. Geosci. Remote Sensing, GE–23, 438–449

Clemence, G.M. (1966): Inertial Frames of Reference. Quarterly J. R. Astron. Soc. **7**, 10–21

Cohen, M.H., Shaffer, D.B. (1971): Positions of Radio Sources from Long-Baseline Interferometry. Astron. J. **76**, 91–100

Cohen, M.H., Jauncey, D.L., Kellermann, K.I., Clark, B.G. (1968): Radio Interferometry at One-Thousandth Second of Arc. Science **162**, 88–94

Collins, C.B., Hawking, S.W. (1973): The Rotation and Distortion of the Universe. Mon. Not. R. Astron. Soc. **162**, 307–320

Corbin, T.E. (1974): Base System of Proper Motions for the AGK 3R. Astron. J. **79**, 885–889

Corbin, T.E. (1985): The Determination of Fundamental Proper Motions. In: *Calibration of Fundamental Stellar Quantities, IAU Symposium No. 111*, D.S. Hayes, L.E. Pasinetti, A.G. Davis Philip (eds.). Reidel, Dordrecht Boston, 53–70

Corbin, E.T., Schwan, H. (1991): Present Status of the Work on the FK5 Extension. In: *Reference Systems, IAU Colloquium No. 127*, J.A. Hughes, C.A. Smith, G.H. Kaplan (eds.). United States Naval Observatory, Washington, D.C., 238–241

Corbin, T.E., Urban, S.E. (1990): Faint Reference Stars. In: *Inertial Coordinate System on the Sky, IAU Symposium No. 141*, J.H. Lieske, V.K. Abalakin (eds.). Kluwer, Dordrecht Boston London, 433–442

CORE (1999): lupus.gsfc.nasa.gov/core

Counselman III, C.C. (1976): Radio Astrometry. Ann. Rev. Astron. Astrophys. **14**, 197–214

Danjon, A. (1960): The Impersonal Astrolabe. In: *Stars and Stellar Systems, Vol. I, Telescopes*, G.P. Kuiper, B.M. Middlehurst (eds.). The University of Chicago Press, Chicago London, 115–137

Danjon, A. (1980): *Astronomie Générale*, Seconde Edition. Librairie Scientifique et Technique, Albert Blanchard, Paris

de Sitter, W., Brouwer, D. (1938): On the System of Astronomical Constants. Bull. Astron. Inst. Neth. **8**, 213–231

Deutsch, A.N. (1954): Utilisation des Objets Extra-galactiques pour l'établissement d'un Système Absolu des Mouvements Propres des Étoiles. Transactions of the International Astronomical Union, Vol. VIII, P.Th. Oosterhoff (ed.). Cambridge University Press, Cambridge, 789–794

Edge, D.O., Shakeshaft, J.R., McAdam, W.B. et al. (1959): A Survey of Radio Sources at a Frequency of 159 Mc/s. Mem. R. Astron. Soc. **68**, 37–60

Eichhorn, H. (1974): *Astronomy of Star Positions.* Frederick Ungar, New York

ESA (1989): The Hipparcos Mission. Vol. I–III, ESA SP-1111, European Space Agency, Paris

ESA (1992): The Hipparcos Input Catalogue. Vols. **1–7**, ESA SP-1136, European Space Agency, Paris

ESA (1997): The Hipparcos Catalogue. Vols. **1–17**, ESA SP-1200, European Space Agency, Paris

Eubanks, T.M., Matsakis, D.N., Josties, F.J. et al. (1995): Secular Motions of Extragalactic Radio-Sources and the Stability of the Radio Reference Frame. In: *Astronomical and Astrophysical Objectives of Sub-Milliarcsecond Optical Astrometry, IAU Symp. No. 166*, E. Høg, P.K. Seidelmann (eds.). Kluwer, Dordrecht Boston London, 283

Fallon, F.W., Dillinger, W.H. (1992): Crustal Velocities from Geodetic Very Long Baseline Interferometry. J. Geophys. Res. **97**, 7129–7136

Fanselow, J.L., Sovers, O.J., Thomas, J.B. et al. (1984): Radio Interferometric Determination of Source Positions Utilizing Deep Space Network Antennas: 1971 to 1980. Astron. J. **89**, 987–998

Fatchikhin, N.V. (1970): Some Determinations at Pulkovo of Absolute Stellar Proper Motions Relative to Galaxies. Astron. Zhurn. Akad. Nauk SSSR **47**, 619–632. English transl. in Soviet Astron. AJ **14**, 495–504

Fey, A.L., Charlot, P. (1997): VLBA Observations of Radio Reference Frame Sources. II. Astrometric Suitability Based on Observed Structure. Astrophys. J. Suppl. Ser. **111**, 95–142

Fey, A.L., Charlot, P. (2000): VLBA Observations of Radio Reference Frame Sources. III. Astrometric Suitability of an Additional 225 Sources. Accepted for publication in Astrophys. J. Suppl. Ser.

Fey, A.L., Clegg, A.W., Fomalont, E.B. (1996): VLBA Observations of Radio Reference Frame Sources. I. Astrophys. J. Suppl. Ser. **105**, 299–330

Florkowski, D.R., Johnston, K.J., Wade, C.M., de Vegt, C. (1985): Stellar Radio Astrometry I. Precise Positions of the Radio Emission of Twenty Stars. Astron. J. **90**, 2381–2386

Folkner, W.M., Charlot, P., Finger, M.H. et al. (1994): Determination of the Extragalactic-Planetary Frame Tie from Joint Analysis of Radio Interferometric and Lunar Laser Ranging Measurements. Astron. Astrophys. **287**, 279–289

Fomalont, E.B., Goss, W.M., Lyne, A.G. et al. (1992): Positions and Proper Motions of Pulsars. Mon. Not. R. Astron. Soc. **258**, 497–510

Fricke, W. (1967): Precession and Galactic Rotation Derived from Fundamental Proper Motions of Distant Stars. Astron. J. **72**, 1368–1379

Fricke, W. (1972): Fundamental Systems of Positions and Proper Motions. Ann. Rev. Astron. Astrophys., **10**, 101–128

Fricke, W. (1974): Plans for the Improvement and Extension of the FK4. In: *New Problems in Astrometry, IAU Symposium No. 61*, W. Gliese, C.A. Murray, R.H. Tucker (eds.). Reidel, Dordrecht Boston, 23–30

Fricke, W. (1977): Basic Material for the Determination of Precession and of Galactic Rotation and a Review of Methods and Results. Veröffentlichungen Astronomisches Rechen-Institut Heidelberg, No. **28**, G. Braun, Karlsruhe, 52 pp

Fricke, W. (1981): Definition and Practical Realization of the Reference Frame in the FK5. In: *Reference Coordinate Systems for Earth Dynamics, IAU Colloquium No. 56*, E.M. Gaposchkin, B. Kołaczek (eds.). Kluwer, Dordrecht Boston London, 331–340

Fricke, W. (1982): Determination of the Equinox and Equator of the FK5. Astron. Astrophys. **107**, L13–L16

Fricke, W. (1985): Fundamental Catalogues, Past, Present and Future. Celestial Mechanics **36**, 207–239

Fricke, W., Gliese, W. (1968): Desiderata for FK5. In: *Highlights of Astronomy*, L. Perek (ed.). Reidel, Dordrecht, 301–305

Fricke, W., Kopff, A. (1963): Fourth Fundamental Catalogue (FK4). Veröffentlichungen Astronomisches Rechen-Institut Heidelberg, No. **10**, G. Braun, Karlsruhe, 144 pp

Fricke, W., Schwan, H., Lederle, T. et al. (1988): Fifth Fundamental Catalogue (FK5), Part I: The Basic Fundamental Stars. Veröffentlichungen Astronomisches Rechen-Institut Heidelberg, No. **32**. G. Braun, Karlsruhe, 106 pp

Fricke, W., Schwan, H., Corbin, T. et al. (1991): Fifth Fundamental Catalogue (FK5), Part II: The FK5 Extension - New Fundamental Stars. Veröffentlichungen Astronomisches Rechen-Institut Heidelberg, No. **33**. G. Braun, Karlsruhe, 143 pp

Froeschlé, M., Kovalevsky, J. (1982): The Connection of a Catalogue of Stars with an Extragalactic Reference Frame. Astron. Astrophys. **116**, 89–94

Giovannini, G., Cotton, W.D., Feretti, L. et al. (1998): VLBI Observations of a Complete Sample of Radio Galaxies. VIII. Proper Motion in 3C 338. Astrophys. J. **493**, 632–640

Green, R.M. (1985): *Spherical Astronomy*. University Press, Cambridge

Grossmann, W. (1969): *Grundzüge der Ausgleichungsrechnung*, 3rd ed. Springer, Berlin Heidelberg New York

Guinot, B. (1979): Basic Problems in the Kinematics of the Rotation of the Earth. In: *Time and the Earth's Rotation, IAU Symp. No. 82*, D.D. McCarthy, J.D.H. Pilkington (eds.). Kluwer, Dordrecht Boston London, 7–18

Guirado, J.C., Marcaide, J.M., Elosegui, P. et al. (1995): VLBI Differential Astrometry of the Radio Sources 1928+738 and 2007+777 at 5 GHz. Astron. Astrophys. **293**, 613–625

Gwinn, C.R., Eubanks, T.M, Pyne, T. et al. (1997): Quasar Proper Motions and Low-frequency Gravitational Waves. Astrophys. J. **485**, 87–91

Hall, D.N.B. (1982): The Space Telescope Observatory. NASA CP-2244, NASA Scientific and Technical Information Branch, 134 pp

Hazard, C., Sutton, J., Argue, A.N. et al. (1971): Accurate Radio and Optical Positions of 3C 273B. Nature Phys. Sci. **233**, 89–91

Herring, T.A., Gwinn, C.R., Shapiro, I.I. (1986): Geodesy by Radio Interferometry: Studies of the Forced Nutations of the Earth. Part I: Data Analysis. J. Geophys. Res. **91**, 4745–4754. A correction to this paper in the same volume, p. 14165

Herschel, W. (1785): Construction of the Heavens. Phil. Trans. Roy. Soc. of London **75**, 213–266

Hofmann-Wellenhof, B., Lichtenegger, H., Collins, J. (1997): *GPS Theory and Practice*, 4th ed. Springer, Wien New York

Hogg, D.E., Macdonald, G.H., Conway, R.G., Wade, C.M. (1985): Synthesis of Brightness Distribution in Radio Sources. Astron. J. **74**, 1206–1213

Hohenkerk, C.Y., Yallop, B.D., Smith, C.A., Sinclair, A.T. (1992): Celestial Reference Systems. In: *Explanatory Supplement to the Astronomical Almanac*, P.K. Seidelmann (ed.). University Science Books, Mill Valley, California, 95–198

Horner, S.D., Germain, M.E., Greene, T.P. et al. (1999): Full-sky Astrometric Mapping Explorer - Astrometry for the New Millenium. In: *Working on the Fringe*, S.C. Unwin, R.V. Stachnik (eds.). ASP Conference Series, San Francisco, California, Vol. 194, 114–120

Hughes, J.A., Scott, D.K. (1982): Results of Observations Made with the Six-Inch Transit Circle 1963-1971. Publ. U.S. Naval Obs. Sec. Series, Vol. XXIII - Part III

IAG (1988): Geodesist's Handbook. Bull. Géod. **62**, 337–340

IAU (1974): (a) Resolution of the IAU Symposium No. 61 'New Problems in Astrometry', (b) Nomenclature of Faint Galaxies and Other Objects. Transactions of the International Astronomical Union, Vol. XV B, G. Cantopoulos, A. Jappel (eds.). Reidel, Dordrecht

IAU (1977): Commission 4: Recommendations to the IAU General Assembly, 1976. Transactions of the International Astronomical Union, Vol. XVI B, E.A. Müller, A. Jappel (eds.). Reidel, Dordrecht, 58–67

IAU (1992): Resolution A4: Recommendations from the Working Group on Reference Systems. Transactions of the International Astronomical Union, Vol. XXI B, J. Bergeron (ed.). Kluwer, Dordrecht Boston London, 41–52

IAU (1996): Resolution No. B5 on the Working Group on Reference Frames. Transactions of the International Astronomical Union, Vol. XXII B, I. Appenzeller (ed.). Kluwer, Dordrecht Boston London, 27–43

IAU (1999): Resolution B2 'On the International Celestial Reference System (ICRS)', Transactions of the International Astronomical Union, Vol. XXIII B, J. Andersen (ed.), Kluwer, Dordrecht Boston London, 39

IERS (1992): IERS Standards (1992). D.D. McCarthy (ed.), IERS Technical Note No. 13, Observatoire de Paris, 150 pp

IERS (1994a): Implementation of the IERS Celestial Reference Frame. 1993 IERS Annual Report, Observatoire de Paris, II-23–II-41

IERS (1994b): Earth Orientation, Reference Frames and Atmospheric Excitation Functions submitted for the 1993 IERS Annual Report. P. Charlot (ed.), IERS Technical Note No. 17, Observatoire de Paris

IERS (1995a): Implementation of the IERS Celestial Reference Frame. 1994 IERS Annual Report, Observatoire de Paris, II-23–II-41

IERS (1995b): Earth Orientation, Reference Frames and Atmospheric Excitation Functions Submitted for the 1994 IERS Annual Report. P. Charlot (ed.), IERS Tech. Note No. 19, Observatoire de Paris

IERS (1996a): Celestial Reference Frame. 1995 IERS Annual Report, Observatoire de Paris, II-19–II-45

IERS (1996b): The IERS Conventions (1996). D.D. McCarthy (ed.), IERS Tech. Note No. 21, Observatoire de Paris, 95 pp

IERS (1996c): Terrestrial Reference Frame. 1995 IERS Annual Report, Observatoire de Paris, II-47–II-59

IERS (1997): Definition and Realization of the International Celestial Reference System by VLBI Astrometry of Extragalactic Objects. C. Ma, M. Feissel (eds.), IERS Tech. Note No. 23, Observatoire de Paris

IERS (1998): Results and Analysis of the ITRF96. C. Boucher, Z. Altamimi, P. Sillard (eds.), IERS Tech. Note No. 24, Observatoire de Paris

IERS (1999): Celestial Reference System and Frame (ICRF-Ext. 1). 1998 IERS Annual Report, Observatoire de Paris, 83–128

Ilin, A.E., Butkevich, A.G., Chubey, M.S. et al. (1997): Project STRUVE. In: *HIPPARCOS Venice '97*, ESA SP-402, B. Battrick (ed.). European Space Agency, Paris, 831–833

IVS (1999): International VLBI Service, 1999 Annual Report. NASA/TP 1999-209243, N.R. Vandenberg (ed.). NASA Center for Aerospace Information, Hanover, MD, 308 pp. Also ivscc.gsfc.nasa.gov

Jacobs, C.S., Sovers, O.J., Gordon, D. et al. (1998a): The Accuracy of the ICRF: An Intercomparison of VLBI Analysis Software. In: *Highlights of Astronomy*, Vol. 11 A, J. Anderson (ed.). Kluwer, Dordrecht Boston London, 320–321

Jacobs, C.S., Sovers, O.J., Naudet, C.J. et al. (1998b): The JPL Extragalactic Reference Frame: Astrometric Results of 1978-96 Deep Space Network VLBI. *Telecommunications and Mission Operations Prog. Rept. 42-133*, pp. 1–55, Jet Propulsion Laboratory, Pasadena, CA

Jahreiss, H., Réquième, Y., Argue, A.N. et al. (1992): The Hipparcos Input Catalogue. II. Astrometric data. Astron. Astrophys. **258**, 82–87

Johnston, K.J., de Vegt, C. (1999): Reference Frames in Astronomy. Ann. Rev. Astron. Astrophys. **37**, 97–125

Johnston, K.J., Seidelmann, P.K., Wade, C.M. (1982): Observations of 1 Ceres and 2 Pallas at Centimeter Wavelengths. Astron. J. **87**, 1593–1599

Johnston, K.J., Fey, A.L., Zacharias, N. et al. (1995): A Radio Reference Frame. Astron. J. **110**, 880–915

Kahn, R., Thurman, S., Edwards, C.D. (1994): Spacecraft-Spacecraft Radiometric Tracking: Signal Acquisition Requirements and Application to Mars Approach Navigation. *Telecommunications and Data Acquisition Prog. Rept. 42-117*, pp. 161–174, Jet Propulsion Laboratory, Pasadena, CA

Kaplan, G.H., Josties, F.J., Angerhofer, P.E. et al. (1982): Precise Radio Source Positions from Interferometric Observations. Astron. J. **87**, 570–576

Keihm, S.J., Marsh, K.A. (1996): Advanced Algorithm and System Development for Cassini Radio Science Tropospheric Calibration. *Telecommunications and Data Acquisition Prog. Rept. 42-127*, pp. 1–20, Jet Propulsion Laboratory, Pasadena, CA

Kellermann, K.I., Owen, F.N. (1988): Radio Galaxies and Quasars. In: *Galactic and Extragalactic Radio Astronomy*, G.L. Verschuur, K.I. Kellermann (eds.). Springer, Berlin Heidelberg New York, 563–602

Kellermann, K.I., Pauliny-Toth, I.I.K. (1981): Compact Radio Sources. Ann. Rev. Astron. Astrophys. **19**, 373–410

Kellermann, K.I., Thompson, A.R. (1985): The Very Long Baseline Array. Science **229**, 123–130

Kellermann, K.I., Sramek, R.A., Schmidt, M. et al. (1994): The Radio Structure of Radio Loud and Radio Quiet Quasars in the Palomar Bright Quasar Survey. Astron. J. **108**, 1163–1177

Kerr, F.J., Lynden-Bell, D. (1986): Review of Galactic Constants. Mon. Not. R. Astron. Soc. **221**, 1023–1038

Kinoshita, H., Souchay, J. (1990): The Theory of the Nutation for the Rigid Earth Model at the Second Order. Celestial Mechanics **48**, 187–265

Kogut, A., Lineweaver, C., Smoot, G.F. et al. (1993): Dipole Anisotropy in the COBE Differential Microwave Radiometers First-Year Sky Maps. Astrophys. J. **419**, 1–6

Kopff, A. (1937): Dritter Fundamentalkatalog des Berliner Astronomischen Jahrbuchs, I. Teil: Die Auwers-Sterne für die Epochen 1925 und 1950. Veröffentl. des Astron. Rechen-Instituts zu Berlin, No. **54**, 117 pp

Kopff, A. (1938): Dritter Fundamentalkatalog des Berliner Astronomischen Jahrbuchs, II.Teil: Die Zusatzsterne. Abh. d. Preuss. Akad. der Wissensch., math.-naturwiss. Klasse, No. **3**

Kovalevsky, J. (1995a): Conclusions. In: *Astronomical and Astrophysical Objectives of Sub-Milliarcsecond Optical Astrometry, IAU Symp. No. 166*, E. Høg, P.K. Seidelmann (eds.). Kluwer, Dordrecht Boston London, 409–432

Kovalevsky, J. (1995b): *Modern Astrometry.* Springer, Berlin Heidelberg New York

Kovalevsky, J., Mueller, I.I. (1989): Introduction. In: *Reference Frames in Astronomy and Geophysics*, J. Kovalevsky, I.I. Mueller, B.Kolaczek (eds.). Kluwer, Dordrecht Boston London, 1–12

Kovalevsky, J., Falin, J.L., Pieplu, J.L. et al. (1992): The FAST Hipparcos Data Reduction Consortium: Overview of the Reduction Software. Astron. Astrophys. **258**, 7–17

Kovalevsky, J., Lindegren, L., Froeschlé et al. (1995): Construction of the Intermediate Hipparcos Astrometric Catalogue. Astron. Astrophys. **304**, 34–43

Kovalevsky, J., Lindegren, L., Perryman, M.A.C. et al. (1997): The Hipparcos Catalogue as a realization of the extragalactic reference system. Astron. Astrophys. **323**, 620–633

Kraus, J.D. (1966): *Radio Astronomy.* McGraw-Hill Book Co., New York Toronto London

Kraus, J.D. (1977): The Ohio Sky Survey and Other Radio surveys. Vistas in Astronomy **20**, 445–474

Lattanzi, M.G., Bucciarelli, B., Bernacca, P.L. (1990): On the Problem of the Hipparcos Reference Frame. Aph. J. Suppl. **73**, 481–488

Laubscher, R.E. (1972): A Determination of the Motion of the Ecliptic. Astron. Astrophys. **20**, 407–414

Laubscher, R.E. (1976a): Dynamical Determinations of the General Precession in Longitude. Astron. Astrophys. **51**, 9–12

Laubscher, R.E. (1976b): Dynamical Determinations of the General Precession in Longitude. Astron. Astrophys. **51**, 13–20

Lawson, C.L., Hanson, R.J. (1974): *Solving Least-Squares Problems.* Prentice Hall, Englewood Cliffs, New Jersey

Lebach, D.E., Corey, B.E., Shapiro, I.I. et al. (1995): Measurement of the Solar Gravitational Deflection of Radio Waves Using Very-Long Baseline Interferometry. Phys. Rev. Lett. **75**, 1439–1442

Lederle, T., Schwan, H. (1984): Procedure for Computing the Apparent Places of Fundamental Stars (APFS) from 1984 Onwards. Astron. Astrophys. **134**, 1–6

Lestrade, J.-F., Jones, D.L., Preston, R.A. et al. (1995): Preliminary Link of the Hipparcos and VLBI Reference Frames. Astron. Astrophys. **304**, 182–188

Lestrade, J.-F., Preston, R.A., Jones, D.L. et al. (1999): High-precision VLBI Astrometry of Radio-emitting Stars. Astron. Astrophys. **344**, 1014–1026

Lieske, J.H. (1979): Precession Matrix Based on IAU(1976) System of Astronomical Constants. Astron. Astrophys. **73**, 282–284

Lieske, J.H. (1985): The Evolution of Adopted Values for Precession. Celestial Mechanics **37**, 209–238

Lieske, J.H., Lederle, T., Fricke, W., Morando, B. (1977): Expressions for the Precession Quantities Based upon the IAU (1976) System of Astronomical Constants. Astron. Astrophys. **58**, 1–16

Lindegren, L. (1991): Hipparcos Data Reduction Overview. Adv. Space Res., **11**, No. 2, (2)25–(2)34

Lindegren, L. (1998): Hipparcos and the Future: GAIA. In: *The Message of the Angles – Astrometry from 1798 to 1998*, P. Brosche, W.R. Dick, O. Schwarz, R. Wielen (eds.). Verlag Harri Deutsch, Frankfurt a.M., 214–222

Lindegren, L., Kovalevsky, J. (1995): Linking the Hipparcos Catalogue to the Extragalactic Reference System. Astron. Astrophys. **304**, 189–301

Lindegren, L., Høg, E., van Leeuwen, F. et al. (1992): The NDAC Hipparcos Data Analysis Consortium. Astron. Astrophys. **258**, 18–30

Longair, M.S. (1979): The Space Telescope and its Opportunities. Quarterly J. R. Astron. Soc. **20**, 5–28

Lortet, M.-C., Borde, S., Ochsenbein, F. (1994): Second Reference Dictionary of the Nomenclature of Celestial Objects. Astron. Astrophys. Suppl. Ser. **107**, 193–218

Ma, C., Shaffer, D.B., de Vegt, C. et al. (1990): A Radio Optical Reference Frame. I. Precise Radio Source Positions Determined by Mark III VLBI: Observations from 1979 to 1988 and a Tie to the FK5. Astron. J. **99**, 1284–1298

Ma, C., Arias, E.F., Eubanks, T.M. et al. (1997): The International Celestial Reference Frame Realized by VLBI. In: *Definition and Realization of the International Celestial Reference System by VLBI Astrometry of Extragalactic Objects*, C. Ma, M. Feissel (eds.). IERS Tech. Note No. 23, Observatoire de Paris, II-3–II-44

Ma, C., Arias, E.F., Eubanks, T.M. et al. (1998): The International Celestial Reference Frame based on VLBI Observations of Extragalactic Radio Sources. Astron. J. **116**, 516–546

Mach, E. (1893): *Die Mechanik, historisch-kritisch dargestellt.* English translation of Seventh Edition, Brockhaus, Leipzig 1912 published in 1960 as *The Science of Mechanics.* Open Court, La Salle, Illinois

MacMillan, D.S. (1995): Atmospheric Gradients from Very Long Baseline Interferometry Observations. Geophys. Res. Lett. **22**, 1041–1044

MacMillan, D.S., Ma, C. (1997): Atmospheric Gradients and the VLBI Terrestrial and Celestial Reference Frames. Geophys. Res. Lett. **24**, 453–456

Manabe, S., Yokoyama, K. (1994): Analysis of VLBI Observations. In: *IERS Technical Note 17*, P.Charlot (ed.). Observatoire de Paris, R-33–R-36

Martin, C.F., van Flandern, T.C. (1970): Secular Changes in the Lunar Elements. Science **168**, 246–247

Marton, L. (ed.) (1976): *Methods of Experimental Physics*, Vol. 12, Astrophysics, Part C: Radio Observations, M.L. Meeks (ed.). Academic Press, New York San Francisco London

Matthews, T.A., Sandage, A. (1963): Optical Identification of 3C 48, 3C 196, and 3C 286 with Stellar Objects. Astrophys. J. **138**, 30–56

Melchiorri, B., Melchiorri, F. (1990): Future Programs in Background Astronomy. In: *The Cosmic Microwave Background: 25 Years Later*, N. Mandolesi, N. Vittorio (eds.) Kluwer, Dordrecht Boston London, 241–254

MERLIN (2000): www.jb.man.ac.uk/merlin

Mignard, F., Froeschlé, M. (1997): Comparison of the FK5 Frame to Hipparcos. In: *HIPPARCOS Venice '97*, ESA SP-402, B. Battrick (ed.). European Space Agency, Paris, 57–60

Mignard, F., Froeschlé, M., Badiali, M. et al. (1992): Hipparcos Double Star Recognition and Processing within the FAST Consortium. Astron. Astrophys. **258**, 165–172

Misner, Ch.W., Thorne, K.S., Wheeler, J.A. (1973): *Gravitation.* W.H. Freeman and Co., San Francisco

Moran, J.M. (1975): Geodetic and Astrometric Results of Very Long-baseline Interferometric Measurements of Natural Radio Sources. In: *COSPAR Space Research XV*, M.J. Rycroft (ed.). Akademie-Verlag Berlin, 33–47

Morgan, H.R. (1952): Catalogue of 5268 Standard Stars. Astron. Papers Americ. Ephem. and Nautical Almanac **13**, Part 3

Morrison, L.V. (1982): Analysis of Lunar Occultations - IV. Rotation of the FK4 Reference Frame. Mon. Not. R. Astron. Soc. **198**, 1119–1125

Morrison, L.V., Argyle, R.W., Requième, Y. et al. (1990): Comparison of FK5 with Bordeaux and Carlsberg Meridian Circle Observations. Astron. Astrophys. **240**, 173–177

Morrison, L.V., Garrington, S.T., Argyle, R.W., Davis, R.J. (1997): Future Control of the Hipparcos Frame Using MERLIN. In: *HIPPARCOS Venice '97*, ESA SP-402, B. Battrick (ed.). European Space Agency, Paris, 143–145

Muhleman, D.O., Berge, G.L., Rudy, D.J. et al. (1985): Precise Position Measurements of Jupiter, Saturn and Uranus Systems with the Very Large Array. Celestial Mechanics **37**, 329–337

Murray, C.A. (1976): The Astrometric Reference Frame. Observatory **96**, 90–97

Murray, C.A. (1983): *Vectorial Astrometry.* Adam Hilger Ltd, Bristol

Murray, C.A. (1989): The Transformation of Coordinates Between the Systems of B1950.0 and J2000.0, and the Principal Galactic Axes Referred to J2000.0. Astron. Astrophys. **218**, 325–329

Newcomb, S. (1898a): A New Determination of the Precessional Constant with the Resulting Motions. Astron. Papers Americ. Ephem. and Nautical Almanac **8**, Part 1, 1–76

Newcomb, S. (1898b): Catalogue of Fundamental Stars for the Epochs 1875 and 1900, Reduced to an Absolute System. Astron. Papers Americ. Ephem. and Nautical Almanac **8**, Part 2, 77–403

Newhall, X X, Preston, R.A., Esposito, P.B. (1986): Relating the JPL VLBI Reference Frame and the Planetary Ephemerides. In: *Astrometric Techniques, IAU Symp. No. 109*, H.K. Eichhorn, R.J. Leacock (eds.). Kluwer, Dordrecht Boston London, 789–794

Niell, A.E. (1996): Global Mapping Functions for the Atmosphere Delay at Radio Wavelengths. J. Geophys. Res. **101**, 3227–3246

Oort, J.H. (1927): Observational Evidence Confirming Lindblad's Hypothesis of a Rotation of the Galactic System. Bull. Astron. Inst. Neth. **3**, 275–282

Patnaik, A., Browne, I.W.A., Wilkinson, P.N., Wrobel, J.M. (1992): Interferometer Phase Calibration Sources, I – The Region 35–75 deg. Mon. Not. R. Astron. Soc., **254**, 655–676

Pearson, T.J., Perley, R.A., Readhead, A.C.S. (1985): Compact Radio Sources in the 3C Catalogue. Astron. J. **90**, 738–755

Perryman, M.A.C., Høg, E., Kovalevsky, J. et al. (1992): In-orbit Performance of the Hipparcos Astrometry Satellite. Astron. Astrophys. **258**, 1–6

Perryman, M.A.C., Lindegren, L., Turon, C. (1997): The Scientific Goals of the GAIA Mission. In: *HIPPARCOS Venice '97*, ESA SP-402, B. Battrick (ed.). European Space Agency, Paris, 743–748

Peters, J. (1907): Neuer Fundamentalkatalog des Berliner Astronomischen Jahrbuchs nach den Grundlagen von A. Auwers für die Epochen 1875 und 1900. Veröffentl. d. Königl. Astron. Rechen-Instituts zu Berlin, No. **33**, 116 pp

Peterson, D., Shao, M. (1997): The Scientific Basis for the Space Interferometry Mission. In: *HIPPARCOS Venice '97*, ESA SP-402, B. Battrick (ed.). European Space Agency, Paris, 749–753

Podobed, V.V. (1965): *Fundamental Astrometry*. The Univ. of Chicago Press, Chicago London

Pyne, T., Gwinn, C.R., Birkinshaw, M. et al. (1996): Gravitational Radiation and Very Long Baseline Interferometry. Astrophys. J. **465**, 566–577

Reid, M.J. (1993): The Distance to the Center of the Galaxy. Ann. Rev. Astron. Astrophys. **31**, 345–372

Robertson, D.S., Fallon, F.W., Carter, W.E. (1986): Celestial Reference Coordinate Systems: Sub-millisecond of Arc Repeatability Demonstrated with VLBI Observations. Astron. J. **91**, 1456–1462

Robertson, D.S., Carter, W.E., Ray, J.R. et al. (1993): Extending the VLBI Celestial Reference Frame to the Southern Hemisphere. Astron. J. **105**, 353–358

Rogers, A.E.E. (1970): Very Long Baseline Interferometry with Large Effective Bandwidth for Phase-delay Measurements. Radio Science **5, No. 10**, 1229–1249

Rogers, A.E.E., Cappalo, R.J., Hinteregger, H.F. et al. (1983): Very-Long-Baseline Interferometry: The Mark III System for Geodesy, Astrometry, and Aperture Synthesis. Science **219**, 51–54

Rohlfs, K., Wilson, T.L. (2000): *Tools of Radio Astronomy*, Third Edition. Springer, Berlin Heidelberg New York

Ronnang, B.O. (1989): Geodesy - VLBI Observables. In: *Very Long Baseline Interferometry, Techniques and Applications*, M. Felli, R.E. Spencer (eds.). NATO ASI Series, Series C, Vol. 283. Kluwer, Dordrecht Boston London, 289–302

Ryan, J.W., Clark, T.A., Ma, C. et al. (1993): Global Scale Tectonic Plate Motions Measured with CDP VLBI Data. In: *Contributions of Space Geodesy to Geodynamics: Earth Dynamics*, D.E. Smith, D.L. Turcotte (eds.). Geodynamics Series, Vol. 23, Amer. Geophys. Union, Washington, D.C., 37–49

Ryle, M., Elsmore, B. (1973): Astrometry with the 5-km Radio Telescope. Mon. Not. R. Astron. Soc. **164**, 223–242

Sachs, L. (1972): *Statistische Auswertungsmethoden*. Springer, Berlin Heidelberg New York

Schaub, W. (1950): *Vorlesungen über sphärische Astronomie*. Akademische Verlagsgesellschaft, Geest & Portig, Leipzig

Schmeidler, F. (1965): Methods in Meridian Astronomy. Vistas in Astronomy **6**, 69–91

Schmeidler, F. (1980): Die Geschichte der Fundamentalkataloge. In: *Astrometrie und Dynamische Astronomie*, W. Fricke, Th. Schmidt-Kaler, W. Seggewiß (eds.). Mitteilungen der Astronomischen Gesellschaft, No. **48**, Hamburg, 11–23

Schmidt, M. (1963): 3C 273: A Star-Like Object with Large Red-Shift. Nature **197** 1040

Schödlbauer, A. (2000): *Geodätische Astronomie*. de Gruyter, Berlin New York

Schreiber, U., Schneider, M., Stedman, G.E., Schlüter, W. (1999): Characteristics of a Ring Laser for Geodesy. In: *Proceedings of the 13th Working Meeting on European VLBI for Geodesy and Astrometry*, held in Viechtach/Wettzell, Germany, February 12–13, 1999, W. Schlüter, H. Hase (eds.). Verlag Bundesamt für Kartographie and Geodäsie, Frankfurt am Main, 278–284

Schwan, H. (1977): Development and Testing of a Method to Derive an Instrumental System of Positions and Proper Motions of Stars. Veröffentlichungen Astronomisches Rechen-Institut Heidelberg, No. **27**, G. Braun, Karlsruhe, 36 pp

Schwan, H. (1983): A Method for the Determination of a System of Positions and Proper Motions of Stars with an Application to the Washington 6 Inch TC Observations. Veröffentlichungen Astronomisches Rechen-Institut Heidelberg, No. **30**, G. Braun, Karlsruhe, 47 pp

Schwan, H. (1988a): Construction of the System of Positions and Proper Motions in the FK5. In: *Mapping the Sky, IAU Symp. No. 133*, S. Débarbat, J.A. Eddy, H.K. Eichhorn, A.R. Upgren (eds.). Kluwer, Dordrecht Boston London, 151–157

Schwan, H. (1988b): Precession and Galactic Rotation in the System of the FK5. Astron. Astrophys. **198**, 116–124

Schwan, H. (1993): Completion of the FK5 Extension and a Preliminary Investigation of the FK5 System. In: *Developments in Astrometry and Their Impact on Astrophysics and Geodynamics, IAU Symp. No. 156*, I.I. Mueller, B. Kołaczek (eds.). Kluwer, Dordrecht Boston London, 339–350

Schwan, H. (1999): Comparison of the FK5 and Hipparcos Catalogues. Astronomisches Rechen-Institut Heidelberg, private communication

Seidelmann P.K. (1982): 1980 IAU Theory of Nutation: The Final Report of the IAU Working Group on Nutation. Celestial Mechanics **27**, 79–106

Seidelmann, P.K., Guinot, B., Doggett, L.E. (1992): Time. In: *Explanatory Supplement to the Astronomical Almanac*, P.K. Seidelmann (ed.). University Science Books, Mill Valley, California, 39–93

Seidelmann, P.K., Johnston, K.J., Urban, S. et al. (1995): A Fizeau Optical Interferometer Astrometric Satellite. In: *Future Possibilities for Astrometry in Space, A Joint RGO-ESA Workshop*, Cambridge, UK, 19-21 June 1995, ESA SP-379, T.D. Guyenne (ed.). European Space Agency, Paris, 187–189

Shao, M., Colavita, M.M. (1992): Long-Baseline Optical and Infrared Stellar Interferometry. Ann. Rev. Astron. Astrophys., **30**, 457–498

Shapiro I.I. (1964): Fourth Test of General Relativity. Physical Rev. Letters, **13**, 789–791

Shapiro I.I. (1967): New Method for the Determination of Light Deflection by Solar Gravity. Science, **157**, 806–808

Shapiro, I.I. (1976): Estimation of Astrometric and Geodetic Parameters. In: *Methods of Experimental Physics*, Vol. 12, Astrophysics, Part C: Radio Observations, M.L. Meeks (ed.). Academic Press, New York, 261–276

Shapiro, I.I., Wittels, J.J., Counselman III et al. (1979): Submilliarcsecond Astrometry Via VLBI: I. Relative Position of the Radio Sources 3C 345 and NRAO 512. Astron. J. **84**, 1459–1469

SIM (1999): Space Interferometry Mission. NASA, Jet Propulsion Laboratory, JPL 400-811 3/99, R. Danner, S. Unwin (eds.). Jet Propulsion Laboratory, Pasadena, California, 139 pp

Smart, W.N. (1953): *Celestial Mechanics.* Longmans, Green and Co., London New York Toronto

Smith, C.A. (1980): The International Reference Star Programs. In: *Astrometrie und dynamische Astronomie*, W. Fricke, Th. Schmidt-Kaler, W. Seggewiß (eds.). Mitteilungen der Astronomischen Gesellschaft, No. **48**, Hamburg, 95–108

Smith, C.A., Kaplan, G.H., Hughes, J.A. et al. (1989): Mean and Apparent Place Computations in the New IAU System. I. The Transformation of Astrometric Catalog Systems to the Equinox J2000.0. Astron. J. **97**, 265–273

Smith, C.A., Corbin, T.E., Hughes, J.A. et al. (1990): The SRS Catalog of 20488 Star Positions, Culmination of an International Cooperative Effort. In: *Inertial Coordinate System on the Sky, IAU Symposium No. 141*, J.H. Lieske, V.K. Abalakin (eds.). Kluwer, Dordrecht Boston London, 457–463

Söderhjelm, S., Evans, D.W., van Leeuwen, F., Lindegren, L. (1992): Detection and Measurement of Double Stars with the Hipparcos Satellite: NDAC Reductions. Astron. Astrophys. **258**, 157–164

Soffel, M.H. (1989): *Relativity in Astrometry, Celestial Mechanics and Geodesy.* Springer, Berlin Heidelberg New York

Souchay, J., Kinoshita, H. (1996): Correction and New Developments in Rigid Earth Nutation Theory. I. Lunisolar Influence Including Indirect Planetary Effects. Astron. Astrophys. **312**, 1017–1030

Souchay, J., Feissel, M., Bizouard, C. et al. (1995): Precession and Nutation for a Non-rigid Earth: Comparison Between Theory and VLBI Observations. Astron. Astrophys. **299**, 277–287

Sovers, O.J., Jacobs, C.S. (1996): Observation Model and Parameter Partials for the JPL VLBI Parameter Estimation Software 'MODEST' - 1996. JPL Publication 83-39, Rev. 6, 151 pp

Sovers, O.J., Edwards, C.D., Jacobs, C.S. et al. (1988): Astrometric Results of 1978-1985 Deep Space Network Radio Interferometry: The JPL 1987-1 Extragalactic Source Catalog. Astron. J. **95**, 1647–1658

Sovers, O.J., Fanselow, J.L., Jacobs, C.S. (1998): Astrometry and Geodesy with Radio Interferometry: Experiments, Models, Results. Rev. Mod. Phys. **70**, 1393–1454

Standish, E.M. (1982a): Orientation of the JPL Ephemerides DE 200/LE 200, to the Dynamical Equinox of J2000. Astron. Astrophys. **114**, 297–302

Standish, E.M. (1982b): Conversion of Positions and Proper Motions from B1950.0 to the IAU System at J2000.0. Astron. Astrophys. **115**, 20–22

Standish, E.M., Newhall X X (1996): New Accuracy Levels for Solar System Ephemerides. In: *Dynamics, Ephemerides and Astrometry of Solar System, IAU Symp. No. 172*, S. Ferraz-Mello, B. Morando, J.-E. Arlot (eds.). Kluwer, Dordrecht Boston London, 29–36

Stein, W.A., O'Dell, S.L., Strittmatter, P.A. (1976): The BL Lacertae Objects. Ann. Rev. Astron. Astrophys. **14**, 173–195

Sullivan, W.T. (1978): A New Look at Karl Jansky's Original Data. Sky & Telescope **56**, 101–105

Takahashi, F., Kondo, T., Takahashi, Y., Koyama, Y. (2000): *Very Long Baseline Interferometry.* Ohmsha, Tokyo (first published in Japanese in 1997 by Takahashi, F., Kondo, T., Takahashi, Y.)

Thomasson, P. (1986): MERLIN. Quarterly J. R. Astron. Soc. **27**, 413–431

Thompson, A.R., Clark, B.G., Wade, C.M., Napier, P.J. (1980): The Very Large Array. Astrophys. J. Suppl. **44**, 151–167

Thompson, A.R., Moran, J.M., Swenson Jr., G.W. (1991): *Interferometry and Synthesis in Radio Astronomy.* Krieger Publication Company, Malabar, Florida

Treuhaft, R.N., Lanyi, G.E. (1987): The Effect of the Dynamic Wet Troposphere on Radio Interferometric Measurements. Radio Science **22**, 251–265

Treuhaft, R.N., Lowe, S.T. (1991): A Measurement of Planetary Relativistic Deflection. Astron. J. **102**, 1879–1888

USNO (1981): The IAU Resolutions on Astronomical Constants, Time Scales, and the Fundamental Reference Frame. G.H. Kaplan (ed.), U.S. Naval Observatory, Circular No. **163**

van Daalen, D.T., Bucciarelli, B., Lattanzi, M. (1987): Rank Deficiency During Sphere Reconstruction. In: *Third F.A.S.T. Thinkshop*, held in Bari, Italy, November 3–6, 1986, P.L. Bernacca, J. Kovalevsky (eds.). Centro Arte Grafiche, Padova, 369–376

van de Kamp, P. (1967): *Principles of Astrometry.* W.H. Freeman and Co., San Francisco London van der Marel, H., Petersen, C. (1992): Hipparcos Great-circle Reduction. Astron. Astrophys. **258**, 60–69

van der Waerden, B.L. (1965): *Mathematische Statistik*. Springer, Berlin Heidelberg New York

van Woerkom, A.J.J. (1943): Note About Galactic Precession. Bull. Astron. Inst. Neth. **9**, 427–428

Vasilevskis, S., Klemola, A.R. (1971): On Determination of Correction to Precession from Stellar Proper Motions. Astron. J. **76**, 508–512

Veron-Cetty, M.P., Veron, P. (1983): A Catalogue of Extragalactic Radio Source Identifications. Astron. Astrophys. Suppl. Ser. **53**, 219–221; also at cdsweb.u-strasb.fr/CDS.html

Vondrák, J., Ron, C. (1993): The Present Status of Preparing the New Reduction of the Past Astrometric Observations to Obtain the Earth Orientation Parameters in the Hipparcos Reference System. In: *Developments in Astrometry and Their Impact on Astrophysics and Geodynamics, IAU Symp. No. 156*, I.I. Mueller, B. Kołaczek (eds.). Kluwer, Dordrecht Boston London, 95–100

Vondrák, J., Ron, C., Pešek, I. (1997): Using the Earth Orientation Parameters to Link the Hipparcos and VLBI Reference Frames. Astron. Astrophys. **319**, 1020–1024

Walter, H.G. (1989): A Compilation Catalogue of Positions of Extragalactic Radio Sources. Astron. Astrophys. **210**, 455–461

Walter, H.G., Sovers, O.J. (1996): Precession and Nutation from the Analysis of Positions of Extragalactic Radio Sources. Astron. Astrophys. **308**, 1001–1008

Walter, H.G., Hering, R., de Vegt, Chr. (1997): Radio Stars for Linking Celestial Reference Frames. Astron. Astrophys. Suppl. Ser. **122**, 529–532

Wielen, R. (1988): Precise Proper Motions and Positions of Stars from a Combination of Fundamental Catalogues with the Hipparcos Catalogue. In: *Mapping the Sky, IAU Symp. No. 133*, S. Débarbat, J.A. Eddy, H.K. Eichhorn, A.R. Upgren (eds.). Kluwer, Dordrecht Boston London, 293–297

Wielen, R., Schwan, H., Dettbarn, C. et al. (1997): Statistical Astrometry Based on a Comparison of Individual Proper Motions and Positions of Stars in the FK5 and in the Hipparcos Catalogue. In: *HIPPARCOS Venice '97*, ESA SP-402, B. Battrick (ed.). European Space Agency, Paris, 727–732

Wielen, R., Schwan, H., Dettbarn, C. et al. (1998): The Sixth Catalogue of Fundamental Stars (FK6). In: *The Message of the Angles – Astrometry from 1798 to 1998*, P. Brosche, W.R. Dick, O. Schwarz, R. Wielen (eds.). Verlag Harri Deutsch, Frankfurt am Main, 123–132

Wielen, R., Schwan, H., Dettbarn, C. et al. (1999): Sixth Catalogue of Fundamental Stars (FK6). Part I: Basic Fundamental Stars with Direct Solutions. Veröffentlichungen Astronomisches Rechen-Institut Heidelberg, No. **35**, G. Braun, Karlsruhe, 209 pp

Wilkins, G.A. (1990): The Past, Present and Future of Reference Systems for Astronomy and Geodesy. In: *Inertial Coordinate System on the Sky, IAU Symp. No. 141*, J.H. Lieske, V.K. Abalakin (eds.). Kluwer, Dordrecht Boston London, 39–46

Wohlleben, R., Mattes, H., Krichbaum, Th. (1991): *Interferometry in Radio Astronomy and Radio Techniques*. Kluwer, Dordrecht Boston London

Woolard, E.W. (1953): Theory of the Rotation of the Earth Around its Center of Mass. Astron. Papers Americ. Ephem. and Nautical Almanac **15**, Part 1, 1–165

Woolard, E.W., Clemence, G.M. (1966): *Spherical Astronomy*. Academic Press, New York and London

Wright, W.H. (1950): On a Proposal to Use the Extragalactic Nebulae in Measuring the Proper Motions of Stars, and in Evaluating the Precessional Constant. Proc. Americ. Phil. Soc. **94**, 1–12

Yatskiv, Ya.S., Kuryanova, A.N. (1990): A New Approach to the Construction of a Compiled Catalogue of Positions of Extragalactic Radio Sources. In: *Inertial Coordinate System on the Sky, IAU Symp. No. 141*, J.H. Lieske, V.K. Abalakin (eds.). Kluwer, Dordrecht Boston London, 295–296

Yoshizawa, M., Sato, K., Nishikawa, J. et al. (1997): An Optical/Infrared Astrometric Satellite Project LIGHT. In: *HIPPARCOS Venice '97*, ESA SP-402, B. Battrick (ed.). European Space Agency, Paris, 795–797

Zacharias, N., Zacharias, M.I., Hall, D.M. et al. (1999): Accurate Optical Positions of Extragalactic Radio Reference Frame Sources. Astron. J. **118**, 2511–2525

Zensus, J.A., Pearson, T.J. (eds.) (1987): *Superluminal Radio Sources.* Cambridge Univ. Press, Cambridge New York

Zverev, M.S. (1963): *Fundamental Astrometry.* U.S. Department of Commerce, Office of Technical Services, JPRS: R-2943-D, OTS: 63-11569. Washington, D.C.

Index

ASTRONOMY AND ASTROPHYSICS LIBRARY

Stellar Physics (2 volumes)
Volume 1: Fundamental Concepts and Stellar Equilibrium
Volume 2: Stellar Evolution and Stability
By G. S. Bisnovatyi-Kogan

Theory of Orbits (2 volumes)
Volume 1: Integrable Systems and Non-perturbative Methods
Volume 2: Perturbative and Geometrical Methods
By D. Boccaletti and G. Pucacco

Galaxies and Cosmology
By F. Combes, P. Boissé, A. Mazure and A. Blanchard

The Solar System 2nd Edition
By T. Encrenaz and J.-P. Bibring

Physics of Planetary Rings
Celestial Mechanics of Continuous Media
By A. M. Fridman, N. N. Gorkavyi

The Physics and Dynamics of Planetary Nebulae By G. A. Gurzadyan

Astrophysical Concepts 2nd Edition
By M. Harwit

Stellar Structure and Evolution
By R. Kippenhahn and A. Weigert

Modern Astrometry By J. Kovalevsky

Astrophysical Formulae 3rd Edition (2 volumes)
Volume I: Radiation, Gas Processes and High Energy Astrophysics
Volume II: Space, Time, Matter and Cosmology
By K. R. Lang

The Sun from Space By K. R. Lang

Observational Astrophysics 2nd Edition
By P. Léna, F. Lebrun and F. Mignard

Galaxy Formation By M. S. Longair

General Relativity, Astrophysics, and Cosmology
By A. K. Raychaudhuri, S. Banerji and A. Banerjee

Tools of Radio Astronomy 3rd Edition
By K. Rohlfs and T. L. Wilson

Tools of Radio Astronomy
Problems and Solutions
By T. L. Wilson and S. Hüttemeister

The Stars
By E. L. Schatzman and F. Praderie

Cosmic Ray Astrophysics
By R. Schlickeiser

Gravitational Lenses
By P. Schneider, J. Ehlers and E. E. Falco

MIX
Papier aus verantwortungsvollen Quellen
Paper from responsible sources
FSC® C105338
FSC
www.fsc.org

If you have any concerns about our products,
you can contact us on
ProductSafety@springernature.com

In case Publisher is established outside the EU,
the EU authorized representative is:
Springer Nature Customer Service Center GmbH
Europaplatz 3, 69115 Heidelberg, Germany

Printed by Libri Plureos GmbH
in Hamburg, Germany